BOLSHOI CONFIDENTIAL

Bolshoi Confidential

*Secrets of the Russian Ballet from the
Rule of the Tsars to Today*

SIMON MORRISON

ALFRED A. KNOPF CANADA

PUBLISHED BY ALFRED A. KNOPF CANADA

Anna Sobeshchanskaya as Odette; Gorsky's "choreographic photo etudes," 1907–09;
Simon Virsaladze, Alexander Lavrenyuk, and Plisetskaya,
Legend of Love, 1972 courtesy of Bakhrushin Museum. The Bolshoi
Theater, May 15, 2015, courtesy of author. All other images
courtesy of Russian State Archive of Literature and Art.

www.penguinrandomhouse.ca

Knopf Canada and colophon are registered trademarks.

Library and Archives Canada Cataloguing in Publication

Morrison, Simon Alexander, 1964– , author
Bolshoi confidential : secrets of the Russian ballet from the rule of the tsars to today /
Simon Morrison.

Includes bibliographical references and index.
Issued in print and electronic formats.

ISBN 978-0-345-81423-4
eBook ISBN 978-0-435-81425-8

1. Bol'sho¨i teatr Rossii. Balet—History. 2. Ballet—Russia—History.
3. Ballet—Soviet Union—History. 4. Ballet companies—Russia—History.
5. Ballet companies—Soviet Union—History. 6. Ballet—Political aspects—
Russia—History. 7. Ballet—Political aspects—Soviet Union—History.
I. Title.

GV1786.B64M67 2016   792.8'0947   C2016-903164-0

Jacket art: © Sergei Fadeichev/ITAR-TASS Photo/Corbis;
Ballet dancers of the Bolshoi Ballet © Olaf Kraak / Stringer / Getty Images
Text design by Faceout Studio
Printed and bound in the United States of America

10 9 8 7 6 5 4 3 2 1

Penguin
Random House
KNOPF CANADA

For Nika, who retired from ballet

before she was five.

. . .

CONTENTS

A Note on Transliteration and Dates

. . .

THE TRANSLITERATION SYSTEM used in this book is the one devised, phonetically, by Gerald Abraham for the *New Grove Dictionary of Music and Musicians* (1980), with the modifications introduced by Richard Taruskin in *Mussorgsky: Eight Essays and an Epilogue* (1993). It renders the Russian letter ы as ï and the аи combination in the name Михаил as Mikhaíl. Exceptions to the system concern some commonly accepted spellings of Russian and non-Russian names and places (for example, Alexei rather than Aleksey, Dmitri rather than Dmitriy, Maddox rather than Medoks, St. Petersburg rather than Sankt-Peterburg) and surname suffixes (Verstov*sky* rather than Verstov*skiy*). For ease on the eye, I favored Ekaterina over Yekaterina and Elena over Yelena. In the bibliographic citations, however, the transliteration system is heeded without exception (Dmitriy rather than Dmitri, and so on). Surname suffixes are presented intact, and soft signs preserved as diacritical apostrophes.

RUSSIA RETAINED USE of the Julian calendar from antiquity until January 1, 1918, when the Bolsheviks under Lenin mandated the conversion to the Gregorian calendar of western Europe. Before the reign of Peter the Great (1682–1725), Russians marked the start of the year on September 1 rather than January 1, and numbered years from the date of the creation of the Earth rather than the birth of Christ. Peter the Great reformed the counting of the years but upheld the use of the Julian calendar in deference to the Russian Orthodox Church. So in effect, before the Bolshevik overthrow of Tsar Nicholas II, the Russian calendar was twelve days behind that of the western European calendar. In this book, dates are specified according to the calendar in use in Russia: Julian before 1918 (abbreviated O.S.), Gregorian afterward.

INTRODUCTION

ON THE NIGHT of January 17, 2013, Sergey Filin, artistic director of the Bolshoi Theater Ballet, returned to his apartment near the central ring road in Moscow. He parked his black Mercedes outside the building and trudged through the wet falling snow toward the main entrance. His two boys were asleep inside, but he expected that his wife Mariya, herself a dancer, would be waiting up for him. Before he could tap in the security code to open the metal gate, however, a thickset man strode up behind him and shouted a baleful hello. When Filin turned around, the hooded assailant flung a jar of distilled battery acid into his face, then sped off in a waiting car. Filin dropped to the ground and cried for help, rubbing snow into his face and eyes to stop the burning.

The crime threw into chaos one of Russia's most illustrious institutions: the Bolshoi Theater, crown jewel during the imperial era, emblem of Soviet power throughout the twentieth century, and showcase for a reborn nation in the twenty-first. Even those performers, greater and lesser, whose careers ended in personal and professional sorrow could justly believe that their lives had been blessed thanks to the stage they had graced. The Bolshoi's dancers transcended the cracked joints, pulled muscles, and bruised feet that are among the hazards of ballet to exhibit near-perfect poses and unparalleled equipoise. Orphans became angels within the schools that served the theater in the first years of its existence; the Bolshoi then nurtured the great ballet classics of the nineteenth century, and more recently the sheer skill of its dancers has redeemed, at least in part, the ideological dreck of Soviet ballet. The attack on Filin dismantled romantic notions of the art and its artists as ethereal, replacing stories about the breathtaking poetic athleticism on the Bolshoi stage with tales of sex and violence behind the curtain—pulp nonfiction. Crime reporters, political and cultural critics, reviewers, and ballet bloggers alike reminded their readers, however, that the theater has often been in turmoil. Rather than an awful aberration, the attack had precedents of sorts in the Bolshoi's rich and complicated past. That past is one of remarkable achievements interrupted, and even fueled, by periodic bouts of madness.

The history of the Bolshoi travels hand in hand with the history of the nation. As goes Russia, so goes the Bolshoi—at least since the Russian Revolution, when the seat of power moved from St. Petersburg to Moscow. Under the tsars in the imperial capital of St. Petersburg, the Mariyinsky Theater (also known as the Kirov Theater) possessed the most prestige; the city of Moscow and its precariously financed ballet and opera house were considered provincial. But depending on who is looking and from where, one theater, one city, one lineage or another might appear in the foreground of a long tradition. In the twentieth century, the Bolshoi assumed pride of place within Russia and on the international stage as the emissary not only of the Russian ballet tradition but also the Soviet state. Bodies speak in Realpolitik. Russian ballet does not privilege abstraction, and those choreographers who, on limited occasion, sought to create non-narrative, non-subjective works erred in imagining that abstraction could be assigned whatever concepts they desired. Looking at the video records of today and sifting through the archival remains of yesteryear affirm that neither the dance nor the music attached to it is, or ever was, considered pure. Boldness and the projection of power are essential to politics and culture, especially within the context of President Vladimir Putin's aggressive nationalist posturing. Today the Bolshoi seeks to regain the preeminence it forfeited after the collapse of the Soviet Union.

Within Russia, from the vaguely defined time of the nation's founding, the rulers of Russia—tsars, Bolshevik revolutionaries, Stalin and his henchmen, the *siloviki* (members of the military-security establishment) of the current petro-ruble regime—have looked to the Bolshoi as a symbol, whether imperial, ideological, or commercial. The theater is about as old as the United States, but has had numerous lives. With Catherine the Great's blessing, a Russian prince and an English showman first raised it up from the marshes of Moscow in 1780 on a plot of land close to the Kremlin; the start-up theater and the seat of goverment have been neighbors through several catastrophes. And fittingly so, given that in Russia politics can be theater and theater, politics.

After a fire in 1853, architect Alberto Cavos turned the Bolshoi into a stone neoclassical paradise of fluted columns, fitted mirrors, and alabaster vases; a sculpture of the Greek muses was installed above the portico. Following the Revolution of 1917, the Bolsheviks considered blowing up the Bolshoi as a decadent icon of the Russian imperial past but pillaged it instead, pulling up the marble floor and painting over the frescoes. The theater became a cultural symbol of the new state, which soon enough had imperial ambitions of its own; indeed, the Soviet Union itself was born at the Bolshoi. On December 30, 1922, it hosted the political congress that voted the Soviet Union into existence.

Stalin ratified the Soviet constitution on the stage of the Bolshoi and delivered speeches before cowed Communist Party officials; no one wanted to be the first to stop applauding. Thereafter it became the site of much Communist Party business, and even served as a polling station until a suitable palace was built inside the walls of the Kremlin. The Bolshoi was the single place where the rulers of Russia and their subjects came into contact. As one Kremlinologist explains, "To put in an appearance in the Bolshoi Theater meant that you belonged to the very highest echelons of power; but to disappear from there was synonymous with a fall from favor and death."[1] At the Bolshoi, ballets began after speeches delivered by officials who had overseen mass murders—the execution, on a staggering scale, of perceived saboteurs, traitors, anti-Soviet "fifth columnists," and other undesirables. "Those who sat on the stage," historian Karl Schlögel reports, "had appended their signatures to the thousands of death sentences approved by the extraordinary commissions and had even become directly involved themselves—in interrogations and the use of physical force."[2]

The repertoire of the State Academic Bolshoi Theater, as it became known, fell under Communist Party control. Its general directors were ordered to produce ballets and operas on approved Soviet subjects. Bulldozers rumbled across the stage to represent the construction of the Communist utopia before audiences of peasants and workers who had to be told when to clap. In 1939, the character of Lenin even appeared onstage in an agitprop opera called *V buryu*, or *Into the Storm*. A photograph from that era shows laborers listening to a performance of Tchaikovsky by way of celebrating the twentieth anniversary of Lenin's secret police. For those directors who could not countenance ballets and operas about collective farms and hydroelectric stations, hewing close to the classics became the one safe, government-santioned alternative.

During World War II, part of the foyer of the theater was destroyed by a German bomb. Repairs were done on the postwar cheap, but the acoustics had earlier been compromised by Stalin, who had ordered the tsar's loge at the center of the first tier encased in protective cement. (A document ordering the special reinforcement was reportedly buried in the wall.) In the 1980s, the Bolshoi fell apart along with the Soviet Union, but the power and majesty of Russian ballet remained, broadcast to the masses as the last vestige of national pride in the bankrupt munitions plant known as the USSR.

WHEN HE SIGNED a five-year contract as artistic director of the Bolshoi in 2011, Filin was the forty-year-old prince of Russian ballet. A Moscow native, he had built a high-profile career as a principal dancer at the Bolshoi and been decorated as a People's Artist of the Russian Federation, the nation's highest artistic honor. His parents were not especially interested in ballet but, seeking to channel the boy's restlessness, arranged for him to learn folk dance. His energy immediately found focus, and at ten years old Filin entered the Bolshoi Ballet Academy, graduating eight years later to claim a position in the professional company. Filin performed his first major role as the impish knave Benedick in *Love for Love*, a balletic adaptation of Shakespeare's *Much Ado About Nothing*. The dance, set to music by Tikhon Khrennikov, is perhaps deservedly forgotten, but the experience sparked Filin's enduring fascination with Shakespeare. The image that he had of himself as a dancer destined for greatness was tempered by Marina Semyonova, his professional coach. She died in 2010 at age 102, the Bolshoi tradition incarnate. During her final decades, she pushed her pupils to overcome the strictures of the Bolshoi style as preached and practiced during the late Soviet period. Filin has singled her out as his most important mentor and confidante. Semyonova told him "things that she didn't share with anyone," and even guided his personal life, cheekily advising him not to marry "this one" or "that one" owing to supposedly "misshapen" limbs or low breeding.[3]

What made Filin a star was chiefly his range: the spectrum he could span between technical displays (as in *Don Quixote*, one of the buttresses of the Bolshoi repertoire), poetic expressiveness, and subtle characterizations. His good looks in his twenties made him perfect for the part of a gadabout, a pleasure seeker; experimental roles came later. Injury forced him from the stage in 2004, but he battled back into the spotlight while also completing a degree at Moscow University in the performing arts. In 2008, at age thirty-seven, he became the artistic director of the Stanislavsky Theater in Moscow; three years later, he was appointed to the same position at the Bolshoi. His job, basically second in command to then general director Anatoliy Iksanov, gave him control over repertoire, casting, appointments, and dismissals. It was a sensible choice. Filin knew the theater and its traditions intimately. Plus he was easygoing, not a firebrand.

BOLSHOI INSIDERS SUSPECTED that the attack on Filin was motivated by professional and personal resentments. So did the police. Yet the Russian media—the government-monitored television channels, plus the less-regulated newspapers and online news portals—teased the public with baroque theories of the crime. The clippings were compiled in a Russian-language book called *Black Swans*, and the American network HBO released a documentary about the attack called *Bolshoi Babylon*.[4] (The behind-the-scenes footage shows Filin, after his martyrdom, being shamed into silence by the new general director in front of the dancers: "I asked you not to speak," Vladimir Urin tells Filin in front of the assembled company. "I'm not going to argue with you. . . . Please sit down.") Gossips and alienated former employees blamed dark elements connected to meddling Kremlin officials—a theory of the crime that did not seem absurd, given that the Bolshoi is a political as well as an artistic institution. Filin denied allegations of extortion, that fees had been demanded for auditions and choice parts. True, he had promoted his own people, as artistic directors are wont to do; he also decided who headlined the programs, who went on tour, and who appeared in the galas—decisions with significant financial consequences for the dancers. There were those who thus coveted his position and thought that he benefited too much from it.

Speculation about the crime centered first on the flamboyant senior dancer Nikolay Tsiskaridze, an indefatigable critic of his employer. For years he had been complaining about everything at the Bolshoi: the five-year, top-to-bottom renovation of the building, the managers, the artistic directors, the stars in the making. But he seemed strangely cheerful in his defense, much too glad to give interviews and declare that he had declined a lie-detector test. When asked about his grievances, Tsiskaridze reminisced about his career and likened himself to other besieged greats of the stage, namely the opera singer Maria Callas, although she was more demure and, onstage, used less maquillage than he did. He recalled his fun-filled, innocent, and lucrative New Year's Eve performances of *The Nutcracker*: "$1,500 a ticket at the official rate," he boasted on the phone, "and Iksanov says I can't dance." In May 2013, his lawyer threatened to sue the Bolshoi in response to the reprimands he had received for his gossipmongering. That June, the nationalist newspaper *Zavtra* broke the news that his two contracts with the Bolshoi, as performer and teacher, had been canceled. He parried with characteristic bravado: "What did you expect? It's a gang there." Fans mounted a protest in front of the theater, inspired by his declaration in the French newspaper *Le Figaro* that "*Le Bolchoï, c'est moi.*"

Tsiskaridze exposed an age-old conflict at the Bolshoi between progressives and conservatives, pitting those dancers who benefited from an archaic patronage system against those who did not. Earlier in the twentieth century, during the era of the Bolsheviks and the Cultural Revolution, Elena Malinovskaya served as director of the theater. An unprepossessing nondescript who rose to fame through Marxist-Leninist political circles, she governed the Bolshoi with a scowl from 1919 to 1935. Occasionally she threatened resignation, claiming that the pressures of the job and the threats she received from disgruntled artists had compromised her health, but her Kremlin protectors kept her at her desk. Although Malinovskaya's survival ensured the Bolshoi's continuing operation, she was reviled for purging the ranks of suspected dissidents. She was further castigated for spoiling the repertoire, accused of making even the classical art of ballet a tool of ideology and so giving it a guilty conscience.

Thus began the struggle between the defenders of the aristocratic tradition and its critics, as well as between those who conformed to official dictates and others who fell silent, knowing it was pointless to resist. The official artistic doctrine of socialist realism obliged ballet scenarists and opera librettists to freight even works about the distant past with Marxist-Leninist content, to taint them with ideological anachronisms. The emphasis on making ballet for the people yielded Cossack, gypsy, and peasant dances not seen on the Moscow stage since the Napoleonic era. The scenarios enforced the simplest binaries: pro-Bolshevik pluckiness versus anti-Bolshevik cowardliness; Soviets versus Fascists; collective farmworkers versus the hot sun and parched earth. Pantomime and peasant exotica were the essence of the repertoire throughout the 1930s and the Second World War.

Tsiskaridze stood with the old guard, those dancers attached to traditional stagings of the Russian repertoire rather than the innovative productions privileged by Iksanov and Filin. His dismissal came as a relief even to his backers at the theater, since it dimmed the spotlight on the scandal. But after a short vacation, he resumed his performance of a persecuted balletic Old Believer. Tsiskaridze had little to fear, it seems, because he enjoyed the protection of powerful interests. Much as Rasputin had bewitched the Empress Alexandra before the fall of the Romanov dynasty in 1918, so too the magnetic Tsiskaridze is understood to have impressed the spouse of the president of Rostec, a government-controlled firm that develops advanced weapons systems. He was not out of work for long. In October 2013, Culture Minister Vladimir Medinsky appointed Tsiskaridze rector of the Vaganova Ballet Academy in St. Petersburg, one of the world's most prestigious schools for dance.

Filin's predecessor as artistic director, Alexei Ratmansky, offered no specific insight into the attack but commented on Facebook that "many of the illnesses of the Bolshoi are one snowball—that disgusting claque which is friendly with artists, ticket speculators and scalpers, half-crazy fans who are ready to slit the throats of their idol's competitors, cynical hackers, lies in the press and scandalous interviews of people working there."[5] Claqueurs are professional audience members, tasked with offering overly demonstrative applause for their favorite Bolshoi dancers in exchange for tickets they can resell. The mysterious balletomane Roman Abramov currently leads this "elegant theatrical protection racket."[6] He appears in the HBO documentary, and boasts of attending hundreds of performances a year.

Ratmansky left the Bolshoi in 2008, after reviving suppressed Soviet ballets and redoing the shopworn classics. He found the pressure from inside and outside of the theater intolerable, especially when brought to bear on creative decisions. To perform the 1930 Soviet ballet *The Bolt*, for example, Ratmansky excised a potentially offensive scene that once would have been comical, even canonically so. It involves a drunken Russian Orthodox priest and a dancing cathedral. The lampoon was politically correct for the godless Bolsheviks of 1930, but heresy to the lords of the new church of 2005. So it was cut. In relocating to New York, Ratmansky hoped to escape the machinations to create what he liked. The Bolshoi lamented his departure, but even the press officer at the theater, Katerina Novikova, empathized with his decision. Tsiskaridze had made his life miserable, she acknowledged. Ratmansky had also put up with bad behavior from other dancers, including the one who would finally be convicted in the attack against Filin.

In March 2013, the police arrested Pavel Dmitrichenko, a lead dancer, and charged him with organizing the attack. He had supposedly paid 50,000 rubles ($1,430) to a thug with a record. Speaking to reporters from his hospital room, Filin confirmed that he had long suspected Dmitrichenko, an irascible, tattooed soloist who harbored a grudge against Filin for passing over his ballerina girlfriend for choice roles. Filin's haute-goth lawyer, Tatyana Stukalova, informed a deferential interviewer on television that Dmitrichenko could not have been acting alone. Soon it emerged that he had two accomplices: Yuriy Zarutsky, an unemployed ex-convict who tossed the acid, and Andrey Lipatov, the driver. Dmitrichenko confessed to organizing the attack but argued that he had merely wanted to frighten Filin, put the fear of God into him. The acid was Zarutsky's idea. Dmitrichenko admitted his "moral responsibility," while carping, wild-eyed, about how he had been wronged.[7] The artistic director had not bestowed the promotions he deserved; his girlfriend, the aspiring ballerina Anzhelina Vorontsova, had been denied the star-making dual role of Odette/Odile in *Swan Lake* as payback for some past slight, notwithstanding the genuine kindness shown to her by Filin and his wife over the years. Dmitrichenko's supporters organized a petition insinuating financial corruption at the Bolshoi—as if that, or anything else, justified maiming someone for life. Filin, blind in his right eye and with 50 percent vision in his left, wept as he testified.

Rights, rules, and regulations can matter little in Russia, and personal connections, or animosities, can make all the difference. Dmitrichenko harbored a grudge against Filin less because he coveted Filin's position (as Tsiskaridze did) than because he resented the obvious conflicts of interest within the *profsoyuzï*, the artists' unions. These were supposed to represent the artists and their concerns to the Bolshoi administration. Yet the unions were headed not by performers but by members of the administration. Thus those running the theater conscripted the artists' unions to their own cause, a problematic state of affairs harkening back to the Soviet era, when Communist minders and KGB operatives headed the unions to keep the artists in check. Dmitrichenko protested Filin's position as head of the dancers' union. Moreover, as journalist Ismene Brown has revealed, Dmitrichenko challenged the system that offered lucrative bonuses to Filin's favored dancers. The "quarterly 'grants' committee," which Filin chaired, "traditionally deferred to his wishes," Brown explains. "It awarded bonuses to dancers for performance, according to a time-honored ranking of what a solo was worth. But dancers not chosen to perform did not qualify. Dmitrichenko, petitioned by the timorous corps de ballet to represent their interests, unceremoniously commanded that all dancers, whether chosen to perform or not, were doing their work as required, and therefore should be entitled to some of the quarterly bonus pot." But Filin "was dissatisfied with the slack attitude of many dancers, who would drift off to do other things or claim sick leave without any notice," Brown reports, and so rejected Dmitrichenko's demands for a proportional distribution of bonuses.[8]

In July 2013, Svetlana Zakharova, the Bolshoi's prima ballerina assoluta and a former cultural representative in the Russian parliament, objected when she learned that she had been assigned to the second cast of John Cranko's *Onegin*. She quit the production, turned off her mobile phone, and left town. The government had had enough of the chaos. Iksanov was asked to step down, with Vladimir Urin, the respected general director of the Stanislavsky and Nemirovich-Danchenko Theaters, becoming his replacement. The Stanislavsky had come to the creative and administrative rescue of the Bolshoi in the past: a case in point being Filin's appointment in 2011. Urin expressed little patience for intrigue and even less for Tsiskaridze and his witches' brew of reactionary invective. According to the journalist, socialite, and former dancer Kseniya Sobchak, Urin replied to the suggestion that Tsiskaridze might return to the Bolshoi with the Russian equivalent of "over my dead body."[9]

As the new general director of the Bolshoi, Urin initiated reforms. Early in 2014, he unveiled a new collective agreement that erased some of the inequities and set out in legal prose what had once been merely understood. The superstar Zakharova, who boasts an international career, heads a charity in her name, and enjoys a driver taking her to and from the studio, exempted herself from the agreement. The haggling over quarterly bonuses was the business of the corps de ballet, no concern of hers. While calm was restored at the Bolshoi Ballet, class conflict remained: between stars and soloists, soloists and members of the corps, those in favor and those who had fallen out. Dancers are defined by their roles—not only in terms of rank, but also by the characters they represent. Before anyone was arrested for the assault on Filin, Bolshoi Theater administrators hazarded that it must have been committed by one of the dancers who took the role of a villain. Filin had performed dashing heroes; the ethnically Georgian, impressively coiffed Tsiskaridze gravitated toward sorcerers. Dmitrichenko appeared in tragic ballets, but also took the role of a gangster in Yuriy Grigorovich's satiric *The Golden Age*. Onstage and off, as it turned out, Dmitrichenko played the part of Tybalt to Filin's Romeo.

Within a year of the crime, Judge Elena Maksimova of the Meshansky District Court in Moscow sentenced Zarutsky to a decade in prison, Dmitrichenko to six years, and the driver Lipatov to four. The three together were also ordered to pay Filin 3.5 million rubles, or $105,000, in damages. (Later, their sentences were trimmed by a year, six months, and two years respectively; and in June of 2016, Dmitrichenko was paroled.) The sight of a popular Bolshoi soloist and two common criminals caged in court, as Russian defendants usually are, recalled earlier, seedier periods in the history of ballet—the lowly state it sometimes fell into in France, Italy, and Russia during the nineteenth century. Then, as suddenly now, the exquisite art seemed compromised by the desperation, exploitation, pain, and toxic rivalries suffered by its artists. Dmitrichenko seemed to embody a pernicious stereotype of the hotheaded, out-of-control artist rebel: He was forced as a child into ballet, he claimed, and had acted "the hooligan," in school, "throwing firecrackers at the teachers."[10] He had riled his peers and railed against the Bolshoi administration. But he did not commit the crime in service of some cliché. Instead, behind the distorted reporting, personal agendas, institutional priorities, and tabloid scandals, lies a basic truth about how business is conducted at the Bolshoi—as in Russia.

• • •

ONCE THE RUSSIAN news cycle turned, shuffling the crime off the front pages in favor of the conflict in eastern Ukraine, this terrible episode seemed soon to be forgotten as but a momentary crisis corrected by installing the unexcitable Urin at the helm. Yet the recent violence surrounding the Bolshoi echoes events dating back to the very founding of the theater in the late eighteenth century. Gripping tales—some lurid, others inspiring—are told in thousands of documents stored in Russian archives, museums, and libraries kept under bureaucratic lock and key; in the recollections of active and retired dancers; and in the distinguished scholarship of Russian ballet experts. The records make for strange reading. However fantastic the imaginings of ballets on the Bolshoi stage, fiction cannot measure up to the truth.

Truth did not exist backstage, declared one of the greatest dancers of the Soviet period, Maya Plisetskaya. An eccentric, explosive performer who moved in and out of official favor, Plisetskaya believed in the Bolshoi, where she danced Tchaikovsky's *Swan Lake* countless times, rhapsodically for some, too showily for others, while also committing to the dark night of the soul known as the agitprop repertoire. Critics were baffled by her iconoclasm. She could be reckless on stage but also mesmerizing, possessing a physical vocabulary that ranged from toreador moving in for a kill to fashion model on the catwalk. In her twenties and thirties Plisetskaya gravitated toward the bad girls of the repertoire, the troublemakers, but also the free spirits. The arrest and disappearance of her parents during the Stalinist purges had left her bereft, defiant, and rude to the KGB officers who trailed her to and from the theater, owing to her romance with a British embassy staffer. Cynicism fueled sedition, but she never defected and largely confined her protests to unorthodox performances. The Soviet regime, desperate for celebrities, needed her both at home and abroad. Still, she was treated coarsely, and remembered recoiling as premier Leonid Brezhnev drunkenly pawed her in his limousine after a performance. "The one time I did go to the Kremlin," she fumed, "I had to walk home across Moscow all alone."[11] In semiretirement, she looked back on her life in the theater with fondness, describing the Bolshoi stage as her guardian. "It was a familiar creature, a relative, an animate partner. I spoke to it, thanked it. Every board, every crack I had mastered and danced on. The stage of the Bolshoi made me feel protected; it was a domestic hearth."[12] She recorded those words in her memoirs, an international bestseller by ballet standards, and one that resonates with the recent drama in the Bolshoi. The dispossessed dancers of 2013, of today, speak from a script that Plisetskaya provided.

The Soviet period still haunts the theater, but the oligarchs of the twenty-first century have taken a vested interest in the Bolshoi, now that the grime has become glitz. In his efforts to restore prestige to the new Russia, President Dmitri Medvedev approved a complete overhaul of the Bolshoi, opening up the coffers of the state-controlled oil-and-petroleum giant Gazprom. The theater closed on July 1, 2005, after the final performance of two Russian classics: *Swan Lake* and the tragic historical opera *Boris Godunov.* Six years later, the gala celebration of the $680-million-plus restoration was a political event of a different order. On October 28, 2011, a nervous-looking Medvedev extolled the Bolshoi as one of few "unifying symbols, national treasures, of so-called national brands" of Russia.[13]

Yet the Russianness of the Bolshoi remains a matter of debate. The very concept is fraught and paradoxical, never quite borne out by the ethnographic facts, and has inspired spurious claims of exclusiveness, otherness, and exceptionalism. Dance critic Mark Monahan swoons over Olga Smirnova's "swan-like neck" and the "unmistakably Russian" undulation in her arms, but her syntax and affect are neoclassical and neoromantic, much indebted to traditions outside of Russia.[14] And what the ballet master Marius Petipa contributed to nineteenth-century Russian ballet has its continuation not in Soviet circles but in the creations of George Balanchine in America and Frederick Ashton in Britain. The annals of the Bolshoi do not bear out claims of Russian exceptionalism. Moscow exceptionalism, perhaps, but even that assertion is debatable, since most of the great Russian dancers, past and present, moved back and forth between the academies and stages of the old imperial capital of St. Petersburg and the new one of Moscow.

Regardless, the Bolshoi as a "brand" remains paramount. The theater and its dancers have always been marketed abroad. Under Khrushchev and Brezhnev, the ballet served the Kremlin as a cultural exchange operation and a conduit for low-level espionage by the agents who kept the dancers in check. Some performers defected, including, at the top of her career, the Kirov prima ballerina Natalya Makarova. So too did the soloist Mikhaíl Baryshnikov, who flourished in the West. In a July 2013 newspaper interview, the still-active Baryshnikov likened events at the Bolshoi, past and present, onstage and backstage, to a "non-stop ugly vaudeville."[15]

In fact, the Bolshoi began its life as a vaudeville hall. Its co-founder and driving force had infamous (at least in the eighteenth century) problems with creditors and was forced, for financial and political reasons, to recruit amateur performers from an orphanage for his fledgling theater. Before catastrophe struck in the form of a fire, boys and girls of the Moscow Imperial Foundling Home took the stage as participants in light entertainments. But the Bolshoi only became the Bolshoi—a symbol of Russia itself— after the Napoleonic invasion of 1812. From the 1830s on, it produced a plethora of superb performers. Since that time, the dancers of the Bolshoi have been stereotyped for their athletic prowess, their physical culture. Yet they are also storytellers, gifted mimes. The first great ballerinas of the nineteenth century were trained by actors, and the admixture of dance-free miming and plot-free dance persisted at the Bolshoi long after it had been abandoned elsewhere.

During these early years, the brightest star on the Bolshoi stage was Ekaterina Sankovskaya, a Moscow-born ballerina who inspired a generation of intellectuals through her freedom of expression and expression of freedom. She performed from the late 1830s into the 1850s, and was seen by her most ardent fans, including liberal students of Moscow University, to imitate, and rival, the illustrious European Romantic ballerinas Marie Taglioni and Fanny Elssler. Her appearances in *La sylphide* inspired a sycophantic cult following, a "claque" whose obsession with Sankovskaya, and ballet in general, worried the Moscow police.

The theater she inhabited came into being as an imperial institution with the opening in 1856 of Cavos's new building, resurrected from the ashes of the devastating fire in 1853. The ballet struggled, however, and was almost liquidated; the dancers from the exploited poorer classes faced life as laundresses, mill workers, or prostitutes, even starvation on the streets. The Bolshoi and its machinist nonetheless, almost despite themselves, hosted a dazzling revival of the swashbuckling ballet *Le corsaire*, along with the premieres of *Don Quixote* and *Swan Lake*. The annual "incident reports" at the theater in the 1860s and 1870s detail the commercial gas wars in Moscow (of concern for the Bolshoi because it was gaslit) along with the eccentricities of the directorate of the Imperial Theaters, which oversaw the Bolshoi's operations under the last tsars. The ballets survive as remote versions of their original selves, which have been lost to the stage and doubtless would have little appeal even if they could be reconstructed from the extant floor plans, lithographs, musical scores, and recollections. Who authored the original libretto for *Swan Lake* was until 2015 a mystery, and indeed Tchaikovsky's music seems to be calibrated for a plot line that no longer exists. The gaps in knowledge are no fault of the official record-keepers, who turn out to have been exceedingly meticulous when it came to realizing the mad and beautiful dreams of choreographers and set designers. The search for a reliable donkey for the 1871 staging of *Don Quixote* was pretext for dozens of pages of conscientious bureaucratic handwriting; finding the props for the act 3 spider scene forced one scribe to overcome his arachnophobia.

Maya Plisetskaya, the vessel of Bolshoi bravura during the Soviet years, died just before her ninetieth birthday, which the Bolshoi marked on November 20 and 21, 2015, in a memorial gala called "Ave Maya." She remains the source of some of the more reductively persistent assumptions about the Bolshoi ballet, including Jennifer Homans's assessment of the Khrushchev-era Bolshoi as somehow "stranger" than other troupes, "more oriental and driven less by rules than by passions—and politics."[16] In honoring one of its greatest ballerinas, a deeply passionate artist both celebrated and constrained by politics, the theater revisited its own troubled history even while still struggling to emerge from the aftermath of the macabre attack on its artistic director.

FILIN COMPLETED HIS contract but remains at the theater in charge of an atelier for up-and-coming choreographers. After months of conjecture, Makhar Vaziev was appointed the new artistic director of the ballet. Vaziev comes from Milan by way of St. Petersburg, and his hiring, as Ismene Brown summarizes, "satisfies both the Bolshoi conservatives' need for a director with a credibly conventional profile and suitable leadership CV to command the dancers' compliance, and the pressure for an acceptable conductor of renovation and refreshment."[17]

The healing of the present divide permits reflection on the ruptures and sutures of the past. The story of the Bolshoi Theater, its ballet, Russia, and Russian politics can only, however, be traced in gestures and revealed against mottled backgrounds in occasional close-ups. This book starts with select scenes from the beginning, but ends far from the end. The focus here falls only on the ballet, although the Bolshoi is, of course, a world-famous opera house as well; opera is excluded from the discussion, except insofar as it might illuminate the ballet, the national brand's signature product. Ultimately, like ballet itself, this book proves paradoxical in documenting at times disenchanting truths—the complicated existences of the dancers, their art, and its venue—in hopes of at least suggesting what might be sublime, what might redeem, what could still elevate us above it all.

BOLSHOI CONFIDENTIAL

· 1 ·

THE
SWINDLING MAGICIAN

FROM THE START, the Bolshoi Theater was rife with political and financial intrigue. On March 17, 1776 (O.S.), Catherine the Great granted Prince Urusov of Moscow exclusive rights for the presentation of entertainments using performers foreign and domestic, including serf theaters. The license was granted for ten years, but just four years later, in 1780, it ended up in the hands of an Englishman named Michael Maddox. He ran the theater, then called the Petrovsky, into the ground. The tale of his mysterious business practices long pre-dates the sensational productions of the Bolshoi, but he made the theater fascinating.

MADDOX WAS EITHER a mathematician or a tightrope walker during his youth, and the theater that he helped to found in Moscow either employed professional actors or exploited the talents of orphans—all depending on what half-remembered tale is to be believed. Actual evidence is scant. Maddox advertised his magic shows in Moscow and St. Petersburg newspapers, signed official papers, and implored government officials for forgiveness when he ran into trouble with his numerous creditors.

The stories about his early years in England have a suspicious amount in common with those of Johann Faust, the traveling magician, fortune-teller, and charlatan best known from Goethe's nineteenth-century play. Just as Faust boasted of his dealings with the devil by way of self-promotion, so too Maddox considerably embellished the facts in the anecdotes he shared about himself. And like Faust, Maddox found himself immortalized in fiction after his death; the Russian writer Alexander Chayanov set one of his gothic short stories in the Petrovsky Theater. Planned for four years but built in just five months, the Petrovsky hosted all manner of entertainments, from ballets to operas to expertly translated Shakespearean dramas to masquerades. Trifling accounts survive about fabulous stage machinery meant to render astonishing meteorological and seismic disturbances. Characters seemed to pass through the floors and walls, while adolescent girls reportedly exposed intimate surfaces in the corps de ballet. Maddox pledged "cumulative" (meaning "harmonious") entertainments, but he ran afoul of the imperial censors and lost some of his greatest actors to a rival troupe in St. Petersburg.[1] He was also competing with the noblemen who maintained serf orchestras, including the magnate Nikolay Sheremetyev, who had the resources to perform, for a few elites, ballets and operas at his estate outside of Moscow. The competition intensified when Maddox, a popular-theater man, reached past burlesque to offer more substantive fare. He failed to increase his audience. Upper nobles had their serfs to entertain them, and the pious, including the old merchant families of Moscow, stayed away. Maddox went bankrupt, and then, in 1805, his theater burned down—as candlelit, coal-heated theaters with wooden roofs were wont to do. His Jewishness was to blame for the fiasco, anti-Semitic gossip held, even if he had been baptized a Catholic.[2]

MADDOX LEFT NO LIKENESS, and no references to his appearance exist beyond mention of the crimson cloak he wore year after year. The description of the theater in Chayanov's fictional story is based on research by the author's wife, Olga, a cultural historian. For Maddox himself, Chayanov relied on his mind's eye, embellishing the contemporaneous accounts of the impresario's "diabolical will" with a reference to "infernal breathing." The protagonist of the story glimpses Maddox during an opera, illuminated by the chandeliers that remained lit during the performance, as was then the custom. He is imagined sitting amid "undulating waves of blue and black tailcoats, fluttering fans and sparkling lorgnettes, silk bodices and Brabant lace capes." Maddox exits the auditorium before the second act; the protagonist follows through vaguely lit corridors, up and down stone staircases, past the dressing room of a soprano singing the part of a shackled slave. Maddox is described as tall, with a dusting of gray hair, dressed in a coat of antique cut, oddly blank in affect. "There were no tongues of fire circling him, no stink of sulphur; everything about him seemed quite ordinary and normal," the novelist writes, "but this diabolical ordinariness was saturated with meaning and power."[3]

Maddox comes and goes in the story, which ends in the slush outside of the theater, the protagonist encased in the Moscow night and an atmosphere of neurosis.

The real Michael Maddox was born in England on May 14,

1747, though he claimed to have ancient Russian roots. His Protestant ancestors had immigrated to Russia in the seventeenth century, the era of the Catholic Stuart monarchy, to escape religious persecution. He was the sole surviving son of the English actor Tom Maddox, "who with all his family and troupe" perished in a cargo-boat crash near the Port of Holyhead—all "except one infant who floated ashore in a cradle."[4] The orphan was raised by his uncle, Seward, a trumpeter. Following in his father's footsteps, Maddox became an entertainer, performing tightrope acts in the 1750s at Haymarket Theatre and Covent Garden in London. He balanced a mere three feet above the stage, less to reduce the danger to himself than to his audience. Toward the end of the act, he would hover on one foot while balancing a straw on the edge of a glass and plinking a fiddle. Other anecdotes from London have him blowing a horn and banging a drum on the slack wire. He also tumbled and conducted unspecified physical and mechanical experiments. Outside of London he acted in saltbox theaters and manipulated fairground puppets, with Punch as his favorite. In York "during race week," he and his troupe performed morning and evening at Merchants Adventurers' Hall, among other venues.[5] In the southwest English town of Bath, he entertained ladies and gentlemen along with the servants who held their places while their masters mingled at Simpson's Rooms. "For a considerable salary," Maddox pivoted and swung above the audience while balancing a coach wheel and juggling a dozen balls.[6]

Lore has it that Maddox was engaged in mysterious business dealings throughout Europe, which perhaps explains his connections to the English and Russian diplomats (George Macartney and Nikita Panin) who brokered his first visit to Russia in January 1767. Notice of his tightrope act appeared in St. Petersburg in October of that year. The language in the newspaper bulletin suggested a certain age-of-curiosities excitement about Maddox's debut in the imperial capital: "Herewith it is declared that the celebrated English equilibrist Michael Maddox will be demonstrating his art in the wood winter home, to which all inclined respectable individuals are invited."[7]

Maddox went to Russia without means—and without knowing the language—but managed, after falsely claiming an Oxford education and some teaching experience, to find work amusing Pavel I, son of the Russian empress, Catherine the Great. Pavel was delighted by his new tutor's *Cours de recréations mathematique et physiques.*[8] Maddox must have exceeded expectations, and Catherine declared her gratitude to him in the form of an official letter of commendation. That kept him away from the rabble of the fairground.

He returned to London to direct a theater, but in the 1770s St. Petersburg lured him back. Maddox shelved the magic shows for clock making and the invention of fanciful automatons, including music-box dancers. In tribute to his benefactress, Catherine the Great, he designed an elaborate clock whose bronze and crystal figurines allegorized her achievements. The figure of Hercules, who represented Russia's suppression of Sweden, stood in the middle of three columns atop a music box. The base was formed by statues of maidens gesturing toward the four corners of the Earth. Every five minutes—the preferred length of meetings at Catherine's court—chimes rang and miniature eagles dropped jewels from the top of the columns into the open beaks of eaglets in their nests. The gilded vignette was meant to illustrate how the Russian empire nurtured its conquered territories. Engravings on the pedestal and atop the music box showed stars, planets, and the rays of the sun. Catherine the Great herself never saw or heard the clock, however, having died of a stroke in 1796, a decade before Maddox completed it. It was privately sold then put on public display, and during the Revolution confiscated by the state. Eventually, in 1929, it ended up in the Kremlin Armory.

The peregrinations of showmen led to appearances in other Russian cities, including the comparative backwater of Moscow, where the nongovernmental university newspaper *Moskovskiye vedomosti* (Moscow gazette) announced an exhibition of Maddox's curiosities. Apparently the show found a following. In a subsequent bulletin from February 1776, he offered (through his Russian-language scribe) heartfelt thanks to the Moscow public for making the show such a huge success, solicitously adding that "after the end of this month the showings will cease, and so as not to deprive pleasure from those desiring to take them in once more, an invitation to attend is with all suitable deference extended."[9] He was mindful of competition from other entertainers. The "mechanic and mathematician M. Megellus" also plied his wares in the same newspaper, advertising exhibitions of "various wonders" at the parish of St. John Baptist for 1 ruble (50 kopecks for the cheap seats).[10] The newspaper is crowded with varied squibs that survey the social, cultural, and economic scene at the time. Notices for French-language history books, translations of English publications about plowing, portrait sales, and land auctions appear beneath epigrams to the empress and verses to the New Year. Besides granting space to Maddox, Megellus, and the occasional freak show, *Moskovskiye vedomosti* printed stories from afar: that of the 175-year-old Argentinian man and the beef-and-millet diet that sustained him, and that of the "girl, age seven or eight, from the French village of Savigné-l'Évêque, who has sprouted hair all over her body and has a beard and moustache hanging from her chin down to her shoulders."[11] Weather reports appeared after the fact: "There was thunder and lightning yesterday afternoon at 5 o'clock and some hail fell, but it did not last for long."[12]

In Moscow, Maddox improvised an existence for himself as an impresario, catering to a public in search of amusement. Entertainment was prohibited during the Orthodox fasting periods, but even at other times, there was little to do. Maddox sought to fill the void by opening a theater and soon came into possession of one. But not on his own, and not without taking on (then running afoul of) dangerous creditors, the Old Believer merchants who had loaned him thousands of rubles in goods for his enterprise and who did not appreciate his refusal to repay them. Maddox became, in their eyes, the Antichrist, and Moscow needed to be cleansed of his presence.

Maddox also clashed with the xenophobic commander of Moscow, and with a powerful politician who had opened a theater of his own on the grounds of the *Imperatorskiy Vospitatel'nïy dom*, the Imperial Foundling Home. Once that territorial dispute was resolved, Maddox came to depend on the talented children of the orphanage to dance in his ballets and sing in his operas. For ever after, Moscow had its theater, and the theater had its school.

THE MOSCOW THAT Maddox made home was harsh, a city of tanneries and slaughterhouses, altogether lacking the stern neoclassical grace of St. Petersburg. Fires presented the greatest hazard, since most of the non-government buildings, including the churches, were made of wood. The dead were also a problem. The bubonic plague of 1771 felled a third of the population, including two of Maddox's potential rivals for control of theatrical entertainments in the city. (At the time, the core of Moscow comprised the area between the white defensive walls of the Kremlin and the outer ditch, gates, and ramparts—what became, by the end of the eighteenth century, the Boulevard Ring.) Cemeteries, like factories, crowded the center until Catherine the Great ordered them relocated beyond the ramparts into the artisan suburbs. The empress disdained Moscow: "besides sickness and fires there is much stupidity there," which recalled "the beards" of the boyars who had ruled it before her time.[13] She and her courtiers invaded the Kremlin for her no-expense-spared coronation, but she otherwise kept her distance. Compared to St. Petersburg, the imperial capital on the Gulf of Finland, thirteen postal stations north, Moscow was dissolute, depraved. Upon recognizing that it needed her divine intervention, Catherine drained the swamp, literally, by ordering the encasement of the tributaries of the Moscow River in subterranean pipes. The empress was benevolent when convenient, repressive when required. She quashed the revolt of 1773, for example, but counseled compassion when it came to the execution of the rebels, whose ranks included peasants, former convicts, religious dissenters, and Cossacks. Torture was discouraged, as was the public display of corpses. But such decorum was not extended to the leader of the rebels, Yemelyan Pugachev. He was hauled to Moscow from Kazakhstan in a metal cage, then decapitated and dismembered in Bolotnaya Square.

Prussian by birth, Catherine ascended to the throne in 1762 after securing the arrest of her puerile husband, Peter III. He had ruled Russia for just half a year, enacting a series of halfhearted reforms that aided the poor but offended the lower noble ranks. They forced him to abdicate, after which he was placed under house arrest in his manor in Ropsha. Catherine allowed him to keep his servant, dog, and violin, but not his lover. In July 1762, he died, cause unknown. Alexei Orlov, the coup-plotting brother of Catherine's own lover, blamed Peter's death on a drunken quarrel with his guards. Catherine attributed his demise to cowardice. "His heart was excessively small, and also dried up," she recalled, after ordering his bruised corpse opened up.[14] She described the day she became empress (before her husband's death) with more warmth:

I was almost alone at Peterhof [Palace], amongst my women, seemingly forgotten by everyone. My days, however, were much disturbed, for I was regularly informed of all that was plotting both for and against me. At six o'clock on the morning of the 28th, Alexei Orlov entered my room, awoke me, and said very quietly, "It is time to get up; everything is prepared for proclaiming you." I asked for details. He replied, "Pacik [Peter III] has been arrested." I no longer hesitated, but dressed hastily, without waiting to make my toilet, and entered the carriage which he had brought with him.[15]

As empress, Catherine rose at dawn to attend to affairs of state, ensuring that meetings did not exceed the five-minute span Maddox would represent in his clock. She maintained a discreet but adventurous love life; the goings-on in her bedchamber later prompted ludicrous Soviet-era gossip about decadent sexual practices, including bestiality. Official records reveal that she overhauled the Russian legal system, pushed the boundaries of the empire westward, and ordered the construction of more than a hundred towns in eleven provinces. Besides the establishment of the Imperial Foundling Home, her educational reforms in Moscow included the opening of two gymnasia under the aegis of Moscow University. The first of these was for the sons and daughters of noblemen, the second for the sons and daughters of commoners. Some of Maddox's eleven children attended the latter.

TO OPERATE HIS THEATER, Maddox needed a partner from the upper noble ranks. He found it in the Moscow provincial prosecutor, Prince Pyotr Urusov. Among the prince's duties was overseeing the masquerades, fairground booths, strongmen, and trained bears of Moscow. In March 1776, the governor general of Moscow, Mikhaíl Volkonsky, granted the prince a decade-long exclusive permit for theatrical presentations. Urusov had earlier collaborated with an Italian impresario, Melchiore Groti, but the relationship soured, and Groti vanished "to God knows where" with the costumes and the salaries owed to the staff.[16] The municipal police could not catch him. Maddox came to Urusov's rescue, convincing him of the financial and logistical benefits of a partnership while also mesmerizing him with visions of fantastic spectacles to be staged in dedicated spaces. Since there was no shortage of unemployed professional actors in Moscow, neither Urusov nor Maddox thought to enlist amateur talent—namely, the girls and boys who were being taught four hours per day, four days per week, on the grounds of the Imperial Foundling Home. The actors from the bankrupt Moscow Public Theater would suffice, along with some serfs.

On August 31, 1776, Urusov and Maddox formalized their relationship. The contract between them was certified by the police and survives in the Russian State Archive of Ancient Acts. It runs just four lines, the first reaffirming Urusov's ten-year monopoly, after which, in 1786, Maddox would be granted a ten-year monopoly of his own. Tucked into the mix was the unusual detail that Maddox was to provide 3,100 rubles a year to the Imperial Foundling Home. His contribution to the drama and music school on its grounds did not mean, at the time, that he could exploit the talents of the orphans. That was a later development that would arise when he fulfilled the last stipulation in the agreement with Urusov: the construction, by 1781, of a proper theater in Moscow. Advertised as entertainment for the entire nation, the theater was to be built of stone and surrounded by a moat for the prevention of fires. Its "accessories" were at once to pamper its patrons and improve the skyline.[17]

• • •

MADDOX AND URUSOV acquired a parcel of land on an ancient thoroughfare in central Moscow. It had once served as the home of lance- and spear-makers, hence the name of one of the cathedrals that dominated the neighborhood: the Cathedral of the Transfiguration on the Spear. The plot was on Petrovka Street, parallel to the half-finished underground tunnel that would, following its completion in 1792, guide water from the north of the city into the Moscow River along what is now Neglinnaya Street. The water had once wrapped itself around the Kremlin, serving as a natural defense against invaders to the east.

Before the theater on Petrovka Street was built, Maddox and Urusov arranged performances on Znamenka Street, in a theater located on an estate belonging to Roman Vorontsov. During the summer Maddox also began to organize Sunday concerts and fireworks in the public gardens on the southern outskirts of Moscow. Admission through the covered entrance into the gardens, which Maddox modeled along the lines of the London Vauxhall, was 1 ruble or 2, depending on whether the visitor sat for tea in the rotunda. The Italian theater manager Count Carlo Brentano de Grianti was charmed by the place when he visited in the 1790s, but since the gardens appealed to tradesmen—cobblers, hatters, and corset-makers—the upper ranks kept their distance. Grianti's description of the gardens is briefer than his accounts of the passions of Russian countesses, Siberian gems, gambling at the English Club, and masked balls at the court of Catherine the Great. But he finds room to mention the great "profit" that "the theater entrepreneur M. Maddox" made in the gardens on holidays.[18]

Maddox sank some of that profit into the Znamenka playhouse, renovating it in time for the premiere of the Russian comic opera *The Miller Who Was Also a Magician, a Swindler, and a Matchmaker* (Mel'nik—koldun, obmanshchik i svat, 1779).

The score is chockablock with buffoonish, rustic ditties of broad appeal, even to non-Russians; the best of the tunes are heard in the central *devichnik* scene, a kind of bachelorette party for the heroine. The music was put together by the violinist Mikhail Sokolovsky, who had been added to Maddox's payroll as a favor to his wife and sister, both talented music-theatrical performers. The opera was a success, lasting much longer in the repertoire than the theater itself.

But the fixes were cosmetic. The Znamenka was a firetrap, and Maddox complained about its flammable flimsiness in a letter to the governor general. Sure enough, "negligent lower servants who lived in the basement" sparked an inferno.[19] The playhouse burned to the ground on February 26, 1780, during an unscheduled intermission in a performance of *The False Dmitri*, a play based on actual historical events in Russia (the cursed period of famine, usurpers, and impostors known as the Time of Troubles). The lead role was played by a court-educated thirty-six-year-old actor named Ivan Kaligraf, who supplemented the income he received from Maddox by giving acting lessons at the orphanage.

Kaligraf, who had survived the bubonic plague in Moscow, perished after the fire. He caught a cold while attempting to douse the flames. The sniffle developed into pneumonia, and then fever of the brain. *Moskovskiye vedomosti* did not report his death and focused instead on the survival of the governor general, the brave servants who saved their masters, and the prompt actions of the police in preventing the blaze from spreading to nearby houses by sealing off the ends of the street. Had the fire spread, scores might have perished, since most of the dwellings in the area were nothing more than collections of tree trunks purchased at market.

An entire article in *Moskovskiye vedomosti* was dedicated to the loss in the fire of a bejeweled chapeau, "on which was sewn instead of buttons a large ring of a single diamond with smaller diamonds sprinkled around."[20] A hunting hat with diamond thread also vanished in the panicked flight from the theater, along with a pair of round earrings and "a silver buckle of gold and crystal."[21] A handsome reward was promised for the return of these items to their owner, an imperial senator. But the newspaper said not a word about the death of one of the best actors in the city.

Urusov suffered a huge financial loss in the fire and was forced to surrender his share of the theater to Maddox for 28,550 rubles. Imperial officials offered to reassign Urusov's rights to Maddox as long as the stone theater was finally built on Petrovka Street. Construction of the theater, the future Bolshoi, had not even begun when the Znamenka burned down. To see the project through to completion, Maddox needed to borrow a huge sum of 130,000 rubles while also settling the bill for the damage to the Vorontsov estate and continuing, per imperial decree, to supplement the budget of the orphanage. Since the fire had deprived him of income, he was forced to borrow repeatedly from the *Opekunskiy sovet*, the governing board, which was established under Catherine the Great for the care of orphans and widows, and whose activities included a pawnshop and a mortgage brokerage.

Maddox had secured an architect for the project, Christian Rosberg, but progress was delayed owing to Rosberg's health problems. In 1778, he suffered from "painful seizures" after being exposed to noxious fumes and had to surrender his position as a building inspector.[22] It took Rosberg four years just to come up with a model for the theater. The pressure from Maddox's creditors was intense. He turned the threat to his advantage by appealing to the highest power in the land, Catherine the Great, for assistance mobilizing a brigade of builders. Work proceeded apace, and the theater was completed by the end of 1780. Maddox was saved—at least for the moment. The governor general found himself obliged to instruct the police, in a disquieting memo from March 31, 1780, "to accord Maddox special reverence and respect and protect him from unpleasantness. . . . Seeking to bestow pleasure on the public, he had traded all of his capital to construct a huge and magnificent theater and remained burdened by debt."[23]

The plans for the theater survive, although most of the images only detail the exterior and surrounding structures. The theater had a single entrance and exit, with three stone staircases inside leading up to the parterre and the three tiers of loges; two wooden staircases led to the galleries above. Later a plank-covered mezzanine and a masquerade rotunda with elaborate garland moldings, portraits, and mirrors would be attached by corridor to the theater. The rough granite square at the front of the theater was on higher ground than the fuel-storage area in the back. Wooden buildings cramped the square to the right and left, spoiling the view of the theater from the distance and posing a fire risk. Maddox occupied one of these buildings; another perhaps served as his horse stable and carriage house. The statelier buildings on Petrovka were held by aristocratic clans. The artists of the theater slept in garrets and frequented the clammy, soiled Petrovka tavern. General Major Stepan Apraksin, destined to be a front-line commander in the war against Napoleon, occupied a residence farther up the street, not far from the carved stone façade, made to look like leaf and vine, of the Church of the Resurrection.

The belief has always been that the Bolshoi Theater was built on the foundations of the Petrovsky, but urban archeology places them 136 to 168 feet apart—the Bolshoi being that much closer to the Kremlin. Much as with the Staatsoper and the old Kärntnertortheater in Vienna, Maddox's stone block theater with slanted wooden roof did not titivate the skyline, but it was impressive for its time, rivaled only by the Senate Palace, the neoclassical building that now serves as the Kremlin residence of the Russian president, and Pashkov House, which became the first public museum in Moscow.

For a description of the inside, there are the piecemeal recollections of the noblemen who attended the six-o'clock performances in the 1780s. From their carriages, which were parked by a watering point to the side of the theater, they ascended a torchlit central staircase past the parterre into their leased loges, 110 in all, and further ascended, during entr'actes, to a buffet of cold cuts catered, according to the records, by a Frenchman. Entrance to the parterre cost 1 ruble, the galleries 50 kopecks. The audience on the floor and in the rafters included bureaucrats, students, merchants, officers, and valets. Mention is made in the sources of commodes for the ladies. The ceiling of the theater was fashioned from canvas-covered planks that, to the dismay of those trying to listen, deadened the sound of the orchestra. Large wax and tallow candles in forty-two chandeliers illuminated the space and mixed an odor akin to singed hair with the smell of the patrons. The light was magnified by mirrors onstage and off; torch dances by masked male and female performers served as rough-and-ready spotlights; handheld candles in the audience were used to read programs. Underground were nooks for the dress- and wigmaker, rooms for making and storing props and panels, and practice spaces for the musicians. Even those who could read music sometimes learned their parts by rote, saving Maddox the cost of a copyist, paper, and ink. Coal stoves heated the theater and the masquerade rotunda.

The hall was Maddox's greatest pride and greatest expense. (Most of the loans he obtained from the *Opekunskiy sovet* went to its construction.) The Englishman Charles Hatchett, an amateur chemist and son of the imperial Russian coach maker, recalled Maddox boasting to him that the masquerade rotunda could hold

5,000 people. Hatchett was either mistaken in his recollection or referring to the number of people who could be accommodated in Moscow's public gardens, which had entertainments of their own. Or perhaps Maddox was simply exaggerating. In truth, the rotunda could hold 2,000 people, excluding the musicians in the rafters, and the theater itself no more than 900. Hatchett further observed that, no matter the size of the crowd, the well-heeled in the loges could preserve their privacy: "The boxes had veils of light silk to draw before the front so that those in them may be seen or not at their pleasure."[24]

Maddox pampered the elite, his season-pass holders, with coal heat and fashion brochures, and he invited them to rent their loges in advance so that they might "decorate them as they saw fit."[25] The seating plan recalled a chessboard, with the queens and bishops stacked at the back, and the pawns, the single-ticket holders, gathered before them. The participants in the masquerades, in contrast, tended to be "idlers and spendthrifts" looking for fun, and "gentry seeking grooms for their daughters."[26] The decadence and occasional tawdriness of the masquerades added to the allure of Maddox's theater and inspired a grisly tale of fiction, "Concert of Demons," whose hero, a former asylum inmate, suffers a psychotic episode in the Petrovsky. Sparks fall from the stars onto the roof of the theater as he wanders past a decrepit lantern-holder into the rotunda, which is illuminated, poorly, by smoking tapers in the chandeliers. The hero peers through the murk and the seductive swirl of red-and-black domino masks to behold, on the orchestra platform, Frankensteinian grotesquerie: "Necks of storks with faces of dogs, bodies of oxen with heads of swallows, cocks with goats' feet, goats with men's hands."[27] The powdered, owl-faced conductor leads the band in a respectable performance of the overture to *The Magic Flute*. The hero is introduced to the ghosts of famous composers. Then he is seized. "In half a minute," the conductor tears his right leg off, "leaving nothing but bone and dry sinews; the latter he began to stretch out like strings."[28] His remaining leg dances to the music before he loses consciousness.

The author of the 1834 tale, Mikhaíl Zagoskin, claimed, in tribute to Maddox, that it was based on actual events.

MADDOX'S INITIAL BUDGET for performers was just under 23,000 rubles, with the cost of operating the theater and the masquerade rotunda, including the salaries paid to the doctor, the coal stoker, and the hairdresser and wigmaker coming to 28,500 rubles. His roster included thirteen actors, seven actresses, and a dozen musicians. There were also seven dancers, three male, four female, who were denied room and board, and who earned pittances: 72 rubles a season in the case of the least-skilled ballerina. His lead actors came from a playhouse that had operated in Moscow in the 1760s under the direction of the composer Nikolay Titov. Nadezhda Kaligraf, widow of Ivan, earned a modest 600 rubles a season for delivering lines such as the following from the German bourgeois tragedy *Miss Sara Sampson:* "A short disappearance with a lover is a stain, it is true; but still a stain which time effaces. In some time, all will be forgotten, and for a rich heiress there are always men to be found, who are not so scrupulous."[29] She parried onstage with Vasiliy Pomerantsev, a subtle Shakespearean actor much coveted by Maddox's rivals—those upper nobles who conspired to pry his exclusive rights away from him. Pomerantsev earned a proper 2,000 rubles for up to a hundred performances a year and did not mind his employer insisting that his lines not be cued from the wings or through a hole in the front of the stage.

The theater opened its doors on the eve of New Year's Eve,

December 30, 1780, with a dramatic prologue that extolled not Catherine the Great, as would have been *de rigueur* in the Imperial Theaters, but Maddox himself. The deities of the arts, Momus and Thalia, are cast out of Moscow when their theater burns down but return incognito aided by other mythological celebrities. A chorus greets them at the entrance to the theater on Petrovka to proclaim the end of their suffering in a boring, unfree world without art. The prologue pokes at the ulcer of theatrical censorship while also boasting of Maddox's talents as entertainer. It was written by the satirist Alexander Ablesimov, the librettist of *The Miller Who Was Also a Magician, a Swindler, and a Matchmaker*, the comic opera that stood as Maddox's biggest success to date. It was a step up from the witty fables that Ablesimov spent most of his time writing.

Next on the program was a presumably recycled, quickly stitched-together piece of pantomime and dance called *L'école enchantée*, or *The Magic School*. Little is known about it beyond a playbill listing the dramatis personae and the names of the ballet master, costumer, designer, and five lead performers. The masks, silks, panels, and screens are long lost. As was typical of ballets at the time, characters came from myth, and their gestures were perhaps derived from picture books, illustrated tales of the ancient world. The inclusion of the magician Mercurius, god of eloquence and commerce in *L'école enchantée*, suggests that it was intended as an allegorical illustration of Maddox's illusion-filled career.

The music, also lost, came from the quill and inkpot of Josef Starzer, an industrious, well-connected Viennese composer credited with dozens of ballets. His collaborations with the influential ballet master Jean-Georges Noverre enhanced his international reputation, as did the itinerant dancers who spread his music around. Starzer fraternized at the Russian court with the Austrian dancer Leopold Paradis, who performed in St. Petersburg for almost two decades before getting a teaching position in Moscow at the Imperial Foundling Home. There Paradis taught classes of fifteen girls and fifteen boys on Mondays, Wednesdays, and Fridays from nine to noon, casting them in "sérieux," "demi-caractère," and "grotesque" roles based on their faces, not their feet.[30] His agreement with the Foundling Home required him to set a new ballet every other year on his students, while also providing instruction in traditional partnered social dances: Polish minuets and contra dances. Those students with natural talent and true zeal were given extra training. The curriculum lasted three years, with an exam after the first year deciding whether students had sufficient suppleness to proceed. Those who flunked were immediately replaced, since Paradis built his entire pedagogical method on classes of thirty.

Paradis was paid 2,000 rubles a year by the orphanage and given a housing, firewood, and candle allowance of another 200 rubles (he had requested 300). He was old-fashioned enough for the orphanage to want him dismissed, but its overseer in St. Petersburg was unwilling to compensate him for the termination of his contract and approve the appointment of a new teacher, so he was kept on the payroll. Meantime, Paradis was involved in a dispute with a former employer in St. Petersburg over wages owed. No one was happy, and complaints flew back and forth on luxury paper bearing florid signatures.

Sixteen of the children in Paradis's class danced in *L'école enchantée*. Their names are not included on the surviving playbill. The names of the adult dancers, the principals, are given, but they must have been traveling performers, since they are nowhere to be found on other Petrovsky Theater programs.

It hardly mattered, since ballet at the Petrovsky Theater was of much less importance to Maddox than opera and drama. It was also derivative, replicating Italian and French practices, and posing no threat to the bigger-budget ballets staged at court in St. Petersburg. The pantomimes Maddox produced had resonant names like *The Fountain of Good and Bad Fortune*, but gauging what exactly occurred onstage is hopeless. There exists the occasional newspaper bulletin about fantastic special effects and elaborate costume changes, as in the case of a ballet from 1781 titled *Harlequin Sorcerer*, whose trickster hero appeared in at least eight different outfits. Maddox also mounted the ballet *Acis and Galatea* at the Petrovsky. The ballet, to music by Franz Hilverding—a composer in and out of debtor's prison—had been performed in the Winter Palace by noble amateurs with amazing (for the time) special effects.[31] The hero, the poor shepherd Acis, falls into the hands of the reprehensible Cyclops Polyphemus, who hurls him through the air toward a mountain. He would have been killed by the blow had he not been saved by Love. Polyphemus goes for the kill again in the second act, this time hurling an entire cliff toward Acis and his beloved, the beautiful nymph Galatea. Love intervenes once more, gathering the shepherd and nymph into his arms and sweeping them through the clouds into his namesake kingdom. Neither the pulleys and ropes used to produce these marvels nor the reactions of the audience to them are mentioned in the sources. It was said, however, that when the ballet was presented at the Winter Palace, the apotheosis brought tears to Catherine the Great's eyes.

Maddox first relied on Paradis as ballet teacher and creator before turning to expatriate Italian talent. In 1782, Maddox enlisted Francesco Morelli, a Milanese dancer who had performed for seven years in St. Petersburg before settling into a teaching position at Moscow University. Morelli's sacrifice to his art left his once-acrobatic legs battered and fragile and his feet (in the opinion of one of his students) "scorched."[32] The official records of his career cannot be trusted, since he suffered amnesia in his dotage and filled them with errors. It seems that, near the end of his life, he taught dance to serfs, but evidence also finds him doing clerical work and engaged in regular disputes with his employer. He married the daughter of a count and lived in the count's home, later boasting that he somehow prevented its destruction by Napoleon's troops. Morelli remained with Maddox for about fourteen years. His tasks included teaching classes and leading rehearsals; ordering masks, costumes, and props; arranging auditions; moving dancers on and off of the stage; and cueing the orchestra. Morelli created ballets about star-crossed love, ancient and modern, on land and sea, but nothing that lasted beyond a single season. His brother Cosmo, a dancer of loose morals involved in several sex scandals, helped him with his work. Morelli's final ballet for Maddox was *The Two-Timed Village Doctor*—an attractive potpourri organized much like a comic opera, but with gesture doing the work of song.

When Morelli became feeble, Maddox turned to Pietro Pinucci and his wife, Columba, who in their three years at the helm increased the number of ballets produced annually at the Petrovsky from twenty-five to thirty-five. Some gained a toehold in the repertoire, but most were forgotten, the two-part dances mixed and matched together for use as entr'actes or interludes under different names.

The role of ballet master thereafter fell to Giuseppe Salomone II, who danced with his much more famous father in London, Vienna, and Milan before finding work with Maddox. He made his debut in Moscow in 1784 with *The Fountain of Good and Bad Fortune*. His name and those of his three daughters, all musicians, recur in the sources. He is the one Petrovsky ballet master with whom some specific principles can be associated, owing to his mid-career tutelage under the Parisian Noverre, who called for the transformation of ballet from a cheerfully banal confection into a plot-driven, narrative art—an art of grittier, grimmer sentiment. Pantomime was to lend the old noble steps gravitas. The theory was put into practice and acquired a name: *ballet d'action*. Salomone set several of Noverre's ballets at the Petrovsky, elevating the genre from simple-minded caprice, but in the process he alienated his audiences. Ballet was supposed to entertain, gaily, with the dancers bursting into street songs, banging drums, and changing their costumes up to eight times per show. It was meant to titillate, not educate—at least not while a retired tightrope walker was in charge.

OVER THE COURSE of his time at the Petrovsky, Maddox produced more than four hundred Russian and foreign ballets, operas, and dramas—including a significant production of Mozart's opera *The Magic Flute* in 1794. The light comic opera *The Miller Who Was Also a Magician, a Swindler, and a Matchmaker* settled into the repertoire, and for those seeking other delights, the masquerade hall proved popular. From the very beginning, however, expenses outweighed receipts, bringing Maddox into serious legal conflict with one of his designers, Félix Delaval, who sued over unpaid wages and the dishonor of having been turned out on the street. Maddox defended himself by impugning Delaval's character. "Mr. Delaval came to the hall to ask me for money," he wrote in a kind of affidavit. "I told him that he had already been given extra, but that if he showed me his mastery I would pay him what he had been promised. He responded with very harsh words and left, but came back two days later and began to blaspheme me in the presence of Captain Alexander Semyonov and the actor Ivan Kaligraf, and also uttered obscenities to Captain Alexander Semyonov, and a few days before that struck the soldier standing on guard."[33] Maddox ended up losing the case and had to compensate Delaval for lost wages, 60 rubles in candles, and 25 rubles in firewood.

Maddox muddled through these and other conflicts, scrimping on salaries, candles, and firewood, and ignoring the resulting complaints about the chilliness in the hall. But in 1783, his third year running the Petrovsky Theater, he faced a grave threat to his livelihood from an unlikely place: the orphanage. The crisis began when Maddox clashed with a senior official in the imperial government, Ivan Betskoy. Betskoy served as personal assistant to Catherine the Great on matters related to educational enlightenment and presided over the Imperial Academy of the Arts. Betskoy had founded the orphanage in 1763 and subsequently demonstrated, in the remaining years of his life, a sincere concern for the children under his care.

The orphanage, an immense quadrangle, was located on a bend of the Moscow River, adjacent to the Moscow market district called Kitay-gorod. The name now translates as Chinatown, but the ramshackle collection of stalls and workshops had nothing remotely Chinese about it. (The archaic Russian word *kita* refers to plaiting or braiding, and it is thought that basket weavers once plied their trade in the area.) The *Opekunskiy sovet* managed the finances of the orphanage, and advertisements for its mortgage brokerage and pawnshop appeared in *Moskovskiye vedomosti*. Funding came from a lucrative 5-kopeck tax on playing cards. (The empress decreed that the packages would show the symbol of the orphanage—a stork—along with the slogan "She feeds her chicks absent concern for herself.")[34] There were also discreet donations from noblemen who had fathered children out of wedlock and a separate tax on public entertainments. Enough money was left over after basic expenses to import musical instruments from abroad, together with colored pencils, "bows," and "screws."[35] The orphans assumed the surnames of the princes and princesses who funded their care (the twenty orphans supported each year at the bequest of Princess Marianna Gessen-Gomburgskaya took the last surname Gomburtsev, for example), but the imperial pedigree did not spare them from manual labor in factories and mills in their adulthoods.

Betskoy had conceived the orphanage as a school of manners for the emancipated children of serfs, those whose parents had died in the bubonic plague, or those who had been abandoned by soldiers and peasants. By improving the lives of these unfortunates, Betskoy imagined fostering a third caste, an enlightened middle class between the nobles and peasants. Inspired by the Enlightenment thinkers Locke and Rousseau, he argued in his elegant fashion that children come into the world neither good nor evil, but like a wax seal into which anything could be etched. The boys and girls at the orphanage were to be imprinted with laudable inclinations: love of hard work, fear of idleness, compassion, politeness, tidiness, and cleanliness. Engineering the heart and soul was as essential as training the intellect. Tutoring in foreign languages and the arts, including dance, music, and theater, was meant to shield the children from baser influences. The first children to learn ballet were the offspring of palace servants. But shocking death rates at the orphanage (even instances of dead and dying babies being left at the door), an epidemic of child abuse, and tales of embezzlement sullied Betskoy's plans. He offered rewards for the rescue of babies from gutters and troughs and could not countenance that the shelter he had opened for them lacked the proper resources—including wet nurses—to keep them alive. Some of the pain he felt on behalf of his older adoptees can be detected in a letter that he wrote to the governing board, protesting the use of corporal punishment and harshness of the cabinet- and textile-making rooms:

> As a result of various rumors circulating here I have learned
> that the wards, especially those of the female sex, are being

brought up in a manner quite disgraceful; I do not mean that they should be taught to be vain and prideful, for true education cannot consist in that, but one ought to find a mean, so that a human being could esteem the human in himself and yet know how to be equal to one's station, whatever that may be, and, allowing no one to treat him as if he were a beast, would wish to fulfill, with diligence and as if it were an honor, all obligations imposed upon him in accordance with said station. Above all they say about those wards who have been apprenticed to manufacturers, and in particular about those assigned to Tanauer, that they are being kept in conditions that are in no way commensurate with human society, and are worse than those befitting servile commoners.[36]

As always, ideals collided with reality, one that clean forks and bowls and napkins changed every three days could not conceal, except for foreign guests, whose impression of the place was that of a Potemkin village, the children dancing around the beaming director in gratitude for their lamb and rice and iron beds. Behind the scenes, maidens were raped by the staff—a serious matter, since pregnant single women risked savage beatings to precipitate miscarriages and the perilous disgrace of banishment to Siberia. For other wards, the experience of the Enlightenment consisted of toiling in overheated, unventilated rooms, winding cotton and spinning flax, being flogged with knouts if their quotas went unmet. Few of them sang; even fewer danced.

Betskoy, the proud, stout representative of the proud, stout empress, ensured that visitors came away with a positive impression. In the autumn of 1786, Sir Richard Worsley (an English statesman and antiquities collector) traveled to Moscow on the back end of a European tour, noting the potholed roads leading into the city but also the "noble view" of churches and palaces from six kilometers out. He dined with Maddox on September 27 and 30, going to the theater after the first meal and raising glasses to the health of counts, countesses, and their children at the noblemen's club after the second. The singers were better than the actors in Maddox's enterprise, Worsley believed, adding that just one of the actors survived the merciless heckling from the parterre to give "general satisfaction." Worsley included a visit to the orphanage on his itinerary, and describes in his memoirs the "innocuous" but soon-to-be "augmented" building that gave shelter to 4,000 orphans "who are taught music, geography and moral history." The girls, he adds, "embroider and make very good lace." The director, Georg Gogel, talked him through the budget: "The expense of the different masters and teachers who overlook the children amounts annually to 40,000 rubles, the fixed pension of this hospital from the crown is 70,000 rubles, besides which they are supposed to have a fund of some 3 million, which they lend out at interest." Overall, Worsley found the place "admirably well conducted, and each child has a bed, the girls are in a ward by themselves, and the dinner throughout the whole is changed twice a week. There is also a small collection of natural history, to instruct those who are to follow that pursuit, a music room and a library. The wards for the lying-in women are in another separate building, where the women may come when they please, and return home without the least expense, nor can any question whatever be asked them." A touch of wryness: "I was informed by the director that great advantage of this part of the institution was taken by the nobility."[37] (Worsley could sympathize: His estranged wife, Seymour Fleming, had given birth to a boy fathered by another man and was rumored to have taken more than two dozen lovers in 1782 alone.)

At least at first, the entertainments put on by the orphans were intended just for the children themselves, their minders, and visiting dignitaries. Little survives of these performances beyond playbills and unspecific anecdotes. In 1778, Count Pyotr Sheremetyev attended a play and a Russian comic opera and was impressed enough to "perpetuate the pleasure he had expressed verbally by donating one hundred rubles" for distribution to "orphans of both sexes in the theater."[38] The children also put on a ballet on a subject of dubious moral content: Shakespeare's lascivious poem *Venus and Adonis*, in which a goddess takes a mortal lover by force. On other occasions they performed "Chinese shadows," which entailed speaking their lines behind screen partitions and waging great battles with their hands and fingers.[39] Since these were private events, the performances did not pose a threat to Maddox. But in 1783 a baron and donor (Ernst Wanzura) petitioned the empress to license the in-house theater for public performances. Catherine agreed, and the orphanage went into the entertainment business, mounting French and Russian dramas, operas, and pantomime-harlequinades.

The English cleric William Coxe supplies a precious, albeit vague, eyewitness account of one of these shows, coupled with an expression of surprise at the absence of "unwholesome smells" in the nursery and the sweetness of the bread baked by the oldest orphans for feeding to the youngest at sunrise and sunset. The performers "constructed the stage, painted the scenes, and made the dresses" for the comic opera he attended. During the performance, they "trod the stage" with ease. "There were some agreeable voices," and "the orchestra was filled with a band by no means contemptible, which consisted entirely of foundlings, except the first violin, who was their music master." Coxe heard the singers but did not see dancers, since "on this occasion the play was not, as usual, concluded with a ballet, because the principal performer was indisposed, which was no small disappointment, as we were informed that they dance ballets with great taste and elegance."[40]

Seeking permission to continue operating the theater, the director of the orphanage boasted of the success of these performances to Betskoy in a letter dated June 13, 1784: "Each day our theater gets a little better, to the greatest satisfaction of the public. The directors of the noblemen's club . . . informed me that their members intend to send a letter of gratitude to the governing board, including 2,000 rubles in this letter to be shared among the orphans who have distinguished themselves in the theater."[41]

Betskoy did not share the noblemen's delight and abandoned his phlegmatic demeanor to voice his outrage. He attended one of the ballets and was appalled, seeing not images of "great taste and elegance" but filthiness, postures fit for a "brothel theater."[42] He feared the orphanage theater becoming like the larger serf theaters operating in Moscow during the period—places of impure pleasures, whose vulnerable female performers did more for their masters than dance and sing.

Unaware that Betskoy was planning to abolish the orphanage theater, Maddox flew into a rage, or at least pretended to, about the violation of his privilege. First he sent the police to warn the publisher of *Moskovskiye vedomosti* against promoting the orphanage theater, and then he took the matter to the imperial court. Long forgotten was Maddox's own plan, back in 1779, for the orphanage to invest in the building of his theater. For his change of heart, Betskoy turned against him and judged his character suspect. Soon Maddox had a different agenda, one that he expressed to the governor general of Moscow, Zakhar Chernïshov. "Lend the hand of benevolence to a foreigner who surrenders his entire being to the justness of your Most Gracious Majesty," he pleaded with fake innocence, and "consider the unfortunate predicament of my family and those who have entrusted their capital to me."[43] The rhetoric did Maddox no good. The governor general took the matter to the empress, who instructed him to settle it on his own. Betskoy, for his part, also sent a letter to Chernïshov, expressing astonishment that a "foreigner who has come to enrich himself" could have the "impudence" to claim control over that which was most "sacred": control of the nation's culture.[44]

The court declared that the orphanage was permitted to operate a theater irrespective of Maddox's exclusive rights. Incongruously, given his initial protests, the decision allowed him to solve his financial problems—at least for the moment. He proposed absorbing the orphanage theater into his own enterprise, pledging to cover the costs of "an apartment and firewood" and restraining himself from "selling" the girls "for money."[45] He also proposed helping those orphans "who wished to pursue happiness elsewhere" by negotiating their contracts with other parties—a sly way of keeping tabs on the competition, but also perhaps an acknowledgment of the miserly salaries and grievous contractual bondage he was offering.[46] Maddox also said that he would hire the dance, music, and acting teachers of the orphanage for the Petrovsky. And he agreed to purchase, for 4,000 rubles, the costumes and props that the orphans had been using.

The sleight of hand was Maddox's repeated insistence on also operating the orphanage theater—but not the orphanage theater that had been in operation for the past year. Maddox proposed to expand his public theater empire by selling that structure and opening another one in Kitay-gorod, one that would be bigger, sturdier, and potentially more lucrative. His conniving drew a heated response from a member of the governing board:

As regards the notion, to my mind unimaginable, that the wooden theater deeded by Her Majesty be sold at a public auction, such stipulations astonish me. For where will our wards, then, perform? Surely not in a theater erected in the auditorium in the orphanage's central corpus? In that case we would have to invite inside the orphanage the municipal police and defer to its authority, since its presence is required whenever public entertainments are staged, with the entire city flocking to the very locale to which no stranger ought to be admitted.[47]

Maddox would drop the idea of building a second theater, though not before securing funding for it from the governing board, earning him the reputation of the cleverest of the clever when it came to financial dealings.

The negotiations lasted several months and were freighted with suspicion by those noblemen who thought the Petrovsky evil, a disreputable place guaranteed to harm the orphans, soil them inside. But after much agonizing and rewriting of the contracts, Maddox got his way: He received fifty ballet pupils, twenty-four actors, and thirty musicians from the orphanage and all but 10 percent of the income from their exploitation. The agreement reflected the notion that bad could be turned into good, that the orphans would cleanse Maddox's theater, rather than being soiled by it. Such had been the justification for involving the orphanage in the selling of playing cards and pawning of jewelry. These sinful activities became noble when used to rescue homeless children from the streets and enlighten the masses. Maddox too was liberated by the idea that the ends justified the means. Financial crimes became pious in the service of the ballets and operas performed at the Petrovsky, or what Maddox began to refer to as the Grand Theater, "the Bolshoi."

Maddox retained his monopoly. Neither the orphanage nor its instructors nor the foreign theatrical troupes that the orphanage had brought to Moscow could operate without his consent. And by bringing the orphanage theater under the aegis of the Petrovsky, Maddox managed to shield himself from his merchant creditors, to whom he owed, they alleged, 90,000 rubles. Some of what he took from them came in the form of cash, but he had also relied on them for building materials and furniture. Banks as institutions did not yet exist in Russia, and the magnates and moneylenders of Poland had not been integrated into the empire. Maddox had no option but to seek loans from a claque of Ryazan-Moscow merchants, who for centuries had been the sole group in Russia with serious amounts of cash at their disposal. The poet Alexander Pushkin borrowed from the merchants, as did the state, but it was unprecedented for a single individual to be so dependent on credit, as opposed to receiving a grant from the empress, to operate a public institution. Having sunk his personal savings from his magic shows and the Taganka neighborhood Vauxhall into the operation of the Petrovsky, Maddox had no practical intention of paying the loans back. He also knew that the barrel-bellied, bearded boyars would seek his hide if he defaulted. His theater—and his safety—rested on receiving the blessing, as well as the protection, of his other creditors: the powerful noblemen of the governing board. Once he had obtained this protection, Maddox took an audacious step. He appealed to the board for additional financing. Apparently Maddox's ambition, not to mention his slyness, knew no bounds.

The confrontation with the merchants was postponed as the financial standing of the existing theater continued to deteriorate.

Between 1786 and 1791 the Petrovsky stagnated. Frustrated by the repertoire choices and miserable salaries, some of Maddox's star performers relocated to St. Petersburg and the Imperial Theaters. Leased serfs and the orphanage provided replacements, including some true talents. Maddox hired Arina Sobakina and Gavrila Raykov, two comic dancers taught by Paradis, as well as the great actor Andrey Ukrasov, purported to be a trendsetter among young Muscovites—but these overexposed, underpaid performers could not, on their own merits, keep the Petrovsky afloat.

Maddox could not pay interest on his debt, much less pay down the principal, and his efforts in 1786 to solicit even more funding from the *Opekunskiy sovet* predictably came to naught. He was branded a deadbeat. His merchant lenders renewed their demands for repayment, raising the interest rates and threatening him with prison. He tried to plead his case in St. Petersburg, "going there during the winter for five months and in the end leaving my petition behind without any hope of it being taken up."[48] Then, back in Moscow that same year before the governing board, he fell to his knees: "Since I have no means whatsoever to settle my debts, that which is owed to the orphanage and my particular creditors," he begged, "I find myself for faithful payment with no recourse but to surrender the entire matter to the governing board, and with it to surrender myself, all of my possessions and the income they provide, in free will to the management of the governing board."[49]

With that, the theater on Petrovka Street, later known as the Bolshoi, became a government operation. The *Opekunskiy sovet* assumed complete control over the building and its finances. Maddox retained the title of general director, along with a budget of 27,000 rubles to pay his performers, the doctor, the furnace stoker, and the hairdresser. His salary was pegged to the success of the ballets and operas that he staged—5,000 rubles if receipts from the performances exceeded 50,000 rubles, 3,000 rubles if not. If, as was expected, expenses outweighed receipts, then he would receive nothing, not even firewood and candles for his apartment. To survive, Maddox appealed to the masses, staging more comedies than tragedies. The rich regarded him with suspicion, but he had a common touch. His repertoire choices showed his preference for exuberant childlike characters, mad dreamers rather than representatives of boring convention. Characters like him.

In the first year of the new arrangement, he earned his 5,000 rubles, relying on the advice of noblemen with an avid interest in the theater when sorting out the season. Some of these noblemen operated private serf theaters and were no less keen to keep tabs on Maddox as he was on them. They approved the good and censored the bad—not just those works that offended etiquette, but also those whose actors failed to emote, or whose dancers botched the *bourrée*.

The government too stepped in. Alexander Prozorovsky, an arch-conservative, anti-Enlightenment figure, took a special interest in Maddox and his business dealings. He had been appointed governor general of Moscow in an effort to prevent a repeat, in imperial Russia, of the fall of the Bastille in Paris. The delights of his command of Moscow included book-burning parties, the suppression of occult groups and non-Orthodox religious sects, the Freemasons in particular, and the recruitment of spies to monitor the comings and goings of potential insurrectionists.

The Petrovsky fell outside of Prozorovsky's control, which made Maddox a target of special investigation. The governor general sought to prove that Maddox had been negligent in fulfilling the duties granted him by the empress, and to negate the exclusive rights that remained in force despite his financial ruin. Confusion dominates his reports to Catherine, and to the noblemen's club, as to whether Maddox's exclusive rights terminated in 1791 or 1796.

Maddox of course defended the latter date, but the proof the governor general demanded could not be found, neither in Maddox's home nor in the files of Mikhaíl Volkonsky, the deceased governor general of Moscow, nor in police records. Maddox claimed that the papers granting him his privilege had mysteriously vanished. When pressed, he argued that the papers had been destroyed in the fire that had occurred back in February of 1780, in the three-sided wooden theater on Znamenka Street. Likewise next to nothing remained of the architectural plan, including the model, of the theater on Petrovka Street. The original architect, Christian Rosberg, informed the chief of police that Maddox had confiscated the model from him, but when the plan and model were demanded of him, by threat of force, all that Maddox managed to produce were the keys to a drawer filled with moldy, indecipherable scraps of paper. In the absence of documents legitimizing Maddox's theatrical activities, the governor general ordered the chief of police to extract an affidavit from Maddox "to add to the file."[50] The noblemen running Moscow under Prozorovsky blanched at the thought of buying Maddox out for 250,000 rubles, as he proposed.

Having failed to discredit Maddox, Prozorovsky resorted to extreme measures. He turned to the court with the unfounded allegation that Maddox's house, which stood on the grounds of the Petrovsky Theater, had been built with embezzled funds. The petition failed, after which, with extreme malice, Prozorovsky directed the police to burn the house down, no questions asked. The order was not carried out. The denouement of the drama involved Prozorovsky ordering a punitive inspection of the theater and scolding Maddox for its deficiencies:

It is my duty to say that you ought to endeavor to keep said theater unsoiled and maintain in it plentiful heat and yet forestall any suffocating fumes. . . . The hall in which you perform is riddled with a multitude of grave errors of architecture, though for this not you but the architect is at fault, and in so great a hall there is but one ingress and egress, and the only other way out is by means of a vile rope ladder. My predecessor had ordered an atrium to be erected, several years have passed, and yet you are not even thinking about it, and so I demand and assert that you must at all costs this coming summer raise that atrium, or else I will order your theater shut down until such time as it is built.[51]

In an attempt to deflect the criticism, Maddox reminded his antagonist of the good things that he had accomplished in his rotting theater, including the absorption of the school for thirty girls and boys and the promotion of the Russian repertoire. Prozorovsky changed the subject in response, shifting his invective from the sagging ceiling to the imperfect personnel:

It surpasses all understanding that your choir master is deaf, and that the German master of dancing in that ballet was lame, or else crooked-legged, and your ballet master is also old, as is his wife likewise, and no good as a teacher, for you have not a single student of either sex who would be at least tolerable in their dancing.[52]

In January 1791 Maddox asked the *Opekunskiy sovet* to free him from his financial obligation to the orphanage (10 percent of the receipts), as a form of "compassion to the oppressed."[53] The money would then be used to renovate the Petrovsky. The request was approved, but ultimately the matter rested with Betskoy. Maddox persisted, listing all of his services to the Moscow public: the building of the theater and its circular auditorium, the masquerades that he arranged in the Taganka Vauxhall, an investment of 100,000 rubles. The Russian (not Italian) ballets and operas that he produced needed to be taken into account, as well as their sets and costumes. The power brokers relented and, as a "good, humane deed," bought out his exclusive rights for just over 100,000 rubles while also relieving him of his 10 percent financial commitment to the orphanage, which he had never actually honored.[54]

Maddox's strongest supporters were dead and gone, and the new generation ruling Moscow proved hostile to his endeavors. He had maneuvered from the start to secure the protection of the crown, and he needed it to survive. In the 1790s his theater fell entirely out of fashion, and he into disrepute. His merchant creditors persisted in their campaign to prosecute him and took the time away from feasting, praying, and abusing their wives to dictate a letter to their literate sons for submission to Nikolay Sheremetyev, the owner of a first-class serf theater who had married, to the shock of the aristocratic establishment, his leading lady. The language of the complaint, dated July 4, 1803, is ornate, stuffed with proverbs, Ryazan dialect, and biblical arcana in the service of invective. The merchants sought to reclaim the 90,000 rubles they were owed, and hoped for Sheremetyev's assistance in imprisoning Maddox, since he had played them for fools for years, "twisting like a snake and a toad" to avoid his obligations, and leaving them "as helpless as crawfish in a shallow" when it came time to collect.[55] Moreover, he had insulted their bushy beards. Arson was not an option. If the Petrovsky was, God forbid, to burn down, the merchants would not recoup their losses. The 90,000 rubles Maddox owed to them—on top of the 250,000 he owed to the governing board—could not be gotten from Maddox's candle and firewood suppliers, who were also victims of his cunning, nor could it be beaten out of the orphans in the troupe, who would protest, should extortion be attempted, that they had earned their wages through hard toil:

> Verily is this Maddox the craftiest of all living beings, and back when we had not yet learned all his ways and taken full measure of his cunning—to wit, that he pays none of his debts and yet keeps putting away all the profit from the Theater into his own pocket on the sly—back then, while begging us for a reprieve in collecting a payment, would he bawl openly in front of us all, so much so that he could draw pity from stones. And what a master of trickery he is—you can be the smartest merchant in the world, and yet until you get to know him inside and out, he'll fool you over and over. And towards the end, having dispossessed us of both our wares and our capital, he set off treating us in an impolitic way: in his house did he curse and shout at us, simpletons, solely for our asking for that which was due to us. "How dare you," he says, "you beard-heads, set your foot in a house of a gentleman? Don't you," he says, "know that I, just like the local gentlemen here, carry a sword? And I am," he says, "made as ever the master of the Theater for all perpetuity." And so indeed we do believe that he is a man of magnitude, therefore, while all the local powers that be, may the Lord keep them in good health, we approach with no fear whatsoever, were we terrified to even think of showing ourselves before Maddox towards the end. For as it says in the Holy Scripture, "poverty doth humble a man," and Maddox is nowadays so proud that no cat will want to sit in his lap, and there's no sign that he is dwelling in poverty, but, he says, "I am only obliged to pay you one and a half thousand rubles a year; that," he says, "is what it says in the paper that the govern-

ing board has. How dare you demand more from me?" And that's his whole argument. Well, simple-minded as we are, we don't buy that kind of reasoning and think to ourselves, "Was it not he himself who made it so that he only has to give us that much?" And so the trustees, in their kindness to us, did judge that "Maddox, as they say, is poorest of the poor, nothing more can be gotten from him, and it's as good an end to a vile state of affairs as can be"—and thought that this would make us content. Will, now, Maddox succeed in having his way with us even here? For if he decided to pay us even one-and-a-half of ten thousand rubles a year, so we are certain as certain can be that the trustees would not hinder him in this but furthermore would commend him for dispensing with grace that which he gathered wickedly.[56]

The merchants wanted Maddox to sit in jail until his attitude improved and he opened his purse. But it was not, in the end, in the interest of the governing board to deprive him of the chance to settle his debts with the orphanage. In terms of his finances, Maddox was as "naked as a falcon," the governing board advised the merchants, but he had the backing of the crown and could not be touched.[57] Their desire to see him in a cold, damp prison cell, tormented by parasites, or sent on foot to Siberia, betrayed their ignorance of the perks of aristocratic relationships. Maddox knew these very well. Connecting the budget of his theater with that of the orphanage had shielded him from arrest, leaving his merchant creditors powerless. He would "dive to the bottom of hell" with the 90,000 rubles they had lent him, leaving their children with "no meat for their soup."[58]

By 1794, he was having trouble meeting payroll and found himself begging his stars to accept, in place of a salary, the chance to perform whatever and whenever they liked and keep a large percentage of the proceeds. The arrangement he made along these lines with Pyotr Plavilshchikov, a pudgy, doe-eyed actor committed to representing the plights of the lower ranks, was advertised in *Moskovskiye vedomosti* on December 13, 1794. "The performance is a benefit for M. Plavilshchikov, who receives no payment from the theater" and asks for "the indulgence of the esteemed public" in "flattering his hope" by attending.[59] He performed, then he quit, taking with him the conductor of the orchestra and leaving the public, which took the side of the actors over Maddox, disgusted.

The crisis deepened in the final year of Catherine the Great's reign and the first years of her daughter-in-law's rise to power as spouse of Tsar Paul I. Receiving word of the strife, the empress consort, Mariya, dispatched one of her spies to report on the Petrovsky.[60] The spy, Nikolay Maslov, wrote back three weeks later, on November 28, 1799, with a long list of calamities. He complained that the theater changed its shows so unpredictably that actors could not learn their lines in time. Their costumes were often ill kempt, or sometimes even performers simply wore street clothes. Plus the theater and dressing rooms were so frightfully cold that the performers often fell ill. "The management, all the while," he continued, "rebukes them harshly."[61]

Mariya expressed genuine surprise that the mistreated actors had not taken matters into their own hands and staged a hostile takeover of the theater. The Petrovsky had been bankrupt for at least three years, she realized. It had died along with her mother-in-law, Catherine the Great. Although Maddox announced business as usual in *Moskovskiye vedomosti* at the end of the official period of mourning for the empress, not even fireworks in the great rotunda could suppress the sad truth. He had nothing in the coffers, no one to clean the stage or bait the mousetraps, no coal to stoke or wood to burn. Still harboring the delusion that he might placate his nemesis, Prozorovsky, he had pledged to repair the theater and offered to heat it in advance of performances, rather than letting the rabble shiver in their stalls. He had also sought to increase receipts with a production of *Pygmalion*, an Ovid-derived melodrama about a sculptor who, having renounced the pleasures of the flesh, falls in love with one of his own creations. (The goddess Venus takes pity on him and brings the statue to life.) Maddox's 1794 and 1796 performances of the drama, to sweet music by the Bohemian violinist Georg Benda, succeeded, but most of his other stagings of the period failed. The entire theatrical enterprise had fallen to pieces, and no one from the Moscow aristocratic establishment wanted to clean up the mess. Maddox sent a long letter to Mariya in 1802 in hopes that the orphanage would assume his debts and he would be allowed to retire from twenty-six years of service to Russian culture with his dignity intact. Following an audit that found both the theater and the orphanage awash in red ink, Mariya ordered the liquidation of Maddox's estate.

The debts to the *Opekunskiy sovet* exceeded 300,000 rubles, which Tsar Paul, Mariya's husband, absorbed on behalf of the crown. The Ryazan-Moscow boyars, for all their colorful invective, did not get their 90,000 rubles back.

The Petrovsky Theater closed, in ghastly fashion, on Sunday, October 8, 1805. At three o'clock, just before a performance of the popular mermaid spectacle *Lesta, or the Dnepr Water Nymph*, a spark became a flame, which became an inferno. The theater burned for the next three hours, a conflagration seen far and wide. The curious gawked; police, theater workers, and firemen milled helplessly around. The cause of the blaze was a subject of speculation. Two eyewitnesses, gentle people in their dotage, proposed that the Day of Judgment had at long last arrived for Maddox and his scandal-singed theater. *Lesta* was a benign thing, a comic opera that retold an old legend of a mermaid who pines for a prince, but the ladies in question thought it was demonic, a horror of the imagination that offended the Christians in the audience. God intervened before the curtain went up.

Most simply blamed the fire on carelessness in the cloakroom. Someone had knocked over a candle, setting the lining of a coat alight; his or her frantic efforts to stamp out the flames had failed. Such would have been typical of Maddox's underpaid employees, the nobleman playwright Stepan Zhikharev explained, "the whole lot, each one being thicker-headed than the next."[62] Zhikharev watched from a distance: "We saw the enormous glow of a fire over Moscow and stood for a long time in bewilderment, wondering what could be burning so intensely. A postman coming from Moscow explained that the theater on Petrovka was on fire and that the fire brigade in all of its strength was unable to defend it."[63]

Maddox was done. He stayed in Moscow for a time, trolling the streets outside of his home in his familiar crimson cloak. There was talk of eviction, but the empress consort intervened to let him keep his house, instead of giving it to his actors. Eventually, he retired to the dacha and garden that he had bought years before, at the height of his powers, in the village of Popovka. He died there on September 27, 1822, at age seventy-five. His dancers and singers had become wards of the state and the Moscow division of the Imperial Theaters. Besides the remnants of Maddox's troupe, the Imperial Theaters absorbed a serf theater with a staff of seventy-four as well as the French public theater operating in the city at the time. Maddox's native Russian actors elegantly assured the empress consort that their pursuit of fame was not affected by "self-investment" but a desire to bring Russian theater to its "highest perfection."[64] Even in its ruin, the forerunner of the Bolshoi staked its claim as a source of national pride. The ambitions—and the failures—of Maddox's theater would also haunt the Bolshoi, which would likewise endure corrosive conflicts between the coldhearted management and the disloyal performers, succumb to government oversight, adjust the repertoire in search of audiences, struggle with stagecraft, and squander huge sums. And the theater would burn, repeatedly, but always be rebuilt.

Maddox retired without a title in the Table of Ranks, but with a generous pension of 3,000 rubles and "six horses to his carriage."[65] Maddox and his wife, a woman of German aristocratic lineage, had, among their eleven children, a son with a stutter whom they turned out for bad behavior. The stutterer in question, Roman Maddox, became the greatest Russian adventurer of the nineteenth century. He spent a third of his life in prison or exile for swindling, assembled a militia of mountaineers against Napoleon's troops, and, it was said, ravished more maidens than Casanova. Banished to Siberia, he conducted geological expeditions. The son's exploits fueled anti-Semitic gossip about the father. The slander increased after his death. Without pretense to subtlety, one Soviet-era source claims that Maddox's posthumous reputation ranges from a "prominent Englishman who was forced for political reasons to abandon his homeland" to a "thieving speculator and money-grubbing 'Yid.'"[66]

In the end, Maddox was no less an illusion than those he created.

· 2 ·

NAPOLEON
AND AFTER

THE CHARRED REMAINS of the Petrovsky Theater moldered in the bog under its former foundation, home again on summer nights to "birds of prey," "lots of frogs," and their music.[1] Maddox's free-enterprise experiment in dance and song had failed; the tsar stepped in, and ballet and opera in Moscow became, with the exception of the serf theaters, a government operation. The Moscow Imperial Theaters administration was established under the control of the St. Petersburg Imperial Theaters and the aegis of the court, which oversaw artistic, educational, and financial matters.

The children were the first order of business. Their training in dance and music had taken place in the Foundling Home before being absorbed into Maddox's operation. The orphanage remained proudly perched on a bend in the Moscow River, but it no longer privileged training in the arts. The Enlightenment educational principles of Catherine the Great and her personal assistant Ivan Betskoy were pursued instead in a separate building. Its name, the Moscow Imperial Theater College, was cumbersome, but it stuck. Throughout the nineteenth century the college expanded, its curriculum encompassing not only the arts but also the sciences, and enrollment increased. In the twentieth century, the prestigious dance division was renamed the Bolshoi Ballet Academy.

In the first half of the nineteenth century, the Moscow Imperial Theater College moved around as it grew: from a building in the market district near the old Maddox theater, to a series of stone manor houses. Three of the manor houses belonged to generals of long and distinguished service, one to a lieutenant colonel, another to a court chamberlain. The residence of the court chamberlain, an elegant structure of yellow pastel that still stands on Bolshaya Dmitrovka Street, housed first the college and then, after 1865, the business office, or *kontora*, of the Moscow Imperial Theaters. Toward the end of the century, a larger space was found in a building on Neglinnaya Street that had once been a canton school, an institution that readied the sons of conscripts for military service with lessons in everything from fortification to penmanship to shoemaking.

When the Imperial Theater College first opened, in 1806, it enrolled fifteen girls and fifteen boys. Far fewer students completed the course of studies in the first years than began it, because many chose to pursue other vocations. Tuberculosis also took its toll, as did personal problems. When the college could not fill the rosters of ballet performances, itinerant performers from the provinces and serf actors from Moscow's manor houses stepped in. The reputation of the art improved, as did the training, and by 1817, the number of students had doubled. Five years later, eighty-six students were in attendance: forty-one girls and thirty-four boys in the dance program, three concentrating in drama, and eight in music. By the end of the 1820s, when the college moved to the manor house on Bolshaya Dmitrovka Street, enrollment exceeded two hundred.

Students entered the college between ages nine and twelve and graduated between eighteen and twenty. Those living in residence included orphaned wards of the state and children of people working for the Imperial Theaters. The college limited the number of boarders to fifty students of each gender; by an odd quirk, those living at home could train in dance but not drama or music. The curriculum for the beginning students included, besides dance, classes in holy law, Russian grammar, arithmetic, handwriting, geography, history, drawing, gymnastics, piano, and violin. Later, mythology, fencing, and mime were added. Once it was codified, the routine in the college was invariant: rise at eight, common prayer, breakfast, dance classes until noon or one, lunch, academic subjects, dinner, carriage to the theater for those performing, permission to visit home on major holidays. Dance rehearsals were often held offsite; on Saturdays, the classes were inspected. Those students who did not, in the end, exhibit talent were given training in costume- and prop-making and the science of set changes. Those with some promise were assigned to theaters in Moscow and St. Petersburg as needed, with an obligation to perform for ten years.

Tales of life in the college are scarce but suggest a no-frills yet nurturing environment. One early graduate described being dressed "disgracefully, ridiculously, in trousers and coats of putrid light green fabric, patched here and there."[2] But the college was not Bleak House. Mikhaíl Shchepkin (1788–1841), a serf actor destined for greatness, taught at the college in the decades after Napoleon. He described his hard work there in a kindly cant: "Having taken on these responsibilities and accustomed myself to performing them conscientiously I seldom missed a day at the school. I soon became acquainted with all of the children, and we lived as friends, study-ing a little, but seriously."[3]

The next concern was rebuilding the theater itself. For the first two years after the fire, Moscow's entertainers performed on estates and in summer gardens around the city. Theatrical life once more ended up in the homes of noblemen, many of whom main-tained private serf theaters within their sprawling compounds. The largest exploited the talents of hundreds of performers, and hosted operas, ballets, and divertissements of foreign (Italian) visual design. With the Petrovsky gone, public theater suffered, and many of the professionals that Maddox had employed lived hand-to-mouth. Only in the spring of 1808 did the actors and dancers of Moscow find a new home in a wooden theater on Arbat Square, designed on imperial commission by Carlo Rossi, the immigrant son of a ballerina.

Its completion had been slow. Ivan Valberg (Val'berkh), the first famous native Russian ballet master, was told that it would be fin-ished at the start of 1808, but work didn't even begin until almost Easter. As he grumbled to his wife, "The theater is not done and the pettiness of the intrigues endless. There are no costumes, no sets; the conditions, in a word, are those of a fairground booth." Valberg found the "squabbling between the sub-directors, actors, dancers, dressmakers, and assorted riff-raff" tiresome and came to regret coming to Moscow from St. Petersburg, where he had held a comfortable position at court.[4]

Most of what is known about the Imperial Arbat Theater is fil-tered through fictional novels and stories. Leo Tolstoy's *War and Peace* includes a scene in which seventeen-year-old heroine Natasha Ros-tova, having just been humiliated by her fiancé's father and sister, goes to the opera; she is joined by the socially ambitious and sexually allur-ing Hélène. At first the fakery of the opera seems all too apparent and fails to impress. But Natasha, needing to lose herself in fantasy, falls under its spell. "She did not remember who she was or where she was or what was happening before her. She looked and thought, and the strangest thoughts flashed through her head unexpectedly, without connection. Now the thought came to her of jumping up to the footlights and singing the aria the actress was singing, then she wanted to touch a little old man who was sitting not far away with her fan, then to lean over to Hélène and tickle her."[5] The opera itself goes unnamed but is generally assumed to be an anachronistic combination of Meyerbeer's *Robert le diable* and Gounod's *Faust*.

The references to ballet in *War and Peace* are also indistinct (Tolstoy disapproved of twirling naked legs as much as he did stout prima-donna singers). Natasha refers to the dancer and ballet master Louis Duport, who performed in St. Petersburg and Moscow between 1808 and 1812, adhering, with majestic bearing, to the strictures of the French classical style. In the novel, Duport symbolizes the French influence on Russian aristocratic life, soon to be shattered by the Napoleonic Wars. It was an accurate depiction of the historical reality: War destroyed the Imperial Arbat Theater, razing it four years after it opened. The last event, on August 30, 1812, was a masquerade ball augmented by a mazurka quadrille performed by students.

War would also transform Valberg's career. "When Napoleon Bonaparte's Grande Armée marched into Russia," he "became the choreographer of the hour."[6] Valberg's transformation can be traced through his portraits. One likeness presents him as a curious man of letters: hair tousled, eyebrow cocked, a hint of St. Petersburg's spires in the background. Another has him looking remote and austere, with bleached skin, pale eyes, and a thin wig pulling back his scalp. The latter is the appearance he cultivated in Moscow as a mature artist, a Russian cultural patriot.

Valberg had begun his career in St. Petersburg, teaching in the theater school there from 1794 to 1801. For a brief period within that span, by capricious decree of Tsar Paul I, men could teach ballets but were not allowed to perform in them. Shoelaces and social dances were likewise banned. The tsar loved rigid drill and martinet discipline and believed that dancers, female dancers, should be more like soldiers—that is, less delicate and more violent in their movements. Ironically, he met his end at the hands of violent soldiers. A cabal of drunken officers confronted him in his residence, pulling him out from behind a curtain and demanding his abdication. When he refused, he was strangled. Few tears were shed in the Imperial Theaters after Paul's assassination. Men returned to the ballet, and the waltz returned to the court.

In 1801, following the ascension of Tsar Alexander I, Valberg traveled to Paris to improve his technique. Charles-Louis Didelot replaced him as pedagogue, raising standards in the corps de ballet and working to make Russian-born talent into "stars."[7] Didelot's officially sanctioned reforms included creating a middle tier of character dancers, or coryphées, between the corps de ballet and the first dancers. He eliminated the "steeplechasers" from the roster of the imperial ballet and replaced them with performers who possessed supple limbs and expressive faces.[8] Ballet historian Yuriy Bakhrushin credited Didelot with putting dancers in flexible, heelless slippers and sandals suggesting "Ancient Greece."[9] Out went the buckle shoes of the past, along with the wigs and rigid frocks that had limited the dancers' movements. Didelot established a strict training regimen and was known as a zealous taskmaster, albeit one with a kind heart and a gentle touch. Both men and women were taught *entrechats* and *battements*, and proper posture was enforced in the classroom through taps to the legs and backs with the baton used to count time. Bruises and loving pats on the head were the measure of a dancer's promise.

One of his most famous disciples, Yevgeniya Kolosova, had first been a student of Valberg's. Her physical expression was considered more nuanced, more natural, than speech. The ballets Didelot conceived for her were lavish productions with elaborate scenarios drawn from a conflation of pseudohistorical sources. He found his ideas in books on history and mythology, which he took to the studio in the afternoons. More than one of his plots pivoted around the rescue of the hero or heroine from boulder-throwing, earthquake-generating brutes. Didelot was also fond of Cupid and virgin sacrifices, and dabbled, toward the end of his career, in Orientalism. He liked to assign himself the roles of powerful gods, in defiance of his skeletal frame and oversized nose.

To simulate great windstorms, Didelot made his dancers flap their arms until dizzy and faint. To suggest spiritual flight, he came up with the idea of suspending dancers from wires and had his technicians raise and lower them with blocks and ropes. Didelot scorned gravity in various other ways. For his 1809 ballet *Psyché et l'amour*, a demon flew up from the depths of the stage and sailed, torch in hand, over the heads of spectators. Venus was once carried into the clouds in a chariot pulled by fifty live doves. Biographer Mary Grace Swift happily ignores the likely carnage: "It is interesting to imagine the care that had to be taken to harness each dove with its little corselet, which was then attached to wires guiding each bird."[10]

In 1811, Didelot was forced out, placed on a leave of absence for what the administration of the Imperial Theaters billed as ill health. In truth, a series of personal disputes resulted in the nonrenewal of his contract. Back from Paris, Valberg took over his overlapping

responsibilities as imperial ballet master, choreographer, and pedagogue. The thirty-seven ballets that Valberg himself created combined the feet placements and body alignments associated with the
French style and the technical displays of Italian entertainers. Valberg also tapped into his humble origins (his father was a tailor) for
creative material. One of his earlier ballets, from 1799, is set on the
streets and in the salons of Moscow. A man from the lower ranks
loves an aristocratic woman, and passion defeats reason with disastrous results. Although it deeply affected the audience, Valberg was
rebuked by the cognoscenti for using modern-day costumes. "Oh!
How the wise men and know-it-alls rose up against me! How, they
asked, could a ballet be danced in tail-coats!" he remembered of the
fracas.[11] He subsequently produced a series of fantastic ballets and
several domestic dramas that served the cause of moral and ethical
enlightenment. In one, a girl named Klara must be educated in the
rewards of virtue; another ballet teaches an American heroine the
price of betrayal.

Valberg came into his own, and distinguished himself from
Didelot, with a folk-dance-based divertissement about a Cossack
maiden who, disguised as a man, becomes a heroic chevalier. Following its successful performance in St. Petersburg, Valberg took it
to Moscow. There followed a series of pieces that combined dances,
songs, and dramatic dialogues expressing love for Russian peasants
and the sacred soil on which they toiled and for which they would
fight. Gone were the pixies, sprites, and chariots of the gods; in
came peasants, soldiers, and peasants-turned-soldiers. The choreographic dimension was reduced, but the overall popular appeal
increased. The most significant of these divertissements dates from
the height of Napoleon's invasion. Just four days after the pivotal
Battle of Borodino, which left both the French and Russian armies
depleted and out of position, Valberg staged *Love for the Fatherland*

(Lyubov' k Otechestvu, 1812) in Moscow. The music was written by Catterino Cavos, Didelot's preferred composer. According to an "eyewitness," *Love for the Fatherland* was so patriotic it convinced audience members to sign up for military duty.[12]

THE GRANDE ARMÉE entered Russia in the summer and fall of 1812. It has been estimated that 400,000 of its troops died for a cause that had lost meaning even before the crossing of the Niemen River of Belarus and Lithuania into Russia. Perhaps the same number of Russians lost their lives, perhaps more. The struggle was not, as it tends to be constructed, ideological, pitting the forces of revolution against monarchic rule. By 1812, Napoleon Bonaparte had declared himself emperor and exercised powers no less absolute than the Russian tsar. His relationship with Alexander I had at times been respectful; their emissaries had mooted the signing of the equivalent of a nonaggression pact. Even the possibility of a dynastic liaison through marriage loomed. But Alexander's decision to move his troops to the western borders of the empire created the pretext for the French invasion. Napoleon interpreted the move as a provocation and used it to recruit Polish forces for the battles in Smolensk, Borodino, and Moscow.

The war was a catastrophe for both sides. Cossack and Russian peasant conscripts under the control of Field Marshal Barclay abandoned their positions over and over again, ceding the soil of Holy Rus to the French without a fight. The behavior was passive-aggressive: the Russians neither laid down their arms nor engaged in traditional warfare. Instead, Barclay ordered the Cossacks to burn everything left behind: food sources, houses, modes of transport, and communications equipment. Barclay's aides, seeing the wasteland of overturned carts and dead or dying horses and men, challenged his judgment. The tsar sacked him, appointing Prince Mikhaíl Kutuzov in his place. Kutuzov was not a brilliant strategic thinker—by most accounts he was inert and rather clueless—but he benefited from being in the right place at the right time. He achieved victory after Napoleon essentially defeated himself by overextending his troops in hostile Russian territory. The scorched-earth practice deprived Napoleon of the spoils of his conquest. Supplies dwindled. Marauding Cossacks harassed the French encampments at night and captured and tortured to death those soldiers caught foraging for food on their own. Napoleon persisted, insisting upon the eight days' march from Smolensk to Moscow. When Napoleon's aides second-guessed his thinking, he fatefully declared, "The wine has been poured, it has to be drunk."[13] The horrendous battle of Borodino delayed, but did not stop, the French siege of the city. The cost in terms of lives and materiel on both sides was exorbitant.

Napoleon's soldiers entered Moscow on September 14, 1812, after exchanging grapeshot and cannonballs with the surrounding Russian positions. The colorful cupolas and golden spires of the city had made a fairy tale–like impression on the French from afar. But the streets were quiet, save for scattered drunkards and assorted ne'er-do-wells. Napoleon established quarters in the Kremlin without fanfare the following morning; he assumed administrative control of the ancient capital without such control having been ceded to him. The tsar and Moscow's ruling class ignored his arrival and refused to meet with him. Tolstoy imagined Napoleon's disappointment in a single sentence: "The *coup de théâtre* had not come off."[14]

Two-thirds of the population of just over a quarter million had evacuated. Before the invasion, the muddle-headed governor general of Moscow, Fyodor Rostopchin, had regaled the population with tales of French sadism. He acted surprised, however, when the terrified masses packed up and left. Rostopchin predicted Napoleon's defeat in his proclamations, but also pledged to leave him nothing but ash. The noble class locked up their stone manor houses and headed to their rural homes. Their carriages clogged the road. They packed up their human goods (cooks, maids, nurses, footmen, and jesters) along with their dressing tables and portraits. The carriages mingled with carts containing merchants and tradesmen and their families, along with injured Russian soldiers and—according to anecdote—deserters disguised as women. "Moscow was shaken with horror," a noblewoman recalled of her pampered exodus. She responded to Rostopchin's exhortations to stay in the city and accusations of treason by planning her "flight" and the packing of her precious objects.[15] The poor had no choice but to heed Rostopchin and take shelter in churches. Shopkeepers guarded their shelves against looting. The governor general ordered saboteurs, traitors, and spies for the French captured. Then he unlocked the prisons and madhouses. He ordered business papers destroyed and treasuries emptied. The looting began.

Rostopchin had been told by Kutuzov that Moscow would not be defended, so he fulfilled his promise to burn it down. The city had been tactically abandoned; sacrifice would be the price of its survival. Rostopchin ordered water tanks drained and charges placed in the granaries, tanneries, dram shops, and storehouses. Small fires illuminated the cart-jammed bridges, the shredded, discarded uniforms, and the human and animal waste on the streets. The flames spread easily in the late-summer breeze, ravaging block after block of wooden buildings, engulfing a hospital, and forcing the rabble onto the river's edge. Voices of the doomed mingled with the echoes of prayer and discordant singing. The flames increased the strength of the wind and the wind the strength of the flames. When the fire threatened his quarters in the Kremlin, Napoleon gathered his precious *articles de toilette* and left. He and his commanders took in the spectacle of the city in self-immolation from a suburban palace.

One of Valberg's (and Didelot's) distinguished students, Adam Glushkovsky, would become the first great ballet master of the post-Napoleonic era; during the war, he served as a teacher and ballet master in Moscow, reporting firsthand from the front lines. Relying on his own memories and those of his peers, he compiled a harrowing true-life account of the Napoleonic invasion.

Nine months before the Napoleonic invasion, in January of 1812, Glushkovsky arrived in Moscow. A mustachioed man with a wide-open face and the wardrobe of a musketeer, he was touted less for his leaps and jumps than for his acting. He danced at the Arbat Theater and taught at the Imperial Theater College, passing the lessons he had received from Didelot on to the children in his classes. He lived at the college but took his meals gratis in the home of the ballet master Jean Lamaral. When word came from the Moscow governor general that he would have to evacuate, he buried a trunk of his belongings in the woods. (The trunk stayed safe; he found it intact upon his return.) He spent his final wages, a bag of copper coins handed to him on the eve of the French attack, on boots and a coat for the road. Then he seated himself in a cart with his students, bound for the church towns northeast of Moscow known as the Golden Ring. The famished horses could barely lift their hooves, and the procession bogged down. He and the students settled for the night in a refugee camp before receiving word that the French would soon be upon them. The convoy lurched onward.

They moved through hamlets to the town of Vladimir, in hopes of taking shelter and refreshing their horses. The town was crammed with Russian soldiers, French captives, and assorted people of rank. The scene was repeated farther along the road, in the town of Kostroma. There the vagabond entertainers performed in the local wooden theater in exchange for food, a bath, and a bed. After just two days, however, the regional governor announced that he could not accommodate the theater school refugees in Kostroma, despite being directed to do so, on official paper, by the theater directorate in Moscow. Housing was instead found in the picturesque fishing village of Plyos. For three months, the students occupied merchant dwellings built into the hill above the Volga River. Glushkovsky and the other teachers who had evacuated (the instructors of holy law, diction, voice, and drawing) settled into buildings on the shore. To the horror of the eavesdropping local crones, Glushkovsky's girls lifted their skirts above their ankles and hopped about while practicing their fandangos with the boys. Word spread of the "unclean spirit" that had taken hold, and of the "devil's helper" teaching them their steps.[16]

Snow fell, and the students sledded down the hill to their classes. News of their presence spread to the aristocratic families residing in the area, and Glushkovsky became the featured entertainment as well as the instructor, in character dancing, of the darlings of the households. He took sick, however, after performing a solo from an Anacreontic Didelot ballet in a cold hall wearing only a light silk tunic. The fever threatened his life, but he declined the treatments offered by the village doctor—tea laced with vodka and bloodletting—in favor of hot wine and chest compresses soaked in vinegar. He convalesced back in Kostroma, where the governor finally found space for him and his students. The governor lived "like cheese in butter," staging operas on birthdays and hosting dance events capped with fireworks displays over the Volga.[17] The students of the Moscow Imperial Theater College continued their education in exile in the governor's private theater. Glushkovsky boasts of having a contented French prisoner as a servant, touting the lad's skills as a basket weaver and tooth puller.

He recorded what he heard from his friends still in Moscow about conditions in the city beset by the French. One of those left behind was a touring violinist, Andrey Polyakov, who told Glushkovsky about the filth and the smell of the invasion, how the fire flowed up and down and all around the boulevards of the city:

> Buildings on both sides of Tverskoy Boulevard burned; the heat was so intense that it could barely be withstood; in places the ground cracked and buckled; hundreds of pigeons rose over the wall of flame, then fell, scorched, onto a bridge girder; the smoke corroded the eyes; the wind carried embers a great distance; sparks fell like rain onto people; the thunder of collapsing walls sent them into terror; the aged and women with babies at their breasts fled their homes moaning and wailing and beseeching God's protection; others, the weak, died in the fire; charred dead dogs and horses littered the road in places; French soldiers fell to their deaths from roofs while trying to put out the fire.[18]

Polyakov's description of wartime Moscow evokes the horrors of Dante's *Inferno* and the divine last judgment. These points of comparison were made knowingly, as a best attempt to get across the inexplicable misery. He did not see everything that he describes, but his account is convincing and in keeping with other eyewitness descriptions of water boiling in wells from the heat of the flames and charred paper falling from the sky far outside Moscow. At the end of Tverskoy Boulevard, Polyakov saw two Russian soldiers hanging from a lamppost. It had been turned by the French into a gibbet. The signs in Russian stuck to their chests identified one as an arsonist, the other a defector to the French side who had second-guessed his decision and so met his end. Upper Petrov Monastery offered another ghastly scene. The sacred fourteenth-century grounds had become an abattoir. Pigskins sagged from hooks in the walls, cattle and lamb parts slicked the floors. French soldiers with bloodstained hands carved and distributed slabs of meat from the altar. Horses whinnied for food from the choir lofts.

After three days the fire had run its course, and the September weather turned glorious. Napoleon returned to the Kremlin, instructing his officers, in between card games and reports from the field, to reestablish order on the streets. Polyakov witnessed French soldiers smoking, eating, and mucking about before forming ranks for morning inspection. One or two trumpets blared; drums rattled. Napoleon himself arrived on a white horse, and the soldiers smartened themselves up. Napoleon gave them a quick, bored glance, ignored their salutation, then released them back to their tobacco. Thus the occupation settled into a routine. Millers returned to their mills, washerwomen to their washing. Theatrical life also resumed, after a fashion, with the performance of six French comedies and vaudevilles in a pleasant serf theater on an undamaged street. The texts were tweaked in honor of Napoleon and the depleted Grande Armée. Among the performers were Frenchmen employed by the Imperial Theaters alongside officers who had once trod the boards in Paris. The audiences were uncouth, with Glushkovsky describing undisciplined adjutants in berets "coolly smoking tobacco from Hungarian pipes with small stems," unresponsive to the performances except during the patriotic speeches, at which point they leapt to their feet to shout *"Vive l'empereur! Vive la France! Vive l'armée française!"* During the intermission they swilled wine and gorged on chocolates and fruit; afterward they remained in the halls of the theater dancing polkas.

Russian forces refused to capitulate, and engaged in a war of attrition. The people of Moscow starved; pigeons and crows were killed for soup. When they had all been eaten, only the sourest of staples remained—cabbage. Napoleon's men roamed the ashes "as pale as shades, searching for food and clothing but finding nothing, wrapping themselves in horse blankets and torn coats," with "either peasants' hats or women's thick, torn scarfs" covering their heads. "It was like a masquerade," Glushkovsky recalled of the weird getups on the streets. Nothing remained of the belief in liberating conquest that had borne the French into Moscow, a city with a texture that they could not fathom. Napoleon ordered the Great Retreat, but not before imagining a heroic return and, in a letter to his aide Hugues-Bernard Maret, vowing to blow up the Kremlin. Rumors of the impending bombing reached Polyakov's mother, who died of fright. Marshal Éduoard Mortier carried out the plan in the middle of the night on October 20, laying the charges to raze the citadel. But rain, or perhaps heroic Cossacks, put out the fuses attached to the barrels of gunpowder. Most of the towers and walls remained intact.

The French retreat was a pitiful sight. Battered, famished soldiers skittered along litter-strewn, stench-filled streets in twos and threes to their formation points. Most made it out; some were killed on the spot, others were captured. Those who had tended to sick Russian babies at the start of the occupation or otherwise demonstrated a human touch were given shelter in cellars. Mobs awaited the retreating soldiers in the forests, seeking revenge for the burning, the looting, the desecration of churches, the butchering of livestock. Tools of iron and wood gouged out eyes and vital organs.

The withdrawal continued into November. The temperature dropped. Subzero winds put out campfires; frozen corpses were cannibalized. Napoleon survived to regroup, but his command was fragile and his straggling forces humiliated. European allies became foes, and after a series of defeats he was forced to abdicate. Ambitions crushed, Napoleon would be imprisoned in exile on the island of St. Helena, where at least the climate was more forgiving.

WHEN DIDELOT RETURNED to St. Petersburg in 1816 from his purported leave, he resumed his duties in an utterly transformed political and cultural landscape. Tsar Alexander I recognized that he had the self-sacrificing Russian masses to thank for rescuing his rule from Napoleon. Their triumph against improbable odds inspired the cultural shift, the enthusiastic embrace of all things Russian. Cossacks took the stage to celebrate Napoleon's defeat. Gypsies and peasants joined them and were paid to give lessons in their native crafts to performers otherwise trained in *pliés, battements, ronds de jambe,* and courtly dances. The new fad for the *prisyadka* squatting position and choral round dances, accompanied by pipes, hurdy-gurdies, and assorted noisemakers, did not last but left an impression nonetheless. Didelot adapted to the patriotic turn by adding Russian dances of the streets and the fields to the pedagogical curriculum of the ballet school in St. Petersburg. In 1823 he staged the second ballet to be based on a text by Alexander Pushkin. Titled *The Prisoner of the Caucasus, or The Shade of the Bride* (Kavkazskiy plennik, ili Ten' nevesti), it included a dark-eyed oriental heroine, lasso-wielding barbarians, a ghost, and, in the final act, a chorus of praise for the tsar. It had little to do with Pushkin, but Pushkin was not in the slightest offended. Rather, he wanted to know everything about it, telling a friend that he had once courted the beloved ballerina in the lead role.

Moscow, the battered survivor of the siege, became the seedbed of the new nationalism. Plans for rebuilding included a colossal theater for ballet and opera, one that would surpass Maddox's long-gone Petrovsky Theater, an enterprise tainted by corruption and its owner's English origins. A proper school would be established, with a proper curriculum, headed by an exceptional pedagogue: Glushkovsky. His first and ultimately greatest contribution to ballet in Moscow was as a teacher, and he carved out a chapter for himself in ballet history. He correctly described keeping his students alive during Napoleon's invasion, providing them with a school (three of them, in fact, between 1814 and 1829, the year of his retirement as teacher), and improving every aspect of the training for everyone.

Glushkovsky formed a professional troupe from his most talented disciples and set about enriching the theatrical repertoire with patriotic pageants, after the example of Valberg, and longer plot-based ballets based on the texts of Pushkin, following Didelot. In his account of the period, Glushkovsky described the installation of boards, straps, and cushions in his classrooms to help the students develop lift and improve their turnout at the hip and ankle. He spoke about the types of movements privileged by his teachers and which of their ballets he resurrected once a new theater was opened in Moscow—ballets that emphasized gracefulness and flow over coarse contrast. The repertoire changed to mirror the newly nativist cultural context. "In 1814, 1815, and 1816," he claimed, "in the Petersburg and Moscow theaters, Russian national dances reigned supreme." These dances supplanted "the French *recherché* manner."[19] The French element eventually reasserted itself, but he continued to make room for folk fare. He blended materials of different urban and rural origins in order to represent magical extremes or the desire to overcome commonplace situations.

Glushkovsky took on overlapping duties and honed his ballet-making skills during the rebuilding of Moscow, its fantastical rise from the ruin of total war. Juggling the positions of dancer, teacher, and ballet master caused him great stress, however, and he begged the directorate for help. Yet in 1831 his duties only increased when he was appointed chief inspector of the ballet and its director. Glushkovsky had to be present at rehearsals and oversee the staging of up to eighteen ballets in a single season, by his own count. He had to haggle for funding, find replacements for ill and injured dancers, and provide both dancers and dances for operas, melodramas, and the ballet groups inserted into vaudevilles, among other things. Out of consideration for the colossal load on his shoulders, the directorate of the Imperial Theaters allowed him and his wife, Tatyana, herself a dancer, to escape Moscow for a month each summer to "correct" what he termed his "ruined health."[20] Having served with what his overseers termed "great zeal" and "commendable behavior," Glushkovsky petitioned for retirement in 1838, at the age of forty-six, and thereafter received a pension of 4,000 rubles along with a parting gift of a pair of diamond rings. The pension was impressive for the middle class, though an abyss below what an aristocrat earned each year from his serf estates.

GLUSHKOVSKY'S CAREER IS associated with the invention of "Russian" ballet, which emerged at once as an assemblage, an orientation, and an ideal. The East Slavic Cossacks brought some of their traditional dances to the theaters and schools of the post-Napoleonic Russian imperial ballet, as did the inhabitants of the interior steppe, Siberia, and the Caucasus Mountains. Glushkovsky and his successors also had access to the dances of nomadic peoples. These were altered and exaggerated, losing their ethnographic substance to become symbols, stylized representations, of the "Russian" empire. Later, the folk fare would be relocated to dream scenes, hallucinations, or the parade-of-nations pageants as found in French ballets dating back to the time of Jean-Georges Noverre and Louis

XIV. "Dances of the peoples" in nineteenth-century Russian ballets would be confined to the margins and would fall out of the plot.

Into the mix of Russian ballet was also added imperial court dances from Europe. The blending of non-Russian elements into Russian ballet seems paradoxical, but such was Glushkovsky's aesthetic—at odds with itself. The more his dancers sought an angelic escape from gravity's pull, the more important it became to have them step on the soles of their feet, flatly, in a flesh-and-blood, human manner. And the more important the plot, the freer the performers felt to shift out of character, to break the emotional and psychological frame for the sake of bravura athletic display. The divertissements of the post-Napoleonic period included a lot of talking and singing; muteness, the defining element of ballet, was surprisingly rare. Ballet in Moscow thus developed along its own lines, reflecting local conditions much like species of birds evolving on a remote island—particular, even peculiar, in its adaptations. Elsewhere, popular ballets and operas imported from the West ensured ticket sales. But Moscow offered a bounded space for Russian ballet, like Russian opera, to flourish.

A new public theater in Moscow was constructed under the administrative umbrella of the St. Petersburg court between 1821 and 1825, toward the end of Glushkovsky's career. It rose from the craggy gorge where the old Petrovsky Theater once stood, yet was meant to represent a clean break from the past and reflect the new nationalist ambitions. Despite the patriotic turn in the arts, however, the spacious new theater, like the performances within, still derived from continental European models. Milan's Teatro alla Scala and Paris's Salle Le Peletier lurked in the conscience of the architect. As a symbol of a city making a new start, a city of the future rather than the past, it needed to be bigger, grander, than the theaters of France and Italy, standing above if not apart from them. Thus Imperial Russia's orientation toward, yet projected dominance of, the West was translated into marble and plaster.

The impetus to build the theater came from Dmitri Golitsïn, who replaced the disgraced arsonist Fyodor Rostopchin as governor general of Moscow. A basic neoclassical concept was approved in 1819, but no specific plans were drawn up until the summer of 1820, when four members of the Imperial Academy of the Arts put their heads together. The lead planner was Andrey Mikhaílov, a senior professor of architecture, with three other members of the academy, including his brother, also participating. The first draft was subject to revision, and the budget went beyond what Golitsïn was prepared to approve on behalf of the court. The extravagant plan needed to be scaled back. Throughout his career, Mikhaílov, who also designed the hospital where Fyodor Dostoevsky was born in 1821, saw numerous building projects either canceled or completed by others, the Bolshoi included. The court indulged him with commissions but recognized his limitations.

Another architect involved from the start, Osip (Joseph) Bové, modified the design with the approval both of Golitsïn and the tsar. Bové had long enjoyed official support and oversaw the post-Napoleonic reconstruction of Red Square and the restoration of façades throughout Moscow. He could not, however, control the imaginations of the private builders contracted for the restoration work, the result being a riot of reds and greens that displeased the tsar, who ordered the façades swathed in paler colors. (These pale colors characterize the older buildings in Moscow to the present day.) For the Bolshoi Theater, Bové exercised restraint, eliminating, for reasons of taste, the nineteenth-century version of a shopping center that Mikhaílov had envisioned for the first floor and lowering the flat roof. He did everything he could to control costs, including contracting the masons himself and transporting stone bases to the site on his own dray. It was also his idea to salvage whatever he could from the detritus of the old Maddox theater; not all traces of the past were expunged. But as the wiser men of the Imperial Theaters directorate had predicted, costs still ran well over budget, from the 960,000 rubles allotted by the treasury to the colossal sum of 2 million.

Construction of the theater lasted more than four years. In July of 1820, the first of the ditches was dug and the first of the thousands of pine logs forming the foundation hammered into place in the bog on Petrovka Street. (Estimates vary on the number of logs pounded into the mire: more than 2,100 for certain, more than 4,000 perhaps.) Construction involved hundreds of laborers in the winters, even more in the summers. It did not end until December of 1824, and then just barely. The zodiac-embossed curtain and scrims were completed after the extended 1824 deadline, and, because of the budget overrun, both Mikhaílov and Bové had to sacrifice the 8,000 rubles in imported chandeliers that they had intended to hang in the side rooms, replacing them with illuminations of papier-mâché and tin fashioned by local craftspeople. Bové also had to forego the giant mirror that he had wanted to hang in front of the curtain, allowing audience members to gaze at themselves; the mere thought of it terrified the directorate, as much for its radicalism as its cost.

The finished building was nonetheless luxurious, with the loges facing the stage drenched in crimson velvet, gold fringe, and braids, and the open boxes on each side suspended, as if from the air, from cast-iron brackets. Columns on pedestals framed the galleries, supporting the arabesque-decorated ceiling, from which a massive crystal chandelier was raised and lowered by pulley. Oil lamps provided lighting, along with two parallel rows of candles fronting the loges. Even Russophobe Europeans were impressed at what had been achieved. "Travelers who visit Russia expecting to find a people just emerging from barbarism are often astonished to find themselves in scenes of Parisian elegance and refinement," the *Illustrated London News* opined. The new theater was the greatest example of this unexpected urbanity. Although the theater was slow to adapt to new technologies—gas lighting was not installed until 1836, in tandem with the building of a special gas plant—the "orchestra and chorus were strong," making the theater "a favorite place of resort of the Russian nobility, who usually wear their stars and ribbons at the opera."[21]

It could hold more than 2,200 people, but demand exceeded capacity, especially in the first years, prompting management to repeat programs and cram additional seats into the auditorium. The side rooms had enough space to host chamber concerts by touring foreign musicians. The entrance was graced with a portico and led to a grand central staircase and ample reception rooms. Five massive semicircular windows provided light for the auditorium and the stage on each side of the theater. Ten paired columns supported the gable at the back. Since it was bigger than Maddox's operation, it was called the Bolshoi—meaning "Grand"—Petrovsky Theater. Over time, the reference to Petrovka Street was dropped. The space in front, Theater Square, acquired a public garden. Later a fountain was added. The ravine and pond that had once been on the site were filled with rock and soil hauled from demolished bastions in Kitay-gorod. Theater Square also came to include a smaller theater for plays, the Malïy, also designed by Bové.

Both the inside and outside of the theater inspired, and were inspired by, national pride. An unsigned article in *Moskovskiye vedomosti* heaps praise on the theater and on Moscow, the rebuilt symbol of "the sword of victory," ready to join the ranks of the great world cities.[22]

> The swiftness and grandeur of certain recent events in Russia have astonished our contemporaries and will be perceived as nothing less than miracles in distant posterity. . . . Our fatherland draws closer to the great European powers with each achievement. Such a thought arises within the soul of the patriot at the appearance of the Bolshoi Petrovsky Theater, whose walls have risen, like a phoenix, in new splendor and magnificence from the ruins. For how long in this place has the eye been exposed to the foul heaps, the remains of horrendous disaster, and the ear to the thumping of the worker's hammer? And now to capture the delighted gaze is a splendid building, an edifice of enchanting taste in height, immensity, and noble simplicity, coupled with elegance, stateliness, and ease. And now the inner walls receive the thunder of the muses; positive inspiration for humanity! Such is the magnitude, in spirit and deed, of Russia's government.

Unlike Maddox's catch-as-catch-can song-and-dance operation, the grand space was conceived from the start as a cathedral to the finest of the fine arts, one that placed the mercantile middle classes and the inhabitants of the Table of Ranks side by side "on the path to Enlightenment."

The nineteen-year-old poet Mikhaíl Lermontov celebrated the construction of the Bolshoi Petrovsky Theater in similarly lavish terms. In his "Panorama Moskvï" (Panorama of Moscow), a meditation on the walls, roofs, and boulevards of the city, he imagined the god Apollo, whose alabaster statue topped the portico of the

Bolshoi, glaring at the crenelated Kremlin walls from his chariot, upset that "Russia's ancient and sacred monuments" were hidden from view.[23] Those monuments had been seriously damaged in 1812, after Napoleon ordered the Kremlin detonated and soldiers looted the decorative insignia and ornaments. Tsar Alexander I commissioned the repairs in a neo-Gothic style, and his successor, Tsar Nicholas I, saw them through. The Bolshoi Petrovsky Theater, in contrast, struck a neoclassical pose: symmetrical, monumental, and harmonious.

The theater opened on January 6, 1825, with a benediction and an allegorical prologue featuring Apollo and his muses. Then "a soothsayer from a mythological world" predicted the nation's future, the triumphs to come. There was also an affirmation of the vastness of the Russian Empire, the terrain it occupied from Poland to the Caspian Sea, from "the mists of Finland" to the "cloud ridges" of the "formidable Caucasus." Bové, the hero of the moment (Mikhaílov was all but forgotten), heard well-earned bravos from the stage. Following the six p.m. opening performance, at eleven p.m. the theater hosted its first masquerade. It was meant to be an elegant occasion; patrons were told not to bring hats or "indecent masks" into the theater.[24]

The opening of the theater brought the peregrinations, if not the hardscrabble existence, of Moscow's performers to an end. There remained the challenge of learning multiple roles for multiple short-lived stagings. Some were made in Russia, others freely imported, in the absence of copyright protection, from Europe. The first years featured burlesque comedies and benefits for individual dancers and singers, but Pushkin also made his presence felt (as source for the ballets *Ruslan and Lyudmila*, *Prisoner of the Caucasus*, and *The Black Shawl*), likewise Cervantes (*Don Quixote*) and Goethe (*Faust*). Pre-ternatural fare put the fabulous machines of the stage to good use.

The repertoire included a balletic version of *Cinderella*, the beloved seventeenth-century folktale about an abused and overworked maidservant who becomes, via a magical helper and friendly critters, the sparkling bride of a prince. It was choreographed for the 1825 opening of the Bolshoi Petrovsky Theater by the twenty-year-old ballerina Félicité Hullen to existing music by her middle-aged husband, Fernando Sor. She was Parisian and he was from Barcelona, but they both ended up in Moscow in the employment of the Imperial Theaters. Their marriage did not last.

Sor's career in Moscow spanned three years. He composed other ballet scores, but is best known for his guitar pieces: studies, sets of themes and variations, transcriptions of songs, and sonatas. The music is discreet, polite, and much indebted to Mozart. Hullen was brasher, flashier. She was mentored in Moscow by Glushkovsky, who promoted her talents as a ballerina and then made her his partner as ballet master at the Bolshoi and pedagogue at the Imperial Theater College. She became Russia's first female choreographer, and included Russian dances in ballets on Russian themes. Like Glushkovsky, Hullen distinguished herself in Moscow by producing comic works on peasant themes that would never have been staged in St. Petersburg, for reasons as much aesthetic as political. Yet Hullen still privileged the repertoire that she had performed as a young dancer in Paris, fueling the criticism from one of the administrators of the Imperial Theaters that she was pushing Russian ballet back in time when it needed to move forward. She serviced her debt to her homeland by introducing features of French Romanticism to Russian ballet. The amalgam she created—of the local and international, from the land, of the ether—helped distinguish ballet in Moscow as something different, something distinct from what was staged in St. Petersburg and throughout Europe.

Hullen's and Sor's *Cinderella*, which was premiered at the Bolshoi Petrovsky Theater during its inaugural season, exemplifies her particular mix of European and Russian influences as well as the distinctive qualities of ballet as revived in Moscow. The familiar European story is clothed in distinctly Russian garb to offer much more than a lesson in protracted courtship or even a tale of personal transformation, whether on the surface, through the heroine's donning a ball gown and glass slippers, or, more deeply, as she learns to distinguish good from evil. Instead, audiences in Moscow (no strangers to cinders) were accustomed to patriotic sentiments being tucked into ballets and operas, so could interpret *Cinderella*, at least in part, as a parable of national striving. No longer revealing a girl's poetic isolation, the ballet now featured Mother Russia as the heroine unwilling to be a maidservant to Europe. Her years of neglect and disrespect had come to an end through the expulsion of Napoleon. The heroes of the war, including the governor general of Moscow, Golitsïn, vie for the role of the prince, and the ball is set in the Russian imperial court. The big new theater also infused the modest folktale with potent grandeur.

The ballets by Valberg, Glushkovsky, and Hullen mark the emergence of a Russianness that would define the Bolshoi Petrovsky Theater for the twenty-eight years of its existence—and not only in ballet. The Bolshoi was (and is) also an opera house, and this same search for Russianness is found in the operas of Mikhaíl Glinka, who was immortalized even before his death as the father figure of the Russian musical tradition. Whereas the choreographers at the Bolshoi made their dances seem Russian by manipulating models from France and Italy, Glinka and his successors relied on exoticisms taken, more often than not, from points to the east. Archaic scales and scale segments came to define Russianness in Russian music, along with invented scales like the whole-tone and the octatonic, church bells, drawn-out lamentations, and, in opera, text settings sensitive to the accents and stresses of the Russian language. Most of these musical novelties were invented, including the tunes supposedly borrowed from the peasants. But by concocting them they became more affecting and alluring, more seductive both to audiences at home and abroad.

Glinka came from a village near Smolensk, but he was cosmopolitan in mind-set, spending as much time outside of Russia as inside. He learned music in Europe and died in Berlin. His first opera, the pro-Russian, anti-Polish *A Life for the Tsar* (Zhizn' za tsarya, 1836) was nonetheless feted as a model nationalist score. (In the Soviet period in particular, it received the blessing of nationalist ideologues, though not before the libretto had been rewritten, to exclude the tsar.) Glinka's second opera, *Ruslan and Lyudmila* (1842), did not fare as well. Its eclecticism ensured it a difficult journey to the stage. Later, however, the concoction was heard with different ears and esteemed for its earthiness. The score blended European styles and genres. It also paid homage to the ancient bardic epic narrative tradition, and thus seemed to reach back to a Russia of yore: Russia before Peter the Great, Russia before Ivan the Terrible—in other words, Russia before Russia.

Real or imagined, the success of Glinka's Russianness was the bane of the existence of his less skilled, less well-trained peers. Among the more resentful of them was Alexei Verstovsky, a prolific composer as well as a central figure in the operations of the Bolshoi Petrovsky Theater. He composed music for the theater, but his legacy rests on his administrative contributions. His career overlaps with Glinka's and picks up where Glushkovsky's leaves off.

VERSTOVSKY (1799–1862) WAS of modest noble lineage and grew up listening to the subpar serf orchestra on his father's land in southeast Russia. He trained as an engineer in St. Petersburg but cared much more about his chief hobby: music. He studied singing, took violin lessons, and realized accompaniments at the keyboard. Engineering bored him, so he decided to offend his father by becoming a part-time composer, an occupation that even he thought beneath his station. Verstovsky's first substantial composition, a vaudeville called *Grandma's Parrots* (Babushkinï popugai, 1819), set a low aesthetic bar. His technique improved thanks to lessons with, among others, the great Italian opera composer Gioachino Rossini. (Legend has it that Rossini gave these lessons to Verstovsky only after Verstovsky agreed to settle his gambling debts.) Patrons of the Bolshoi Theater flocked to see Verstovsky's Slavonic devil opera, *Pan Twardowski*, but it was ridiculed by operagoers in St. Petersburg for its vacuousness and two-dimensional characterizations. It also paraphrased the scariest pages in Carl Maria von Weber's German devil opera, *Der Freischütz*.

Verstovsky found greater success with a clever blend of love songs, horror effects, and comic minstrel tunes entitled *Askold's Tomb* (Askol'dova mogila, 1835). Set in the ancient days of Kievan Rus, the opera involves two lovers, a witch, and an unnamed character seen lurking, in the first act, around the grave of a pagan prince. Dark forces keep the lovers apart, but the witch ensures the rescue of the heroine and her reunion with the hero through some well-timed spells cast around a cauldron, with black cat and owl looking on. The unnamed character helps as well, but ends up drowning in the River Dnieper. *Askold's Tomb* played to nationalist sentiments both on the level of Russian medieval plot and archaic musical elocution, and it received hundreds of performances in Moscow and St. Petersburg, becoming arguably the most popular Russian opera of the nineteenth century. Even after it was dropped from the repertoire, the dances survived (Verstovsky joked about the dancers taking them to their graves). Had Glinka not come along with his canonic Russian operas, Verstovsky might be regarded as a central figure in Russian music history. He ended up in the margins.

His failure to top the success of *Askold's Tomb* left him bitter, especially after the ascent of Glinka. Jealous, he grumbled that Glinka's 1836 opera, *A Life for the Tsar*, failed as a piece of drama: "One does not go to the theater for the purpose of praying to God," he declared in the middle of his hotheaded critique.[25] Verstovsky thought of himself as the greater pioneer, but was stymied in his pursuit of fame, and thus laid down his pen, becoming a bureaucrat and politician. Positioning himself in the right place at the right time, Verstovsky toadied up to people in power so as to move up the bureaucratic ladder of the Moscow Imperial Theaters from music inspector to cast and crew inspector and then to repertoire inspector. Eventually he took over the Moscow directorate altogether.

The image that emerges from his employment records is that of a poor gentleman who constructed an administrative career for himself from scratch with no great successes or failures. Despite never loving his work, he was unable to devote himself to leisure for financial and social reasons. On the other hand, his letters reveal a much more vivid persona, bordering at times on the outrageous. He comes across as a jolly good fellow, a lover of gossip (about brides and the doddering "old mushrooms" in the civil service), teasing, and outrageous puns.[26] His pen and his tongue could be cruel, however, and he did not hold back when deriding critics and censors and all of the other people who had crossed him. He wrote in extreme haste but fluidly, especially when he vented spleen about his various peeves. These included same-sex relationships. In his letters from the late 1830s, he mocks the effeminate manners of male dancers, some openly homosexual, others not, by using feminine endings and misspellings to describe their behavior: "A new

dancer has come to us in the theater with the grandest of preten-
sions; I don't like him and most of our decent people agree with
me entirely. Most of all I don't like his girlish ways. He prances
around as if to say 'I'm sooo tired!' 'I daaanced until I practically
faaainted on the stage!'"[27] Verstovsky could not help but wag his
caustic tongue about the perceived lesbianism of the ladies in his
circle as well: "The former actress Semyonova and Princess Gaga-
rina have the most passionate correspondence, one can't live without
the other—it's magical, simply magical!"[28] His letters often include
strange drawings altogether unrelated to the subjects under discussion: a chap with a rooster's comb bowing like an ape to a baroness;
a Chinese man with an umbrella riding an elephant; the pope bap-
tizing three babies in a pot.

The group of nobles running the theaters of Moscow and St.
Petersburg was small and tight-knit. The librettist of Verstovsky's
opera *Askold's Tomb*, Mikhaíl Zagoskin, was director of the Moscow Imperial Theaters from 1837 to 1841. Soon Verstovsky agitated to replace Zagoskin, pledging "to repair all of the cracks in
the directorate" that had appeared under his leadership.[29] The largest, he complained, had been created by the choreographer Hullen, who was not, in his opinion, a progressive force at the Bolshoi
but someone who had "pushed things back by five years, goaded
by Zagoskin, and completely destroyed the ballet company. Many
fine dancers dispersed and those who stayed were spoiled."[30] The
slander did not, however, help him to get the job, at least not immediately. He continued to report to the governor general of Moscow,
Dmitri Golitsïn. Thus he was required to attend parties at Golitsïn's
home, which he found tiresome, "more like dusks than evenings,"
and worse than the enervating occasions at the English Club that
rounded out his social calendar. The older "bastards" at the parties
"pranced like cranes"; the bearded, "greasy" youth put on a dissatis-

fied affect, pretending that they had better places to be.[31] The social scene improved when the sovereign visited Moscow, at which time the city became like an "excavated anthill," everywhere "busybodies sweeping and repairing," "beards getting trimmed, moustaches already shaved, everyone cleaned up and sobered up!"[32]

Zagoskin was replaced, first by Alexander Vasiltsovsky, an anxious, humble individual much prone, in his letters to the court, to protestations of worthlessness. Finally, after Vasiltsovsky took sick and could no longer fulfill his duties, Verstovsky assumed the directorship of the *kontora* of the Moscow Imperial Theaters. He served in the position from 1848 until his own retirement in 1861, a year before he died. He did not like Moscow; its provincialism was not a virtue. But as he confessed at the start of his administrative ascent, "the grace of expected rewards" kept him there. Certainly he was able to reward himself by keeping his opera *Askold's Tomb* in the repertoire. And when the management structure of the Bolshoi shifted, returning control from Moscow to St. Petersburg, Verstovsky gladly cast himself in the role of a dedicated public servant and hands-on reformer.[33]

Throughout the nineteenth century, the directorate of the Moscow Imperial Theaters reported to the directorate of the St. Petersburg Imperial Theaters—except between 1822 and 1841, when the Bolshoi and Maliy Theaters were overseen by the governor general of Moscow and the *Opekunskiy sovet*, the governing board of the Imperial Foundling Home and its bank, to which the Moscow theaters still owed money from the Maddox era. After 1842 the administration of the Bolshoi and Maliy Theaters resembled that of the main theaters in St. Petersburg. Repertoire was reviewed by the (initially) three-member Censorship Committee established within the Ministry of Education in 1804, and budgets were set by the State Treasury of the Ministry of Finance—all under the supervision of the

Ministry of the Imperial Court and His Majesty the Emperor. Control of the Bolshoi and the Maliÿ Theaters reverted to St. Petersburg in 1842, when the elderly Golitsïn's health began its final decline.

The impetus for the administrative restructuring in 1842 was a report ordered by the Ministry of the Imperial Court on the condition of the Bolshoi. The report was compiled by Alexander Gedeonov, the director of the St. Petersburg Imperial Theaters, and by painting a picture of neglect, it suited Gedeonov's needs—namely, placing the Moscow theaters under his personal control. The extremely biased conclusion was that Bové's architectural marvel had not been properly cared for since its opening in 1825. The water tanks were empty, which created a serious fire hazard; the "mechanism" under the stage was insufficient for performances involving frequent set changes; there were not enough stagehands, and they often found themselves double-booked, scheduled to work at the Bolshoi and the Maliÿ on the same night; the costumes used by the opera were threadbare; those used by the ballet were newer but had been stitched together by a "rather mediocre tailor."[34] The Maliÿ had a modest "shop" on its premises to store its costumes and props, but the Bolshoi was forced to lease "temporary wooden sheds in total disrepair." Other difficulties at the Bolshoi included poor lighting. "All of the oil lamps are in a dilapidated state," Gedeonov commented, "leaving the stage dark" even during performances. The ends of the ceiling beams in the hallways were rotting, posing an obvious danger, and the "retreats" (meaning the latrines) produced a noxious stench.

He saved his harshest words for the Moscow Imperial Theater College, which supposedly existed in a state of "total destruction." The students who did not live on the premises outnumbered those who did, and the non-residents caused the directorate difficulties: "They missed rehearsals and performances owing to bad weather, sickness, or even just problems in their homes attributable to their extreme poverty." The college itself was inadequate for the needs of its residents, owing in part to the lack of water for bathing (which had to be brought in from the street and carried up a narrow staircase) and improper sanitation; such squalor, according to the college doctor, "caused the students colds and other serious illnesses with potentially lethal consequences." The boys who fell ill were confined to a room with four beds on the second floor of the college, with a nurse and attendant next door. A thin wall made of wooden planks was all that separated the patients from the stage used by the students, so that "the dances and other activities held there throughout most of the day cause great concern to the patients and much harm." The girls' sick room was on the third floor and much roomier, but the windows had been installed less than a third of a meter above the floor, posing a safety hazard. "Obsessed with fever, suffering intense delirium and disorientation," the report conjectured, "a patient might, irrespective of all precautions taken, potentially meet misfortune by jumping through the window." And the teapot in the boys' sick room had gone missing.

Gedeonov commissioned two independent inspections of the Bolshoi and Maliy Theaters and the Theater College in support of his claims and soon found himself in charge of the entire theatrical complex, along with a summer theater in Petrovsky Park in Moscow. When he took over, he arranged for the payment of the debt owed by the theaters to the *Opekunskiy sovet*. Since he also had to oversee the St. Petersburg Imperial Theaters and could not be in two cities at the same time, he relied first on Vasiltsovsky and then Verstovsky to provide him with regular reports on the situation in Moscow. The offices of the Moscow directorate operated in a three-story stone building in the Arbat neighborhood before moving to quarters on Bolshaya Dmitrovka Street, just steps from the Bolshoi. According to one source, the bureau contained a small room known as a "lockup," where artists and employees suspected of malfeasance could be placed under arrest.[35] Thus was discipline enforced.

The first order of business in the reports for Gedeonov was financial: an accounting of box-office receipts. This was followed by a description of the success or failure of individual productions, followed by, in the case of the Bolshoi, mention of the health of dancers (who in the ranks had pulled a muscle or sprained an ankle), minor or major accidents (the broken ribs suffered by a musician who fell asleep on the sill of an open window), and the status of repairs to the theater. When praised for their work or asked about their personal affairs, Vasiltsovsky and Verstovsky swooned, grateful for the attention from on high. Gedeonov had a short wick and wore a scowl, but he cared about his employees, guaranteeing salaries for performers in the first and second ranks and granting special privileges after two decades of service. Housing was a never-ending concern, both for the artists and the staff as well as for their families. Gedeonov's kindness was felt by the eldest daughter of Verstovsky's clerk; she had been living across from a "filthy kitchen and yard in a room next to laundrywomen" and an actor who "dried and ironed his black underwear" in plain sight. (According to her father's appeal to Gedeonov, the poor girl also had to endure the "perverse company" of middle-of-the-night card players and horn blowers.) Verstovsky rescued her from the squalor. For such consideration, Gedeonov earned the love and affection of his employees, who praised him, with "sincere souls and contrite hearts," as "a Father and Benefactor of the human race."[36]

Gedeonov had angled for control of the Bolshoi, and though he managed it with care he was also a micromanager, personally involved in ticketing (in general he refused to provide comps to Bolshoi Theater performances, even to high-ranking nobles) and matters as seemingly trivial as the cost of the bouquets tossed at dancers and singers during benefits. He even pursued the case of a mal-feasant who, in November of 1845, tossed an apple at the stage during a benefit performance. He took pains to return a beloved pipe that a German count had left in a loge and haggled over the prices for a hurdy-gurdy and carpets imported from Scotland. In addition to setting the salaries of the artists in the Imperial The-aters, he facilitated the granting of vacations and medical leaves.

Once he had been promoted to director, Verstovsky endeav-ored to prove that he was up to the task of keeping Moscow's larger and smaller stages running by regaling Gedeonov with up-to-the-minute descriptions of Bolshoi and Maliy Theater operations, plac-ing much greater emphasis on ballet and opera productions than concerts—though he made special mention of Franz Liszt, a com-poser and pianist he deeply admired and whose recitals in Mos-cow proved lucrative. Verstovsky inserted himself into all of the operations of the Bolshoi Theater orchestra, insisting on auditions and precise tuning, making sure that bows were repaired and rosin stocked. The music sounded wonderful, as Gedeonov admitted in his otherwise damning assessment of the condition of the Bolshoi Theater in April of 1842. Verstovsky had an obvious personal inter-est in keeping his own works on the stage and shamelessly pro-moted *Askold's Tomb*, which stayed in the Bolshoi repertoire exactly as long as he remained employed by the Moscow Imperial Theaters. His position enabled him to postpone or problematize the Moscow premieres of works by his rivals, including Glinka.

Verstovsky also took a personal interest in improving the educa-tion provided by the Imperial Theater College, complaining in 1841 that "the voice teacher, M. Gerkulani, has yet to have them open their mouths in his classes and teaches solfeggio on the keyboard, which is quite curious. And even more amusing, the dance teacher in the school, M. Peysar, has lame hands. Sitting, he demonstrates what he wants his students to do with just his feet."[37] In truth, the situation was never as bad as he described, and the problems he identified improved after the restructuring. Energetic young teachers were appointed to the staff, ensuring that instruction lived up to the needs of the college and the theaters it supported.

Verstovsky cultivated the image of a hearty good fellow for his superiors, but not for the artists under his supervision, who found him standoffish. The long-time Bolshoi Theater decorator and technician Karl Valts remembered him

> inevitably being on the stage before performances, standing before the curtain, and everyone having to come up to him to bow. He never wore the mandatory uniform at the time, but was always dressed in a short jacket and dark grey pants. He was almost bald, but a few unruly hairs remained stuck to his crown, like Bismarck. In conversation with the artists he always kept his hands in his pockets and addressed them in the familiar form. Beside him, like a shadow, arose the figure of the inspector of the Theater College.[38]

Although he generally treated the artists of the theater with cold derision, Verstovsky fell head over heels for one of them: the beautiful, talented, and overextended singer Nadezhda Repina. She was lowborn, the daughter of a serf musician, but had a proud prima donna career on the stage of the Maliy Theater and inspired some of Verstovsky's songs, including the most eloquent of his Russian Romances. He married her.

Given the customs of the time, however, it was not an easy marriage to maintain. Rumor had it that, for political reasons, Repina was forced to retire in 1841. Verstovsky signed the resignation papers behind her back just before control of the Moscow Imperial

Theaters reverted to Gedeonov. Repina's feelings on the matter are unknown, but it was said that she returned home from a triumphant performance to learn from her husband that her career was over. She fainted and took to drink.

Verstovsky must also have been distraught at what he had been forced to do. He adored his wife and would not be parted from her, just as he would not be parted from his true self—that of an artist, a composer, not a bureaucrat. Out of frustration with his lot, his paperwork, and the intrigue that he himself had promoted, he would one day wish the Bolshoi away.

But the Bolshoi was now more than a building. It stood as the symbol of a pursuit: the struggle for national identity through cultural identity. Because Moscow had borne the brunt of Napoleon, because it had burned and been rebuilt, because its populace had endured and finally triumphed, the formerly brackish backwater claimed the mantle of national purpose from the imperial capital of St. Petersburg. Bureaucratic wrangling between Moscow and St. Petersburg aside, Moscow found itself ascendant. Its distance— from St. Petersburg, from Europe—proved a benefit rather than a hindrance. Even before it became the seat of power in the twentieth century, Moscow in the nineteenth, after Napoleon, began to assume importance. The Kremlin, and the Bolshoi, could bide their time on the bend of the river along trading routes that the government could only pretend to govern.

The struggle to represent Russia in the arts continued through the imperial Russian era, through the Soviet era, and into the present day; surely, it is a struggle without end, Romantic in the extreme for its investment in ideals of the people and the nation. Yet the Bolshoi could lay claim to that most clichéd of concepts: the Russian soul.

· 3 ·

FLEET AS LIGHTNING:
THE CAREER OF
EKATERINA SANKOVSKAYA

ALEXEI VERSTOVSKY LEFT behind a long paper trail as first
the inspector and then director of the Moscow Imperial Theaters.
The performers under his control did not. Neither did their performances. What survives from the first half of the nineteenth century
are music scores, scenarios, the recollections of eyewitnesses, and the
images collected, over time, by devotees such as Vasiliy Fyodorov,
an art historian and director of the Malïy Theater Museum under
Stalin. But even these collections are selective affairs, labors of love
with huge chronological gaps that no scouring of archives, kiosks,
and libraries could fill. The first half of the nineteenth century, the
era of the Bolshoi Petrovsky Theater, is even less well represented
than the Maddox era—but for the case of the Moscow-born dancer
Ekaterina Aleksandrovna Sankovskaya (1816–1878), whose career
extended from October 1836 to November 1854. A diva before the

phenomenon of the diva existed, Sankovskaya rivaled her illustrious European contemporaries Marie Taglioni and Fanny Elssler in both lightness and precision.

Yet her name, unlike theirs, has faded from the annals of ballet history, to the extent that the details of Taglioni's performances in St. Petersburg from 1837 to 1842, and Elssler's in St. Petersburg and Moscow from 1848 and 1851, are better known, even though Sankovskaya's career was no less illustrious—and no less controversial—than theirs. Russian critics fawned with great ardor over Taglioni; one of them, Pyotr Yurkevich, even claimed her as St. Petersburg's own: "Our incomparable sylphide, with one wave of her little foot, rends asunder all the heavy theories of encyclopedic construction," he enthused, further waxing that she was "beautiful and unattainable, like a dream!"[1] Knickknacks bearing her likeness appeared on the streets of the imperial capital, and a patisserie conceived an elaborate tartlet in her honor. The most famous, or notorious, piece of lore surrounding Taglioni's guest appearances in St. Petersburg has her fans purchasing her dance shoes at auction for 200 silver rubles and then sautéing them for a feast.[2] The behavior was odd, but it was not without precedent, as Sankovskaya herself would have known.

From her European role models, Sankovskaya adopted the distinctive features of Romantic ballet: the all-white, unadorned costume, including the tutu, and dancing with heels off the ground. For choreographic exotica, she donned pantaloons and Turkish-style slippers. Before her time, moving *sur les pointes*, or on the knuckles of the toes, had been an acrobatic feat, invented by Italian gymnasts and then adopted, for expressive purposes, by such French dancers as Fanny Bias and Geneviève Gosselin.[3] Excluding the winsome oil portrait that hangs in the Bakhrushin Museum in Moscow, the extant images of Sankovskaya are fanciful, showing her floating, hovering. The lithograph that Fyodorov preserved of her comes from a staging of *Le corsaire* in 1841, when she was at the height of her powers. She is either landing from a jump with toes extended, or in *piquée arabesque*. She looks "as fleet as lightning" in the ballet—radiant for an instant, then gone forever.[4]

Little is known about her life, besides mention of her mother and sister, also a dancer, and the quarrels she had with rivals in their looking-glass world. Born in Moscow in 1816, Sankovskaya entered the Moscow Imperial Theater College when she was nine, on the petition of her mother. She boarded at the school as a *kazennaya vospitannitsa*, a nonpaying, state-supported pupil. Before learning character dances, she studied the mazurka, the quadrille, and other social dances considered indispensable for the perfection of bearing and posture. The most important initial instruction came from Mikhaíl Shchepkin. He was the dominant presence at the Malïy Theater, devising a method of acting that privileged emotion and sensation over thought. He rejected two-dimensional representations and stock characterizations, instead encouraging his students to connect as intimately as possible with their subjects. Although Shchepkin at first had doubts about Sankovskaya's potential as a performer in his idiom, labeling her "talented, but capricious" in one of his notebooks, he became her mentor, instilling in her a commitment to naturalness of expression that she maintained throughout her career.[5]

Sankovskaya first danced small roles in ballets on historical and mythological themes, including Charles Didelot's *The Hungarian Hut* (Vengerskaya khizhina), in which she appeared disguised as a boy, nerves setting her arms and legs atremble. Sankovskaya's first solo appearance was at the Malïy Theater in 1831, at age fifteen, in the role of a smitten milkmaid. The ballet, one of Didelot's more trifling concoctions, pits the milkmaid and the peasant lad she loves against her grandmother. In the role, Sankovskaya impressed the litterateur Sergey Aksakov. Despite grumbling about the corps de ballet coming too close to the front of the stage in the concluding village wedding dances and the lack of soulfulness in the pantomime, Aksakov noted a tremendous improvement in the teaching at the Theater College. Sankovskaya and her onstage partner "were sweet and captivating," he wrote. "They will mature, and their gifts will bear brilliant fruit."[6]

In 1836, Sankovskaya's teacher, Félicité Hullen, decided to take her to Paris for the summer, "for the betterment of her talent."[7] The Imperial Theaters granted permission for the trip but did not fund it, so Hullen footed the bill. Little is known about the adventure. In Paris, Sankovskaya seems to have been brought into direct contact with Fanny Elssler, who saw in her less a performer in her own style—earthbound, *tacquetée*, defined by intricate footwork—than the likeness of Taglioni, capable of creating the illusion of supernatural lightness in her jumps, as befitted her slight build. According to a writer for the ephemeral arts and politics journal *Moskovskiy nablyudatel'* (Moscow observer), "the spirit of the Parisian sylph [Taglioni] enlivened that of the petite Muscovite."[8] Sankovskaya absorbed the impressions gained from her time abroad into her own style, one that assimilated each step, each combination, into a single image. She returned to Moscow a professional, a Bolshoi ballerina.

The unknown author of the think piece in *Moskovskiy nablyudatel'* noted that, owing to inexperience, Sankovskaya "sometimes sacrificed herself and her art by indulging an ungracious tour de force," but that, nonetheless, each movement, each lift and fall of her torso, "was sheer delight."[9] Officialdom cleared her path to greatness; two months after her return from Paris, Sankovskaya received word of the successful completion of her studies at the Theater College and her appointment to the Moscow Imperial Theaters as a "dancer of the first rank," "première danseuse."[10] The official who signed the papers pointed to her performance in *Fenella* as justification for the appointment, "Mademoiselle Sankovskaya performed with exceptional distinction in the ballet *Fenella* and, on two other occasions, in divertissements. After the last of these performances Madame Hullen was called to the stage; the public of Moscow wanted to express gratitude to her for nurturing such a wonderful dancer."[11]

Fenella uses an abbreviated arrangement of the music of a grand opera, *La muette de Portici* (The mute girl of Portici), by composer Daniel Auber and librettist Eugène Scribe. Set in Naples in 1657, the plot concerns a love triangle during a period of rebellion and volcanic eruption. Alphonse, the son of the Spanish viceroy of Naples, is betrothed to a princess, Elvire, but has seduced the fishermaid Fenella. The death of Fenella's brother prompts her, at the end, to throw herself into burning lava. Neither the composer nor the librettist of the original 1828 opera intended for the heroine to be silent, performing only in mime, but the atypical absence in Paris of a suitable soprano for the role, and the presence of an alluring ballerina, Lise Noblet, led to the switch. Reviewing the score, Hullen decided that *La muette de Portici* should have been a ballet in the first place and so enlisted an arranger (Erkolani) to help her choreograph it for the Bolshoi. Fenella mimes rather than sings in the original five-act version for the Paris Opéra; in Hullen's four-act version, she dances rather than mimes. Gesture is the domain of the other characters, those who tell the story; Fenella becomes an idealized conception. She feels and expresses her feelings in movement, but also reaches for higher spiritual values. Hullen gave the part of Fenella to another dancer for the April 15, 1836, premiere, with Sankovskaya, listed as a student on the playbill, in supporting parts. Soon thereafter, the starring role was hers.

Sankovskaya was contracted to dance in ballets, operas, and

divertissements as instructed by the Imperial Theaters and as her strength and stamina permitted. Her first solo dance at the Bolshoi was a *pas du fandango*. Announcements in *Moskovskiye vedomosti* have her partnering in a new Parisian *pas de châle* on November 27 and December 28, 1836, and appearing in the lead role in the one-act ballet *La servante justifiée* (The serving girl justified) on December 11. Eleven announcements for Sankovskaya's performances appear in 1837 and encompass everything from benefits to appearances in masquerades. Her talent and popular appeal convinced the directorate of the Moscow Imperial Theaters to make her promotion retroactive; it was moved back from the opening of the 1836–37 season to the opening of the 1835–36 season. She earned 800 rubles per year in the first three years of her professional career, along with 200 rubles in housing allowance. She was also granted a shoe budget, but it was rescinded in 1845, when she was told that she would have to pay for her footwear herself, and also absorb the growing costs of her dresses, gloves, tights, and hats. An impressive stack of documents from 1845 finds her urging the release from customs of the twelve pairs of "white silk shoes" she had ordered from Paris, but the specifics of the design of the footwear, essential to the understanding of Sankovskaya's technique, are not listed.[12] The assumption is that she skimmed the stage, like Taglioni, on some combination of half-, three-quarter, and full pointe, but the sources are vague. As a student, the dancer Anna Natarova recalled seeing Sankovskaya in *La sylphide*. "She astonished everybody by running around the stage and going through her *pas*, all on pointe," Natarova claimed. "This was new at that time."[13]

Tsar Nicholas I took a special interest in Sankovskaya, as did many nobles with Moscow ballerinas, the imperial ballet being during his reign a harem of sorts for the court. Upon signing her first contract, Sankovskaya received an oversized diamond from the tsar and a lump-sum bonus of 150 rubles. Sexual affairs with dancers were a rite of passage for an adolescent nobleman, and it was not uncommon for older nobles to rely on the ballet school for lovers, plucking them from classes like fruit from hothouse gardens. Nicholas's son, the future Tsar Alexander II, inherited his father's tastes, and there is evidence to suggest that he took one of Sankovskaya's rivals as a mistress. Besides personal pleasure, however, Nicholas found within the corps de ballet a model for obedient troop behavior. And vice versa: For a performance of the ballet *The Revolt of the Harem* (Vosstaniye v serale) in 1836, he assumed the duties of a ballet master by assigning the dancers weapons training.[14] He broke down their initial resistance to the idea by making them rehearse outside in the snow.

The extent to which the Bolshoi Theater became a seraglio, and whether Sankovskaya was abducted by infatuated noblemen, will never be known. It is clear, however, that she existed above and apart from the lesser, poorer dancers whose futures lay in the laundries or on the streets as licensed prostitutes, dressed in yellow, carrying medical checkup forms of the same color. The term "ballerina" and the Table of Ranks for dancers (first dancer, second dancer, coryphée, corps de ballet) had not yet been codified by the Imperial Theaters, but there is no doubt Sankovskaya rose to the top, and stayed there. She far surpassed her teacher to become the finest Russian dancer of the first half of the nineteenth century. The administration of the Moscow Imperial Theaters recognized her talent early, increasing her bonus to 500 rubles and then 1,000 rubles upon the signing of contracts in 1838 and 1839. Later, she earned bonuses based on the number of times she starred in a ballet, seven rubles per outing in 1845, rising to ten, fifteen, eighteen, and finally twenty-five in 1851. Her contracts also guaranteed her an annual benefit or half-benefit performance, a lucrative perk, and for one of them she tried her hand at choreography, restaging the 1845 ballet *Le diable à quatre* (The devil to pay), which Joseph Mazilier had originally choreographed to music by Adolphe Adam, for presentation at the Bolshoi at the end of 1846. The subject of class conflict (a hot-tempered marquise magically trades lives with the good-hearted spouse of a cobbler) might have explained its appeal to Sankovskaya, but it was also chockablock with madcap caprice, including an episode in which a hurdy-gurdy player has his instrument broken over his head. Sankovskaya also performed in St. Petersburg and in 1846 toured abroad to Hamburg and Paris, among other cities—a first for a Moscow-trained dancer.

Bohemian students idolized her for reasons both religious and philosophical, as did the prominent theatrical observers Sergey Aksakov, Vissarion Belinsky, Alexander Herzen, and Mikhaíl Saltïkov-Shchedrin. Appraisals and descriptions of her performances in the press are nonetheless few and far between, since the theatrical review had only just been legalized in 1828 for the semiofficial culture and politics newspaper *Severnaya pchela* (The northern bee), and strict rules were put in place, by the Minister of Internal Affairs and the Moscow police, about who could write reviews and how it was to be done: nothing anonymous, nothing unsolicited, and so nothing troublemaking. The gaps in critical thought were filled by periodicals like *Moskovskiy nablyudatel'*, diaries, and memoirs. Sankovskaya's devotees saw spiritual liberation in her movement and found it difficult to believe that she was merely human, prone to injuries. Injuries excited alarm but also, like Taglioni's and Elssler's infirmities, increased Sankovskaya's allure.

She had rivals, both early in her career and later on, and gossip raged, as it tends to, about her efforts to damage their careers. The first in the long list of competitors was Tatyana Karpakova, who had also trained with Hullen and had also been taken to Paris for exposure to the more rigorous lexicon of the Parisian repertoire. Karpakova danced from childhood and had sufficient nuance and timing to earn parts in theatrical comedies, though a critic of the time lamented her refusal to surrender cliché, the crass jumps that dancers recycled from ballet to ballet. Two years after graduating from the Moscow Imperial Theater College, Karpakova married a classmate, Konstantin Bogdanov. She had children whom she did not raise, ceding their upbringing, in keeping with the habit among artists, to the Theater College. As Karpakova slowed down, her name faded from the repertoire, and, after Sankovskaya's ascension, the theatergoing public forgot about her altogether. In 1842, tuberculosis sentenced Karpakova to a premature death around age thirty.

KARPAKOVA HAD A DIFFICULT time escaping the strictures of academic classicism: her pantomime was considered cold, impersonal. Sankovskaya, in contrast, performed with passion, exhilaration, the seeming naturalness of her filigreed movement disguising a brutal training regimen. Her health suffered the strain even in her twenties, and she found herself unable to do all that was expected of her, which brought her into conflict with the administration of the Moscow Imperial Theaters. For all her fame, she remained a servant of the state, forced to do as she was told and obliged to explain every bruise, sniffle, or absence to her employers. Requests for time off needed to be submitted long in advance, likewise appeals for long-term medical treatment. As director of the Moscow Imperial Theaters, Verstovsky grew tired of her complaints, suspecting that she was exaggerating or inventing her health problems. He accused her of reveling in the attention generated by her absences from the stage and noted that she quickly returned to form whenever another dancer challenged her position.

In March of 1843, her doctor recommended that Sankovskaya be permitted to travel to Bad Ems, Germany, the preferred summer retreat of the European and Russian nobility, to take the thermal mineral waters and sea salts. She was suffering from myriad ailments: frail nerves, gastrointestinal disorder, irritation of the liver, persistent low-grade fever, and constant back pain. The request was rejected because Sankovskaya had not herself discussed her situation when she was in the offices of the Moscow Imperial Theaters to arrange a benefit performance, and because the doctor's report did not explain how the facilities in Bad Ems could help. She filed the same request in March of 1844, by which time the back pain had increased and Sankovskaya had developed a cyst on the inside of her left thigh above the knee. In addition, she had a hernia, the result of a pulled groin. Her doctor also noted abdominal pain and the discoloration of the skin characteristic of jaundice. On April 10, Sankovskaya was given leave to travel abroad and issued a foreign passport for four months of treatment in Bad Ems, her pay suspended for the duration, from May to August. Before leaving, she had to prostrate herself before the intendant (director-in-chief) of the Imperial Theaters in St. Petersburg, Alexander Gedeonov, pledging, once she had recovered, to dedicate herself to justifying his benevolence. She perhaps did not need to go so far, since Gedeonov was, as the ballet master Marius Petipa recalled, a "very kind" man. Though he seemed harsh, earning the nickname "grumbler benefactor," he generally forgave bad behavior. (Petipa relates the case of a "bit player" who turned up drunk for a performance and threw up onstage. Gedeonov admonished the "disgusting creature" but allowed him to keep his pension, even after the actor pulled a pair of pistols on him.)[15]

The thermal mineral springs, despite their reputation as a fountain of youth, did little to alleviate the abuse Sankovskaya's body had suffered through the years. Her health continued to decline. In August of 1848, she was fined 259 rubles and 54 kopecks for failing to perform; she had been out sick for three months. When she finally returned to the Bolshoi, she was upstaged by a visiting dancer from St. Petersburg.

Her health problems obliged her to work, for a period, without a contract. She took her last bow near the end of 1854, having established the benchmark for subsequent generations. Official papers exchanged between the Moscow and St. Petersburg Imperial Theaters indicate that, to Verstovsky's consternation, she received special treatment in her final years onstage. Sankovskaya retired past her peak but not conspicuously so, beloved by the Moscow public as "the soul of our ballet," a hometown girl made good.[16] A farewell benefit was arranged at the Maliy Theater but canceled, due again to her health, but also to a decline in the size of her audiences. Verstovsky thereafter started to promote her protégés, especially the bright young Praskovya Lebedeva—the one dancer, in all his years of correspondence, to earn his genuine praise. Sankovskaya received another diamond and a pension equivalent to her salary in the late 1840s. After leaving the stage she taught social dances to girls and boys in gymnasia and manor houses. One tale has her setting a "sailor's dance" on the future great method actor Konstantin Stanislavsky.[17] His technique owed much to Sankovskaya's childhood instructor Mikhaíl Shchepkin. Before her death on August 16, 1878, her career had come full circle.

Five years after Sankovskaya's retirement from the stage, a tribute of sorts was published in the journal *Otechestvenniye zapiski* (Notes from the Fatherland) under the title "Recollections of a Moscow University Student."[18] The text is autobiographical, but it is drenched in mystical perfume and meanders from what is known about Sankovskaya's career. The student in question, Nikolay Dmitriyev, exhausts superlatives in describing the effect on him of Sankovskaya's dancing during a glum time in his life. He recalls her performance in 1837 of the lead role in *La sylphide*, an early staple of the repertoire first choreographed by Filippo Taglioni in Paris in 1832 for his daughter, Marie, who overcame serious physical challenges to serve as her father's muse. *La sylphide* was profoundly influential, providing the archetype for, as an obvious example, the act 1 madness scene and act 2 dance-love-nexus of *Giselle*. At its most basic level, *La sylphide* concerns striving for the ideal, but it ends in grief and leaves open the question as to whether the effort merited the sacrifice. Marie Taglioni was in St. Petersburg performing the part of the ethereal heroine on the exact same night that Sankovskaya danced the ballet in Moscow. This was neither a scheduling coincidence nor a conflict but what Sankovskaya's teacher, Hullen, had conceived as a duel in satin slippers.

Sankovskaya triumphed—at least according to Dmitriyev. In his recollections, he arrives at the Bolshoi in a foul mood, burdened, like Goethe's Werther, by suicidal thoughts caused by boredom, loneliness, and the harsh autumn frost. He seeks distraction, but there is no Academy of the Arts in Moscow for entertaining edification, no Hermitage. For "aesthetic feeling," he has recourse to the theater alone. His spirits sink further when he realizes that the program for the evening is neither a play nor an opera but a benefit for a ballerina. There is no point in returning to the "dreariness," "grief," his neighbor's "stupid mug," and the "inescapable samovar" of his room, so he surrenders the seven rubles in his pocket, a colossal sum, for a ticket. The crowds in the side rooms of the theater beam obtuse happiness, and he grinds himself into his seat thinking that they have all been duped. The orchestra interrupts his recollection of Lermontov's verses on the torments of ignorance.

And then he sees her. The curtain rises to reveal a house in a mythical elsewhere (Scotland) and a man flopped in an armchair, napping, or in Dmitriyev's description, tugged to sleep by forces beyond his control. Sankovskaya comes into view in a window above the stage and then glides down over the railing of a ladder to the floor, her skin and tulle white as the moonlight. She kneels before the armchair and then, again in Dmitriyev's description, rises to dance for the man, expressing her unreserved willingness to submit to his desire. Then she disappears, as ungraspable as "air's pure translucence."

The man in the chair, James, is soon to be wed, but he is dissatisfied with his intended bride, Effie, a conservative, salt-of-the-earth type. He seeks the escape symbolized by the sylph, the enchanting other, and falls in love with her. Dmitriyev too became smitten with Sankovskaya, waiting for her to return to the stage with his heart stopped and then, when she did, watching her skim across the floor, rapt. He grew aware of the interloping temporalities, the places where the music ends but the dancer continues her delicate runs, and appreciated the special visual effects: the sylph's ascent into the ether with her partner at the end of the first act, and her disappearance through a trapdoor in the second. Nothing is said of the tragic ending of the ballet, when James, desperate to possess the sylph, flees his bride for the forest (the realm, in the Moscow staging, of benign witches illuminated by street lamps). There in the woods James grasps the sylph, trapping her in his cloak. She loses her wings, the source of her power, and dies. A writer for the fashion journal *Galatea* provides the detail Dmitriyev excluded: "The expression on her face as she battled death was uncommonly affecting."[19]

Beyond noting the perspiration that accumulated on Sankovskaya's body like "spring dew," Dmitriyev revealed little about the specifics of her dancing: how high Sankovskaya jumped, how often she rose up en pointe, whether or not she soared above the stage with wire supports, the thickness of the leather on the heels of her slippers. The details were apparently incidental to the spell that she cast on him and his fellow students and professors.

La sylphide was the centerpiece of Sankovskaya's career, but Dmitriyev believed that her dancing was most true to herself in the Ballet of the Nuns scene from Giacomo Meyerbeer's supernatural opera, *Robert le diable* (1831). The scene was made famous in Paris by Marie Taglioni, who on at least three occasions took the lead role in a shocking spectacle: The ghost of the abbess Helena (Taglioni) leads her sisters, also risen from the grave, in a morbid seduction ritual. The abbess comes not from some benign spiritual beyond but from the lower depths of hell. She and her sisters have been condemned to the underworld for succumbing to unclean thoughts and are forced forever to do the bidding of the Evil One. The opera's protagonist, Robert, is lured into their lair in search of the magic branch that will allow him to reclaim his true love. He resists the necrophilic temptations and, through the intervention of his angelic half-sister, survives Taglioni's—and Sankovskaya's—balletic night of horrors.

In Paris in 1831, the ballet was cast in an eerie green light produced by a long row of gas jets lit one by one by an attendant. The garments worn by the dancers, catching the light, made strange shapes. The effect was dangerous (Taglioni's pupil Emma Livry died in horrible fashion when her skirt brushed up against a gas jet on the stage) but alluring, transforming the Ballet of the Nuns into an etheric bacchanale. On the ghost abbess Helena's cue, the ghost nuns remove their habits to reveal, in the ethereal moonlight, translucent tulle and the pale skin beneath it. Edgar Degas immortalized the scene in 1876 in an impressionistic painting. The ghost nuns are seen processing to the front of the stage, swooning and flopping onto their knees in supplication. A reviewer for the Parisian *Journal des débats* described the wraiths dropping "their veils and their long habits, revealing only their light ballet tunics. Each of them drinks deeply of Cyprus wine or Val de Pegnas to refresh her mouth in which spiders have perhaps been spinning their webs; this gives them the courage to dance, and here they are spinning like tops, dancing rounds and the farandole, and dispensing themselves like women possessed."[20] The spectacle also possessed Dmitriyev, though his description does not come from an actual gaslit performance of the Ballet of the Nuns in Moscow; at the time of his writing, in 1859, the technology had not yet been installed in the Bolshoi. The nuns he saw would have moved in dimness. Dmitriyev insists, against the historical record, that Sankovskaya surpassed Taglioni in the role of the ghost abbess and that she calibrated it perfectly, exposing the dangers of her art, its seductive Satanism.

Dmitriyev was sufficiently captivated by Sankovskaya to turn up night after night at the theater hoping to see her perform again, but she never did. That led him to conclude she had left for Paris, again, or London, or had perhaps even suffered the bittersweet fate of the sylph. His account is emblematic of the love she received from liberal Moscow students, who crowned her their own personal tsarina, while also attesting to the reverence with which critics of the period described each step and gesture in her embodiments of Esmeralda, Giselle, and Paquita. Certain sensational details are omitted from his tribute, including the evening when the police were called to the Bolshoi to restore order after the ovation from the fawning students threatened to exceed acceptable decibel levels—the theater being no place for mass demonstrations. The noise ordinance came directly from Tsar Nicholas I, who had quashed the uprising that followed his ascension to the throne, in December of 1825, and thereafter maintained order in the empire through callous means. His was a rule of censorship, intolerance, and the persecution of the foreign, the nonconforming outsider. Sankovskaya, the made-in-Russia emblem of spiritual freedom, was, for the social class most ground down, a light in the dark.

The adoration of youthful audiences, both for Sankovskaya the great artist and Sankovskaya the perspiring human being behind the pirouettes, brought the French phenomenon of the claque (taken from the French word for clapping) to Moscow. Her devotees—her claque—could be counted on to applaud, cheer, and stomp their feet at the end of intricate sequences, giving her a moment to regain her balance and sneak in a breath. The rest of the audience some-times followed their example, making the success of the evening so resounding that no critic could quibble. In Paris, the claque could support or sabotage a performance, by talking or hacking or clapping off-beat, if the dancer fell out of favor with the claque or refused to provide free passes to the performance. There is no evi-dence to suggest that Sankovskaya ever offended her fans; their ado-ration lasted from 1836, when she made her debut, to 1854, when she left the stage.

INDEED HER FANS remained so overcommitted to her as to make the Bolshoi stage perilous for actual or potential rivals, and Sankovskaya was spared the indignities suffered by lesser lights. One of them was her own sister, the lesser-known Alexandra, who had a modest career in Romantic roles, together with folk fare and masquerades. But during her years at the Imperial The-ater College and on the Bolshoi Theater stage, Alexandra—billed as

Sankovskaya II—was bullied for her imperfections at the barre and, once to great alarm, abused in front of the entire theater.

The villain was the thirty-four-year-old ballet master Théodore Guerinot, a native of rural France who had danced in St. Petersburg for four years before accepting a renewable three-year position in Moscow in the fall of 1838. He specialized in mime and was touted for superb acting, his facial mannerisms extolled as "polysyllabic."[21] His behavior behind the scenes, however, lacked such nuance. He was, frankly, a cad. Guerinot enjoyed betraying his lover, the French dancer Laura Peysar, sometimes feigning innocence when caught in the act and at other times placing the blame on whatever insidious seductress had forced herself upon him that evening. Peysar exorcised her personal anguish by literally throwing herself into her art. She took on dangerous roles requiring elaborate stunts and almost killed herself when a boom holding her above the stage collapsed. She broke her leg in the fall. Her career ended, and Guerinot left town.

His debut in Moscow included the saltarello from the second act of the popular comic opera *Zampa, ou la fiancée de marbre* (Zampa, or the marble bride). Though the saltarello has benign rustic Italian origins, Guerinot and his onstage partner, Alexandra Voronina-Ivanova, made the quick triple-meter steps seem like devil's work. He was hailed by an anonymous reviewer in *Moskovskiye vedomosti* for performing as though each phrase was an on-the-spot, in-the-moment invention. Guerinot provided "excitement in the randomness" of the phrases, "giving the dance a new look each time. . . . You begin to think, in truth, that he is dancing on impulse, that each rapid change in his movement is the product of a rush of imagination, rather than being a requirement of this inventive dance."[22] After making this memorable first impression, Guerinot was appointed "ballet master and first dancer of mime" at the Bolshoi Theater in October of 1838.[23]

In Moscow he worked alongside, and then replaced, the Napoleon-era ballet master and pedagogue Adam Glushkovsky, who chose to retire from his position at the same time as Sankovskaya's mentor, Félicité Hullen. Guerinot brought French ballets from St. Petersburg to Moscow and, for 17,000 rubles a year, masculinized them, making the roles of the men as compelling as those of the women. His productions at the Bolshoi included *La fille du Danube* (The daughter of the Danube), which Filippo Taglioni had choreographed for his daughter, Marie, as well as the slave-girl drama *Le corsaire* and *Le diable boiteux* (The devil on two sticks), whose Paris premiere featured Fanny Elssler in a Spanish castanet dance called the cachucha. Guerinot partnered with Ekaterina Sankovskaya in several ballets, and both of them were lauded in the press for their performances, though the critics in question lamented the underbudgeted, dreadful-looking sets and costumes in the Moscow version of *La sylphide*, as opposed to the lavish Taglioni version in St. Petersburg. Guerinot was as expressive and evocative in his mime, demonstrating that "male dancing can be significant in its own right." Sankovskaya was "gentle" and, despite the disappointing staging, the ideal of grace. She might not have "floated through the air" and "glided through the flowers" as captivatingly as Taglioni, and her white tunic and wreath might have been a bore, but in the end she received five curtain calls—the same as Taglioni.[24] And Sankovskaya was the better actress of the two dancers.

Trouble for Guerinot came in 1842 with a staging of Rossini's opera *William Tell*, which has dancing in the third act. Since the opera concerns a rebellion against a repressive regime, in this case Austrian, the Censorship Committee of the Ministry of Education delayed approving it for production, having detected hints of revolution. To reach the stage, the opera had to be renamed *Charles the Bold* and the libretto reworked to enhance its patriotic as opposed to insurrectionist elements. The flash point, both onstage and off, was an aggressive *pas de trois* performed by Guerinot and the two Sankovskaya sisters. As soon as the dance ended, Alexandra ran off, her bladder full. She did not hear the call back to the stage and arrived late for her bow. She was supposed to enter the stage ahead of Guerinot and her sister, whose ranks exceeded hers, but since she was slow getting back, the order had to be reversed. Guerinot lost his temper. He went into the wings, grabbing Alexandra by the arm, and dragged her onto the stage. She stumbled and had to pull herself free to keep from falling. Backstage, he slapped and kicked her in front of the chorus. She fainted and took to bed for six days.

Alexandra's account of the attack, which she turned into an official complaint against Guerinot, prompted an investigation and interviews with audience and staff members who had witnessed the incident or heard about it. The slap was described as but a flick in the comically muddled recollection of a certain Captain Lieutenant Mukhin, who recalled Guerinot "lifting his hand and flicking her on the left cheek right next to her eye." Her "astonished and enraged visage" prompted him to conclude "that she had indeed been affected by the flicking." But, he mused,

whether or not M. Guerinot kicked her in the shins, or she him, as M. Guerinot testifies, that I did not see, for I was looking above their legs. Yet, in all likelihood, and given that she was ahead of him, she would have had to direct her kick behind her to M. Guerinot. Still, I cannot say anything definitive about this. Upon returning backstage, I, as a person external to the proceedings and having no obligation to say anything, refrained from doing so until the Repertoire Inspector, Court Counselor Verstovsky, arrived, declaring: "M. Guerinot has quarreled with Mlle. Sankovskaya; she has called him a swine." To which I, as an eyewitness to the event, deemed myself obliged to rejoin immediately: "And so is she justified, for M. Guerinot flicked her."[25]

The case went to St. Petersburg for a ruling. Guerinot was fined two weeks' pay by the minister of the court for his behavior—an indication, perhaps, that such incidents were somewhat routine. He was also made to apologize to his victim, which he did to her satisfaction, and advised that further incidents might lead to the termination of his employment. That the Russian word for "kick" is spelled with a soft sign in the Moscow records of the assault but without a soft sign in the St. Petersburg records—*pinka* instead of *pin'ka*—might seem a trifling detail, but it proves telling. People spoke differently in the two cities. Muscovites retained a domestic dialect that the court had abandoned; the Russian language was spoken more gently in Moscow than in the capital. But the art had a harder edge.

GUERINOT'S REPUTATION DETERIORATED. He was disparaged by the director of the Moscow Imperial Theaters, Verstovsky, who joked in a letter to his supervisor in St. Petersburg that "no matter how much one tries to teach Guerinot—to behave himself—he never ceases being a scoundrel."[26]

His swan-song benefit was on October 29, 1845; next came the expiration of his contract and what decorum obliged those in the know to call "unpleasantness." The unpleasantness, however, extended beyond Sankovskaya's sister to another dancer, Luisa Weiss, whose beauty helped to compensate for her technical limitations. Weiss had begun her career in Darmstadt, Germany, dancing in the theater built by the grand duke of Hesse, and then relocated to London, where she performed, depending on the source, either to great acclaim or partial success. Prince Alexander Nikolayevich (the future Tsar Alexander II) had a strong connection to Darmstadt, having married Princess Marie of Hesse in St. Petersburg in 1841. He invited Weiss to Russia and showed an intense interest in her performances at the Bolshoi—so intense, in fact, as to suggest that the dancer from Darmstadt was his mistress. Gedeonov also expressed interest in her, editing the letters that she wrote to the Moscow Imperial Theaters in hopes of a more lucrative contract. Weiss's ties to the court, and the special treatment she received, including imported footwear and payment in advance for her performances, made her a subject of gossip, as did her falling-out with Sankovskaya. The tattle within the theater was that Sankovskaya considered Weiss a threat and was conspiring with Guerinot to bring her down.

As part of the October 29, 1845, benefit for Guerinot, Weiss performed *La sylphide*, to constant, loud applause from most of the audience, the exception being Sankovskaya's claque, who tried to drown out the clapping with catcalls. There were several curtain calls—ten according to one count, fifteen in another. During the last of them, an apple was thrown at Weiss from the loges, plopping unceremoniously down at her feet.

The next day, Verstovsky reported the incident in lavish detail to Gedeonov, noting that the apple toss was unprecedented and that he had ordered an investigation above and beyond what the officer on duty in the theater reported. Weiss, he added, refused to dance again at the Bolshoi, and her mother and brother, who lived with her in Moscow, were very upset. Thus was compromised his attempt to "counterbalance public opinion in relation to Mlle. Sankovskaya, who is an obvious attraction for the ballet but cannot always be relied upon by the directorate due to poor health."[27]

Since Prince Alexander was Weiss's benefactor and would hear about the incident from her, Gedeonov decided that he needed to get involved. He wrote a letter to the prince explaining what had happened in language suitable for a child, first mentioning that, in recent times, audiences had engaged in the commendable custom of gently lobbing bouquets of flowers onto the stage, and that, in both Moscow and St. Petersburg, audiences tended to behave themselves. Though the apple had caused no damage, he stressed the need to find the person who threw it. Prince Alexander took the matter seriously, appointing a special officer to investigate on his behalf.

Subsequently Gedeonov reported that Guerinot had distributed a large number of free tickets to students, including those of the fencing instructor in the theater. He also learned that, on the morning of October 30, a day after the apple toss, Guerinot was overheard asking one of the students whether the performance, including the final curtain call, had gone according to plan. The silliness of the drama escalated when Verstovsky decided to get involved. He interviewed everyone who might have had anything to do with the incident and then expressed frustration at the discrepancies in their accounts. One eyewitness claimed that Weiss had encountered the apple after her third curtain call, not her tenth, and that it was half eaten, chewed, in fact, right down to the core. Surviving chunks of apple served as evidence to prove that it had actually posed no threat to Weiss's safety. Verstovsky dismissed this account as biased, coming from a dancer who "placed Mlle. Sankovskaya incomparably higher than Mlle. Weiss in all respects."[28] His investigation revealed, even less helpfully, that the apple had been thrown from a loge registered under the alias Zolotov. "A person by that name does in fact exist," Verstovsky explained to Gedeonov, but he was a deeply spiritual man, "an Old Believer from the other side of the Moscow River, and does not attend the theater."[29]

Someone else asserted that the apple had been thrown after most of the audience had departed, as the chandelier was being raised. But the chandelier, Verstovsky replied, was fixed in place.

Since Guerinot had a bad reputation (Verstovsky never forgot the flicking episode), he was blamed for disgracing Weiss, but Verstovsky also had extremely harsh words for Sankovskaya, whose alleged conspiracies against younger talents had exhausted his patience. "I am quite willing to accept that as long as she remains in the Moscow Theater she will constantly disrupt the order and disturb the peace with her tireless intrigues," he fumed. "After several days discussing her benefit and all of her incessant whims all I wanted to do was collapse in bed!" The twilight of her career consisted of "making others feel sorry for her, as if she were some downtrodden waif or pig in the poke." This was no way to treat his star dancer, Verstovsky knew, but he had had enough of Sankovskaya's self-centeredness and the "little illnesses" that led her to petition for a reduced workload, performances of parts of ballets—a solo variation here, a *pas de deux* there—rather than entire works.[30] She lay in her bed all covered in bouquets, claiming to be at death's door but refusing to see a doctor.

Verstovsky was no less disgusted with Guerinot, who had taken sick leave for—he claimed—a bad leg but found time to go to the ballet school each day to "whisper in Sankovskaya's ear for an hour or two."[31] He wanted both of them removed, especially Guerinot, and rejoiced at the thought of a twenty-two-year-old dancer and ballet master from St. Petersburg, Irakliya Nikitin, replacing him at the Bolshoi. The news of Nikitin's coming to Moscow "finally lets the stone roll from my heart," he told his supervisor.[32]

Weiss submitted a complaint of her own, accusing Sankovskaya of conspiring with Guerinot against her, just as she had conspired against two other dancers in fits of pique. Given that Weiss had not succeeded in mobilizing the public against her, Sankovskaya purportedly hatched a plan with her partner to humiliate her during the October 29 benefit. But the catcalls from the "450" students who had received free tickets failed to quell the enthusiasm of the general public, who called her to the stage fifteen (not ten) times after the performance of *La sylphide*. The apple was "huge," Weiss recalled, "and it was thrown at me with such force that it broke into small pieces when it struck my breast, and certainly would have killed me had it hit my head."[33]

That was the end of Guerinot. Gedeonov refused to renew his contract. Sankovskaya, too, was removed from the Bolshoi, but just to give tension over the apple attack a chance to dissipate. Gedeonov dispatched her to St. Petersburg, where she performed *La sylphide* at the Great Stone Theater before touring abroad. She triumphed. Although Verstovsky engineered her departure, he regretted the significant loss to ticket sales and recognized that nothing could compensate for it. Sankovskaya's Moscow fans remained feverishly committed to her while awaiting her return; they exacted revenge for her banishment by pulling pranks on those who presumed to take her place—pranks that were far more bizarre than the dancers themselves ever contrived.

Weiss recovered from the apple attack, performing two weeks later on a program that featured *Zampa, ou la fiancée de marbre* to sustained applause from the auditorium and the loges. "After my performance yesterday I was received very warmly," she informed Gedeonov with gratitude; "1,000 rubles in bouquets were tossed to me by the local nobility."[34] She remained in Moscow (there is reference to her performing in an 1846 vaudeville depicting "a day in the life" of a hapless theater prompter, *Ein Tag aus dem Leben eines alten Souffleurs*), and she must also have appeared in St. Petersburg. Toward the end of her run, she suffered the minor misfortune of having a scarf and gold bracelet stolen from her Moscow apartment, after a man posing as an administrator with the Imperial Theaters lured her and her mother to an official meeting. Another long investigation followed.

The claque dreamt up their worst prank, however, against another, much more gifted dancer, Elena Andreyanova, who had the double misfortune of rivaling Sankovskaya and partnering with Nikitin, the dancer who had replaced Guerinot.

Like Sankovskaya, Andreyanova performed in a manner evocative of Taglioni and Elssler and came into prominence at the time that those two ballerinas, the twin poles of the Romantic era in dance, visited St. Petersburg. She was nicknamed the "northern Giselle" when she toured in the role to Paris, but she suffered terrible nerves and, according to a corpulent theater observer named Jules Janin, "trembled like a northern birch tree" when she made her first entry on the Paris stage.[35] The consensus among critics was that Andreyanova had tremendous power in her limbs and had committed herself to a heroic bearing. Her chiseled facial features, thick brows, and dark eyes added to her expressiveness. Comparisons between Andreyanova and Sankovskaya inevitably emphasized the former's boldness, resolve, and strength, and the latter's gentleness, lightness, and smoothness in transitions. The distinction was that of the real versus the ideal, with Andreyanova revealing the effort, making her triumph over hardship explicit. Sankovskaya, in contrast, concealed it.

In Moscow, Sankovskaya's supporters found Andreyanova lacking in refined lyricism, the gift of being able to sing a phrase with her body. But she was celebrated in St. Petersburg and received special treatment from Gedeonov, who lavished food and wine on her. Once she became his mistress, she was protected from other officials and officers of the court and felt sure that she did not need to purchase support, as had Sankovskaya, from a claque. The old balletomanes of St. Petersburg fell hard for her, as they did for other dancers, seating her in her carriage after performances before retiring to oysters and Champagne in private dining rooms to luxuriate in unrequited love, but they were harmless compared to the zealots in Moscow.

Aware of Gedeonov's intimate relationship with Andreyanova, Verstovsky made sure to praise her talent to the heavens when she performed *Giselle* at the Bolshoi Theater at the end of 1843. He also felt obliged to ridicule Sankovskaya—and her fans—after her appearance in a vaudeville by Jean-François Bayard, as part of a December 17 benefit performance for the actor Alexander Bantïshev:

> Although M. Bantïshev's benefit brought him only 2,000 rubles, the public, especially the upper ranks, shouted to their hearts' content. No sooner had they caught sight of Mlle. Sankovskaya than they let out three hurrahs! If someone had been brought into the theater blindfolded and asked where he was, doubtless he would have said that he had been brought to the public square just as a high-ranking general had arrived, the hurrahing being of just such a distinction! Desiring to show that she had been moved to tears by the ovation, Mlle. Sankovskaya made of her body a pose so filthy that I would be embarrassed to name it. Then, upon making her typical coarse gestures, those that rope-climbers make as they climb up ropes, she began to dance in a manner so unseemly that I couldn't bear to look at it, especially now that we have come to love Mlle. Andreyanova's dances.[36]

Verstovsky acknowledged that Sankovskaya was a skilled entertainer, amusing a broad swath of the public in the up-tempo, satiric grab bags of "music, singing, dancing, *calembours* [puns], *marivaudage* [affectation]," and ridiculous happenings that defined the French vaudeville and its Russian derivations.[37] But, he claimed, she had a disastrous outing on December 17. Trolling for laughs, she went too lowbrow, embarrassing herself before the merchants and audiences in the crowd. Verstovsky made it seem as though she had given the vaudeville a bad reputation by crossing the thin line in her performance between delicate ballerina and bawd. He would make the same invidious comparisons to Andreyanova—and repeat his tales of conflicts with Sankovskaya over dressing rooms and costumes—in 1845 and 1848, when Andreyanova returned to the Bolshoi Theater as part of extensive tours around the Russian Empire. He was unable, however, to change the minds or tame the behavior of the ballet-goers known as "Sankovisti."

His decision, in February of 1845, to assign Sankovskaya additional vaudeville appearances at the Maliy Theater while Andreyanova starred at the Bolshoi backfired. There were no apples thrown or flicks administered, but Andreyanova was subject to jeering from the free-ticket-holders in the galleries. The noise threatened to drown out the legitimate applause from the gentlemen in the seats and dampened the enthusiasm of the ladies, who expressed their approval through the vigorous shaking of their kerchiefs. Meanwhile, at the Maliy Theater, bouquets covered Sankovskaya's ankles as she took her last bow. Andreyanova rightly anticipated trouble for her subsequent engagement at the Bolshoi in November of 1848 and reserved even more seats than she had in the past for her fans from St. Petersburg.

According to the nineteenth-century journalist Mikhail Pilyayev, the incident occurred during Andreyanova's benefit performance of *Paquita*, a ballet best known for its Grand Pas *classique*, which exists in various versions in the present-day repertoire.

The full-length version danced at the Bolshoi in 1848 was choreographed by Marius Petipa and Pierre-Frédéric Malavergne, to music by Édouard Deldevez and Ludwig Minkus. The three scenes and two acts told of the love of a Spanish gypsy for a French officer during the Napoleonic Wars. The gypsy discovers that she is of noble blood and, as the fates ordained, the cousin of the officer, which allows the two of them to get married. The *pas de trois* of the first act and grand classical *pas* of the second were created with Andreyanova's skills in mind, sculpted, as it were, onto her body. She danced the 1847 premiere in St. Petersburg before bringing the ballet to Moscow.

The "agent of the antic" directed against her at the Bolshoi was a tradesman who had been given a free ticket and a few rubles by a student named Pyotr Bulgakov, the leader of the Sankovskaya claque, for the favor of flinging an offending object onto the stage from a stall on the right-hand side. Pïlyayev intimates that the tradesman was a blockhead, but he had good aim and impeccable timing. A dead cat landed at Andreyanova's feet at the end of the *pas de trois*. The cat had a note pinned to its tail, or to a ribbon attached to its tail—the anecdote is fuzzy on this point—that read *"première danseuse étoile."*

The French dancer in the role of the French officer, Frederic Montessu, picked up the feline and, cursing at the audience, sent it sailing into the wings. Andreyanova shielded her face in horror; "it was evident from the convulsing of her chest and shoulders that she was in tears," Pïlyayev recalls. Confusion reigned. The entire cast filled the stage; noblemen shouted, banging the feet and arms of their chairs; noble ladies waved kerchiefs with even more vigor. Petals rained down on the star as the sound of her sobs reached the loges. The police arrived and nabbed the culprit. The performance continued, but Andreyanova refused to dance; an alternate took her part. Still, she was thrice summoned for a curtain call by the public.[38] For Andreyanova's sake, Bulgakov was banished from Moscow and police placed at the front of the stage for her subsequent appearances, after which, as Petipa relates, "the public literally overwhelmed her with flowers and valuable gifts."[39]

More is known about the scandals than the glories of the Moscow stage, because the scandals generated heaps of documents, and the glories, at least at this point in time, inspired nothing more specific than poetic tributes, bouquets of words: "Sankovskaya in *Sylphide* / Is so sweet / Lord forgive the sins / That have been committed."[40] She was the most radiant figure in recollections of ballet of the period, and as the case of the altogether unknown teenage dancer Avdotya Arshinina demonstrates, the celebrated performers faced many fewer hardships, and many fewer threats to their well-being than the dancers in the shadows, whether in Russia, Europe, or America. Arshinina doubtless lacked Sankovskaya's skills and never had a chance of becoming a dancer of the first rank, but the sins committed against her put all of the tales of kicks in the shin, apples, dead cats, and the antics of the Sankovistï into the ghastliest of contexts. Those were elite-dancer problems.

On January 5, 1847, Arshinina was dumped at the door of a hospital experiencing "fits of madness" and "constant delirium."[41] Pale and emaciated, she had severe injuries on her head and body as well as bruised, infected, "blackened" genitalia.[42] The crime was the talk of the town and the subject of discussion in legal circles for years. It exposed a wretched economy wherein lesser-skilled dancers were promised access, through their art, to aristocratic circles, only to become sex slaves. Bribes were essential to the enterprise, along with drugs, masquerades, and small black masks.

The first person to be arrested in connection with the assault was Arshinina's own father, a mediocre fiddler on the books of the

Moscow Imperial Theaters. He had been living in a pitiful state, the police reported, with his three young daughters in a cold, damp apartment, unable to care for them after his wife's death, with no money for food or clothing. Desperate, he "sold" Arshinina, his oldest daughter, to a "master," Prince Boris Cherkassky, for 10,000 rubles.[43] Before taking formal possession of her, Cherkassky showered her with gifts: enamel earrings with diamonds, a gold bracelet, a cloak of fox fur with sable collar, indoor silk fabrics, sweets, and more than 2,175 in rubles that Arshinina asked a sister to hide away for her. Her father was bribed into the sale with a coat and a silver snuffbox. The actor who introduced Arshinina to the prince was paid, along with the proxies who purchased sedatives for the prince at pharmacies on Arbat Street.

The events leading up to the crime were pieced together from police interrogations conducted at all hours of the day and night. Essential information came from the prince's custodian, who revealed that, on New Year's Eve of 1846, Cherkassky and Arshinina attended a masquerade at the Bolshoi. Hidden behind a mask, Arshinina danced and made the rounds of the theater on the arms of several noblemen until the stroke of midnight, at which time she was returned to Cherkassky. Three of the people who had promenaded with her—a college registrar, a teacher, and a merchant—joined her and the prince at his home. They dined and drank vodka and Champagne. The glass given to Arshinina contained a sedative. She was raped, first by the prince and then, after the prince had fallen asleep, by the others. Arshinina returned to consciousness during the assault and managed to tear herself free. She ran into the yard wearing just a blouse but was caught and dragged back inside. The next morning she was taken to her father's apartment, bloodied and unresponsive. He and the prince's physician tried to restore her health before taking her to the hospital. The evidence of the violence she had suffered—her clothes and the bottle containing the sedative—was burned in a stove. The bottle shattered; the chemical compound it contained turned the flames different colors.

The head physician of the hospital noted her "loss of innocence" and "highly morbid condition."[44] Cherkassky rejected Arshinina's accusation that he had forced himself upon her in a demonstration of "extreme passion"—despite the fact that, from her bed in the hospital, she was heard crying out "Prince! Prince! What are you doing to me! Have you no fear of God!" and "Father, why have you ruined me?"[45] Before her father was arrested, he arranged (through Verstovsky) to see her in the hospital, where he heard her shrieking, "Why is this happening to me?" among other incomprehensible ravings.[46] She died of her injuries thirteen days after arriving in the hospital.

Fearing prison less than the humiliation of a conviction, Cherkassky tried to place the blame on Arshinina herself. He first attributed the inflammation in her lower abdomen to improper menstrual hygiene, then to excessive horseback riding, and, even more feebly, to dehydration caused by dancing. Cherkassky's liaison with Arshinina had been consensual, he argued, as had been his relationships with other Imperial Theater dancers. He paid them not for the favor of sex but out of pity for their poverty.

The case took another bizarre turn when Cherkassky accused an interrogator of abusing his power by pulling on his beard, but the senior medical officer in the case found the prince's facial hair to have "perfect integrity."[47] Cherkassky also drew attention to the "magnitude" of his member; the medical officer concluded it was not as huge as he had boasted.[48] The prince sat in custody for months but was not, in the end, convicted, owing to trivial discrepancies in the eyewitness accounts. Arshinina's father was sentenced to prison in Siberia for two years and banished from Moscow.

• • •

SANKOVSKAYA HEARD ABOUT the crime, as did everyone in the Moscow Imperial Theaters. The director noted the date of Arshinina's death in a report sent to the court in St. Petersburg, adding the hope that she might rest in peace. The crime, however, belonged to the realm of the dispensable underclasses, not to the court. Fyodor Dostoyevsky made this realm the subject of his novels, raging against its cosmic injustices and commonplace brutalities. Sankovskaya and her rivals escaped it, both onstage and off.

Her world was one in which, according to a historical meditation published in the second-to-last year of Soviet power, "actors, singers, dancers, the professoriate, students, and literati resembled a tight-knit family of distant lineage—one that preserved, before it began to die, the antiquated psychology native to the centuries-old Russian capital."[49] The sentiment is appealing, making the Romantic era in Russia less lonely for great, elite artists than the Romantic era in France and Germany. But it cannot compensate for the lack of data about Sankovskaya's achievement, the fact that most of the records of her career went up in flames. The reviews are inspired but insubstantial, lacking specifics. There is no known information about what her parents did, whether she got married, the nature of her foreign appearances, her teaching and training regimen, and what she did in her free time. Perhaps the lack of day-to-day details is justified. Perhaps little is known about her existence because there is in fact little to know, her life and art having been one.

There survive just two letters, one of trifling content—congratulations and best wishes on a Name Day—and the other substantive. They were both written, in elegant prose and in an elegant hand, near the end of her life, when she and her sister Alexandra, by then also retired from the stage, were living in the house they had purchased in the village of Vsekhsvyatskoye, now part of north-central Moscow. Sankovskaya had the letters hand-delivered by coachman to the dancer Mariya Manokhina, the daughter of one of her onstage partners, at the time of Manokhina's debut at the Bolshoi in the ballet *Satanilla*. The substantive one, containing an exceedingly precise lesson in pantomime, offers insight into how Sankovskaya perceived her art and how things had changed since the days of her greatest triumphs.

Satanilla dates from 1840. It was choreographed in Paris by Joseph Mazilier before being revived by Marius Petipa and his father Jean-Antoine Petipa. The score came from two Frenchmen, Napoléon Henri Reber and François Benoist, as overhauled by a Russian conductor, Alexander Lyadov. Sankovskaya performed a version in 1848 at the Bolshoi, and remembered the role in sufficient detail to coach Manokhina through the essential moments in the plot, a tale of love, hell, and mortgaged souls. A female sprite, Satanilla, is entrusted by Beelzebub with the undoing of a count in his old, haunted castle but instead loses herself to love. She burns the bond that had condemned his soul to damnation, despite the fact that he will never love her back, his heart belonging to a mortal, whom Satanilla, in an act of selflessness, allows him to wed. She earns in exchange for her sacrifice the blessing of heaven and liberation from the powers of darkness.

Sankovskaya insists that Manokhina listen for her cues, and that she not crumple her crimson gown by accident or step onto the trapdoor leading to hell too soon. That would spoil everything. If a final rehearsal has not been scheduled, Manokhina should at least walk through her part backstage with her partner, Dmitri Kuznetsov. He and other dancers did not know their music, Sankovskaya recalled from the rehearsal she had seen, and rushed their dances. Since Manokhina was in the lead role, she would bear the blame if the stage action ended too soon. About the bond-burning scene, and the heartbreak that Satanilla suffers when she realizes that the count loves another, Sankovskaya was meticulous:

> Begin to weep when you hear the cue, not before, and after four measures let go of his hands. Go to light the paper the second time not with your back to the table. Just turn your head to Kuznetsov. Toss the paper at the tremolo. Point to it at the cue and say that you are going to die, but do so quietly, weakly. Yesterday the paper burned properly. If it burns too slowly in your hand, wave it down, and if too quickly, raise it.[50]

Sankovskaya tells Manokhina at the start of the letter that she feels too weak to take a coach to the Bolshoi for the performance and, in her compromised physical condition, could no longer demonstrate the steps in *Satanilla* as she remembered them. She passed the torch to Manokhina in the same manner that, back in 1836, Félicité Hullen had passed the torch to her—professionally, dispassionately. "I don't know if you'll understand what I've written to you, but try to remember that you are not performing as a schoolgirl, have more confidence in yourself, and, mainly, listen to your music, then all will be well. The dances are all very good, but don't be upset if they don't come out as you intend. I suggest that you congratulate Gerber at the end, since he'll still be conducting even if he's not very good. God be with you."

To the extent that most ballets tend to be about ballet to some degree, *Satanilla* might be seen as a parable about the devil's bargains and sacrifices that dancers have to make. To succeed in the art, Sankovskaya advised Manokhina, she needed to "forget everything," losing herself in the depiction of a character that desires to escape the bonds of the underworld and ascend, by means of the clasp in the back of her corset, into brightness.

SANKOVSKAYA DIED A few months after writing the letter and was buried near the church that gave her village its name, All Saints. The graveyard no longer exists; the church grounds were eliminated by the Soviets in favor of apartment buildings. The embers of *Satanilla* include her performance notes, published plot summaries, and, in the music archive of the Bolshoi Theater, the violin rehearsal score and a complete set of parts from the 1890s.

The fire that consumed the physical records of her career in the Bolshoi Petrovsky Theater began on March 11, 1853. During a rehearsal at nine thirty that morning, according to a breathless article published in *London Illustrated News*,

a dense cloud of smoke was observed from one of the fire-station towers of Moscow, issuing from the roof of the large Imperial Theatre. . . . It was soon found that the immense building was burning inside and that the fire had already spread itself with an amazing velocity in all directions of the interior. The flames burst forth from the fallen roof and from the windows: black smoke rose high in the air, and, sweeping over the northern vicinity of the theatre, obscured the light to such a degree that people could not well see what they were about. Innumerable firebrands flying in the air, threatened to set fire to the whole neighborhood. Had there been more wind at the time, and had there not been snow lying deep on the ground and the roofs of the houses, the catastrophe would have been inevitable.[51]

The mechanic who discovered the fire was "scorched." The newspaper added that "from the number of *employés* permanently living with their families in the house, many lives were lost." Firefighters battled the flames for two days, but the effort was futile, and the theater surrendered to the "greedy element." There was an act of courage from a typical Russian man of the people: an unemployed roofer and boilermaker named Vasiliy Marin. The tale of his exploits was repeated in Russian publications far and wide, from Moscow to Yaroslavl, and soon immortalized in folklore in the form of a colored woodcut, or *lubok*. In the gloss published in *London Illustrated News*, the "peasant" Marin "nobly distinguished himself" by scaling the frozen rain-gutter with a rope and hook in his waist in order to rescue a man trapped near the roof. Three of his friends in the crowd of onlookers had tried to hold him back, but he broke free and ran toward the inferno nonetheless, claiming that he could not "bear the sight of a Christian soul thus perishing." For his good deed, he supposedly received a medal, 150 rubles, and an embrace from the tsar.

The theater collapsed; six carpenters died, among them serfs belonging to the notorious Prince Cherkassky. Eighteenth-century costumes were lost, along with decorations, an archive of financial and personnel documents, music scores, and rare instruments. The intricate official reports (including Verstovsky's) chronicle the burning of floors, ceilings, lamps, and sofas; the collapse of the roof; even the denting of the boiler-room pumps. They also pinpoint the exact locations of the employees of the theater from seven in the morning until noon, and include the testimonies of the seventeen boys and twenty-three girls who had been taking dance and music classes inside. The cause of the fire was never determined; none of the eyewitness accounts indicated arson. It apparently began in a tool room located on the right side of the stage beneath the staircase leading to the women's restrooms. A technician with a key reported that he used it to store stage materials and warm clothes. The actors on the stage first saw sparks and smoke and then felt a massive explosion that shook the ground like an earthquake. Neither fuel nor gunpowder nor explosives had been stored in the theater. Flames overwhelmed the water tanks; the boiling water released huge plumes of scalding steam. The police noted the rescue of three bags of copper coins from a safe by the treasurer; a girl who'd lost two teeth falling down a staircase; a boy who'd left to buy a bagel just minutes before the inferno would have engulfed him; a man who'd leapt from a window in fright but then ran back into the theater to save a woman; a custodian who unrepentantly acknowledged failing to report the smell of smoke before finishing his shift and heading home; and an administrator who'd forgotten to take his mother with him when he fled their apartment in the theater.

The smoke cleared after three days, exposing the foundations and subterranean corridors underneath the part of the theater that had been destroyed. A feeling of desolation overtook Moscow, the loss affecting even those who interpreted the flames as the divine retribution of Holy Rus against the corrupting evil of ballet and opera—even though the small vaudeville house across the way survived. The part of the Bolshoi that still stood could not be saved. Vegetation encased the remains over the summer as the pagan force of nature worked to reclaim the temple of culture. The birds and frogs moved back in.

THE THEATER WOULD be rebuilt again in 1856, assuming its present-day appearance; Sankovskaya's protégée danced in *Satanilla* on the new stage. Verstovsky remained in his post, cantankerous as ever, and continued to treat his dancers like serfs. But he could count on them to make his productions sensational—so much so that, before retiring, he would proudly confront the first documented instance at the Moscow Imperial Theaters of ticket scalping. The Bolshoi had cultivated a repertoire, partly imported, partly home-grown, but entirely for Russian performers. Ballet attracted large audiences drawn from Moscow's middle and upper classes, and dancers appeared before adoring audiences. After 1856 nothing— not fire, slashed budgets, scandal, not even war—could erase its achievements.

· 4 ·

IMPERIALISM

THE BOLSHOI PETROVSKY THEATER was gone, but Alexei Verstovsky did not much miss it. Nor did he see the point in rebuilding it.

The decision was not his to make. The Imperial Court in St. Petersburg approved and oversaw the reconstruction, leaving the cantankerous bureaucrat running the Moscow Imperial Theaters powerless. Verstovsky heard about the project from one of the architects involved in the planning. "Five million bricks" and "three million in silver rubles" had been budgeted, Verstovsky learned. "Doubtless it would be more cost-effective in the present circumstances for Moscow to resist building such a massive playhouse," he argued, "which, even in its best years, had been filled no more than a dozen times." The three million rubles would be better allocated to the railroad, he confided to a colleague, "and that is the indisputable truth!"[1] Yet Verstovsky no longer had the stamina to fight for the truth; his "eyes were refusing to serve" and his handwriting "getting worse and worse."[2] In 1861 he surrendered his post to Leonid Lvov, brother of the composer of "God Save the Tsar," the Russian national anthem for most of the nineteenth century. Less than a year after retiring, Verstovsky died of a heart attack.

The Bolshoi was rebuilt in time for the 1856 coronation of Tsar Alexander II in Cathedral Square at the Kremlin. Its opening was integral to the festivities. The budget and design of the Bolshoi bore the imprint of political and cultural aspirations to restore national esteem. The Crimean War, waged between 1853 and 1856, had proved a devastating and humiliating defeat for the Russian Empire. Disputes in Bethlehem and Jerusalem had prompted Russia to march into present-day Romania and threaten the Ottoman Empire. With France and Britain aligned against Russia, a bloody front opened on the Crimean Peninsula near Sevastopol. The city fell to European and Ottoman allies, forcing Russia to sue for peace. (In 2014, as part of a campaign by President Vladimir Putin to right perceived historical wrongs, Russia retook the Crimea from Ukraine. Sevastopol remains in dispute today.)

After the loss of hundreds of thousands of lives and more than a billion rubles in the Crimean War, Alexander II grasped the orb and scepter in 1856 with a fresh start in mind and a new stage for the celebrations. There had been no unrest before his ascension, no regicide, no coup, and no evil omens—although the crown did slip from the empress's head during the ceremony. Rumors that the previous tsar, Nicholas I, had committed suicide proved false (he died of pneumonia), and the throng at the Kremlin greeted the new sovereign without excessive cowering. Worries about his youth and inexperience were tempered by the sense, from liberals, that Russia needed reform. Reason, it was hoped, had been placed on the throne.

The Bolshoi Theater of 1856 lies at the heart of the Bolshoi of today. Some tsarist swank was added in the second half of the nineteenth century, when the heating and lighting were also upgraded. In 1917, the Bolsheviks smashed windows, swiped fixtures, and shut off the heat. The theater became a space for political functions—serious events, no fun at all, full of jabbering about everything but ballet and opera. The Soviet Union itself came into official existence at the Bolshoi. The workers of the world were commanded to "unite!" as children rushed across the stage in agitprop spectaculars. During World War II, a German bomb damaged the façade; repairs did nothing to improve the acoustics. Upkeep lagged, then ceased as the Soviet Union went bankrupt. The scuffed parquet floors sagged, the outer walls cracked and peeled. But the Bolshoi did not burn down, and its performers continued to be venerated by the public. Five hundred meters away, the occupants of the Kremlin regarded the theater as a potent weapon in the Soviet diplomatic arsenal. Fidel Castro attended the ballet, as did Ronald Reagan. The Bolshoi at present remains an elaborated version of what the St. Petersburg architect Alberto Cavos had imagined in a fevered dream.

Cavos, the son of an Italian opera singer and grandson of an Italian dancer, unreservedly pursued his passions for beautiful women, the cities of Italy, Renaissance painting, antique furniture, mirrors, crystal, and bronze. The fineries he desired informed his architectural choices, and vice versa. When his first wife died of tuberculosis after the birth of their fourth child, he remarried, taking as his spouse a seventeen-year-old. Together they had three children and nine or more grandchildren, but Cavos routinely cheated on her and the marriage collapsed. He retired to the Grand Canal in Venice with a mistress, leaving his wife nearly destitute and eldest daughter without a dowry. The commissions that had made him so rich (and, at his death, his mistress) included the Bolshoi Theater in Moscow and the Equestrian Circus Theater in St. Petersburg. The latter indeed hosted the circus as well as opera. In 1860, it was rebuilt and renamed the Mariyinsky, after the wife of Tsar Alexander II, Mariya Aleksandrovna.

For all his fame, the commission to rebuild the Bolshoi did not magically fall into his hands. Cavos competed in 1853 with three other architects, his chief rival being the Moscow neoclassicist Alexander Nikitin. Cavos triumphed by correcting the most glaring flaw in the design of the old theater: the potentially dangerous pileup created by the stairs blocking the doorways to the lower-floor stalls and seats. Nikitin had proposed keeping the interior of the old theater intact, but, in hopes of preventing another inferno, suggested replacing everything once made of wood with iron and cast iron (excluding the floor and ceiling of the auditorium) at a cost of some 175,000 rubles.

Cavos also sought to improve the Bolshoi's acoustics, which the intendant of the Imperial Theaters, Alexander Gedeonov, lamented. Cavos wanted the inside of the new theater to be like the body of a string instrument, a Stradivarius violin. He proposed removing the curved brick walls behind the loges and replacing them with panels that projected rather than absorbed sound. Iron trusses in the ceiling would suspend, from the seams, a resonant pinewood plafond decorated with a painting of Apollo and the Muses. Gedeonov discussed Cavos's proposals with the minister of the court, Count Alexander Adlerberg, taking into account, of course, the opinion of the tsar: "His Majesty had no wish to demolish the present stone wall of the corridor; but since the wall is not entirely trustworthy Cavos accommodated a new one in his plan." The architect also sought to ensure that the fireproofing had no "communication" with the auditorium—no effect, in other words, on its acoustics. Cavos won the contest, and construction began.[3]

Cavos made the Bolshoi the most sumptuous theater in the world, and in record time. Construction began with the sinking of bundled beams into the mire in May 1855. When the exterior was completed at the end of 1855, Cavos presented the estimates for the cost of the fittings, draperies, and velvets, likewise the price of the lamps and chandeliers, including the astonishing three-tiered chandelier of crystal pendants suspended in the auditorium. The chandelier was more than eight meters in height and had more than 20,000 parts. But since it dripped wax and oil, only the poorest sods ended up sitting (or standing) beneath its splendor.

The tsar's coronation was the spur in the builders' sides. On its eve, just fifteen months after groundbreaking, only a hill of trash remained to be cleared. Cavos's achievement, everyone recognized, was miraculous, unparalleled in theater design. Yet there was a problem, one that would haunt the Bolshoi into the twenty-first century. The foundation still sat on the bog below. Water, the bane of wood and masonry alike, seeped into the oak pilings, rotting them away and leaving the theater, a century later, standing on crumbling brick.

On June 16, 1856, two months before the opening, a serious problem arose. Cavos received an unsubtle warning from the minister of the court about an unstable wall behind the front gable: "It behooves M. Cavos to ensure that what he has allowed to transpire through his lack of care does not cause him to be held accountable."[4] The wall was repaired. Installing the heating and lighting left little time to gild the foyer and pad the seats, much less hire polite or literate ushers. But the Bolshoi was complete.

The theater opened to the public on August 20, 1856, with a staging of Vincenzo Bellini's opera *I Puritani* (The Puritans) starring a cast of internationally recognized singers, including Enrico Calzolari, Frederick Lablache, and Angiolina Bosio, a twenty-five-year-old coloratura soprano much admired by Tsar Alexander II. There was no thought of performing a Russian opera, since the court had long preferred Italian ones—the more exuberant the better—and the first ballet would be staged only at a special, invitation-only gala on August 30. The court dithered as to which Italian opera should be performed for the public opening, first considering Rossini's *Il barbiere di Siviglia* (The barber of Seville) and Verdi's *Rigoletto* before settling on *I Puritani*. For a moment, it seemed that Gaetano Donizetti's comic opera *L'elisir d'amore* (The elixir of love) would inaugurate the new theater, but it was pushed back to the private performance ten days later. So it was Bellini at the Bolshoi on opening night.

In Russia, the politics of the theater sometimes mirrors the happenings of history, especially in periods of tumult, of which Russia has had a surfeit. Following Napoleon's invasion in 1812, deriding the French became modish in the Imperial Theaters. Later in the nineteenth century tastes would turn against the German Empire and Prince Otto von Bismarck. After the Great October Socialist Revolution of 1917, when Russia flipped over on herself and everything good in the past turned bad, the repertoire transformed as well. Glinka's *A Life for the Tsar* morphed into *Hammer and Sickle* to match Communist aesthetics; Puccini's *Tosca* emerged from the Bolshevik coup as *The Battle for the Commune*.

But in the war- and revolution-free year of 1856, the bond between art and politics loosened. The choice of *I Puritani* for the opening of the Bolshoi Theater and crowning of the new sovereign had nothing to do with the world beyond the stage. It was picked simply because it was the newest on the list of available operas, and because it would be sung by the popular Bosio, star of an Italian opera troupe in St. Petersburg. The plot is actually anti-aristocratic. Unlike the Soviets, however, who scoured libretti, listened to music, and looked at dance for signs of sedition, Tsar Alexander II feared nothing from the theater. The sordid goings-on in Bellini's scores, or anyone else's, posed no threat to imperial rule.

Likewise the first ballet selected to honor the monarch was meant to showcase a talented performer: *La vivandière* (1844) featured Fanny Cerrito, an Italian ballerina of marvelous technique, delightful in her execution of *batterie*, as precise in her rapid turns as a spinning top. Her partner—the no less renowned dancer, choreographer, and ballet master Arthur Saint-Léon—was also her husband. Her steps are lost to time, but one of the group dances, a *pas de six*, survives in Saint-Léon's notation, and offers a sense of his impressive technique.[5] Cerrito played the early nineteenth-century Napoleonic equivalent of a Girl Friday, a maiden who serves French soldiers by writing letters on their behalf, bandaging their wounds, and managing a canteen. She sells food and provisions to the troops at a discount, but preserves her virtue; the soldiers covet what is forbidden to everyone but her true love, the tavern-keeper Hans. Army life did not allow for easy *pliés*, and Cerrito was required to execute hard one-foot landings with jugs and utensils strapped around her waist.

Press reports about the new Bolshoi were effusive. Reviewers gushed about the expansive façades, the intricate mosaics on the lobby floors, and the mélange of "floral ornaments, rocailles, cartouches, meshes, rosettes and plaits" in the tiers.[6] Cavos had reimagined the Bolshoi in a "Byzantine-Renaissance style," with entrance columns of milk-white limestone, loges of crimson velvet, and foyers full of fitted mirrors and grisaille squares.[7] The seats were padded with horsehair and coconut matting—the latest in comfort. Fine gold leaf overlaid papier-mâché moldings in the auditorium.

Ingredients for the gilding included clay, egg, and vodka. Paint-brushes were fashioned from the fine hair of blue (perhaps brown) squirrels' tails, excellent for the application of thick, rich color.

The history of the nation was allegorized on the second curtain, painted with the image of a crucial event from 1612. In that year, according to Kremlin legend and official propaganda, the Russian masses united for the first time against their enemies, a band of Poles and Lithuanians. Besides fouling Russian land, the invaders sought to convert the peasants and merchants to Catholicism, a fate considered worse than death. A salt peddler named Kuzma Minin and a prince named Dmitri Pozharsky prevented the tragedy. The curtain shows the two men entering Moscow on horseback, intent on inciting the people to rebel. The message was as obvious in 1856 as it is today: As long as we are united, we the Russian people can defeat anyone. Foreign occupiers will always be expelled, and those who treacherously side with them will likewise be vanquished. The curtain elicited praise from both Russian critics and those foreign-ers who saw in it less an endorsement of xenophobia than an hom-age to Italian theatrical design. It hung in the Bolshoi Theater until 1938, when Stalin decided to make 1917, rather than 1612, Rus-sia's favorite year. The curtain vanished from the premises. Politics mandated its restoration in 2011 based on a sketch and a photo-graph preserved in the Bolshoi Theater Museum. Vladimir Putin and his Kremlin lieutenants have invoked the year 1612 to stoke fears of foreign invasion and arouse a nationalist spirit while tem-pering dissent.

For his contribution to the nation, Cavos was awarded the cross of Vladimir the Great, ruler of Kievan Rus, and granted an annual pension of 6,000 French francs. A loge in the theater was dedicated to him after his death.

• • •

TEN DAYS AFTER the public opening, the Bolshoi was handed over to the nobility for a private performance, an occasion like no other. On August 30, 1856, the Imperial Court aspired to make a spectacular international impression, celebrating its own reconstitution as much as the theater's with an exclusive gala performance. Donizetti's opera *L'elisir d'amore* offered the kind of preposterous bubbliness that the tsar enjoyed, and spread a message of goodwill to all those in attendance. As one expert on his reign notes, it expressed things close to his heart: "sentimental faith in the magical power of love, creating good feelings and healing wounds—joy and infatuation conquering disbelief and making for a sense of common humanity."[8]

A reporter on hand that evening, William Howard Russell, described the event in a feature piece for the *Times* of London. He extolled the pale and delicate sea-green interior, the orange- and fuchsia-perfumed side rooms, and the sparkling and twinkling from the rays of candles that proved too dazzling, in their aggregate, for sustained viewing. He gushed about the diadems donned by the noble ladies in the loges, the discipline exhibited by the officers of the parterre, including their perfectly harmonized cheers when the tsar and tsarina arrived at eight thirty p.m., and the exotic distinctiveness of the Turks, Georgians, and others in attendance from across Eurasia. The notion that they were all a part of the ever-expanding Russian Empire, an empire with coasts on the Pacific and Arctic Oceans as well as the Baltic, Black, and Caspian Seas, shocked even its rulers. Uniforms of white and gold, blue and silver, crimson, black, and scarlet turned the parterre into the richest of flower beds. Russell described the scene to his British readers:

A Roman amphitheater was probably grander, but it could not have been a more brilliant sight. A gorgeous and magnificent crowd filled the theatre, but the arrangements were so good that there was neither hustling, confusion, nor noise. There were no ladies in the pit, so that the effect of the many splendid uniforms was homogenous, but the front rows of the first tier of boxes were occupied by the mistresses of creation in full dress—such diamonds, in coronets, circlets, earrings, necklaces, bracelets, brooches, in all the forms that millinery and jewellery could combine those precious stones they were present—looking their best, and filling the house with an atmosphere of flashes and sparks in the rays of the wax lights. The grand ladies of the Russian Court . . . were there, rich with the treasures won, in ages past, by their hard-pated ancestors from Tartar, Turk, or Georgian [lands]. Some of these ladies are very beautiful, but if there could be any portion of womankind which, as a rule, could be said not to be exquisite and of resplendent charms, it might be safely affirmed that they lived in Russia. The exceptions to such a remark are very conspicuous. There is one little head which always attracts any eyes that may be near it—a baby mignon face, with the most peach-like colour, enveloped in a wild riotous setting of flaxen hair, which bursts from all control of band or circlet, and rushes in a flood over the shoulders. It is such a face as inspired the artists who operated on old Dresden china, and it belongs to a young Russian Princess, who has just burst upon the Moscow world. Another lady near her is Juno herself—a statelier and more perfect beauty could not be seen. A little further on there is a lovely young Moldavian, married to a Russian Prince, who has just been sent off to the Caucasus—three months after the wedding. . . . But the catalogue . . . must cease here for the present, for the crowd in the pit increases, and the Emperor may be expected every moment. In the front rows of the pit are placed the Generals and Admirals, Privy Councilors, Officers of State, Chamberlains, and personages of the Court. Behind these are similar officers, mingled together with members of the foreign missions, and the strangers who were invited to be present. There were not half-a-dozen black coats in this assemblage of distinguished people; all the rest were in full uniform. Lord Granville was already in his box in the grand row on the left-hand side of the Emperor's state box. M. de Morny and the French Embassy were placed in the box on the right of the Tsar's. The other Ministers and Ambassadors were provided with places in the same row, and the attachés who had no room above were accommodated with seats in the pit. It was past 8 o'clock when the Emperor appeared, and the instant he was seen the whole of the house rose as if thrilled by an electric flash, and cheered most vehemently again and again. The Tsar and Tsarina bowed, and every salutation was the signal for a repetition of the enthusiastic uproar, through which at last the strains of "God Save the Tsar" forced their way, and the audience resumed their places.[9]

Ultimately the excited reporter ran out of space, so promised his readers another, even more detailed, chronicle of the occasion. Famous for reporting on the Crimean War, Russell had permission to write at length for the *Times,* and his article on the Bolshoi ran on to 5,250 words before even mentioning the bad manners of the Americans in attendance or considering the difference between the polonaise as performed in Russia and its birthplace in Poland. Also omitted were the Russian medals and ribbons pinned to the chests of the ambassadors, the tiaras that blocked the views of the plumes, the jealousies and wounded feelings occasioned by a St. Petersburg princess being seated beneath a certain Moscow countess. More important—most important—was the building itself. The Bolshoi was now an Imperial Theater in appearance, not just in name.

Before the century's end, it would host two more coronations: that of Tsar Alexander III in 1883 (for which Tchaikovsky provided the *1812 Overture*, among other ostentatious *pièces d'occasion*) and Tsar Nicholas II in 1896. The coronation in 1883 came after an assassination. Alexander II was killed by a bomb in St. Petersburg thrown by a member of a band of anti-autocratic zealots called People's Will. He had survived several assassination attempts in the past, but in this instance two explosives were lobbed at him; the second landed at his feet as he emerged from his carriage, shredding his legs. His death brought an end to a period of economic, agricultural, and social reforms, including the emancipation of the serfs (motivated by the tsar's reading of the agrarian populist Alexander Herzen) and a certain degree of freedom of expression in the press and the universities. The reforms had not gone far enough, however. Liberated serfs were dragooned into leasing land from their former masters or reenslaved in factories. Activists seeking to form labor unions or political parties were jailed or killed, adding fuel to the fire that would become the 1917 Revolution. There was no thought of issuing a constitution or forming a parliament. The strife at the fringes of the empire spread to the center.

The long-delayed ascension of his son became the subject of anxious speculation, but after months of seclusion, Tsar Alexander III was enthroned without incident. A secret police force, the *okhranka*, had been formed for the purpose of infiltrating and liquidating subversive organizations. The coronation ceremonies at the Bolshoi affirmed, in response to the terrorist violence, an abiding love of the nation, the Russian Orthodox Church, mystical traditions, and the "Muscovite origins of imperial power."[10] During the festivities, Alexander III represented himself as a heroic knight amid the boyars, but for him, as for his predecessor and successor, such "people-mindedness" (as would become the watchword of the Soviets) ended as soon as he and his massive entourage returned to St. Petersburg. The tsar imposed a series of reforms that sought to assert the power of the throne at the expense of the people—at least those people who did not suit the definition of a "true Russian."[11] There were pogroms. Jews, the scapegoats of Russian history, were banished from Moscow, their expulsion hastening after Alexander III appointed his brother, Grand Duke Sergey Aleksandrovich, the governor general of the city in 1891. The lore surrounding the derring-do of the Don Cossacks, perennial heroes of Russian history, was promoted, and new churches were built in ancient Russian Orthodox style. Even the language changed, as archaic eighteenth-century expressions became popular again in the press and bureaucratic missives.

For the 1883 coronation, the Bolshoi hosted a partial performance of the 1613 coronation scene from Glinka's opera *A Life for the Tsar*, composed in the first half of the nineteenth century. The intentional mixing of politics and theater featured marching soldiers, hundreds of choristers, and a late-arriving, dry-throated soprano in peasant garb. She had been circling the theater in her carriage, trying in vain to enter past police and soldiers blocking the doors. Having stood up the tsar, already seated in the central loge with his family, she arrived onstage in hysterics, trembling from head to toe and crying, "Ice! Ice!" to the stagehands, hoping to cool down her head, if not her vocal cords.[12] The opera got going, and, at the patriotic highpoint, the floorboards of the stage shook to the strains of "Glory, glory, holy Russia!" There followed the performance of an allegorical ballet by Marius Petipa, *Night and Day*

(Noch' i den'), about renewal. The Queen of the Night, Evening Star, comets, planets, ferns, swan maids, mermaids, and dryads join hands in the first half; then the Queen of the Day cavorts with the Morning Star, birds, butterflies, bees, and flies. An assortment of nationalities comprising the Russian Empire appears—from Finns and Georgians and Poles to Don Cossacks and Siberian shamans, each greeting the dawn as a symbol of the coronation. Mother Russia enters as a plump matron in the middle of the friendship-of-the-peoples round dance. It was an Olympian spectacle, combining ballet, parade, and circus with soldiers in review. The St. Petersburg ballerina Ekaterina Vazem notes, however, that the "ballet's music, written as usual by Minkus, lacked for quality."[13]

The opulent ceremonial performance was a signal, if still faint, of things to come. It demonstrated that the Bolshoi, the Imperial Theater of the ancient Russian capital, could serve ideological purposes. The divertissement at the Bolshoi blurred the identities of the ethnicities in a simulacrum of autocratic subjugation. *Night and Day* offered a parable of national unity and the power of the empire. Tsar Alexander III ended up being sufficiently flattered by the ballet in his honor to order it performed again two days later, exclusively for his family.

AFTER THE IMPERIAL INSIGNIAS were removed from the entrance and the roof, the Bolshoi Theater catered once again to Moscow audiences and their more down-to-earth tastes. Although Moscow and St. Petersburg had been connected by rail since 1851, the bumpy two-day ride never brought the cities closer together. Moscow retained its essential rustic character even after having been rebuilt post-Napoleon. It was grittier, grimier, and, being under the control of merchant guilds, more thuggish than the imperial capital to the north. As the ancient capital, it nonetheless considered itself the real, true Russian center, and put its own stamp on Russian culture, building a monument to the writer Pushkin before St. Petersburg did, for example, even though Pushkin did not spend much time in Moscow. The Imperial Gendarmerie maintained order (and, beginning with Tsar Alexander III, supervised the *okhranka* secret-police station). Bulbous cathedral domes floated above narrow, curving, muddy, smelly streets; fish and game markets supplied coarse meals for raucous subterranean *kabaki* (taverns) and quieter street-level inns (*traktiri*). There were, roughly speaking, two separate citizenries. Nobles of ancient lineage, privileged members of the Table of Ranks, successful merchants, and affluent industrialists frequented social clubs and arts salons, dined on haute cuisine in fine French restaurants, and strolled through the pleasure gardens of Moscow. The workers—poor, illiterate, or semiliterate—lived their short lives in modest dwellings lit by candles and kerosene lamps. For both classes, and the functionaries mediating between them, there were holiday treats, street fairs, and the rituals of the liturgical calendar. Love for their red-bearded, hard-drinking ruler equaled, among Muscovites, love for the Russian Orthodox Church.

The monarchists of St. Petersburg held Tsar Alexander III just as close to their hearts but the Church at greater distance. Government ministers, bureaucrats, and courtiers were more secular in outlook, and indeed colder and more hypocritical in their interactions than the salt-of-the-earth types of Moscow. The residents of St. Petersburg imagined their imperial capital, an improbable network of palaces and canals spilling into the Gulf of Finland, as a portal to Europe. Moscow, in contrast, hewed close to its Eastern, Byzantine roots and expected as much of its ballet and opera house, despite its neoclassical façade.

Cavos had transformed the Bolshoi in grand aristocratic style, but Moscow audiences still wanted to be entertained. Comedies, folk fare, and bric-a-brac divertissements remained as popular as ever. Ballets that had succeeded in St. Petersburg fell flat in Moscow, even when the same performers were involved. Ballet master Alexei Bogdanov, a St. Petersburg transplant, tried staging spectacular *ballets-féeries*, including one that received close scrutiny from the censors: *The Delights of Hashish, or The Island of Roses* (Prelesti gashisha, ili ostrov roz, 1885). The initial buzz from this colorful, colonialist banquet filled the Bolshoi for two or three performances, after which ticket sales sagged and the production had to be struck. The reviews were slight and focused more on the plot, lighting, and chemical explosions than on the dancing. *Teatral'nïy mirok* (Theatrical world) praised Bogdanov for his "energetic" approach to the group dances, including the "Dance of the Bees" that was performed by the youngest members of the cast, and credited him with "at last raising up the fallen art of choreography in Moscow." *The Delights of Hashish* "caused a furor."[14] The group dances earned the adjective "tasteful" in an article in *Teatr i zhizn'* (Theater and life), which does not much assist the cause of choreographic reconstruction.[15] Elsewhere, the corps de ballet was likened to a "bouquet of assorted roses." The reviewer appreciated strong Italianate emotions in dance and lauded the budding talents of the Bolshoi Ballet. Lidiya Geyten indulged the Africa of the imperial Russian imagination, performing "the kaftan dance with the wild passion and the fire of an actual African."[16] Some of the other solos, such as the "Chinese" dance, were deemed a pleasant surprise, suggesting that worse had been expected of Bogdanov.

Platitudes were the fate of another such potpourri, *Svetlana, the Slavic Princess* (Svetlana, slavyanskaya knyazhina, 1885), which Bogdanov put on the stage after demanding a raise. "I expect better reward appropriate to the responsibilities of ballet master and director," he wrote to his supervisors in St. Petersburg, enclosing within his letter a postcard of a ballerina from Dresden whom he wanted to hire "for a small performance fee." It would be "an experiment," he argued, for the purposes of "refreshing" the Bolshoi Ballet.[17] His greed, along with his obvious bias toward foreign dancers and the garishness of his productions, did not sit well. The dramatist and Bolshoi repertoire inspector Alexander Ostrovsky derided Bogdanov for his "circus performances" and sought to have him fired. Meanwhile the administration of the Imperial Theaters in St. Petersburg debated whether "new and vulgar" performances in Moscow were better than "old and miserable" ones.[18]

As the ballet master at the Bolshoi, Bogdanov enforced greater discipline in the ranks, requiring attendance at morning dance lessons in the theater. The quality of the dancing improved. Yet the repertoire imported from France and Italy failed to attract audiences. Critics gnashed their teeth, and much to the dismay of the bookkeepers of the Imperial Theaters, the Bolshoi Ballet did not turn a profit. The accounts were audited, and administrators were no sooner hired than fired or, when bureaucratic rigor mortis set in, had their duties ghosted, covered by others.[19]

For a time, no one seemed to be in charge of the Bolshoi, as evidenced by the trivial but telling case of the insulted wardrobe manager, Semyon Germanovich. He did not know to whom to complain, in 1882, about the "epithet" thrown in his face by Vladimir Pogozhev, then the acting intendant of the Imperial Theaters in St. Petersburg and Moscow while the actual intendant, Ivan Vsevolozhsky, traveled to Europe. Pogozhev used his time in charge to rid the Bolshoi of independent-minded administrators, sending financial auditors to Moscow and accusing Germanovich and others of cooking the books. "Seven female costumes" for Richard

Wagner's opera *Tannhäuser* were purchased but never seen, and the batteries ordered by the machinist to illuminate Anton Rubinstein's opera *The Demon* were fewer in number and weaker in voltage than invoiced.[20] Germanovich's nasty clash with Pogozhev left a "horrible stain" on his good name.[21] He hoped the court would rinse it out, but to no avail. Pogozhev fired him, and it took a long time (eight years, in fact) for the former wardrobe manager to recoup the wages he was due: 90 rubles, 38 kopecks.[22] The sourest of grapes fermented in his mind over this matter, and his dislike of the Bolshoi Theater administration turned pathological.

Germanovich's successor was the twenty-four-year-old Anton Vashkevich, whose mother was a railroad crossing guard. Pogozhev had worked for the railroad before serving the court, which perhaps explains how the lad got the job. Vashkevich held the rank of *kollezhskiy registrator*, the bottom of the imperial Russian nomenclature, and frankly had no business taking on a senior position at the Bolshoi. His hiring provoked resentment, and he was accused of stealing the salaries meant for the tailors and fitters, spending some of the money on "half bottles of vodka, perhaps more" at a tavern and some more of it on a prostitute picked up in the Moscow Hermitage Garden, before losing the rest. Only the last part of the tale was true, Vashkevich insisted. Although he had taken to drink to calm his nerves, he never, he swore, drank to excess. He had meant to pay the tailors and fitters, but because they were not in the theater at the time, he kept the money on his person. He had been robbed, he claimed, after falling asleep. Vashkevich too had suffered abuse from Pogozhev and feared for his job. "He had been living in a constantly agitated state," an investigation concluded, "expecting changes in the staffing of the theater."[23]

On October 1, 1883, financial problems at the Bolshoi resulted in the shocking dismissal of more than 100 dancers—almost half of the entire roster. The March 27 memorandum laying the groundwork for the purge is merciless:

> In view of the expected abolition of the Moscow ballet troupe, the Office of the Imperial Theaters respectfully requests of Moscow the establishment of a Commission to be chaired by the Office of the Moscow Imperial Theaters, inviting ballet master Petipa and chief régisseur [stage manager] L. Ivanov to travel from here to Moscow as participants, and inviting Smirnov from the artists in Moscow—for the purpose of compiling a list of those artists who, qualified for their pensions, could be dismissed from service, as well as those other persons who, through weakness of talent or inability, are no longer of use and would therefore be subject to abandonment by the state.[24]

The dancers received the news at a most inopportune time—in the middle of a performance of *The Demon*. Just as they "lifted their left feet in order to run across the stage on the toes of their right ones, a guard approached them to tell them they were out. The stunned dancers fainted, awaking just in time to disturb the peace and calm with their crying and yelling." Dressed as angels, they fell down in a heap from their wires and were injured. "But still they resisted being fired!"[25] Nineteen of the dancers joined the Mariyinsky, only after passing an exam to prove that their legs were not too plump. The dancers learned of their promotion to St. Petersburg by telegram. Older "soloist artists" received their pensions and a modest buyout. The younger, fitter dancers retained by the Bolshoi saw their salaries cut, which was less a problem for the "married ladies" than the single women, who had to assume "the keeping of cows and the selling of milk" to make ends meet.[26] (One of the novice milkmaids reportedly canceled a rehearsal to tend to the birth of a calf.) The scandal was sneeringly lampooned by the writer Anton Chekhov, who ridiculed the administration for getting rid of the dancers "politely, quickly, and most importantly, all of a sudden."[27]

The upheaval was part of an effort to improve the operations of the Imperial Theaters. A committee formed by Vsevolozhsky, the intendant in St. Petersburg after 1881, arranged for greater oversight of the repertoire plus substantial pay and honoraria increases.[28] In some of the theaters morale improved, but not at the Bolshoi Ballet, which, as the March 27 memorandum reveals, seemed all but doomed. The dairy business could not save it, nor the rush to the altar that inevitably followed "any flirtation" between female dancers and affluent Moscow merchants.[29] The director of the Moscow Imperial Theaters, actor Pavel Pchelnikov, made it clear in his correspondence that both he and his overseers preferred opera to ballet, and that the best ballets were those that were danced as part of operas. One year after the dismissals, however, he proffered a glimmer of hope, arranging for a handful of the "unfortunates" sacked in 1883 to be rehired for a salary of 300 rubles.[30] It was not a living wage but certainly better than "starvation" or "sleeping rough."[31] The reprieve had come from Vsevolozhsky and, through the minister of the court, Tsar Alexander III. Vsevolozhsky argued for the survival of the Bolshoi Ballet, specifically the retention of the older dancers, out of sympathy. They had no other skill besides dancing, he argued; it would be "too harsh" to leave them "without a crust of bread" amid the celebration surrounding the coronation of Tsar Alexander III.[32] The tsar found cause to agree with Vsevolozhsky, and allowed the Bolshoi Ballet to continue. The art became an essential decoration for his reign—a reign that, in general, privileged appurtenance and embellishment, a case in point being the Fabergé eggs he gave to the tsarina on special occasions beginning in 1886.

How specifically to keep the Bolshoi Ballet operating was left for Vsevolozhsky, the minister of the court, and, to a lesser extent, Pchelnikov to determine. First, however, an impresario of sorts—the machinist Karl Valts—stepped forth with the idea of privatizing the ballet. He proposed funding performances himself and pocketing two-thirds of the proceeds. Although Vsevolozhsky thought the proposal "beneficial" (given how little the ballet earned compared to the opera, even Russian opera), he fretted over the Imperial Theaters "entering into these type of transactions with its employees."[33] The proposal, which recalled the era of Michael Maddox, was declined.

By August 8, 1884, a deal had been brokered to keep the Bolshoi Ballet operating as a state enterprise, with a budget of 100,000 rubles per year (compared to 217,000 rubles allotted to the Mariyinsky Ballet). The roster was first set at 100 dancers, 71 women and 29 men, but then, owing to special pleading, the number was slightly adjusted to 102: 63 women and 39 men. Vsevolozhsky grumbled that, before the reform, the Table of Ranks in the Bolshoi Ballet made about as much sense as the Table of Ranks in the court. Most of the dancers, greater and lesser talents alike, had been earning 100 to 150 rubles a year, although a select few had seemingly won the Moscow Imperial Theater "lottery," earning more than 10,000 rubles among them. The "inequalities" and "injustices" in remuneration were not entirely corrected, but talent, as opposed to personal connections, came to matter more in making promotions.[34] Soloists now earned an average of 600 rubles, character dancers 500, and members of the corps de ballet 400. The ballerina Lidiya Geyten earned the highest salary, at 3,300 rubles. That kept her in Moscow, as opposed to decamping to St. Petersburg or Europe.

The Bolshoi Ballet lost much of its "autonomy" in the shake-up, ballet historian Yuriy Bakhrushin notes, but at least it carried on.

"Fortunately," he adds, "the 'reform' did not affect the Moscow ballet school, which continued operating as before."[35] Indeed, for Vsevolozhsky, the school was sacrosanct. Setting aside 7,000 rubles for "the teachers of ballet, ballroom dancing, and mime" would prevent a recurrence of the stagnation of recent decades and both replenish and revitalize the ranks.[36] The students of the school were to receive proper training, be brought into contact with guest choreographers (Petipa, first and foremost), and take occasional trips to St. Petersburg to be part of the better-funded Mariyinsky Theater.

DESPITE THE TUMULT of these years, the Bolshoi managed to stage ballets of note, three of which stand out not only in their own time but also in ballet history: *Le corsaire*, *Don Quixote*, and *Swan Lake*. All were jumbled affairs at the start, but each has earned a place in the international repertoire thanks in large part to choreographer Marius Petipa.

He had fled to Russia in 1847 from Spain, where his tomcatting, including a tryst with a mistress of a diplomat—or perhaps the daughter of the mistress, sources are uncertain—prompted his flight to escape prosecution. Petipa had already avoided a thumping after kissing a ballerina on the cheek, only to be challenged to a duel with pistols by the envoy whose honor he had insulted. The results of the duel are recorded in his memoirs: "He shoots—a miss; and my bullet shatters his lower jawbone."[37] It was safer to chase the girls in St. Petersburg, where Petipa created one ballet for each year of his service along with incidental dances for French operas, galas for courtiers, and various divertissements. His disciples notated his important ballets in his final years, and Petipa's own surviving sketches, etched on pads in colored pencil, illustrate his obsession with order, balance, and logic. But he also became famous for his national dances, solo variations, presentations of mime, and the celestial orbs, sunbeams, and blooming flowers represented by his corps de ballet. His fastidiousness made him prone to profane outbursts (either in French or ungrammatical Russian) when reality fell short of his vision. Underperforming dancers were sent packing in tears; opponents and those who would dare to restage his ballets were derided in his bitter memoirs as "conceited ignoramuses" with "twisted brains."[38]

Petipa had his professional foes, and on one occasion was taken to French court for plagiarism. After choreographer Jules Perrot proved that a *pas* he had conceived for a ballet in Paris could not by chance have recurred intact in a ballet by Petipa in St. Petersburg, Petipa was declared liable and required to pay 300 francs in damages.[39] The incident, an embarrassment, raises a question about the source of Petipa's inspiration. Was his innovation sui generis, sprung fully formed like Athena from the head of Zeus, as was sometimes claimed in later years? In Paris and London, he had made little impression, his choreographic work overshadowed by that of his older brother Lucien. Not until Petipa arrived at the Russian court did his star begin to shine, but that light may have been powered by purloined and plundered sources. His classicism could perhaps best be defined as *ars combinatoria*, a Renaissance-era term that describes an assemblage of what already exists into something new: the achievement not of invention but refashioning. Moreover, his taste in music is, in retrospect, a puzzle. Petipa had dependable but lesser-skilled in-house theatrical composers at his disposal for most of his career. Only in his seventies did he set the music of Tchaikovsky. Could he not have branched out earlier than he did? Was innocuous music in boxy rhythms easier for him to handle than great music of filigreed textures and more frequent odd-numbered counts?

Regardless, the arriviste Petipa built an empire for himself at the Mariyinsky. Tsar Alexander II and his successors indulged the Imperial Ballet of St. Petersburg under Petipa's control. The school benefited: Dormitories were made more comfortable, and the sixty or so students in residence were scrubbed up and trotted off to "chapel" before their lessons.[40] The ruler's largesse funded Petipa's ambitions. Ballets were set in Egypt and India, heaven, and the afterlife, moving beyond the exotic through the dream of the exotic and into the dream of the dream of the exotic. In *The Pharaoh's Daughter* (Doch' farona) from 1862, mummies come alive, and a parade-of-nations episode is set in the Kingdom of the Rivers. (To his credit, Petipa resisted, at least most of the time, the impulse to have his dancers move in two-dimensional profile, noting in his memoirs that "the Egyptians certainly walked as we do.")[41] His representations could be stunning. In *La bayadère* (1877) a winding procession through the Kingdom of the Shades features forty-eight women in white; the absence of color symbolizes death (as well as purity) in the Hindu tradition. Typical of Petipa's backwards-forwards phraseology, each dancer steps ahead into *arabesque*, then retreats into *cambré*, then straightens and moves ahead two steps. The *cambré* is done with *bras en courronne*, the arms curved to suggest, depending on the lighting, a glowing halo around the head. It is as meltingly beautiful a dance as has ever been imagined for the art. Petipa assigned it to the Russian-born, Russian-trained dancers in his corps, as opposed to the foreigners. In his ballets, the court of St. Petersburg saw its own magnificence, its own imperial dominion.

THE BOLSHOI HAD nowhere near the budget of Petipa's operation and no one of his skill in charge. Moscow had to endure a string of imported ballet masters, beginning with the Italian Carlo Blasis. A high-minded stickler for precision and proportion, he improved the ballet school but, as one eminent historian bluntly concludes, "added nothing significant" to the repertoire.[42] His Czech and Belgian successors fared no better. The distance between Moscow and St. Petersburg only increased. Lamentably, as another historian writes, "between the retirement of Adam Glushkovsky and Félicité Hullen-Sor in 1839 and the appointment of Alexander Gorsky at the end of the century, there was no resident ballet master of distinction assigned to the Moscow ballet for long enough to improve standards, and for years at a time no permanently assigned ballet master of any kind."[43]

Because the Bolshoi did not have an in-house genius, it had to work around the idea of genius by creating ballets in a more communal fashion. But when Petipa became involved with the Moscow troupe things changed. The freer collective spirit remained, and informed his thinking, but dramatic content and concept improved.

An exception was *Le corsaire*, which remained happily confused even in Petipa's hands. The thinnest of plots—a tale of a handsome pirate's love for a ravishing slave girl—serves as pretext for an ambitious, inconsistent spectacle set in a bazaar, a grotto, a pasha's palace, an enchanted garden, the pasha's palace again, and on the high seas. Sword fights? Of course. Magic sleep-inducing rose? The stronger the fragrance the better. Shipwreck that leaves the lovers clinging to a rock? The only way to bring down the curtain. Audiences in Moscow flocked to see *Le corsaire* repeatedly, in different guises, throughout the nineteenth century. The first version (starring Ekaterina Sankovskaya) was choreographed by Marie Taglioni's brother, Paul, in 1838; the second by Joseph Mazilier in 1856, and the third by Jules Perrot in 1858. Subsequently it was undertaken by Petipa, who presented it in four different versions, each more elaborate than the last.[44] Verstovsky groused about the "jostling" and "crush" to secure tickets for the Perrot version of *Le corsaire*, and likewise of the profits made by the servants of nobles from the resale—the scalping—of tickets in restaurants and on Theater Square.[45] But somewhere inside his intemperate self, he must have been pleased by a popular ballet done on the cheap that still had everything.

Everything except modern lighting, which had yet to be installed in the Bolshoi Theater. Cavos had exhausted the budget of the Moscow Imperial Theaters to rebuild the Bolshoi, but production standards lagged behind those of the ballet and opera houses of Europe, where lighting had long been provided by gas. Russia had developed pioneering technology for the use of gas in streetlamps and homes even before the Napoleonic War, but its implementation in the theaters of St. Petersburg and Moscow was much delayed. Cavos proposed installing gas in the Bolshoi in 1856, but his estimate was high, and the plan shelved. *Le corsaire* was left strangely in the dim, if not the dark.

In 1863, Makar Shishko was hired to install gaslights at the Bolshoi, having done the same in St. Petersburg the year before. A self-made man, Shishko had come to Moscow from the provinces with just a copper in his pocket, earned an education in medical chemistry, and married a dancer in the corps de ballet. (He would marry again after her death and in his retirement, to a bride of just twenty-three.) Before becoming a gas entrepreneur, he specialized in pyrotechnics, color illuminations, and sparklers. He hoped to bring his experience to the Bolshoi and Malïy Theaters.

Yet disputes with a French mechanic, a Russian gas engineer (Mikhaíl Arnold), and a Russian gas supplier (Pyotr Shilovsky) left Shishko sidelined. He summarized his travails in a dejected but graceful letter to the directorate of the Moscow Imperial Theaters:

Rumors have recently reached me to the effect that several members of the gas alliance persist in their intrigues against me and, in each instance, cast me in shadow. Such a systematic campaign to paint me in black should naturally awaken indignation among all who are virtuous in thought and honest in service, especially when the fate of an entire large family, rather than just a single person, depends on that service.

Shishko had three daughters and a son with his first wife. Each of them needed medical treatment in warm climates, hence his complaint about the "semi-official denunciations" by his enemies in the gas alliance. He was pleased that the charges of corruption leveled against him had been judged baseless, but the "sad events" still stung, and he felt obliged to ask the directorate for the "protection from accidents" accorded other artists of the theaters.[46]

In the end, credit for the installation of gas lighting in the Bolshoi goes to no one and everyone, with huge sums disappearing in the process. And soon after the theater was finally equipped, a gas war erupted among vendors, each in search of a monopoly. On October 7, the gas was inexplicably extinguished at the end of a play at the Maliy Theater. That same evening, it ceased flowing during the entr'acte of a performance of the aptly titled ballet *The Flame of Love, or the Salamander* (Plamya lyubvi, ili Salamandra). The Bolshoi Theater was plunged into darkness, scaring its patrons, who fled the hall before sufficient lamps and candles could be lit. Again on November 20, the gas supply in the Bolshoi was mysteriously cut off. Reopening the valve that fed gas to the chandelier solved the problem, without causing concern to the audience. The eight gas regulators on the payroll of the theater were investigated after Shishko blew the whistle on them.

Having lost the gas war, Shishko returned sadder but wiser to his duties as master of fireworks in Moscow. He remained involved in the operations of the Imperial Theaters, watching for the next big thing in theatrical mechanics in Europe, then encouraging its adoption in Moscow.

There followed the importation of the equipment needed to direct intense flames of oxygen and hydrogen toward cylinders of quicklime, bathing the performers in limelight. In the mid-1870s, carbon-arc lamps attached to batteries came to be used in the Bolshoi Theater. Batteries began to be mass-produced during the period, spurring the invention of the strangest of gadgets, from electric pens to doorbells meant to be rung from within coffins to prevent being buried alive—replacing "breathing tubes" and a bell-ringing "line to pull" from six feet under.[47] To date, the use of batteries in ballets and operas had been limited, but the machinist relied on them. Battery-produced light was eerier than that from gas, both the kind supplied to the theater from pipes and from compressed-gas containers. For more than a decade, until the late 1880s, batteries and gas operated side by side, with the batteries powering the special effects (chiefly macabre) and gas feeding everything else. The documents describing this aspect of Bolshoi operations are technical and financial, but also full of drama. Fear of progress within the court ran repeatedly up against the aggressive ambitions of foreign and Russian companies.

When it came to the Bolshoi, the court cared much more about scrimping than splendor. Imperial finances were increasingly strained, owing to the horrendously costly defeat in the Crimean War, the horrendously costly victory in the Russo-Turkish War, and the increasingly futile effort to tamp down insurgencies and rein in the forces of chaos along the ragged borders of the empire. Even given the government's budget problems, the ballet and opera house of St. Petersburg fared better than the Bolshoi.

The differences between the two theaters were described in

detail by Grigoriy Volkonsky, a Moscow University chemist, in a letter to an imperial official. Volkonsky, a slightly mad scientist prone to setting his lab on fire (and so roasting his beard, nose, and cheeks), had been dispatched to St. Petersburg in February of 1888 to evaluate the lighting systems at the Mariyinsky and recommend improvements at the Bolshoi. He was "struck not only by the grandness of the electric lighting as well as the effectiveness and orderliness of its operation, both during rehearsals and performances. The transitions in the theater from full illumination to near total darkness are carried out almost instantly, consistently and without irregularities." He hoped that in the near future the Bolshoi might be given "just a part" of the Mariyinsky's lighting equipment. Still, he had a criticism. Although the electric "tinted-glass shielded Bunsen cell lamps" employed by the theater were impressive, he wondered about their cost-effectiveness. Gas produced brighter, stronger light, and the Mariyinsky had an ample supply at low cost. Volkonsky did not, however, have a problem with the cost of the fireworks that had been designed by Shishko, for whom he had warm words.[48]

The letter prompted some updates at the Bolshoi. A German firm, the V. K. Von Mekk & Co. Partnership of Oil and Petroleum Gas Lighting and Heating, sought to install its systems in Moscow at discount rates, no price gouging. The gas lighting inspector instead seems to have steered the contract for the upgrade to his friends at the Theater and Theater College Gas Lighting Company. The batteries were improved but remained problematic. They were expensive to charge and recharge. Any mishandling resulted in acid burns, and they could be embarrassingly inconsistent. Mephistopheles did not look half as frightening when the Bunsen cell shining a red light on him conked out in the middle of a performance of Charles Gounod's opera *Faust*.

The Theater and Theater College Gas Lighting Company

remained in control of the Moscow Imperial Theaters until 1892, when the lighting, heating, and ventilation were again overhauled, under the direction of Bengardt Tseytshel, a merchant from the first guild of civil engineers of St. Petersburg. He was paid 325,000 rubles in three installments to obtain the necessary people and equipment to bring the Bolshoi up to date. Some of his planning was deemed "irrational," and tempers flared about dust and dirt, radiators, recurring cracks in the brick-lined tunnel connecting the Bolshoi and the Malïy, and the water needed to cool the steam machines.[49] On December 16, 1893, power demands exceeded expectations for a simultaneous performance of a play at the Malïy and an operatic double bill at the Bolshoi (Tchaikovsky's *Iolanta* and Leoncavallo's *Pagliacci*), causing a blackout at a clubhouse for noblemen that purchased amps from the same electric station. Holiday lighting also taxed the system. Power did not flow everywhere in the Bolshoi, and Tseyshtel had to put up with the inevitable quarrels about who truly "needed an electric current" and who could do without.[50]

The transitions from coal to steam, oil to gas, and from Bunsen cells to Schuckert generators were all overseen by the Dresden-trained decorator and technician Karl Valts, a fastidious, obsessive type who was hired by the Bolshoi at the age of fifteen as a set painter and seldom left the premises thereafter, rising to the rank of chief machinist in 1869 and receiving several awards for his work. He did not exaggerate when he titled his memoirs *65 Years in the Theater*. Valts learned some of what he knew from his father, Fyodor Karlovich Valts, who had begun his career as the conductor of a serf orchestra before learning theater mechanics and assisting Makar Shishko in his fireworks exhibitions. Valts Jr. had a bigger, bolder imagination than Valts Sr. and earned the nicknames "magician" and "sorcerer" for what he brought to the Bolshoi, budget permitting. He hoisted horses onto clouds colored with harsh chemicals, and irrigated gardens of tropical plants with waterfalls and fountains. Critics loved his effects but complained about the earsplitting din.

Between productions, Valts dabbled in composition, producing a polka and a waltz. He also authored scenarios for operas and ballets, which he connived to bring to the stage through exotic, corrupt means, promising, for example, ballet masters jobs with the Bolshoi in exchange for productions of his pet projects. Valts boasted of his achievements in his memoirs, but only vaguely, leaving the reader wondering how, for example, he went about wrecking the galleon in *Le corsaire*, twirling the windmill in *Don Quixote*, and whipping up the tempest in *Swan Lake*.

Of interest regarding Valts's creativity are the recollections of Yevgeniya Kavelina, daughter of Pavel Kavelin, who oversaw the Moscow Imperial Theaters from 1872 to 1876 or so. (He appears to have hung on to his position longer than contracted.) Kavelina observed firsthand the challenges her father faced on the job and dished about the appalling behavior of noblemen—their ethical lapses, sordid liaisons, and grandiloquent sleaze. Her recollections must not have been penned for publication. Dirt is a theme, likewise excrement. She accuses the family of a state councilor of soiling the tsar's loge; apparently, her father's first order as head of the Bolshoi was to have the box thoroughly cleaned. Then she recounts the retirement of the opera singer "Madame Aleksandrova," who was presented with a gift from the parterre after her swan song. The diva fainted upon opening the foul box, filled with "non-horse [human] manure."[51]

Kavelina's account of *Le corsaire* is interspersed with remarks about her father's successor, Lavrentiy Auber, whom she describes as "a nice old man, a Frenchman who had a place in our loge, always slept during the performance but woke up just in time for the inter-mission." She repeats the tattle of ballerinas from the orphanage who claimed him as their father for the sake of prestige, leaving him with a "huge paternity" of a "legion of imagined children with no end." In 1876, the same year that Auber was placed in charge of the Moscow Imperial Theaters, Kavelina's father hosted the shah of Persia, Nasser al-Din, during his first visit to Moscow. The shah had never been abroad before, she notes, and acted like a "pure savage." His attendants butchered sheep in his Kremlin guest suite, leaving the floor and furniture in such a shocking state that the rooms had to be renovated as soon as he departed. When the shah attended a ball, he became the talk of the town after affronting the wife of Moscow's lieutenant governor by asking her, in broken French, "Why for you, ugly woman, the ball?"

Kavelina escorted the shah to a Bolshoi performance of *Le cor-saire*. It was his first time at the ballet, and he "fell into a state of indescribable ecstasy, especially after the shipwreck, when he nearly jumped out of his chair and began to bellow and wail for all the theater to hear." The gale lessened; the hero and heroine took shel-ter, and the curtain came down. Impressed, the shah awarded the director of the Moscow Imperial Theaters the Persian Order of the Lion and the Sun. The ballerina Anna Sobeshchanskaya took home a shawl.

The shipwreck scene also intrigued Kavelina, who asked her father how it had been done. He told her that Valts had relied on the talents of the poor and homeless—"street rabble," in her blunt telling—to create the illusion. The children huddled underneath a canvas that stretched across the stage; they lay on all fours, and then flexed and unflexed on cue, causing the canvas to roil and seethe around the ship. Meanwhile the din from the equipment powering the lights evoked the howling wind. The mast of the ship snapped, and all was lost.

OR NOT QUITE. The pirate and the slave girl survived to love again, of course, and the ballet's run continued. Performances of *Le corsaire* alternated in certain seasons with the successful *Don Quixote*, the first ballet of its size expressly intended for Moscow. It was created by Petipa to meet the desperate need at the Bolshoi for new productions and stanch the near-constant complaints to the minister of the court about the absence of a permanent ballet master in Moscow. Talk came and went about transferring Petipa to the Bolshoi, especially in 1867, but Petipa resisted. He ended up spending large amounts of time in Moscow during the second half of 1869, even foregoing part of his contractually stipulated summer leave to be at the Bolshoi. He appears to have stayed in Moscow from July through November 1869 and used his time in residence to do something bold.

Knowing the different tastes of audiences in Moscow and St. Petersburg, Petipa conceived two versions of *Don Quixote*, an act of cleverness meant to send a message to the competition—although by the time the second version premiered in St. Petersburg, there was no competition. Petipa had begun his choreographic career as second ballet master of the Imperial Theaters of St. Petersburg (the first was Arthur Saint-Léon, with whom Petipa competed for resources throughout the 1860s) but soon proved himself peerless.

Although Petipa created *Don Quixote* with Moscow in mind, he turned to a trusted St. Petersburg composer, Cesare Pugni, for the music. Pugni had moved around from Milan to Paris to London during his most productive years before turning up in St. Petersburg. He lived in comfort or deprivation, depending on the state of his alcohol and gambling addictions, and although he often composed according to a formula, humming Italian opera composers like Bellini in some of his tunes, he produced some all-purpose hits, including the "Opera House Polka" of 1844. His melodies often collapsed into pedestrian gestures, but in select contexts he produced music of poignant grace, with "sunniness and innocence" being pricked by "tears."[52]

Pugni, however, was nearing the end of his self-abusive life in 1869 and could not finish the music for *Don Quixote*.[53] The resident composer of the Bolshoi Theater, Ludwig Minkus, stepped into the breach, saving the ballet and earning distinction for himself as a result. Minkus hailed from a tiny town in Moravia and had received his musical training in Vienna, where his father, a Jewish Moravian wine merchant, had opened a restaurant. In his youth, Ludwig (also known as Aloysiu, Alois, Lois, Louis, Léon, and Luigi) worked as a violinist in several European cities, and came to Moscow by way of an Italian opera company in St. Petersburg. Minkus signed his first contract with the Bolshoi in 1862, serving as in-house composer and conductor as well as the music inspector for theaters throughout Moscow. He compensated for a receding hairline by growing a beard of old-fashioned trim, covered twinkling eyes with gold-rimmed glasses, and enjoyed cigars and the fresh butter and milk sold on the streets of Moscow. He was affable but capable of flashing a terrible temper. He slid into idle depression when overwhelmed, prompting his employees to accuse him of laziness.

Both Pugni and Minkus approached their tasks like bakers, cutting their scores, in the words of one balletic gourmand, "like so much pendent pastry on a pie-dish, to a pre-existent shape."[54] That shape included narrative scenes, solos, duets, and group dances for the corps de ballet with musical phrases no longer than a mid-nineteenth-century dancer's stamina could permit. The music was likewise fitted to the plot, the dancers' feet, and even the Bolshoi Theater props. One of the prop makers had contrived tears of laughter rolling down the face of the moon, which are heard in the down-bows of the violins during one of Quixote's mad fantasies. The overture is dreamlike, the music avoiding the beat. That changes when the curtain goes up and the dancers appear. Then, as in Pugni's ballet scores, the beat becomes very important.

Owing to the suddenness of the commission, the "speed" with which Minkus was "obliged to compose the music for the new ballet *Don Quixote*," he was late in finishing the score.[55] Petipa seems to have had the violin rehearsal score in hand a month and a half before the scheduled premiere, but time ran out for the orchestral parts to be made. Minkus's "continued lateness" exacerbated the financial problems at the Bolshoi. Desperate for income, the Bolshoi performed, in the interregnum, a short and sweet ballet from 1868, *The Parisian Market* (Parizhskiy rïnokh), which "positively" earned back the 925 rubles and 4 kopecks spent on it.[56] According to a letter of November 3, 1869, from Saint-Léon, Minkus was "on the point of finishing his *Don Quixote* for Petipa," but he missed the deadline and ended up "quarrelling with everyone" with his famously "beastly temper."[57] Once the furies had subsided and the *Don Quixote* parts had at last been prepared by an assistant, Minkus expressed pride in his score. Petipa too nodded in satisfaction.

In setting *Don Quixote*, based on the novel by Cervantes, Petipa reached back to his youth as a dancer with the King's Theater in Madrid, Spain. He filled his ballet for the Bolshoi with exciting, up-tempo Spanish dances of the kind that he had learned to perform in Madrid and that might appeal in Moscow. Petipa seems to have conceived *Don Quixote* in the spirit of a masque, a sixteenth-century improvised comic entertainment involving amateurs. The original version, long gone from the stage, was an admixture of slapstick and colorful exotic dances that elaborated, at heart, a mere three sentences from the source novel—the sentences that summarize the contents of part 2, chapters 19 through 21. Set in and around Barcelona, these chapters tell of the intrigue among Kitri, the daughter of a tavern owner; her beloved Basilio, a barber; and Camacho, the old but rich man whom Kitri's overbearing father demands that she wed. Don Quixote deludes himself into thinking he can help Kitri and her lover to be together, but he ends up needing their help after he is injured in a battle with a windmill he believes to be a giant. During his convalescence, he dreams that he defeats a giant spider and enters a magic garden, where he sees his ideal woman, Dulcinea.

The rest of the novel, all but one episode from part 1 and most of part 2, is missing, and with it, the central concept. *Don Quixote* was written in response to the misrepresentation of Spain in chivalric books, *Los libros de caballerías.* As Cervantes himself remarked, the adventures that fill his masterpiece bear "only a negative relationship" to other stories of Spain "and the chivalric spirit that informs them."[58] *Don Quixote* parodies tales of knightly deeds by knightly men. The title character is poor, middle-aged, and insecure, defending himself with a sword and shield made of cardboard—not much of a knight at all, and doomed to endless thrashings. His heroic-sounding name, Don Quixote, is a fabrication, and he needs his addled squire to give him confidence. The trifling tale of Kitri, Basilio, and Camacho is but one plot among several, none of them plausible.

Petipa set the story as a ballet in four acts totaling eight scenes, or skits, with the penultimate one (act 3, scene 7) involving a magic garden and Don Quixote's vision of an ideal beauty: Dulcinea. She performed a group *pas* with an elegant Cupid and the corps de ballet, which included eight little girls, all outfitted as dryads. Most of the rest of the dancing, including that by the peasant heroine Kitri, referenced rustic traditions. The playbill lists a *muiñeira*, the Spanish equivalent of a jig, a generic *zingara* (gypsy) dance, a jota, a couples' dance with castanets held high, and a Spanish Rose dance, which might have been like the habanera in Georges Bizet's gypsy-themed opera, *Carmen*. The Bolshoi was full for the four performances. The picadors and sword dance appealed to Moscow's audiences, as did the laughter of the moon and the gallop performed by a lark-catcher, who snapped shut the door of the cage in time with the music. Don Quixote battled dragons, crocodiles, and a spider. There was even a performance within the performance: a puppet show, put on by the comedians of the Barcelona marketplace that Kitri calls home. Reviewers lingered on the food props—the piece of cheese swallowed by one of the clowns, the plate of soup busying a devil— and the "delight, horror, rage, and joy" etched onto the face of the dancer in the lead role, Wilhelm Vanner.[59] The first performance was a benefit for Anna Sobeshchanskaya, the Bolshoi's best dancer at the time (she had been dancing for the Imperial Theaters since 1858 and age sixteen) but not an especially enchanting one. Sobesh-chanskaya reportedly lacked "fire" and "chic" in her performance as Kitri, although she succeeded in "making short skirts fashionable for ballerinas."[60]

Minkus did not conduct the premiere on December 14, 1869. The task fell instead to Yuliy Gerber, who needed more time to rehearse the orchestra than Minkus had allotted. Gerber had great skills as a violinist and talent comparable to Minkus as a composer. But, being prone to attacks of nerves and even fainting spells, he was not the most able conductor, as evidenced by his rough night at the podium for a performance of *The Pharaoh's Daughter* in January 1870. It elicited a howl of protest from a reader of the newspaper *Russkiye vedomosti* (Russian gazette), who wrote the following screed to the editor: "He doesn't know to pace properly, fails to notice when any of the ballerinas mistake counts, and can't coordinate their movements with the orchestra—because he stares fixedly at his score, paying absolutely no mind to the dancers' feet. We saw for ourselves yesterday as the choreographer, Petipa, stood in the wings gesturing any which way for M. Gerber to make the orchestra under his control play *accelerando* and *ritardando* according to the character of the dances. But the gesturing went unnoticed: M. Gerber waved his baton as he liked; the orchestra performed as it liked; and the dancers jumped as they liked."[61]

Yet *Don Quixote* somehow held together, and the general success of the bravura ballet eased Minkus's promotion to in-house composer of the Imperial Theaters of St. Petersburg—a big step up from Moscow. There his pay doubled to 4,000 rubles, a commendable sum. He retired in 1886, when the position of house composer was abolished, with a pitiful pension well less than allotted dancers of the corps de ballet.

Petipa returned to Moscow for short stints, transferring ballet productions from the Mariyinsky to the Bolshoi, but never thinking of relocating. For an obvious reason: On September 2, 1870, Arthur Saint-Léon fell over dead at the Café de Divan in Paris, the victim of a stroke. Petipa now enjoyed total command of the Imperial Ballet of St. Petersburg and great influence over its poorer cousin in Moscow.

IN NOVEMBER 1871, Petipa brought *Don Quixote* to the St. Petersburg stage. The folk fare of the Moscow production, he decided, would not appeal to the court. Petipa also suppressed some of the slapstick, eliminating, for example, the laughing moon and the bird catcher. But the far-flung fantasies were spared. The budget for the Mariyinsky production allowed for the making of a "flying spider" by a professional sculptor, "three cacti," and "three dragons."[62] The spider was pulled up and down by puppeteers hired for the job at about the same salary as the production's hairdresser.

Petipa even added a fifth act for a duke and a duchess, instructing the dutiful Minkus to write new music, and an epilogue on the subject of Don Quixote's death. The melancholic ending contradicted the original comic intention of the ballet. Petipa expanded the roster for the dream scene from twenty-eight dancers to seventy-two, including three "lines" of children.[63] Bringing them to the theater required hiring four carriages and ten pairs of horses. And, crucially, he made Kitri and Dulcinea one and the same character, to be performed by a single dancer. In the dream scene, the peasant girl becomes an image of divine perfection: a classical Russian ballerina.

Petipa also decided that Don Quixote's faithful servant, Sancho Panza, needed to enter and exit the stage on a donkey, an important character in the source novel by Cervantes, but just a prop in the ballet. This was not the first time that the Imperial Theaters got involved in donkey procurement. Back in 1853 the famous French actress Mademoiselle Rachel (Élisa Félix) had administrators running around in circles trying to obtain a donkey for her. The directorate assumed that she needed it for a Christmas play, obliging her to explain to the déclassé Russians hosting her that she needed donkey milk for digestive and cosmetic purposes. Somehow, her request for the lactating jennet was granted.

The idea of costuming and putting makeup on a horse was rejected, and so a search began in earnest for a donkey strong enough to carry the bulky Sancho Panza. The quest ended in disaster. A jennet was acquired from a burlesque house by the theater stable keeper for 200 rubles a season, but the beast was much too old and jittery for show business and collapsed. A veterinarian attributed her death to brain fever, "inflammation of the meninges," but that was a cover-up.[64] The ballet itself was the cause.

Soon after the premiere of the new version of *Don Quixote* in St. Petersburg (a dubious success, in the opinion of the visiting Danish ballet master August Bournonville), Petipa brought the ballet back to Moscow.[65] This time, the disaster with the donkey was avoided, thanks to the excessive attention brought to the matter by both the imperial court and the Moscow Imperial Theaters. The bureaucrats in charge of the new Bolshoi staging took pains to ensure that sufficient funds were allocated for a stable, oats, hay, and "treats in the form of bread."[66] The cost of bridles, training, and a minder were also taken into account. The going rate for a donkey was 40 rubles, but the *kontora* of the Imperial Moscow Theaters was honored to report to St. Petersburg that a male donkey, or jack, had been obtained for free from the zoo, with its keeper agreeing to ride him to and from the Bolshoi for 75 kopecks a day. The papers were signed and the ballet staged. The donkey basked in applause before retiring, after the final curtain, back to the zoo.

That was in 1873. By the end of the year, Petipa's *Don Quixote* had been performed at the Bolshoi seventy-five times, the bravura feats cheered night after night. The antics onstage sometimes paled in comparison to the caprice backstage, as attested by the annual incident reports—the compilations of accidents, arrests, protests, foiled arson attempts, and strange goings-on in and around the theater, including bookkeepers being vengefully accused (by the illegal ticket sellers they had caught) of accepting sacks of sugar as bribes. The ballerinas of the Bolshoi, like those of the Mariyinsky, were upset to be reminded of the need to shave their armpits. A popular subject in the reports is the ruckus caused in the galleries by Moscow University students, likewise fisticuffs in the orchestra, stagehands getting tangled in ropes, the children whose smelliness barred them from being hired as footmen, and the mishaps that tended to befall the supernumeraries: tripping over props, backing into lamps, and setting their tunics aflame. Sometimes, to the exasperation of the administration, the incidents interrupted performances.

The report for 1869 is especially colorful. It begins with a recurring problem: violations of the thirteen-year-old ban on smoking in the loges and parterre. The directorate of the Moscow Imperial Theaters reported that "so-called" solicitors from the Moscow regional court, together with several other officials, responded to the ban by filling the theater with acrid fumes from hand-rolled cigarettes and mauling the usher who asked them to stop. The master of the loges arrived to plead with the men, who cursed him and promised him a thrashing. The police were summoned, but they did not turn up until after the theater had emptied. The Moscow chief of police was mortified and promised that, in the future, officers would patrol the theater to ensure that smoking was confined to the side rooms. The brouhaha spoiled the December 26 performance of *Don Quixote*.

Confrontations occurred within the ranks as well. The previous March, the theater's sweeper, Alexander Fyodorov, was insulted and "pushed in the chest" during an argument with the mechanic's assistant. The sweeper took the matter to court, and, to his satisfaction, the mechanic's assistant was jailed for a week.

Then there was the matter of the December 1 performance of *Faust*, which was disrupted by "a member of the lower middle classes," Egorov Shaposhnikov, who began whistling during the first act from his seat in the third row of the balcony on the left side. He confessed to being offended by the representation of Mephistopheles, whose costume resembled that of church clerics. By whistling, he hoped superstitiously to bring misfortune to the theater for its act of sacrilege.

The funniest incident, which tickled even the sober-minded officials running the Moscow Imperial Theaters, concerned a performance of the French grand opera *Robert le diable* on November 4. A provincial poet, Nikolay Ogloblin, disguised himself as a "commoner," a technician summoned to the theater to inspect the gas jets in the alcove holding the chandeliers. The guard at the backstage entrance failed to detect the ruse and unlocked the vestibule leading into the alcove. The poet carried a satchel stuffed with copies of a jingoistic ode, "The Voice of Russia." During the Ballet of the Nuns in the third act of the opera, the pages rained down on the heads of the baffled audience. After he had emptied his bag, Ogloblin fled down the staircase between the fifth and fourth tiers into the coffee room. There he was detained, along with the inattentive, "intoxicated" guard.[67] Ogloblin claimed that he had nothing against opera or the dancing nuns, but had simply hoped to bring his patriotic art to the public's attention. He was imprisoned for hooliganism.

Opera continued to dominate the Bolshoi stage, although Russian opera struggled to find an audience while French and Italian works flourished. Ballet productions remained "a strange assortment," according to Bournonville, but in 1874 he thought he saw the future of Russian ballet in a brief interlude. "The talented actress who played the role of the village girl lent it quiet sorrow which turns into madness," he raved, "and ends with the death in the waves—a masterly piece of tragic interpretation."[68]

SORROW, AND TRAGIC PATHOS, came to Russian ballet thanks to composer Pyotr Ilyich Tchaikovsky.

Petit bourgeois in everything besides his craft, Tchaikovsky gave to Russian ballet the death in the waves and so much more. He was a regular sort, of the usual tastes for his time, sometimes

requiring the poison of alcohol to soothe the nerves, prone to complaining about the weather and his aches and pains. The tragic,
flaming Romanticism attributed to his existence is less fact than
fantasy, the invention of biographers who cannot countenance that
a homosexual man could in fact live a positive, purposeful life full
of failures and successes, illustrious in helping elevate Russian ballet to dominance.[69] Tchaikovsky did not strive to become famous.
Decorum instead counseled him to impose limits on himself, to
remain within the comfort zone of a gentleman who preferred to
be non-involved, telling absurd jokes, swapping amusing cartoons
of the tsars, playing cards, but keeping his life thin and reserved.
He taught counterpoint and orchestration, composed for a Moscow
pyrotechnic exhibition in 1872 and for other municipal occasions,
and set banal poems. He attracted the attentions of a patroness and
the court, and thus, almost despite himself, found himself obliged
to serve his brilliance.

The Bolshoi gave Tchaikovsky his start as a theatrical composer
after his education in St. Petersburg, but his career ended up everywhere, his works appearing on all of the important stages around
the world. The marvel of his music resides in the guilelessness of
his basic materials: traditional two- and three-part forms, themes
and variations, rising and falling scales, the major and the minor,
thirds and sixths. These building blocks are essential to even his
most cosmic scores, lending them their most human aspects: the
grief before the disarticulation of the body, the dissolution of the
spirit. When he included vernacular elements (age-old songs about
hills, dales, birch trees, and the like) in his compositions, he transformed them, enriching their harmonies and dispersing melodies
through the upper registers of the orchestra. Thus from the streets
of the boyars' town emerged the accompaniment to angels dancing
on their toes.

In 1869, the same year *Don Quixote* was first staged, smoking patrons proved unrepentant, and poems fluttered through the theater, Tchaikovsky's first opera, *The Voyevoda*, premiered at the Bolshoi. Like *Don Quixote*, it was meant to appeal to Moscow audiences. But *The Voyevoda* lasted just five performances, being reviled as much for the slipshod nature of the production as the insubstantial plot, about a provincial governor who steals the daughter of a merchant away from her suitor, who in turn steals her back. Tchaikovsky was embarrassed by the failure and tossed his score into the stove. Two semi-successful operas later, he accepted a commission for his first ballet. He had to be persuaded to do so by the Imperial Theaters, since composers of distinction did not, at the time, write ballet music. (That was the domain of lesser-skilled ballet specialists like Pugni and Minkus.) Tchaikovsky risked affronting his peers, since the opera lovers in his circle scorned ballet, yet the composer wanted to see if he could turn prettiness into profundity. He was also broke. "I accepted this task partly for the money," he told composer Nikolay Rimsky-Korsakov, who did not express much interest in ballet, "and partly because I have long wanted to try my hand at this sort of music."[70] Tchaikovsky began by resurrecting the best tunes from *The Voyevoda* and recycling some music that he had improvised at the piano for a children's party. This compilation would become the most beloved ballet of all, at the Bolshoi as in history.

Swan Lake premiered at the Bolshoi Theater in 1877 under circumstances that remain murky, owing to the loss of records about the unprecedented commission, the sources for the scenario, and the original staging. In the end, Tchaikovsky was conflicted about his achievement, writing in his diary that a performance of *Swan Lake* represented "*a moment of absolute happiness.*" In a letter to a colleague, however, he said he was "ashamed" of the score.[71]

There was little happy about the first staging of *Swan Lake*, which flopped with the reviewers, if not the public. The dances, mounted by the ballet master Wenzel Reisinger, were described as bland, boring, and, in Tchaikovsky's opinion, wryly amusing. "Yesterday, the first rehearsal of some numbers from Act I of this ballet was held in a hall at the Theatrical School," he wrote to his brother Modest on March 24, 1876. Although the orchestration was not finished, Tchaikovsky was keen to gauge the reaction to his music. "If you only knew how comical it was to watch the ballet master creating dances with a most serious and profound air to the sound of one little violin. At the same time, it made one envious to watch the ballerinas and danseurs casting smiles at an imaginary audience and reveling in the easy opportunity for leaping and whirling about, thereby fulfilling their sacred duty." Then the crucial point: "Everyone at the theater raves about my music."[72]

Except Reisinger and his dancers. The choreographer fought with the score, and the premiere of the ballet was postponed from November–December 1876 to February 20, 1877, in part to give him more time to prepare his dancers, but also because Italian operas were taking up most of the rehearsal time. The onstage product failed to impress. *Ports de bras* looked like windmills, the lifts and bends like gymnastic exercises. A reviewer insisted that the character dances, the best part of Reisinger's *Swan Lake*, must have come from other ballets, and remarked that "only a German could have mistaken the pirouettes excreted by Mlle. Karpakova as a 'Russian' dance."[73] Three days later, the critic for *Sankt-Peterburgskiye vedomosti* almost begged the Bolshoi to hire another ballet master. Weaker dances "could not be imagined," he blustered, and thank goodness the audience "paid no heed at all to them." He found it galling that Reisinger "presumed to have his name printed on the poster" and "took a bow before a public that had no thought or imagining of calling him to the stage. Is not this pointless waving of the legs for four hours a form of torture?"[74]

Reisinger was used to such attacks. He had long been hounded by Moscow critics, who could not accept the presence at the Bolshoi of a provincial ballet master known more for failure than success at his previous post in Leipzig. He was not in demand; no one of influence had lobbied for his hiring, and anti-German sentiment in Russian newspapers was at an all-time high. (It reflected increasing anxieties about the emergence of a powerful, increasingly industrialized German Empire under Prussian leadership.) The machinist Valts took credit for bringing Reisinger's name to the attention of the minister of the court. They were friends from long back, roomed together near the Bolshoi, and ducked out for pints of beer between acts. Before staging *Swan Lake*, Reisinger had feigned affection for Russian myth and legend, enduring caustic reviews but bringing in a modest profit with a production of a ballet about an immortal sorcerer (*Kashchey the Deathless*), to forgettable music by Wilhelm Mühldorfer, a composer he knew from Leipzig. Yuliy Gerber, the Bolshoi Theater principal violinist, also contributed to the score, more successfully. The positive response to Reisinger's staging of *Cinderella* in 1871, to a scenario by Valts and music by Gerber, seems to have prompted his full-time appointment as ballet master.[75]

In truth, Reisinger filled the position of ballet master from 1873 to 1878 because there was no other choice. Carlo Blasis had resigned without a successor, leaving the ballet rudderless. When the minister of the court, Alexander Adlerberg, visited Moscow in August of 1873, he frowned upon the sloppiness of the Bolshoi corps de ballet. The directorate of the Moscow Imperial Theaters came to the unhappy conclusion that "in the absence of a more capable ballet master," Reisinger must be hired.[76] Even so, the commission overseeing the directorate informed him in 1874 that it had "no intention of renewing" his contract that year.[77] Yet he stayed for four more years.

Reisinger lacked imagination, had a tin ear, and made a hash of Tchaikovsky's *Swan Lake*, now considered a musical masterpiece. He survived in Moscow thanks to his skill at selling tickets to stitched-together productions that appealed to the middle class, and his success in cleaning up the ragged, radically underpaid members of the corps de ballet. As a habitual recycler, a champion of ready-made choreography, he could make do with hand-me-down décor shipped to Moscow from St. Petersburg. He was thus the best the Bolshoi could do given its chronic financial constraints.

As premiered by the Moscow Imperial Bolshoi Theater in 1877, *Swan Lake* follows the fate of Odette, a beautiful, guileless princess with an evil stepmother who wants her dead. Odette is protected by the crown that her grandfather gave her, but she and her girlfriends nonetheless live in disguise: at night they are free to be human, inhabiting the ruins of a chapel, while during the day they transform into swans on a lake of tears—the tears shed over the death of Odette's mother. Odette can be saved by a declaration of love from someone who has never been in love before. That someone is Prince Siegfried. He is aimless, restless, and unattached. His mother, the queen, has made it clear that it is time for him to find a bride, so she arranges a matchmaking ball. Meanwhile, he and a companion, the knight Benno, spy a wedge of swans passing overhead and take to the hunt. The birds settle on the lake of tears, led by a majestic swan wearing a crown. Siegfried prepares to sink an arrow into the swan's heart, but just then Odette appears, in human form. She explains her sad plight, and Siegfried falls in love with her. They agree that she will attend the ball, where he will choose her as his bride and thus break the spell. Siegfried awaits Odette, but instead her double appears, Odile, an agent of the

demonic Baron von Rothbart. Mistaking her for his true love, Siegfried declares Odile his bride. The stage plunges into darkness; the
deception is exposed, leaving both Odette and Siegfried shattered.
Odette returns to her companions on the lake of tears. Siegfried
begs her forgiveness, to no avail, and Odette dies in his arms. Her
stepmother, in the guise of a screeching red-eyed owl, flies overhead, gripping the crown that Siegfried, in despair, has thrown into
the water. A storm sweeps the thwarted lovers under the waves.

The plot offers up a series of oppositions: swans versus humans,
lake versus castle, day versus night, good versus evil, truth versus
deception, freedom versus enslavement. The standard interpretation has Siegfried seeking escape from the oppressive social order
through communion with the ideal. Odette is the ideal, Odile her
demonic, carnal opposite. But the plot has its excesses and inconsistencies. Why, for example, is the knight Benno involved in the first
and second acts of the 1877 version, but not the third and fourth?
Why do we need both a sorceress and a demon? Do all the swan
maidens share the same curse? The biggest problem is the pitiless
ending. In productions after 1877, a solution would be found in the
music. Tchaikovsky's score concludes with an Orphic apotheosis: a
halo of strings suggests spirits still commingling after death, even
ascending to heaven.

The inconsistencies suggest decision-making by committee,
and it was long unknown who put the scenario together. The story
of *Swan Lake* was published without attribution in *Teatral'naya
gazeta* on October 19, 1876, close to the time of the intended
but postponed premiere. There are distant echoes of Ovid in
the plot, likewise the Brothers Grimm and the stories of Johann
Musäus. A Pushkin poem is a possible source, and details derive
from Richard Wagner: the hero is named Siegfried, perhaps after
the dragon slayer in Wagner's *Siegfried*; the swannishness calls to

mind *Lohengrin*; and when Wagner's Flying Dutchman declares that the feeling in his breast might not be love but the desire for redemption, he seems to be voicing what Odette's longing leaves unsaid. Wagner also stages a flood, at the end of *Götterdämmerung*. Some plot devices can be found in other famous ballets, suggesting that Reisinger might have been the author. (The magic crown that Odette wears can be likened, for example, to the wings of the sylph in *La sylphide*, which also cannot be removed without causing death.) Tchaikovsky changed the scenario, adding some details in his musical manuscript. Later, his brother Modest, a dramatist and librettist, would revise it, making the concept of self-sacrificing love explicit. The Soviet ballerina Ekaterina Geltser liked to credit her father, a Bolshoi Theater ballet master, with compiling the scenario, but there is no evidence to support her claim beyond a copy of the text with his name on it.

The author turns out to have been Vladimir Begichev, a scenarist who served as repertoire inspector for the Bolshoi and, for a few months in 1881–82, as the director of the Moscow Imperial Theaters. He descended from ancient noble lineage and had studied at Moscow University, holding a series of positions in finance before petitioning for posts in the Imperial Theaters. He had long known Tchaikovsky, who once tutored Begichev's prodigiously musical stepson. Begichev had earlier arranged for Tchaikovsky to write incidental music for a drama called *The Snow Maiden* and had nurtured the composer's interest in ballet as part of an effort to expand the Bolshoi repertoire. A colleague and accurate memoirist claims that "V. P. Begichev himself wrote the scenario for the ballet *Swan Lake*; the composer endorsed the subject—he initially expressed an interest in a fantasy involving knights—and agreed to compose the music for 800 rubles."[78] Case closed, except for the fact that the comment came with a disclaimer: "If I'm not mistaken."

But he wasn't. Begichev excluded his name from the published scenario because he did not want to be seen promoting himself in the imperial service. And ballet work lacked prestige.

The music has a distant antecedent in a children's ballet that Tchaikovsky improvised into existence in 1871 to entertain his nieces (his sister Sasha's three daughters). It was rustic theater of the type that had once been performed by serfs, and the composer gamely demonstrated pirouettes amid wooden cutouts of swans. The plot might have been inspired by the Russian folktale *The White Duck*, about a witch who turns a queen into a duck in order to assume her place on the throne. Four years later, when Tchaikovsky began composing the adult version of *Swan Lake*, he recycled a violin and cello solo from an abandoned operatic project about a water sprite who, to gain a soul, marries a knight. It was called *Undine*, and it links *Swan Lake* to an entire cosmos of mermaid stories, including Hans Christian Andersen's *The Little Mermaid*. The storm and swan song that inspired the ending of the score was inspired by the tales collected by Alexander Afanasiev under the title *Poeticheskiye vozzreniya slavyan na prirodu* (Poetic Slavic representations of nature, 1866–69).[79]

Though he knew some ballet steps, loved *Giselle*, and did his homework, Tchaikovsky's knowledge of the genre was slight. The music gets at the theme of longing and the pursuit of an ideal, but it seems to ignore the practicalities of moving bodies around a stage. (The lakeside entrance of the swans and the *pas de deux* are exceptions.) Even in those places where he seems to be thinking about the dance, the character of the music is at odds with the dramatic situation. The climactic, devastating exposure of Rothbart's trickery in act 3 is assigned mere seconds of music. The passage is jarring, a dense chromatic field, but much too brief to have an impact. The ballet critic Arlene Croce has deduced that, although Tchaikovsky "sought advice from his choreographer, the kind of advice which he was later to obtain from Petipa for *The Sleeping Beauty* and *The Nutcracker*—he appears to have been on his own most of the time. The score, unlike the two later ones, is badly organized in terms of theater logic and stagecraft."[80]

The problem with this assessment is that of the realities of making ballets at the Bolshoi in 1877. It remains unclear what Reisinger, with his limited skills, intended for the music and how he changed that intention. He also had in mind different dramatis personae, and different emphases in each of the acts. The act 1 *pas de deux*, which later choreographers transposed to the act 3 episode where Odile seduces Prince Siegfried, was assigned in 1877 to Siegfried and a character called "villager 1."[81] The lush violin solo is freighted with the kind of mild dissonances—augmented seconds and augmented fourths—heard in gypsy music, suggesting that Siegfried and the girl had some kind of attraction to each other. Although much is made of the Odette/Odile opposition in the plot, Reisinger, like Tchaikovsky, seems also to have been thinking of an expanded cast wherein this village love interest might parallel a supernatural one. According to the 1877 advertisement, "villager 1" was performed by the Bolshoi soloist Mariya Stanislavskaya, a St. Petersburg–trained ballerina who had been a soloist with the Bolshoi since 1871. Stanislavskaya danced in four of the seven numbers of the original act 1, including two dances not labeled as such in Tchaikovsky's score: a polka and a gallop. It may be that Reisinger, baffled by the longer dances in the score, dismissed them as "awkward" and replaced them with easier dances taken from other ballets.[82] Tchaikovsky objected, and Reisinger relented, but only to a point. The crowd-pleasing, ticket-selling polka and gallop remained.

The original violin rehearsal score and other materials from the first eight years of the ballet's existence contain some unusual details, such as the inclusion of a dance for "12 German women" recycled from an 1874 Parisian ballet titled *Le tour du monde*, after Jules Verne's great adventure novel *Le tour du monde en quatre-vingts jours* (Around the world in 80 days, 1873). The second section of the dance is labeled a *"Pas de seduction à 8."*[83] It became part of *Swan Lake* on the insistence of another ballet master, Joseph Peter Hansen, who succeeded Reisinger at the Bolshoi.

Some of the passages that tend to be cut or relocated in current stagings actually took pride of place in the original ballet at the Bolshoi. One such number, critic Alastair Macaulay notes, is the "beautifully poignant *andante con moto* section, which builds up into a tragic climax that makes the ballet's scale seem briefly cosmic." As Macaulay explains, "If you listen to this number with the knowledge that Tchaikovsky intended it as part of the enchantress Odile's dances, you find it completely transforms our idea of her; this music is as poignant, doom-laden, and huge-scaled as anything written for Odette."[84] Yet just who was meant to dance this poignant episode remains unclear. In the rehearsal score, the *andante con moto* is called a *pas de six*. The 1877 playbill, however, lists it as a *pas de cinq*, and a playbill from 1878 as a *pas de dix*, performed by the two principles and eight apprentice dancers. In later years it was cut altogether.[85] There are other examples of this sort. Indeed, apart from the principal characters, their conflicts, and the appeal of Tchaikovsky's music, little was or is stable about *Swan Lake*.

For all his limitations, Reisinger ended up being easier for Tchaikovsky to work with than the two ballerinas who played the dual role of Odette/Odile.[86] The first of them was Pelageya Karpakova, the second Anna Sobeshchanskaya, who took the part of Odette/Odile beginning with the fourth performance on April 28. Neither dancer made much sense of the role, but the 1877 reviews of *Swan Lake* agree that Sobeshchanskaya, who had long carried the Bolshoi repertoire on her shoulders, was the better actress and technician. The knock against Karpakova had long been the "hesitation" and "lack of power in her movements, of proper speed, exposing a general absence of strength in the muscles." Her poses and turns lacked definition. A critic had also called them "soft," *ne tverdo*, though a typographical error, or joke, spelled the phrase in question *net vedro*—"not worth a bucket." Karpakova was beautiful and worked hard, but the critic fretted that time and physical training (*vremya i gigienicheskiye sredstva*) might not be enough to correct the deficiencies.[87]

They were not. Of her performance in *Swan Lake*, the theatrical observer Dmitri Mukhin remarked that Karpakova "tried as much as she could to represent the fantastic role of the swan, but being a poor mime, she did not leave much of an impression."[88] He also observed that Tchaikovsky's music vexed most of the cast, being too symphonic, with no clear sense of where numbers began and ended. Then a crucial detail, one that has entered *Swan Lake* lore as proof of malfeasance in the choice of Karpakova over Sobeshchanskaya for opening night: "It became clear in the staging of [*Swan Lake*] that some evil force had begun to have an adverse effect on Mlle. Sobeshchanskaya. For her April 28 benefit she had to settle for the fourth performance of this ballet, but as a principal dancer she justifiably should have been given a new ballet to premiere."[89]

The mystery of the casting decision—Why wasn't Sobeshchanskaya given the premiere?—persisted until Karl Valts stepped forward with an explanation. In his memoirs, he tells the "dark and unpleasant" tale of the rise and fall of Sobeshchanskaya, whose career began like a fairy tale but ended as a nightmare.[90] In her youth she had been pampered by high-ranking court officials. She was "brought to the attention of the eternally bored Tsar Alexander II," who helped to arrange for her to perform in *Don Quixote, The*

Pharaoh's Daughter, and other ballets by Petipa. She also came to know the governor general of Moscow, Vladimir Dolgorukov. He was well into his sixties and declining physically but decided to try to add her to his collection of mistresses, offering her affection and protection along with his family's jewels. From Valts's account, the aged Dolgorukov seems to have imagined Sobeshchanskaya in the role of Madame de Pompadour to his Louis XV. But he did not have the means to maintain the charade. Years of squandering had left him "as poor as a flea." He had to dip into his sister's famous collection of diamonds and emeralds to decorate his adopted ballerina.

Sobeshchanskaya exercised reasonable tact throughout her career but was "careless enough" to fall in love with a young Polish dancer named Stanislav Gillert while Dolgorukov was still in her thrall. Sobeshchanskaya and Gillert had long partnered onstage, and they married. This turn of events did not go over well with Sobeshchanskaya's influential patron, especially after Gillert began pawning the conspicuous baubles that Dolgorukov had given to the ballerina. "A huge scandal brewed that required great effort to cover up, and Sobeshchanskaya lost her access to the highest spheres," according to Valts. Her career ended after "just 17 years of service" to the Bolshoi. She forfeited her privileges and was even deprived of a benefit performance to raise money for her retirement. Valts adds that Sobeshchanskaya, the "former glory of the Moscow ballet," ended up selling candles and soap for a living in the market at Red Square.

Her scandalous marriage supposedly cost her the lead role, and the premiere of *Swan Lake* on February 20, 1877, featured Pelageya Karpakova with Sobeshchanskaya's husband, Stanislav Gillert, in the role of Siegfried. Karpakova had a powerful patron of her own. In 1873, she married the head of the Moscow Savings Bank, millionaire Konstantin Milioti. Supposedly thanks to his influence,

Karpakova was promoted to first dancer when she might otherwise have been confined to character roles.

But here lore parts company with truth. Newspaper stories from the months leading up to the premiere of *Swan Lake* reveal that Milioti was under investigation for embezzlement, meaning he was more of a liability than an asset for his wife. And the romantic intrigue surrounding Sobeshchanskaya did not in fact end her career. During the 1870s, she dominated the Bolshoi stage and retained her coveted position as an official court dancer (much as Tchaikovsky would serve, in his later years, as the official court composer for Tsar Alexander III). In 1876 she was invited to perform for the Danish king, his daughter, and the king and queen of Greece for an event arranged and attended by her former patron, Dolgorukov. Later the same year she danced for Tsar Alexander II during his visit to Moscow. Sobeshchanskaya held enough sway to demand—and obtain—compensation even when performances were canceled or postponed. Like Karpakova, she received numerous gifts from Tsar Alexander II and his family, including jewels and their value in cash on the occasion of the marriage of the tsar's daughter to the Duke of Edinburgh. Sobeshchanskaya retired with a comfortable pension in a comfortable home. The candle-and-soap story involving her husband is an exaggeration of his failed attempt to operate a candle-and-soap-making factory in St. Petersburg. Sobeshchanskaya ended her career in the teaching studio, where among her students was the first great Soviet ballerina, Ekaterina Geltser. That Sobeshchanskaya was assigned the fourth performance of *Swan Lake* thus had nothing to do with her personal relationship with Moscow's governor general. She was just more interested in performing another ballet, *La bayadère*, which Petipa was preparing for premieres in St. Petersburg and Moscow.

Another dancer, Lidiya Geyten, was offered the role. A gray-eyed brunette, Geyten possessed enchanting mannerisms and a filigreed technique. Petipa acknowledged her talent by assigning her a role in *Don Quixote* when she was but twelve years old. In 1874, she joined the Bolshoi as first dancer after graduating from its school. Two years later she was offered the lead role in *Swan Lake*. The music was not the fairy tale she wanted to dance, however, for reasons she laid out late in her career in an interview. "Tchaikovsky wrote his first ballet (*Swan Lake*) for me," she claimed, "but I refused to dance in it, because [he] did not know the technical side of ballet and because it was uninteresting."[91] The composer certainly was unproven at the time, but would go on to write two other ballets for St. Petersburg, each a wonder of acoustic design: *The Sleeping Beauty* (1890) and *The Nutcracker* (1892). When Geyten heard those later scores, she changed her mind about his talents. Yet she still dismissed Tchaikovsky's music as "unrewarding" for dancers, since he was, in her opinion, first and foremost a symphonist. (She thought the same of Alexander Glazunov, who supplied the music for the canonic Petipa ballet *Raymonda*, from 1898.) Geyten also proposed, insolently, that everything Tchaikovsky learned about ballet composition came from Yuliy Gerber's ballet *The Fern* (Paporotnik, 1867). "Tchaikovsky took the score to his estate and mislaid it. This is why the wonderful ballet *The Fern* isn't staged anymore," she explained. There is no proof to her story, but she enjoyed telling it.[92]

Third on the list behind Sobeshchanskaya and Geyten was the older, less-skilled Karpakova, who accepted the premiere of *Swan Lake*. She danced the lead role as a benefit, which pegged her earnings to box-office receipts, minus performance costs (artists' fees, lighting, props, makeup, copyists, tailors, porters, carriages, gendarmerie, alcohol, and posters). Receipts for Bolshoi Ballet performances during this period were poor—often far below the cost of the production. Such was the case with *Swan Lake*, which cost precisely 6,792 rubles to stage, much less than the operas, but still not enough to turn a profit over the course of its run, despite a decent public reaction. The first night, Karpakova took home 1,957 rubles, which was about half of the box-office receipts.[93] For the fourth performance, Sobeshchanskaya arranged to be paid in advance and took home 987 rubles. Once the novelty wore off and ticket prices were reduced, however, the box-office receipts shrank to less than 300 rubles a night. The mediocre earnings further signaled that the Moscow Imperial Theaters required financial restructuring. The Bolshoi Ballet could not be allowed to continue racking up losses.

Critics agreed that Sobeshchanskaya danced much better than Karpakova, but, like Geyten, neither ballerina found merit in Tchaikovsky's score. Both gave the composer headaches by demanding that he change his music. Karpakova insisted that he provide her something special for the act 3 ball scene. The composer complied, producing an up-tempo Russian dance that stayed in the ballet no longer than Karpakova did.[94] Sobeshchanskaya wanted a variation of her own for the third act, but ran to Petipa, rather than Reisinger or Tchaikovsky, with her demand for the solo. Petipa agreed to choreograph a new dance for her in act 3 and asked Ludwig Minkus to compose the music.

When Tchaikovsky discovered what was being done to his score behind his back, he saw red. He calmed himself down by composing a variation of his own for Sobeshchanskaya, with the same tempo, structure, and number of measures as Minkus's insert, so Sobeshchanskaya could dance what she had worked out with Petipa—but to Tchaikovsky's music. She was pleased and even asked Tchaikovsky to compose yet another variation for her. The two variations morphed into a new *pas de deux* for the end of act 3, one that Sobeshchanskaya had willed into being, and one that she danced with her husband as Siegfried. For a while, it replaced the *pas de six* of act 3. Later, the *pas de deux* found its way into *Le corsair*, and the *pas de six* was restored. There were further changes to *Swan Lake*, more demands. Even Tchaikovsky could not keep track of them.

That the ballet was performed thirty-nine times in the first six seasons at the Bolshoi is less revealing than the fact that box-office receipts dwindled for the twenty-seven performances in the first two seasons, after which Reisinger was dismissed from the Bolshoi. Hansen replaced him, and the ballet was reworked for productions in 1880–81 and 1882–83. The second run ended when the sets began falling apart, and the Moscow Imperial Theaters lacked the funds for repairs. "It's all so pale and depressing," Tchaikovsky's patroness complained, seconding the critics. Still she thought the music "a delight," but the reviewers of the 1877 Bolshoi premiere considered it otherwise.[95] Like the décor and like the dance, the music came across as uninflected, devoid of contrast. It did not help that, for the premiere, there were "just two rehearsals" with the "imprecise" orchestra.[96] The conductor overindulged Tchaikovsky's penchant for bombast, and the principal violinist hacked at his solo while letting the string section disintegrate.

Such was the sentiment expressed in the newspaper *Russkiye vedomosti* and, in better detail, *Sovremennïye izvestiya* (Current news), whose theater writer made it clear that, in his opinion, ballet was a despicable art. It appealed to children and to lechers—the "distinguished bald-pated devotees of youth, beauty, and . . . various risqué pictures."[97] The serious theatergoing public preferred the plays staged in the Malïy Theater, which was the one venue for the arts that another newspaper in town, *Moskovskiye vedomosti*, thought deserving of attention. Street fairs received greater coverage than the ballet, and notices of performances at the Bolshoi appeared alongside curious advertisements from, for example, a seller of dwarf animals, goldfish, and turtles imported from America, and a clockmaker seeking (inexplicably) to purchase a female elk.

The critic for *Sovremennïye izvestiya* began with the plot of *Swan Lake*, then turned to the music, skipped past the dance, and concluded with the décor. He expressed bewilderment that the Bolshoi had commissioned Tchaikovsky to write music for a ballet based on a "ponderous," "content-free" German fairy tale as opposed to something from a Russian source. There was too much water, for one thing, and the prince's love for a swan with a crown on her head was absurd. Most of the plot followed the rules of ballet, though not, to his surprise, the end. The thunder and lightning and drowning of the prince and swan princesses was "sad, indeed remarkably so, because ballets tend to end to everyone's satisfaction"—that is, merrily. Knowing little if anything about choreography, the reviewer reduced Reisinger's contribution to *Swan Lake* to a single sentence: "There were dances with and without flowers, and dances with and without ribbons." Later he added that "the character dances needed more character." He had little praise for the orchestra: "There was a nice violin solo, but it was spoiled by M. Gerber. How is that an instrument, and that a soloist? Dragging an unoiled carriage across the stage would have afforded greater pleasure. M. Gerber's creaking spoiled the pleasant impression produced by Mlle. Eichenwald's harp playing." The judgment is harsh, a far cry from the perfumed politeness of theater reviews of the past, before Tsar Alexander II allowed for greater freedom of expression in the press.[98] The invective was tempered only at the end, with the reluctant admission that, despite all its flaws, "the ballet was a success and the public liked it." Tchaikovsky bowed shyly, and Karpakova received "a basket of flowers in the shape of a swan."

The budget was spent on the climactic tempest, as cleverly designed by Valts. In his memoirs, he congratulated himself, deservedly, for making the lake of tears "overflow its banks to flood the entire stage; on Tchaikovsky's insistence I created a true-to-life wind storm; branches and twigs snapped from the trees into the water to be carried along the waves." Odette and Siegfried bob at the back of the stage. At daybreak, the damaged trees become "illuminated by the rays of the rising sun."[99] Observers confirmed his description and, despite scorning the overall production, praised Valts's special effects, including the mechanical construction that allowed wooden swans to swim. He relied on some old tricks, like explosives, as well as the new technology of battery-powered carbon-arc lamps. Valts employed colored electric lighting for Odette's first appearance in act 2 and the famous storm scene. The innovative lighting proved more successful than the wind and wave machines, which drowned out the music, even though, according to the critic for *Russkiye vedomosti*, this was the scene to which Tchaikovsky paid the most attention. For a composer of operas and symphonies to be involved in ballet was unusual, even radical, and the critic was eager to hear the result. But he could not: The score had several wonderful moments, but was "perhaps too good for ballet" and, unfortunately, swallowed up at the end, "owing to the routine, absurd custom of accompanying any fire, flood, etc., on our stage with noise and din such that you would think that you were present at a large artillery drill or gunpowder explosion."[100]

The fad for amazing weather eventually subsided. Future versions of the ballet would avoid the storm scene. Odette and Siegfried perish, but their spirits endure as love eternal. The famous swan theme, the B-minor emblem of tragic desire, brings down the curtain as the lovers are seen, in most representations, moving along the surface of the lake.

Odile has come to be known as the black swan, but she did not dress in black in these early versions, nor was she as malevolent a counter to Odette as she has since been made out to be. (The black-swan idea dates from the Second World War.)[101] Odile was, however, meant to be an enigma. The poster for the 1877 premiere assigns Karpakova the role of Odette but does not give the name of the performer of Odile. In its place there is just an ellipsis—three dots. The dancer in the role is not listed, even though the names of dancers in all of the other parts, even the trifling ones, appear. The absence bears a certain intrigue, but it is obvious from at least one account that Karpakova (and beginning with the fourth performance, Sobeshchanskaya) appeared in both roles—at once the "good" girl and the "bad" one, the femme fatale.

Leaving out the name of the performer in the role of Odile seems like a tease intended to keep the obsessed balletomane guessing until the middle of act 3. This is the critical juncture in the plot, when Karpakova, having offered up the naïve, sweet side of her craft as Odette, arrives on Rothbart's arm disguised as Odile. But she did not look that much different, and no one was fooled into thinking that another dancer was putting the moves on Siegfried. The costume records for the third act have Karpakova in "tutu of maline lace, embroidered with gold stitches. Half-skirt with bodice of straw-colored satin, decorated with sequins and gilt mesh." For the Russian dance, she wore the same-colored tutu, but "decorated with colored velvet ribbon" and with a "headpiece of different-colored satin ribbons."[102] In the familiar, Petipa-based version of the ballet, Odile seduces Siegfried (and the audience) with power, speed, and needlepoint footwork. Hard angles replace soft curves. The contrast between Odile and her alter ego is obvious en pointe. But such dazzle was not part of the original 1877 plan and, as reviewers never tired of saying, actually lay beyond Karpakova's range. Sobeshchanskaya's too. The principal attraction of act 3, therefore, was not Odile's appearance but the effects. Valts plunged the stage into darkness to mark the moment Siegfried learns that he has been deceived, corrupted. When the lights come back on, Rothbart is a demon, dressed in red.

IN 1895, TWO YEARS after Tchaikovsky's unexpected death at his St. Petersburg residence, Petipa and his assistant, Lev Ivanov, reconceived *Swan Lake*. Their setting was a tribute of sorts to the composer, who, judging from a letter to Valts in 1892, had at least one more ballet score in him when he died—one that was intended for the Bolshoi.[103] Tchaikovsky had not aged well: he was white-haired, yellow-teethed from tobacco, and beset by digestive troubles before he reached the half-century mark. But his service to his art had only increased over time. He suffered his creative gift but attended to it with ever-greater urgency. In the weeks leading up to his death, he showed himself in fine form, dismissing all talk of the "repulsive snub-nosed monster" of death. "I feel I shall live a long time," he boasted.[104]

That did not happen. Asiatic cholera spread through Russia in 1892. The first cases were detected around Astrakhan, on the Caspian Sea. The field hospitals that had been opened along transport routes proved ineffective, since rural types, including peasants and Old Believers, viewed urbanites—ministers, cashiers, copiers, doctors, and lawyers—with suspicion. There were antigovernment riots and bizarre stories about people dying after digging for potatoes in infected soil and putting dirty money in their mouths. According to a report prepared by a British epidemiologist, "On July 25, two peasants from Rostov-on-Don, where cholera had prevailed for nearly a month, came to the house of a peasant named S— in the village of Egorovka in order to pay him a debt. The coins were held by S— in his mouth for a considerable time. . . . On the following day S— died from cholera."[105] The disease moved upstream along the Volga River until it reached the underperforming sewer and water systems of St. Petersburg.

There, the homes of the ill were disinfected with lime and chlorine, but the disease could not be eradicated. It lingered for more than a year, taking the lives of ne'er-do-wells, manual laborers, rank-and-file bureaucrats, and eventually nineteenth-century Russia's greatest composer. Cholera bacillus was even found in the pipes leading into the Winter Palace, residence of the tsar, alarming those in the upper ranks who considered themselves immune to the disease by virtue of their avoidance of untreated water, and regular intakes of camphor oil and alcohol-and-ether-based Hoffman's Drops. Tchaikovsky did not fear the disease, even though cholera had killed his mother when he was fourteen, shattering his childhood. He contracted it by imbibing unpurified water at (it is presumed) one of the restaurants he frequented with family and friends. Loss of appetite led to headache, nausea, diarrhea, and cramps. His heart stopped. Tchaikovsky's doctor was vilified for his flat-footedness in treating the composer with hot baths and doses of musk.

Memorial concerts in February 1894 included a little-noticed performance of the second act of *Swan Lake*, after which Tchaikovsky's brother was enlisted by the intendant of the Imperial Theaters to revise the entire scenario of the ballet. Petipa was seventy-five when he proposed staging *Swan Lake* in St. Petersburg, and had himself been brought low in previous years by serious illness, suffering from the skin disease pemphigus. The itching depressed him, and it persisted for years, right up to the year 1905, when rioting broke out in the streets of St. Petersburg and he could not make it to the drugstore. It cannot be said that he brought the same level of energy or imagination to *Swan Lake* that he had brought to *The Sleeping Beauty* in 1890. Petipa had also left most of the 1892 St. Petersburg staging of Tchaikovsky's last ballet, *The Nutcracker*, to his amiable second in command, Ivanov. Tchaikovsky died soon after the premiere of *The Nutcracker*, as did Tsar Alexander III, who had doted on the composer, granting him a generous government pension and bestowing the favor of the entire Imperial Theater establishment on him. Tchaikovsky died a national icon, and his music animated Petipa at a time in his life when the choreographer might otherwise have considered retirement, thinking less about suffusing the stage with splendor and more about his second wife, children, and grandchildren. Instead, Petipa increased his dictatorial control over the St. Petersburg Imperial Ballet.

Petipa and Ivanov's *Swan Lake* was performed sixteen times during the 1894–95 season, including three performances at the Bolshoi Theater. The premiere concluded the official period of mourning for Tsar Alexander III, and the three performances at the Bolshoi celebrated the coronation of Tsar Nicholas II. *Swan Lake* survived—and has endured—thanks to the coherence, the sharpness of image and sound, that the first and second ballet masters of St. Petersburg brought to it, and because the role of Odette/Odile has been passed from one eminent ballerina to another, entering the international repertoire as an expressive and technical showcase, a star vehicle. But for that to happen, Tchaikovsky's score had to be changed yet again, the creative script passed first from Petipa to Ivanov, who respected Petipa's guidelines, and then from Petipa and Ivanov to their dancers. The drama between Karpakova and Sobeshchanskaya that had shaped the Bolshoi Theater premiere of *Swan Lake* in 1877 would be iterated by the St. Petersburg ballerinas Pierina Legnani, whom Petipa privileged, and Matilda Kshesinskaya, a dancer for whom he had less charitable feelings, referring to her in his diaries as "spiteful" and a "nasty swine."[106]

Petipa's *régisseur*, or stage manager, Nikolay Sergeyev, helped to record the basic shape of the dances using dotted arrows, small circles, and boxes atop musical notation. These materials highlight Petipa's trademark obsession with the orderly arrangement of bodies onstage (he preferred even numbers to odd) as well as an interest in the overall look and feel of the production. The synesthesia of *Le corsaire* and *The Sleeping Beauty* infused the décor and props of his *Swan Lake:* The décor for the opening included "little garden seats" in the form of small red and green stepping stools.[107] The Venetian guests at the ball come prepared with castanets, mandolins, and tambourines and gather around a table littered with multicolored cups and bottles. Before the end, Petipa imagined six nymphs and eight naiads frolicking alongside the swans—but crossed out the thought. Another thought, elaborated by a technician in red ink, calls for an unspecified number of owls to swoop silently across the stage behind luxuriant arches of forest green. The queen of the owls—that is, Odette's evil stepmother—was to appear in the weeds near the front of the stage, where she eavesdrops on the passionate exchange between Siegfried and Odette.[108] Rothbart, too, lurks about, comically hoping to remain unseen as the owls flit from side to side.

Prior to the grand waltz of the beginning, twenty-four peasant women were to enter the stage holding flower baskets. Twenty-four peasant men would march in holding "little batons, with ribbons of several shades at their ends; by pressing a button a large bouquet would come from the baton."[109] But Petipa needed to "see the effect" before committing to it; later he rearranged things so that the baskets and batons were held by girls and boys rather than adults. The entire stage was to be in bloom. From the galleries, the dancers composed a single flower, each one a petal; closer up, from the parterre, that flower comprised a kaleidoscope of blossoms in hues of gold and blue. Color took on more meaning as the concept developed. The outdoor springtime colors darkened in the lakeside scene as the action turned inward.

Petipa and Ivanov combined the first two acts of *Swan Lake* into one so the audience could gaze upon Odette and come to know her plight before the first intermission. They also heightened the contrast between the rustic coming-of-age celebration and the formal ball at the palace. Spatial and linear repetitions revealed that outside forces controlled the characters—including the force of predestination as something externally imposed rather than inherently realized. The soloists existed in a realm of their own, where time is fluid, unmeasured, and the lovers escaped into the interstices, the liminal, the elsewhere opened up by the music.

That music, however, was changed. The conductor and resident composer with the St. Petersburg Imperial Ballet, Riccardo Drigo, edited the score in accord with Petipa and Ivanov's choreographic intentions. Tchaikovsky's music was nipped and tucked, and three new numbers added from a set of his piano pieces. The original score was heavy with foreboding but now, in this new conception, needed to suggest hope for the lovers in the beyond.

The role of Siegfried was assigned to a middle-aged Pavel Gerdt, that of Odette/Odile to a muscular Italian import named Pierina Legnani, who had earlier starred in the partial performance of the ballet mounted for the Tchaikovsky memorial. She turned *Swan Lake* into a technical showcase, recycling the thirty-two *fouetté* turns, triple pirouettes, and rapid runs en pointe with which she had earlier, in the role of Cinderella, mesmerized the St. Petersburg public. Odile's *fouetté* turns are singularly unmusical, but audiences love to clap and count along with them. Legnani made them seem effortless and fun. The teenage girls of the ballet school were inspired to imitate her, resulting in sprained ankles and knees. (Dizziness was the chief culprit: to perform *fouetté* turns, dancers need to "spot," to maintain a fixed point of focus on the audience while whipping around.) Legnani held her power in check as Odette, projecting a chaste ideal apart from the fluffing and preening of the other swans. Her back was expressive, her *bourrées* strings of pearls. But as the brazen Odile, she challenged Petipa's strictures and threatened protocol by performing encores (by imperial decree, three encores were the maximum permitted). Petipa did not resist, since, at the twilight of his career, his success depended on hers.

Legnani's role may have increased, but as in *Le corsaire* and *Don Quixote*, some of the smaller character dances in *Swan Lake* disappeared as the art of ballet evolved. Moreover, the *grand pas de deux* for the principals, which resolved their amorous intrigue, was moved up so that plot, expression, and technique all reached their climax at the same time. The grand *divertissement*, the group masquerade, became less important as attention shifted ever more toward the soloists, who executed their own *spécialités de la maison*, bringing something unexpected to their roles even if it meant breaking the dramatic frame. The changes allowed Legnani to include the thirty-two *fouetté* turns, and other "blinding effects" of her invention, in her seduction of Siegfried. "She was riveted to the floor," the critic Akim Volynsky enthused, "and without leaving it during her rotations she constantly faced the public with her joyfully radiant face, which showed absolutely no fatigue. According to the sense of the entire act, a she-devil is before us, who entices another woman's fiancé into her net."[110]

Legnani defined the role between 1895 and 1901, after which she retired from the Imperial Ballet of St. Petersburg to a villa on Lake Como. Following Legnani's farewell benefit, the part went to the sloe-eyed Matilda Kshesinskaya, a black swan capable of extreme malice before the idea of the black swan had even been devised.

Kshesinskaya was beloved by the public for exactly that which upset Petipa: her unruliness. She was also bewitching. Tchaikovsky purportedly told her that he would write a ballet for her, and otherwise sophisticated reviewers suffered memory lapses under her spell, claiming that she invented technical feats actually devised by her predecessors. "The *fouetté* is the apogee of Kshesinskaya's choreographic art," Volynsky recalled, forgetting all about his earlier thrill at Legnani's circus trick. He gleaned from Kshesinskaya's movements "an inner noise and murmuring, full of thunder, full of great and subtle ideas that are transmitted to the public and ignite it with unheard-of ecstasy."[111] There was no froufrou in her art, he insisted, and "for all the imperfection of the structure of her legs," she was "a great artistic figure of truly phenomenal power."[112] Legnani had been surpassed, at least in his eyes.

Kshesinskaya learned the alphabet of ballet with Ivanov (who loved his violin more than his pupils, she huffed) and then, as an adolescent, trained with bravura Italian dancers. She ascended through the ranks of the Imperial Theaters, frequently complaining about Petipa countermanding performance opportunities. She connived to dethrone her predecessor and rival, Legnani, and appropriated most of her repertoire, including Odette/Odile in *Swan Lake*. In her reminiscences, Kshesinskaya cites a critic to the effect that she had been crowned, like Legnani before her, the "prima ballerina assoluta" of the Imperial Theaters—suggesting, in her Russian balletic context, that she had gained "supreme" importance.[113]

This does not seem to be the case. Kshesinskaya joined the corps de ballet of the Imperial Ballet of St. Petersburg on June 1, 1890. She moved up to second then first coryphée, then from second to first dancer, and finally, on October 26, 1896, to ballerina— no prima, no assoluta. Throughout her career, exquisitely timed colds, fevers, and gastrointestinal inflammations got her out of roles she considered beneath her station. Thus she found herself accused of "interfering with the repertoire" and was forced to implore the intendant of the Imperial Theaters "not to rob me of ballets" when Legnani was hired as her replacement.[114] Ultimately both Kshesinskaya and Legnani danced the greatest roles of the time, from the clever Swanilda in *Coppélia* to the beautiful gypsy maiden Esmeralda in the ballet of the same name (Petipa's adaptation of Victor Hugo's *The Hunchback of Notre-Dame*), to Sleeping Beauty and, at their technical zenith, Odette/Odile in the 1895 setting of *Swan Lake*.

Whereas Legnani had Petipa to indulge her whims, however, Kshesinskaya had the imperial court. She enjoyed a three-year affair with the future Tsar Nicholas II, cavorting with him in the presence of grand dukes during his premarital period of "sanctioned waywardness."[115] She gave birth to a child of noble lineage. (Her son never knew his father, but current consensus points to Grand Duke Andrey, rather than Tsar Nicholas.) Before the inevitable bitter denouement of the relationships, Kshesinskaya relished a life of outrageous lavishness that the rank-and-file dancers of the Imperial Theaters, paid just enough to live in poverty, could never imagine. She dined on caviar and pineapple, vacationed in picturesque European villages, gambled, showed up late for the start of the ballet season, received a French golden palm award and a medal from the king of Persia (the same king who lost his mind over the shipwreck scene in *Le corsaire*), and decorated her St. Petersburg mansion in rare stone and wood. Its neoclassical main hall was big enough to host performances; beneath it, according to farfetched rumor, a secret tunnel led from the mansion to the official residence of the tsar, the Winter Palace, on the other side of the River Neva. Kshesinskaya hoarded diamonds and emeralds, but she had particular tastes and returned those gifts from the imperial collection she considered inadequate. She patiently explained in her reminiscences that the jewels habitually given to dancers on the day of their benefit performances lacked sparkle. She asked one of the grand dukes in her stable to raid the imperial collection for something special: "a magnificent brooch, a kind of serpent in diamonds coiled into rings and bearing in the middle a large cabochon-shaped sapphire."[116] She received it.

When told to perform in an eighteenth-century hoop skirt that she deemed unflattering, Kshesinskaya threw a temper tantrum in the offices of the Imperial Theaters. She was fined, but instead of relenting took her complaint to the tsar. The fine disappeared, the administrator responsible was reprimanded, and Kshesinskaya permitted to dance hoop-free.

The incident proved fateful for Petipa. He had built his career in St. Petersburg under Ivan Vsevolozhsky, the distinguished, long-serving intendant of the Imperial Theaters, but then had to withstand two of his successors. First came Sergey Volkonsky. He and Petipa put up with each other for the two years that Volkonsky served as intendant, from 1899 to 1901. Next to the position was Vladimir Telyakovsky, a former colonel in the Horse Guards who had been promoted from director of the Moscow Imperial Theaters to intendant in St. Petersburg. He saw in Petipa a frail relic long past the age of retirement. Petipa found himself alone and defenseless. Repertoire meetings were held without him; carriages failed to turn up at his house to take him to rehearsals. His last ballet flopped, and the one that he hoped to stage thereafter was canceled. In his diaries, Petipa blames old age for his inability to do anything about his situation. But he also blames Kshesinskaya.

She never lost her preposterous sense of entitlement—even after she had her son, her ankles swelled, and her joints began to ache. In 1904, just after turning thirty-one, she was named an "honored artist of the Imperial Theaters."[117] Two years later, the honored artist was reduced to enacting pathetic revenge on a ballerina who had been promoted above her by releasing live chickens on the stage as her rival performed.[118] Only in her fifties, long past her prime, did Kshesinskaya find some measure of self-awareness. By that time, she was no longer in Russia, and the Russia she knew no longer existed. The capital had moved from St. Petersburg to Moscow, and the Bolshoi had taken the place of the Mariyinsky as the theater privileged by the government.

ON MAY 14, 1896, Nicholas II took the throne. Whereas his grandfather, Alexander II, had been named tsar at the nadir of Russia's international standing, Nicholas assumed control of a thriving empire, rebuilt—like the Bolshoi itself—under the severely autocratic reign of Alexanders II and III. Yet Nicholas was not necessarily prepared to take power: In November 1894, his father died suddenly at age forty-nine. Nicholas was twenty-six and only recently engaged. His intimacies with Kshesinskaya were long over, at least for him. Her heart remained in grievous bondage throughout the coronation in Moscow. Less out of love than geopolitical considerations, Nicholas II had married Alix of Hesse, canonized Alexandra the Passion-Bearer a month after his father's death. By the time of the coronation, they had already had a daughter, Olga. Empress Alexandra cared little for operas and ballets, preferring to devote her time to the church (both the Lutheran Church of her upbringing and the Russian Orthodox Church she adopted) and affairs of state. She would bear a son, Alexei, but the child suffered from a little-understood blood-clotting defect, Hemophilia B, passed down to him from his great-grandmother, Queen Victoria of England. The slightest cut could cause him to bleed to death, and, at age eight, after stumbling in a boat, he almost did. The tsarina enlisted an unwashed Siberian mystic faith healer, Grigoriy Rasputin, in hopes of curing her son. Rasputin lingered at court for years and exerted, according to historical consensus, nefarious influence over the tsar, tsarina, and affairs of state during the First World War. Though prone to exposing himself in public and debauching noblewomen, there is no basis to the tales, traded on the streets of St. Petersburg, of his sexual conquest of the tsarina (a notorious, pseudo-pornographic cartoon to this effect was published on a broadsheet); nor did he cure Alexei's illness, of course. The mere presence of the fake monk at the court is thought to have been a catalyst for the end of autocratic rule in Russia. Monarchist assassins ensured that he himself did not live to see that end.

Kshesinskaya traveled from St. Petersburg to Moscow in 1896 to dance in the gala for Tsar Nicholas II on May 17 and appear in what she termed "normal performances" at the Bolshoi Theater. The coronation festivities included, per custom, a banquet for the dignitaries and a massive outdoor feast for the people, plus concerts, fireworks, an opera, and a ballet. The audience for the gala was pompous. Men in medals, ribbons, and uniforms sat in the parterre, and their nonreaction to her performance only increased Kshesinskaya's disquiet. "There I was, alone, torn by two conflicting feelings—my joy in sharing in the patriotic joy of all Russia," she recalled, "and the stifled, solitary cry of my love."[119] Following the now-traditional performance of the Moscow scenes from Glinka's opera *A Life for the Tsar*, the *pièce d'occasion* was Petipa's *The Pearl* (Zhemchuzhina), a one-act ballet narrating the Genie of the Earth's trip down to the ocean floor to abduct the White Pearl, the most precious, most perfect pearl of all, as an adornment for his crown. The dramatis personae also included the Russian export commodities that, in the subjugated territories of the Caucasus, abused laborers dug from the ground in dangerous conditions. (Their long shifts, miserable pay, lack of food, and premature deaths were nowhere represented in the performance.) Men danced dressed as pieces of gold, silver, bronze, and iron. The Italian Legnani took the role of the perfect pearl in a costume of flame and shell. Kshesinskaya appeared as one of the White Pearl's less perfect sisters, the Yellow Pearl, but not before the dowager empress tried to have her removed from the program to protect the chasteness of the coronation. She had reason to intervene. The ballet concluded with "a scene of semi-nude sea nymphs and sirens, looking out languorously as they bathe before an Adonis-like Triton." Somehow it was meant to illustrate the tsar's love for his "flawless, irresistible" wife.[120]

Nicholas's grandfather, Tsar Alexander II, had been crowned to fireworks celebrating his ascension and the opening of the newly rebuilt Bolshoi Theater. For the crowning of Nicholas, there were "hundreds of little electric lights"—emissaries from the spirit world, as Kshesinskaya imagined from her hotel room. The switch used to turn on the lights was hidden beneath a bouquet of flowers presented to the tsarina at the Kremlin Palace at sunset. It "gave a prearranged signal to the Moscow power station," the forsaken ballerina reported, after which "the illuminations started up everywhere. I tried to go and see this, but soon had to give up, for it was impossible to find a way through the enormous crowd which had invaded the streets. But I was able to admire the main part of the illuminations on the Palace of the Kremlin."[121] Like the hundreds of foreign correspondents on the scene, Kshesinskaya perhaps sensed the strange disjunction between the modern, electrified glitter, which also included "huge illuminated fountains," and Moscow's "jumbled medieval landscape." The excess was meant to ennoble the poor; hardship had never looked so good. The bedraggled commoners who queued to throw kopecks into collection plates acquired, in the opinion of Count Vladimir Lamzdorf, "an exalted halo of true dignity and majesty."[122]

But then disaster: the massive but underpoliced feast for the people organized northwest of Moscow in Khodïnskoye Field resulted in the deaths of more than thirteen hundred people in a stampede to secure a souvenir enamel goblet (rumored to contain a gold coin), along with sausage, gingerbread, and beer. People stumbled into the ditches that had been dug to channel the crowds toward the booths and were crushed. Yet the great loss of life merely "darkened" the festivities surrounding the coronation, according to the tsarina's personal valet, and did not, despite some hesitation within the tsar's inner circle, prevent Nicholas II from attending a splendid ball that same night.[123] It was a foolish decision and an ominous portent.

MOSCOW WAS A "stupid city," "a city in name only," and an "oversized playground for dogs," complained Pavel Pchelnikov, the director of the Moscow Imperial Theaters before and after the coronation of Tsar Nicholas II. He was an old-fashioned bureaucrat, the kind who would not allow performances to begin until he had taken his seat and signaled, with a certain tremor of his head or jingle of his medals, for the downbeat. His once malign neglect of the ballet grew benign as he filled his days with nonsense, prattling in official letters about everything other than his job. Pchelnikov wrote of acquiring a "two-wheeled bicycle" as a "good means of getting around for those who dislike walking," the change of light in autumn, his wife's flu, his daughter born out of wedlock, the shortage of seltzer water, and his pride in learning to type but his fear that overusing his Remington typewriter in his correspondence with the imperial court might insult those unready for the age of mechanical production.[124] He cared about his artists to the extent that he did not want to have to deliver bad news to them—on one occasion he requested sick leave, with pay, to get out of the task—and his foot-dragging kept some of them in their jobs.[125] His report on the suicide of a Bolshoi physician is beyond indifferent. (Pchelnikov had "the honor to inform" Vsevolozhsky that Alexander Zhivago, a doctor as well as a supernumerary, had "hanged himself in his apartment.")[126] Pchelnikov lauded Tchaikovsky's operas, especially *The Queen of Spades*, but said little about his ballets—or even ballets in general, excluding his handwringing over the expense of bringing Italian ballerinas to Moscow. He noted Tchaikovsky's passing as the end of an era, but shared no thoughts on what might come after.

By the time Pchelnikov semiretired in 1898, circumstances at the Bolshoi had changed for the better. The ballet was no longer in pitiful shape, no longer a victim of the financial constraints imposed by the court. The drastic cuts of the previous decade had improved the bottom line, and new investments were made. Tired, tacky décor was replaced, lighting and special effects upgraded. An invasion of Italian ballerinas had secured the financial success of Russian ballet productions at the Bolshoi while local talent was being groomed in the private theaters that had opened in Moscow. Sentiment shifted to the idea that the Bolshoi Ballet might one day become fashionable, glamorous enough for visiting dignitaries like Franz Ferdinand. The Bolshoi nurtured the dancers Lidiya Geyten, Lyubov Roslavleva, Adelina Giuri (a Milan-born, Moscow-trained dancer of "crystalline brilliance" and "flawless lines"), and Ekaterina Geltser, and would later offer up Vasiliy Tikhomirov, Mikhaíl Mordkin, and even the Ballets Russes artist Léonide Massine.[127]

The ballet master Alexei Bogdanov might have lacked Petipa's brilliance, but he possessed a certain ribald showmanship, as did his immediate successors: the Spanish ballet master José Méndez, who devised the fashionable exotic *ballet-féerie India*, and Ivan Clustine, who invented the unfashionable exotic ballet *Stars* (Zvyozdï), to a scenario by the Bolshoi Theater machinist Valts. Clustine was a decorous individual who presented himself somewhat above his merit; he referred to himself in his dealings with the *kontora* not as an artist with the theater but as one of its most beautiful attractions.[128] As a reflection of his refined sensibilities, his ballet was set during the time of Louis XIV and relied on old-fashioned group dances. Clustine took the lead role, that of a grandee who abandons the beautiful Claremonde (danced by Giuri) upon falling in love with the Morning Star, Venus (danced by Roslavleva). Pantomime interrupts the reveries: the grandee is challenged to a duel by Claremonde's brother, then wounded, and then returned to his forgiving bride.

Pchelnikov signed the contracts for these performances before leaving the Bolshoi Theater to become a censor in the private theaters. His successor as director of the Moscow Imperial Theaters, Telyakovsky, discovered a "peaceful and calm" but ultimately boring "patriarchal ambiance" in the Bolshoi Ballet at the time of his appointment. "There was no excitement, no rows or incidents, people did not even fight hard for certain positions in the company since the members of the troupe were kind, charming and modest, and significantly, in Moscow, the St. Petersburg breed of loud and expansive balletomanes was unknown."[129] Telyakovsky stirred things up in Moscow by appointing a young ballet master of promise to the Bolshoi, Alexander Gorsky. In so doing, he secured the future of the Bolshoi Ballet—and thus an essential tradition and repertoire.

BORN IN 1871, GORSKY was destined for a life no longer than Tchaikovsky's. He was frail and often infirm as a child. When he was eight years old, his father, a bookkeeper, enrolled him in the Commercial School in St. Petersburg, but his sister's success as a student at the St. Petersburg Ballet School led her brother to audition and enroll. Gorsky's father paid for his tuition the first year, after which the aspiring dancer received a scholarship on merit. His first trip to Moscow came in 1896, where he joined the lovelorn Kshesinskaya on the stage to celebrate the coronation of Tsar Nicholas II. He appeared as a piece of bronze, one of the elements doing battle on behalf of the Genie of the Earth against the King of the Corals and the forces of the sea. On June 1, 1889, Petipa adopted Gorsky into the corps de ballet at the Mariyinsky, where he danced as Prince Fortuné in *The Sleeping Beauty* and in the Chinese dance of *The Nutcracker*. Through Petipa, he fell into the circle of Vladimir Stepanov, inventor of a choreographic notation system codified in *L'alphabet des mouvements du corps humain* (Alphabet of movements of the human body, 1892). In 1896, Gorsky used the Stepanov system to notate Petipa's *The Sleeping Beauty*. Since he received no financial support from the Imperial Theaters for the project, he had to pay his assistants out of pocket. He then used the notation during the nine days and seventeen rehearsals it took him to stage the ballet at the Bolshoi in 1898. There were problems, but his effort flabbergasted the ballet master at the time, Clustine, and Gorsky declined an invitation to become first soloist at the Mariyinsky in order to serve as Bolshoi *régisseur*.

He had little experience as a choreographer and no real interest in being one until he began to consort with a group of artists— furniture and ceramics makers, silk weavers, easel painters, and the writer Chekhov—who frequented the estate of the industrialist and arts enthusiast Savva Mamontov. In time, they were joined even by an archeologist, and together developed a neonationalist, folk-fantastic style that fueled Gorsky's creative imagination. He began to search for a more Muscovite ballet aesthetic, and found it in the original Bolshoi Theater version of *Don Quixote* from 1869. There the gap between how Russian peasants and French courtiers danced was narrowed. Gorsky staged a naturalistic version of *Don Quixote* at the Bolshoi Theater on December 6, 1900.

The props for Gorsky's *Don Quixote* came from St. Petersburg, and dozens of pages of official paper were devoted to the transport of the reservoirs for the fountain, arrows, quivers, the spider, the black iron shield, and the essential bridle and saddle for the donkey/horse. The tutus also came from St. Petersburg, though the dancers in Moscow, possessing a slightly different choreographic vocabulary, referred to them not as *tyuniki* but as *pachki*. The Bolshoi sets were altogether different, however, from those used in the north. The Mamontov-sponsored designers Alexander Golovin and Konstanin Korovin saturated the Bolshoi stage with color, transporting the title character past his old jokes and creaky gestures into a fresher realm of pastel green, blue, and pink. Gorsky sought a real-life look and feel, with the actions motivated by dramatic concerns instead of being fitted into geometrical shapes, the ideal under Petipa in his dotage, if not his youth. The new *Don Quixote* privileged crowd scenes, hubbub, over tight-knit ensembles. The standard Petipa formula remained in place: "plot in the first act, the vision scene for the female corps de ballet and soloists—where the men trespass only in their dreams—and, finally, a marriage celebration."[130] But in Gorsky's hands, as in those of his twentieth-century successors at the Bolshoi, Moscow's balletic "exuberance" supplanted St. Petersburg's balletic "academicism."[131]

The production sparked a heated debate in the press and sent Petipa, the original choreographer, into hysterics. (Gorsky is one of the "ignoramuses" referred to in Petipa's memoirs.) This *Don Quixote* offended, and the ancien régime fought back in the pages of

Peterburgskaya gazeta, the mouthpiece of Petipa's balletomane supporters. Gorsky was accused of sacrificing dance to the other arts and dogged with accusations of plagiarism—"dirty hands"—and bad taste in the changes he imposed on the music. He was called a "decadent" and a "Moscow schismatic" who took his best ideas from vaudevilles and singing cafés (*cafés chantant*).[132] Elsewhere, he was told that he had "destroyed the centuries-old traditions of the art of ballet," "an art no less ancient than love." To this, he responded that "we know nothing about ancient dances, excluding the dozen or so wondrous poses on which our art was built—by us."[133]

Although the drubbing in the press rattled him, it did not cause him to deviate from the course he had set. His style attracted a ballet-averse public to the Bolshoi; the theater went from being typically half full or less to sold-out. Beyond attracting audiences, *Don Quixote* earned Gorsky critical support among the younger dancers of the Bolshoi, whom he lectured in fatherly fashion on his vision for the free-flowing future of ballet as represented by the enduringly popular variation that he created for Kitri and her fluttering fan in the final act.

In 1901, Gorsky staged *Swan Lake*, preserving much of Petipa and Ivanov's version while imposing his own thoughts. It would change further, both inside and outside of Russia, sometimes owing to budget problems or an acute shortage of swans or swan costumes, at other times to more serious political considerations. The Soviets abolished both the mysticism of the ballet and its tragic ending. A close with a silver lining was devised, then taken out, then put back in. The ballet provided rich material for feminist critiques and Freudian analysis, but it has also been taken to be a parable about ballet itself—the softness of its materials, its abused, fragile performers, the fact that the ballerina dies if she fails to break free, if she adheres to the rhythms of the score rather than generating her own, if she repeats phrases rather than developing them. Ballet serves to define the beautiful, the youthful, and the divine and so suffers more than the other arts from the delusion of an original ideal, the contention that the first version, however audiences may have reacted to it, must be the best.

There are no definable versions, however, and no ideal to be found, much less preserved. Certainly the merits of *Swan Lake* cannot be based on the awkward Reisinger-Tchaikovsky collaboration of 1877. The ballet became famous only after several transpositions: first at the Bolshoi in Moscow and the Mariyinsky in St. Petersburg, then everywhere abroad. That which goes by the title *Swan Lake* in the world's theaters is an estranged and abstracted version of what was imagined by Petipa and Ivanov and Gorsky; Tchaikovsky and Minkus and Drigo; Karpakova, Sobeshchanskaya, Legnani, and Kshesinskaya. The dancers retired as the heroines of an art that sought their destruction, one that requires new bodies in order to perpetuate itself.

Gorsky's efforts to transform the art exacerbated the anemia, attacks of nerves, and heart problems that had plagued him since childhood. He continued to emphasize naturalism—in one instance swapping out tutus and pointe shoes for robes and sandals. His less fanciful, more muscular style came to define the dancing at the Bolshoi, which finally, by the end of the nineteenth century, stood as a solid theater with a notable past and promising future. The series of coronations—three within forty years—had put Moscow and the Bolshoi in the spotlight as the city and the stage hosted nobility from St. Petersburg and around the world. The theater itself now had actual spotlights, its lighting and equipment having been modernized along with the ballet technique and training. Some of the greatest dancers and dances of the century were nurtured at the Bolshoi in the years after 1883, when it was spared from being shuttered. By the turn of the twentieth century, the Bolshoi could lay just claim to its own tradition, apart from St. Petersburg and from Europe.

When Petipa died in 1910, Gorsky became the most important choreographer in Russia. He had already outgrown the Stepanov system of dance notation as a way of recording and preserving movement. The musical symbols at its basis proved inadequate for denoting physical space. As an alternative, Gorsky began to photograph his dancers for the purpose of assessing precision in their poses. His interest in the camera became an obsession as he filled an album with "choreographic photo-etudes." He departed from the "neutral" photographic conventions of the day by poeticizing facial expressions in subtle interplays of light, in luminous impressions.[134] The images are blurred, ghostly, preserving the traces of ephemeral gestures.

Gorsky became the most important choreographer in imperial Russia, tsarist Russia. There followed the Revolution of 1917. The choreographer to whom he is most often (and invidiously) compared, Michel Fokine, left his home base in St. Petersburg to join the Ballets Russes in Paris. One of the grandchildren of the Bolshoi Theater architect Alberto Cavos, Alexandre Benois, provided designs and costumes for the expat Paris troupe. Gorsky traveled too, but remained attached to Moscow. He died, bearded and ragged, in a sanatorium in 1924. He is remembered less as a successful reformer than as an icon of the glorious Bolshoi Theater—as newly imagined by the Soviets.

· 5 ·

AFTER
THE BOLSHEVIKS

THREE YEARS INTO World War I, the Russian Empire collapsed. It would be reconstituted under the control of the Soviets
rather than the emperors and empresses of the House of Romanov. Tsar Nicholas II surrendered power on March 2, 1917, under
pressure from the people as well as his advisers. His abdication
came after a decade of strikes in the cities, havoc throughout the
countryside, disasters on land and sea (in the Russo-Japanese War),
shortages of food and fuel, and a program of anti-Jewish pogroms.
In 1905, the tsar had reluctantly decreed a parliament into existence, but the Duma, as it was known, did nothing to quell the
unrest. Marius Petipa recalled the most ominous of the pre-1917
revolts, Bloody Sunday, in his memoirs, complaining, in declining
health, about the inconveniences it caused.[1] The Russian Revolution that followed was, in truth, a coup d'état in two phases: The

first took place from February 23 to 27, 1917, and led to the establishment of an ineffective, unelected provisional government; the
second, on October 25 and 26, 1917, brought to power a band of
socialist zealots under the spell of Vladimir Lenin, an anti-tsarist
political activist from the city of Simbirsk, on the Volga River. (His
real surname was Ulyanov, and Simbirsk would one day be called
Ulyanovsk. He adopted "Lenin" as his insurrectionist moniker
after spending time in a tsarist prison on the Lena River.) Lenin
served as the ideological arbiter of the hardline Bolshevik (meaning
majority) faction of the Russian Socialist-Democratic Labor Party.
His group was fanatical. In its version of communism, there was to
be no intermediate, bourgeois phase in the transformation of Russia into a socialist state. Lenin's pseudo-Marxist political posturing
had no practical basis. It was a utopian fantasy, and like all such
imaginings, destined for tragedy. He and his followers clung to a
belief in the inevitable, dialectical-materialist triumph of socialism
over all other forms of political thought while promising justice to
the presumed victims of the rotten, decadent, autocratic system.

The Great War, the abdication of Tsar Nicholas II, the formation of a provisional government, the rise of regional socialist parties, divisions among the Bolsheviks, their antipodal Mensheviks,
and the Left Socialist Revolutionaries between them—together,
these forces spread chaos across the Russian Empire. Lenin could
not rein in what he had unleashed but managed to exploit the power
vacuum to his advantage. Having sown disorder, he and his accomplices presented themselves as the sole possible solution. Lenin
justified his monstrous achievement with impressive rhetoric, but
when words failed and he faced being shunted aside or strung up,
he turned ruthless, ordering his agents to liquidate real and imagined counterrevolutionaries along with the anarchists, including released prisoners, who had occupied Moscow's great houses

during the tumult. "The filth was indescribable," a British agent, Bruce Lockhart, said of one of the mansions after the routing of a group of anarchists, a political force much feared by Lenin. "Broken bottles littered the floors, the magnificent ceilings were perforated with bullet-holes. Wine stains and human excrement blotched the Aubusson carpets. Priceless pictures had been slashed to strips." The anarchists had been hosting an orgy, Lockhart concluded, unpoetically. "The long table which had supported the feast had been overturned, and broken plates, glasses, champagne bottles, made unsavoury islands in a pool of blood and spilt wine. On the floor lay a young woman, face downwards," a "prostitutka" with a bullet hole in her neck.[2]

One man took to the task of liquidating the opposition with exceptional ruthlessness. Ioseb Besarionis Dze Jugashvili, a Georgian-born disciple of Marxist-Leninist politics who spent his boyhood in religious schools and his youth in tsarist prison, is better known by his adopted moniker, Joseph Stalin.

After the Russian Empire had unraveled at the edges and collapsed at the center, Lenin became its leader. The country lay in ruin. Factories and farms ceased operation in 1917. The banks failed, along with the transport system. Towns and cities lost contact with one another. Out of desperation, Lenin encouraged the surrender of Russian territory to the Germans, French, and British, then simply hoped for their eventual, exhausted withdrawal. But the end of the Great War coincided with the start of a civil war that pitted, generally and reductively speaking, anti-Bolshevik "Whites" against pro-Bolshevik "Reds." (The color scheme refers to the Jacobins and the Socialists in the French Revolution.) The essential function of Lenin's barely functioning government was to confiscate fuel and food supplies from foreign armies and the anti-Bolsheviks. Yet soon it began to turn against its own. The epithet "enemies of the people" was applied to those who resisted sacrificing their belongings, properties, and lives to the regime.

Under the threat of a German invasion of Petrograd (as St. Petersburg was renamed during the First World War) in March of 1918, Lenin, his wife, his guard, and his inner Bolshevik circle relocated to Moscow. Street fighting, shortages, and unusual cold had reduced life in the city to survival. Yet for political and practical reasons, Moscow became the capital of Soviet Russia and, after 1922, of the Soviet Union. (The term "Soviet" derives from a word for council, as in the councils of workers and soldiers that came into being in the run-up to the revolution and had undergirded the provisional government after the abdication of the tsar. Lenin brought these groups into his fold under the slogan "all power to the Soviets.") The Bolsheviks took over the gilded offices and apartments of the Kremlin, which a pro-Bolshevik militia had confiscated in November 1917 from imperial government officials. They also crowded into the opulent Metropole and National Hotels as well as the sequestered mansions of noblemen. The Cheka, the all-powerful political police established by Lenin in December of 1917, established its headquarters in the offices of a former insurance firm. Its mission was quashing resistance.

An obvious target was Tsar Nicholas II. On the night of July 16, 1918, he and the tsarina, their son and four daughters, their cook, doctor, valet, and their pet spaniel were led into the cellar of a merchant's house in Ekaterinburg. The tsarina asked for a chair; two were brought in. Family members were arranged in rows as if to have their picture taken, and then, after a single sentence decreeing their death was read aloud, they and the others were executed by a twelve-member firing squad. The bullets careened off of the chests of the girls, who had sewn diamonds into their clothes for safekeeping. Bayonets and rifle butts finished the job. The corpses were loaded onto a truck and driven into a forest, stripped naked, doused in acid to disguise their identities, soaked in gasoline, lit on fire, and buried in a shallow grave. Lenin learned of the killing in his Kremlin office, marking the report "Received. Lenin."[3]

Through it all, the Bolshoi Theater, an opulent symbol of the tsarist empire and host in 1896 of the murdered emperor's coronation gala, stood in place across from the Metropole Hotel and close to the Kremlin. The composer Sergey Rachmaninoff, who left Russia for good in 1917, departing Petrograd for Helsinki on an open sled, recalled the theater's imperial twilight. He had conducted at the Bolshoi for a couple of seasons and gilded his memory of the experience, noting the beauty of the annual concerts for veterans, the "fantastic" staging of Glinka's *A Life for the Tsar* (the clinking of the spurs worn by the Polish dancers drowned out the orchestra, he quipped), and the cat that wandered onto the stage to take in an aria sung by Feodor Chaliapin before a packed house.[4]

The cat stayed, but Rachmaninoff left, slamming the door "noisily" behind him as he departed, in the midst of conflicts with the musicians and the administration of the Bolshoi.[5] He mentioned none of that in his golden recollections—an acknowledgment of sorts that his challenges were trivial compared to what his successors confronted after the revolution.

The Bolshoi itself suffered only modest damage in 1917: a few windows were smashed, some cash stolen from a desk. One of the younger dancers, Anastasia Abramova, made it seem as though the coup had merely disrupted her schedule, telling the *New York Times* that "Oh, yes, the revolution was terrible—it interrupted the work of the ballet school three whole weeks." Abramova had to miss class a few days. So much for "one of the greatest national convulsions history ever recorded."[6]

The Bolsheviks made the Bolshoi an essential part of their government, both in an effort to cleanse it of imperial associations and because they needed the space for political meetings. Lenin took the stage to explain, in his 1918 constitution, how the "Rights of the Working and Exploited People" were to be defined and defended.[7] The theater hosted the biannual gatherings of the All-Russian Congress of Soviets, the chief governmental organ of the Russian Soviet Federative Socialist Republic (RSFSR), whose members were elected by regional councils (soviets) of people's deputies. The executive committee of the congress, headed by Lenin, directed the affairs of government and defined the responsibilities of the people's commissars, who ran the ministries. Lenin tamed the congress, purging his opponents from the membership.

The most serious and fearless among his foes was Mariya Spiridonova, who had cut her teeth as a defender of the working people by pumping five bullets into the body of a peasant-abusing provincial councilor in 1905. Her punishment included beatings, rape, and a long jail term. ("Swearing terribly," she recalled of her Cossack interrogators, "they would beat my naked body with their whips and say, 'Come now, my fine young lady, give us a stirring speech!'")[8] Spiridonova's political organization, the Left Socialist Revolutionaries, had fallen out with the Bolsheviks after Lenin capitulated to the Germans. In an effort to scuttle the peace treaty, Spiridonova arranged the murder of a high-ranking German official in Moscow. On July 5, 1918, a grenade exploded in the upper tiers of the Bolshoi during the fifth meeting of the All-Russian Congress of Soviets. According to the British agent Lockhart, who had been attending the congress with dozens of other prying foreigners, the grenade exploded by accident, having been "dropped" by a "careless sentry." Knowing that the theater was ringed by troops and the doors barred, another British agent, along with a French one, tore up and swallowed the secret papers in their possession. Other potentially incriminating items were "shoved down the lining of the seat cushions." "The situation was too tense for us to appreciate its comic side," Lockhart added.[9]

The Left Socialist Revolutionaries were subsequently outlawed by Lenin as a political organization. Later Stalin would have Spiridonova, the onetime heroine of the socialist cause, arrested and executed.

THE ABDICATION OF the tsar and the formation of the provisional government prompted an immediate reorganization of the Bolshoi as a state enterprise, ending its existence as an imperial theater but preserving the imperial repertoire. The nineteenth-century opera *Eugene Onegin* was to be staged in March of 1917, but on March 1, the schedule for the theater announced "no rehearsal on account of revolution." The next day, another notice: "bloodless revolution, performance cancelled."[10] The Bolshoi sputtered back to life, concluding the season with the comic ballet *La fille mal gardée* (The wayward daughter) before a largely empty hall.[11] *Don Quixote* was staged during this period, likewise *Le corsaire* and, for the opening of the 1917–18 season, *The Sleeping Beauty*. During the Bolshevik conquest of Petrograd on October 25–26, the Bolshoi performed Alexander Gorsky's version of *La bayadère*, a decadent imperialist ballet with a "slow-beating pulse" that defied the times—though, politics aside, the colors were glorious and the ensembles liberated, breaking through the temporal and spatial frames Petipa had once imposed on them.[12] Rimsky-Korsakov's fairy-tale opera *Kashchey the Deathless* joined Tchaikovsky's *Iolanta* on a double bill.

The revolution would neither be danced nor sung in the theater for many years. Yet there was one balletic nod to the ongoing events, which came at the order of the commissar of the state theaters. A tableau vivant titled *Liberated Russia* (Osvobozhdennaya Rossiya) was stitched together by Gorsky, who remained ballet master at the Bolshoi until the year of Lenin's death, 1924. Russian cultural heroes were celebrated—especially those who had run afoul of the imperial censors or, even better, had done time in tsarist prison. Gogol, Lermontov, and Pushkin were depicted onstage, likewise Dostoyevsky, whose semiautobiographical novel *The House of the Dead* recalls his four-year stint in a Siberian labor camp, the sick minds of the guards and his fellow convicts, and the brutalities everyone suffered. Actors portrayed the Russian nationalist composers Mussorgsky and Rimsky-Korsakov, even performing a group sing-along with laborers, peasants, sailors, students, soldiers, and revolutionaries. A plainly attired figure of the motherland held up her broken shackles to the strains of the French insurrectionist anthem "La Marseillaise."

The March 13, 1917, performance also included Alexander Gretchaninoff's setting of "Long Live Free Russia!" (Da zdravstvuet Rossiya, svobodnaya strana!), a poem by Russian symbolist Konstantin Balmont. The magazine *Iskrï* (Sparks) noted "the tears in the eyes" of the audience.[13] Gretchaninoff penned his hymn in half an hour and donated the proceeds from the printed edition to "liberated political prisoners."[14] In 1925, hardship forced him to immigrate to Paris. Balmont had already left five years earlier. Gorsky, stuck in Moscow, would find himself between two stools, castigated as too eclectically "left" by the defenders of the imperial tradition and as too stagnantly "right" by those who sought the reconstruction of ballet along new, proletarian lines.[15] The Bolshoi was, Gorsky complained, "a stone box with chaos inside."[16] In the spring of 1918, "severe neurasthenia, accompanied by insomnia, frequent headaches, and weakening of the heart" forced him to take a leave of absence from the Bolshoi.[17] Still, his contract as ballet master continued to be renewed. Gorsky had to straddle past and present, performing his versions of the imperial repertoire while also sanctioning productions of modernist ballets by choreographer Michel Fokine and composer Igor Stravinsky that had been performed in Paris by an émigré company, the Ballets Russes. Gorsky deemed the cultural trends of the early 1920s—including Nikolay Foregger's machine dances, the ballet-gymnastic hybrids at the Sokol sports clubs, and the erotic night bazaars—too radical. Although he loosened tradition, he did not want to do away with it. Instead he sought, through ethnographic realism, to revitalize the Russian ballet heritage. Cultural revolutionaries ridiculed him in the immediate aftermath of the coup, but his approach ultimately helped rescue the Bolshoi Ballet. It survived as a Soviet institution thanks first to the ideological redecoration of the classics, then to the commissioning of grand new ballets on Soviet themes. The Bolshoi would not have lasted as a proletarian cabaret, which is how the radicals reimagined it—and, ironically perhaps, as it had been at the time of its founding.

In 1917, the noblemen who ran the *kontora* of the Moscow Imperial Theaters disappeared. One of the last, Sergey Obukhov, took a well-timed vacation that summer, never to return. The *kontora* was searched by the Bolsheviks, and peccadillos were revealed. A hidden passageway was discovered in the loge reserved for "balletomanes of rank." It led through a corridor to a peephole, disguised as a vent, through which men of means could watch the ballerinas putting on their makeup (the dressing room was elsewhere). Investigators felt compelled to confirm that the peephole offered such pleasures, so they gazed through it during an actual performance.[18] There was nothing more to see, however, once performances began to be canceled and replaced by political speeches accompanied by renditions of "La Marseillaise."

To run the Bolshoi, the provisional government chose an opera singer, the lyric tenor Leonid Sobinov. At first there was nothing for him to run. He railed against the political takeover of the theater. "As the elected manager of the theater," Sobinov declared, "I protest its fate being seized by irresponsible hands." The hands in question belonged to the revolutionaries in Petrograd, who struggled to manage the departments and institutions formerly run by the Ministry of the Imperial Court. "Let them deal with the equerries [the *konyushennoye vedomstvo*, or Office of the Master of the Horse], the wine-making estates, and the plant that makes playing cards," he insisted, "but let them leave the theater alone."[19] The lesser entertainments of horse riding, drinking, and gambling were one thing, he seemed to be saying, ballet and opera quite another. Exasperated, Sobinov submitted his resignation, but since no one had the mandate to accept it, he remained on the job.

He traveled to Petrograd and there received guidelines from the provisional government for restructuring. In June 1917, the Bolshoi became an autonomous institution, administered by a council that included the opera and ballet directors, their conductors, the choirmaster, four soloists (two from the opera, one each from the ballet and choir), and members of the technical and design crew—nineteen in all. The council sent a representative to the joint committee of Moscow's public and social services unions. The joint committee supported the provisional government but dreaded and despised the Bolsheviks, interpreting the events of that October in apocalyptic terms.

On October 27, the night after the coup d'état, the opera *Lakmé* was performed. Afterward the theater closed its doors. The November 10 meeting of the joint committee predicted, accurately, "searches, arrests, and violence," the beginning of a "long civil war," the "loss of free speech, a free press, and freedom to assemble," and the hastening of Russia's "economic and financial implosion."[20] The meeting concluded with the public services union resolving not to recognize the Bolshevik takeover. The Bolshoi's staff and artists debated whether the best form of resistance to the "invaders" and the "orders and actions of the Bolsheviks" was "to go on strike" or, "on the contrary, to open the theater."[21]

On November 17, the artists and staff decided that their work needed to continue, so there were no acts of "sabotage," no "arrests."[22] The theater reopened after a three-and-a-half-week hiatus with *Aida*, the grandest of grand operas. There was just one incident, a telling one, after it was announced that members of Mossovet (Moscow Soviet of People's Deputies, the equivalent to city hall) would be using the former tsar's loge. Hecklers began hurling homemade projectiles into the loge from the floor. Soldiers were summoned, the exits blocked, documents checked, and people searched. Revolvers and Finnish knives were found on the "battlefield" of the stalls.[23] The performance in the seats overshadowed events onstage, as pro- and (chiefly) anti-Leninist factions clashed. The theater's agitprop potential had been unleashed, albeit, in this instance, to the detriment of the Bolsheviks.

The theater soon fell under the control of a jocular Swiss-educated Marxist named Anatoliy Lunacharsky. ("His features are not attractive," one of his petitioners noted, "and he speaks with a slight burr, as children do.")[24] He was involved in the Comintern, nickname of the Communist International, reaching out to leftist organizations in France. As the People's Commissar for Enlightenment, Lunacharsky toiled to keep the Bolshoi and other state theaters open; he signed orders ensuring the distribution of ration cards to artists and the procurement of footwear for ballet dancers. Between 1917 and 1919, the cost of silk and leather for ballet slippers grew from 6 rubles and 50 kopecks per pair to 250 rubles. The Bolshoi Ballet used about 500 pairs a season but, after 1917, had no choice but to economize, leaving the dancers' shoes and feet in tatters. Shoe theft became a serious problem. The difficulties obtaining ballet shoes, as discussed by the fitters and stitchers and Lunacharsky's minions, absorbed thirty-four single-spaced pages.

Under the Bolsheviks, the volume of paperwork generated by the Bolshoi Theater, and the government in general, massively increased. The former *kontora* of the Moscow Imperial Theaters was filled with functionaries who much preferred to sit in meetings and debate protocols than shiver in their flats or, as the cause of freedom forced them to do, march in the streets. Hundreds of pages were required to name and re-rename Cavos's architectural marvel from the State Academic Theater of Opera and Ballet in 1919, to the State Academic Bolshoi Theater in 1930. Deliberations continued even when conditions had deteriorated to the point that the operations of the theater had to be suspended, perhaps for good.

The revolution found its way into the theater a year after the fact, on November 7, 1918, when the Bolshoi hosted a gala celebrating the first anniversary of the October Revolution. (The "October" Revolution occurred in November according to the new, Gregorian calendar, adopted on Lenin's orders.) The theater threw open its doors to the sons and daughters of the working people, as well as commissars, deputies, delegates, and lesser functionaries. The Russian version of the French socialist anthem "L'Internationale" was performed, followed by Alexander Scriabin's visionary 1910 score, *Prometheus: The Poem of Fire*. Hallucinogenic in conception, it calls for an enormous orchestra, solo piano, organ, a wordless chorus (representing the primordial cries of transformed man), and an electronic colored-light instrument. The music is orgiastic, ultra-dissonant, and, as reviewers in 1918 fancied, futuristic. There followed the popular assembly (*veche*) scene from Rimsky-Korsakov's opera *The Maid of Pskov*, whose plot highlights the repressiveness of Tsar Ivan (Ivan the Terrible). He torches the rebellious city of Novgorod but leaves the rebellious city of Pskov in peace, because its most fetching maid, Olga, turns out to be his long-lost daughter. She is shot, tragically, and dies in her father's arms. The long evening concluded with a ballet by Gorsky to music by Glazunov. Titled *Stenka Razin*, it concerns a Cossack insurrectionist who, in real life, killed, raped, looted, and stoked peasant unrest in the lawless southern borderlands of the Russian Empire in the 1660s. For his all-around nastiness, which Alexander Glazunov's music tries very hard to ignore, the rebel was quartered on Red Square in Moscow. The Bolsheviks embraced him as one of their own. The ballet version of his exploits was inglorious, as weirdly benign as the music, with dancers dressed in costumes recycled from the opera. Notably, though, it marked a turn away from balletic classicism and offered a hint of something new: a ballet whose hero is reflected in, and defined by, the collective. The program was repeated on November 12, as part of the sixth meeting of the All-Russian Congress of Soviets.

The anticipation of a fresh start after breaking from the court patronage system, and the fantasy of democratic elections, ceded to disillusionment. For the ballet and opera, the loss was very real. The records of the Moscow Imperial Theaters had been stashed for safekeeping in the Troitsk Tower of the Kremlin, which was damaged during the shooting in October of 1917. The papers that survived ended up being divided between the Russian State Archive of Ancient Acts and the Russian State Archive of Literature and Art—without any logical organization. The records of Petipa's time at the Bolshoi were likewise spoiled. Soldiers squatted in his Moscow apartment, and when his daughter Nadezhda returned, she faced a nightmare: "Everything was turned out of the cupboards and chests. Papers, letters, documents, Marius Ivanovich's entire archive was scattered on the floor, trod and laid upon, crushed and torn."[25] The official records, those that were not kept in the apartment, might have been culled by the Soviets owing to their tainted associations with the decadent imperial era.[26]

The Bolshoi itself was stained as an emblem of imperial power, and thus the new government in 1917 debated its continued existence both in private and in public. An article asked the question "Should the Bolshoi Exist?"[27] The answer provided in follow-up publications was no, not at all, but closing the theater, it was argued, might be more expensive than keeping it open. Pensions would need to be paid, and the building itself maintained to prevent vandalism. But the question kept coming up, both from financial and ideological perspectives, especially during the crisis of 1918–19. As Vladimir Galkin, the commissar overseeing Moscow's grade schools, asked during a meeting, "Whose aesthetic interests have our theaters been serving up to now? . . . *Carmen, Traviata, Eugene Onegin*—these are all bourgeois operas. Nothing for the people, laborers, the Red Army." He argued that "the scaffolds of the Bolshoi Theater would be better serving agitation and propaganda." And given the shortages of fuel that winter, he wondered, pointedly, "Are we still of the mind to keep allowing precious fuel to be thrown into the voracious furnaces of the Moscow State Theaters, tickling the nerves of diamond-clad baronesses, while depriving heating stoves of the wood that could save hundreds of laborers from illness and death?"[28]

The People's Commissar for Enlightenment, Lunacharsky, missed the meeting, leaving no one to defend the Bolshoi from Galkin's snarling attack. Lenin put the matter to a vote, but not before deadpanning, "To me, it seems that comrade Galkin has a somewhat naïve conception of the theater's role and significance. We need it less for propaganda than to give rest to our workers at the end of the day. And it's too early yet to put the bourgeois artistic heritage in an archive."[29] Lenin had spoken. The vote went against Galkin.

There remained the question of closing the long-neglected, underfunded ballet school, or at least ending the subsidies for room and board. The school had survived the revolution, and was shuttered, as Anastasia Abramova remarked, for just a few days during the shooting. The ballet committee demanded that it remain open to prevent the stars of the future leaving the country and ending up in the service of foreigners. The director of the (Imperial) Theater College, of which the ballet school remained a part, insisted on preserving the pre-1917 academic curriculum, which included lessons in "the Holy Gospel in Old Slavonic, God's laws, and moralistic spiritual readings"—all anathema to Marxism.[30] The financial problems, the director's recalcitrance, and freezing temperatures in the classrooms forced the school to close through the winter of 1918–19. A committee was appointed to overhaul the curriculum according to the new political realities. It proposed abolishing the Table of Ranks for dancers, the aristocratic system that placed the corps de ballet, akin to working-class dancers, at the bottom. The coryphées, the bourgeoisie, rested in the middle, and the soloists sat at the top as the noble elite. Character dancing would be emphasized, likewise athleticism, "physical culture." The school would also, in time, privilege the teaching of regional dances. Some of these dances purported to be authentic, imported from the campfires of the provinces, but most of them were abstracted and estranged from their sources, made more folk-like than the folk. Fantasy was better than the real thing, and so under Stalin, dancers and singers from Moscow would be sent to the provinces to teach the locals their own eccentric traditions. Thus in terms of how they sang and danced, the peoples of Armenia, Azerbaijan, Georgia, Uzbekistan, and the other Soviet republics would be made into caricatures of themselves.

The council governing the Bolshoi Theater proved inept. Basic administrative questions about benefits, leaves, and performances in other venues were left unanswered. It was dissolved, only to be replaced by another, equally ineffective council. Eventually Lunacharsky recognized the need to bring order to the Bolshoi—both for his own sake, as Lenin's overworked culture and education minister, and for the Bolshevik cause. In 1919, he named a new director of the Bolshoi, the loyal Bolshevik functionary Elena Konstantinovna Malinovskaya (1875–1942). Stern, stout, and flush-faced from nicotine, she knew nothing of culture besides tutoring the basics and helping her husband, an architect, in building a "People's House" to offer free lectures and public concerts in her hometown of Nizhniy Novgorod. To her credit, she never pretended to know, and so she tried, in her duties at the Bolshoi, "to let the dancers dance as they like," even when doing so resulted in the coarsening and cheapening of time-honored solos.[31]

Her political climb began in 1905, when she joined the Russian Social Democratic Workers' Party (of which Lenin's Bolsheviks were a faction) and began involving herself in agitprop activities. Moving to Moscow landed her a position in the cultural-enlightenment division of Mossovet. She lived in the building where she worked, spending long hours at a desk concealed by telephones, never raised her voice (even when shouted at), and demonstrated unsmiling trustworthiness in her duties. A caricature captures her grimace along with the fashion for silk and felt hats in the early 1920s; the caption reads, "Today she's gloomy."[32]

The Bolshoi's older artists resisted her efforts to lift the rock of imperialist repression from their backs and forced her, more than once, to resign. She was accountable to the artists in word, but to Lunacharsky (and above him, Lenin) in deed.

Thus the theater's artists discovered that their professional unions, or *profsoyuzï*, which supposedly represented their interests to the directorate, were actually powerless. Any decision required Lunacharsky's approval. Minutes from the meetings of the dancers in June 1918, October 1919, and December 1919 reveal the depths of their discontent. Some soloists quit; others floated the idea of separating the Bolshoi Ballet from its theater. But despite deep resentment of Malinovskaya they elected a representative to the directorate: Vladimir Kuznetsov, an 1898 graduate of the ballet school, who both danced with the Bolshoi and acted in silent films—four in all. Other side activities included adjudicating a contest for best female legs for a satirical magazine (the contestants submitted photographs of their exposed calves for his sophisticated assessment). An affair with Sophie Fedorova, Gorsky's preferred ballerina and a future member of the Ballets Russes, aided his modest career. He appeared in Gorsky's version of *The Hunchback of Notre Dame* and danced the gopak (Cossack dance) in *The Little Humpbacked Horse*; a photograph also shows him costumed for the mazurka in, presumably, *Swan Lake*. His signature role was the Chinese doll in *Coppélia*, who dances in the second act until his clockwork runs down. Then he sits on a bench upstage, facing the audience. Kuznetsov once wagered that he could get through the entire act without blinking; he won the bet by painting fake eyes on his eyelids and keeping his real eyes shut tight. Besides makeup, magic tricks, and comic roles, Kuznetsov loved practical jokes, causing a stir in 1914 by masquerading as Gorsky during a performance of *The Little Humpbacked Horse* to commemorate the ballet master's quarter century in the theater. Kuznetsov was a congenial bon vivant and was praised by his peers for his "sense of justice."[33] But he does not seem to have been politically savvy, given that he taunted Malinovskaya as a Bolshevik factotum ignorant of the arts. Being right did not help him, and neither did redoubling his insults.

Lunacharsky resisted the election of Kuznetsov to the directorate—claiming, in typical *kompromat* fashion, that Kuznetsov had been detained in the commissariat for "drunkenness" and had even, according to the sadistic charges, hosted "orgies" in his "tavern."[34] Lunacharsky's accusations repeated those leveled, in another context, against the bohemian Stray Dog Café in Petrograd, which the imperial government had closed in 1915 for the unauthorized selling of spirits. But the "tavern" was in fact an atelier, a basement dining room of sorts near the Bolshoi, where skits, humorous tales (by Chekhov, among others), dances, and songs of different genres were performed. Kuznetsov put together the programs and enlisted the entertainers, who worked for food, one free meal per show; they were denied booze, sex, and the delights of hashish—just kasha and cutlets for them. Kuznetsov defended himself from the slander to the satisfaction of his colleagues at the Bolshoi. No one believed he could have been "arrested in a drunken state."[35] But to keep the peace he eventually withdrew from the election. The third and final vote of the Bolshoi dancers, in December 1919, went to Gorsky's disciple, Vladimir Ryabtsev.

Kuznetsov continued to attack Malinovskaya on behalf of the union, underestimating the director's ties to Lunacharsky. In the first of her several acts of revenge against the artists under her control, especially the more charismatic ones, she accused Kuznetsov of sabotage. He had, she told Lunacharsky, incited the troupe to go on strike before the start of the 1920–21 season. Lunacharsky, in response, turned to the head of the Cheka, Lenin's political police.

Kuznetsov was arrested but spent just three days in prison. His colleagues signed a petition asserting his innocence. After his release, the feud continued. Lunacharsky, no longer the congenial Bolshevik the artists had believed to him to be, filled Kuznetsov's Cheka file with fictions about his basement bordello, alcoholism, and "morally dubious past."[36] Lunacharsky informed the chief of the secret police that "disloyal and demagogic agitation persists" in the Bolshoi, with roots in "the ambition of a group of dubious types who seek election to the directorate." He pointed to Kuznetsov as the perpetrator of "a series of clear criminal acts," including agitating the collective to demand better rations and encouraging the dancers and singers to "disrupt spectacles and close the theater." "From my personal meetings with Kuznetsov," Lunacharsky continued, "it became obvious that this individual seeks to lay the path for himself to the highest positions in the theater and he will not desist in his damaging campaign unless he is eliminated in the severest fashion possible. In light of Kuznetsov's criminal actions I ask the M. Ch. K. [Moscow Cheka] to immediately place him under arrest. This will in and of itself sedate the troubled personnel, bringing the matter, once investigated, to a proper conclusion."[37] Kuznetsov blamed the prudish Malinovskaya for his downfall, never suspecting Lunacharsky's involvement. But the commissar harbored an intense, almost intimate, hatred for him.

Kuznetsov was forced to quit the Bolshoi after the 1920–21 season. His Cheka file labeled him a "sulky element" with no right to work in a state theater.[38] At forty-two years old, he was past retirement age for a dancer, but since he had been voted head of not just the ballet union but also the combined union for all of the artists in the theater, he technically had the right to work until old age. Lunacharsky expelled him nevertheless, and then instructed everyone to breathe a sigh of relief that the subversive demagogue was gone. Kuznetsov recovered from the blow. After the Bolshoi, he found employment in Soviet cultural groups and cabarets, giving dance lessons and, in the mid-1920s, staging a frolicsome entertainment about mythological satyrs titled *The Goat-legged* (Kozlonogiye). He also remarried, divorcing his first wife for a nineteen-year-old Bolshoi ballerina.

The dire housing shortage forced Kuznetsov, his new wife, his ex-wife, and his ex-wife's new lover into a communal apartment. Nerves frayed; tensions within the *ménage à quatre* increased. Kuznetsov foolishly brought home émigré newspapers and even read aloud favorite passages within earshot of his ex-wife. She and her paramour denounced him to the Cheka, and he was locked up for possessing subversive material. Apparently his jailors had gentle hearts, and after two months of interrogations they allowed him to plead ignorance. His punishment was relatively mild. Kuznetsov was banished from Moscow and denied the right to live in any of Russia's five largest cities. For a dozen years he lived in Malinovskaya's hometown, Nizhniy Novgorod, after which he was arrested for a third and final time. He had opened his mouth in the presence of the director of the Soviet Palace of Culture in Novosibirsk, declaring Soviet culture inferior to that of his golden, tsarist youth. It was 1938, the height of the Stalinist purges, the Great Terror. Kuznetsov was convicted of treason under Article 58 of the Soviet penal code and assigned to a labor camp in Tomsk. He died in 1940.

CONDITIONS DETERIORATED IN the theater, as in Moscow, during the frigid winter of 1919. The civil war prevented food and fuel from reaching the city. Sewage entered the water system; typhoid, flu, and cholera spread. There were shortages of pine for coffins and plots for burial. Despite being illegal, bartering for peat moss, flour, and potatoes flourished, as did thefts from factories. Some were slyly retrofitted to produce items that employees could sell for food, including "stoves, lamps, candlesticks, locks, hatchets, and crowbars."[39] Dancers rehearsed in the cold, their breath visible as the temperature fell close to freezing on the stage and well below that in the ballet school. Audiences sat in coats and gloves. Curtain times were moved up an hour to save heating costs. Power failures curtailed performances. Instead of hiring part-time workers to clear snow, the theater had the artists themselves do the shoveling. Performers and technical staff scattered, leaving altogether or, between rehearsals and performances, taking on hackwork for bread ("black bread" from rye, Malinovskaya notes, since white bread from wheat could not be found in Moscow at the time).[40] Verdi's *Aida* and Wagner's *Die Walküre* had to be pulled from the repertoire due to lack of resources. Bolshoi orchestra musicians entertained soldiers for rations, sometimes playing on rare, historical instruments that had been confiscated from the homes of noblemen by the music office of the People's Commissariat for Enlightenment. Nationalizing the instruments, the thieves argued, kept them from being sold for hard currency or smuggled abroad.

Salaries were cut, save for the highest-ranking employees. (One of them was the machinist Karl Valts, whom Lunacharsky thought "an exceptional talent." His pay increased from 4,800 to 8,000 rubles in the spring of 1919.)[41] The belt-tightening meant wages were paid through the winters of the revolution and civil war, but not the summers. Malinovskaya and her bookkeeper came up with an unusual scheme to make payroll, taking advantage of the limited free-market reforms of Lenin's New Economic Policy (NEP), including permission to earn a profit and the encouragement of entrepreneurship. A new elite appeared on the streets of Moscow: speculators, or "gold diggers," who bought and sold the essentials of life, plumping themselves up with their profits at cake shops. "Speculators' wives are usually fat, red-cheeked, with heavy hanging hair, and much fur and diamonds," the *New York Times* reported in an exposé of the women of "Red Russia"—from the no-nonsense spouses of Lenin's inner circle to the ragtag tram-car ticket takers. "She wears what she has and in the winter everything she has," the reporter observed of one of the non-uniformed tram-car conductors.[42] NEP ended after seven years, and Malinovskaya expressed loathing for its capitalist components in her memoirs. At the time, however, she took advantage of the system by asking the government for permission to organize a Bolshoi Theater lottery. Her bookkeeper calculated that selling 5-ruble tickets for a chance at the 10,000-ruble jackpot would increase the salary pool by 200,000 rubles. For that to happen, however, the artists would need to hawk tickets to the theater's patrons. Malinovskaya hectored them into doing so, all the while recounting her difficulties getting the Moscow trade union council to allow the event at all.

Throughout the crisis, she represented herself as a heroic warrior doing battle with unnamed foes of the Bolshoi. "The B. T. is surrounded by enemies; fighting those seeking to get their hands on it takes great effort," she wrote.[43] The most serious threat to the theater came from the hardline Bolsheviks who, for financial, political, and aesthetic reasons, saw no reason to finance the arts—especially during a time of cold, hunger, and civil war. Her job was to enact Lunacharsky's harshest decisions and accept blame for them, while he pivoted between the artists and the authorities, trying to placate both sides.

Everyone found a cause to rally around in the first successful revolution-themed ballet, a work by and for children. The Soviets made children, both guttersnipes and those from proper homes, the sole privileged class in the Soviet Union; in terms of staging a new art to suit the changed times, agitprop for kids was a safe bet. The children's ballet-pantomime *Ever-Fresh Flowers* (Vechno zhivïye tsvetï, 1922) earned sincere praise from Lunacharsky. The commissar was so impressed that he even urged Lenin and his wife to attend the second performance, the first having been reserved for children, some of them orphans of the revolution, the civil war, and the Cheka. *Ever-Fresh Flowers* was both rustic and constructivist, representing meadows and mountains, ribbons and garlands, bees and butterflies, fresh-baked buns and cakes, harvesting and blacksmithing, sickles and hammers, marching and singing, and the spelling out of political slogans with letters held up on sticks for all to see. It opened with the children in a ship at sea, threatened by a thunderstorm, and ended in an orchard under the sun. The score offered up a miscellany of accessible classics, boys' and girls' songs, and marches. The elders in the cast explained to the children onstage, and everyone in the production then to the audience, that the flowers in the title represented the new start of the revolution, now five years old. The sets and costumes were done by Fyodor Fyodorovsky, an inspired designer, in a "bright [agitprop] poster style."[44] The apotheosis of *Ever-Fresh Flowers* involved more slogans, more marching, and a hymn to toil—a hit with the fresh-faced audience and, for Gorsky, an uncontroversial success.

And yet the question remained: "Should the Bolshoi Exist?" In some sense, the direst moment of crisis had passed. Its finances had begun to improve, and Russia had begun to rise back up on her feet, leaving time to consider the survival of the theater from an ideological perspective. The theater remained suspect as an imperial institution. It staged operas and ballets, the most elite entertainment. Also it seemed it could not be controlled at a time when lack of control was most threatening. From the perspective of the government, there was too much freethinking in the theater. Lunacharsky tried to fulfill his promise that the Bolshoi would be made to serve the regime. Thus those artists who were the most true to themselves, the most artistic, the most spontaneously and individually inspired and motivated, needed to be suppressed. The bind that the Bolshoi, its artists, and its management found itself in would inform the plots of its greatest "Soviet" productions: sacrifice of the individual for the collective.

Lunacharsky and Malinovskaya defended their actions like woodcutters letting chips fall where they may, arguing that risk-taking belonged outside of the government, in the looser domain of the proletarian cultural groups, and that the path taken by government-funded organizations needed to be narrower, straighter. The Cubists, the Futurists, the Cubo-Futurists, the likes of Kuznetsov, and the riskier experiments of Gorsky's disciples, if not Gorsky himself, belonged elsewhere. To be inspired by the revolution was one thing, but to support Bolshevism quite another. One existed in the realm of ideals, the other as a regime. To let the iconoclasts run free even within the world of the theater would be to risk the ire of the Old Guard within the ranks as well as the rulers within the Kremlin. The theater remained open, but only in the shadow of another threatened rebuilding—this time as a political convention center.

IN MAY OF 1922, Lenin suffered the first of the three strokes that, two years later, would end his life. His wife, Nadezhda Krupskaya, a former schoolteacher, did her part at the typewriter to make it seem as if he were still in command. Lenin had already anointed Stalin as general secretary of the Communist Party, a position that allowed Stalin to establish an enormous political support structure for himself and eliminate his real and imagined foes. Meanwhile the architect of the revolution would be confined to his residence in the woods outside of Moscow, unable to speak, enfeebled, and only dimly aware of his protégé's machinations. After Lenin's death, on January 21, 1924, Stalin would become the ruler of Soviet Russia and the Soviet Union.

Malinovskaya suffered serious health problems of her own but, even while battling fatigue and stress, hung on to her position. In November of 1922, she announced that she had reached an agreement with Lenin's accountants to keep the Bolshoi Theater operating, thanks to lotteries and other such gimmicks as borrowing from the maintenance budget, selling properties, reducing or canceling royalty payments, even selling the "two hundred jars of perfume and cosmetics" from storage.[45] She and Lunacharsky were both fighting to save the theater, under threat from the Central Committee, essentially the board of directors of the Communist Party. A chain of harsh, if contradictory, resolutions had come down. First, there was the decision to close both the Bolshoi and Mariyinsky Theaters, then to establish a "liquidation commission" to consider the possibility of closing them, and then to keep them open but drastically reduce their subsidies.[46] Lunacharsky defended the Bolshoi against them all, citing the Russian cultural legacy and importance, pleading ignorance of the resolutions, protesting being excluded from meetings in which they were made, and denying allegations that he had leaked confidential information to Malinovskaya.

The Soviet government, unlike the tsars, could not afford to make up the difference between income and expenses, which had been more than a quarter of the budget in the past. Having spared Lunacharsky a Central Committee lynching by bridging the gap, Malinovskaya informed the fourteen hundred employees under her direct control that she was overwhelmed with joy at the news that the theater would remain open and expressed her heartfelt gratitude to the artists for performing their duties with "great diligence and discipline."[47]

The troublemakers had left or been expelled, but the ranks still needed to be purified and loyal young Soviet artists enlisted, brought up from the reopened school and recruited from properly proletarian venues. A vision crystallized; a plan came into focus. The Bolshoi would become the people's ballet and opera house, serving the hammer and sickle and the court in the Kremlin. It would imagine a glorious past for itself, beginning in 1825 with its resurrection after the Napoleonic siege and ending with the premieres of Tchaikovsky's treasured balletic and operatic classics. The composer's imperial service and the troubles throughout the theater's long history would be forgotten, except when the tsars could be blamed. The Bolshoi would retain select glories from previous eras while also creating new ones. Henceforth the Mariyinsky in Petrograd/Leningrad, the first imperial stage, would be the second Soviet stage. One regime had succumbed to another, the seat of power had shifted from one city to another, and likewise the weight of the Russian—now Soviet—tradition had moved from one theater to the other, the Bolshoi.

But first a further cleanup operation: Malinovskaya began to impose fines on the dancers and singers for feigning illness, for tardiness, moonlighting, leaving cigarette butts smoldering after meetings (the dancers smoked, both to keep their weight in check and in defiance of the general atmosphere), and giving unauthorized interviews to newspapers. Members of the ballet, the opera, the chorus, and the orchestra were sacked for real and fictional misdemeanors, with special attention paid to those who seemed to undermine the foundations on which the theater was being rebuilt and instead pursued a "dangerous, anarchic path."[48]

The ranks thinned but the workload increased, the number of

performances almost tripling between 1917 and 1924. Evening performances of the nineteenth-century repertoire alternated with children's matinees and "experimental" works. On Malinovskaya's order, special commissions of artists reviewed the rosters, deciding which performers needed to be promoted, demoted, or sent packing. One of the dancers was released in the spring of 1923 because her looks had grown "completely unsuitable for the stage; she's stopped dancing; and she's old." Others lost their jobs owing to "inertia" on the stage, "weak" pantomime, "plumpness," or not showing up for class. "Hysteria" and "political provocations" ended the careers of two of the choristers.[49] Some died; others became soldiers. Still others found work abroad. The chorus and orchestra proved the hardest for Malinovskaya to manage, but she also had problems with the Bolshoi's stars, the ballet dancers and opera singers at the top. Their freethinking, self-centeredness, and unhappiness about the reduction (not loss) of perks and privileges affronted the collective spirit of the revolution.

She purged the ranks as well as the talent. Once it became clear that aesthetic innovation or artistic entrepreneurship would not be permitted in the ballet, she lost choreographers and their favorite dancers to chamber theaters, children's theaters, cabarets, circuses, and the cinema. Gorsky stayed but lost his mind. He was placed in a mental hospital in 1924 after being found naked and babbling to himself in the corridors of the Bolshoi. Other, much more inventive, talents quit for fear of having their experiments rejected by the Old Guard. Progressive standard-bearer Kasyan Goleyzovsky took his talents to the Bat cabaret, silent film, the studio of the theater school, and proletarian cultural spaces. He set almost-nude dances to the music of Scriabin and produced mean-spirited, Max and Moritz–like entertainments for children. The Bolshoi brought him back into the fold more than once, but his projects continued to be rejected. His *Red Masks* (Krasnïye maskï), based on a tale by Poe, was to have marked a brave new direction for the theater. The sets and costumes invoked the masquerades of the Bolshoi's past. It was meant to be tense, sexual, and violent, but also transparently allegorical, representing the destruction of the feudal order by a force majeure, the plague. The message of the source text—that death is the great equalizer, even in a luxuriant castle—was to be applied by the audience to the last days of the Russian Empire under Tsar Nicholas II. But *Red Masks* never reached the stage. Malinovskaya recalled the rehearsals being "nervous," the ambiance no less ominous than the black-and-red room onstage. Goleyzovsky was disorganized, grew hysterical, and soon became the subject of rumors about "pornography."[50] Malinovskaya formed a commission to investigate the kerfuffle.

Red Masks ended up being replaced by a much tamer ballet, *The Nutcracker*—Gorsky's version of *The Nutcracker*, in fact, which suppressed the sadder sentiments of the original and excised the Sugar Plum Fairy. Two years later, Goleyzovsky was pardoned and granted permission to stage a biblical parable, *Joseph the Beautiful* (Iosif Prekrasnïy). The dancing was free and diverse, a kaleidoscopic fusion of shapes and styles, some fluid, others sculpted. The elaborate set comprised multiple platforms connected by bridges at strange angles. Yet once the ambition, and ambivalences, of the project became clear, the ballet and its creators were banished from the Bolshoi, consigned to an "experimental" affiliate.[51]

Malinovskaya did not lament the loss of talent, and an argument could be made that, even if her arch-conservative attitudes harmed the theater during the free-for-all cultural revolution, it spared the Bolshoi from serious attacks during the Stalinist era. A short-term loss perhaps ensured a long-term gain. But the restless spirit of the 1920s proved her downfall when the lesser talents of the theater, the artists who kept the place running, began to leave for artistic as well as financial reasons.

During the 1922–23 season, for example, fifty-seven members of the orchestra decamped to Persimfans, an orchestra that performed without a conductor. Instead of watching one director on a podium, the musicians faced one another in a circle, cuing their own entrances and keeping time together. Other musicians from the theater found work in cafés and restaurants. When Malinovskaya threatened them with dismissal, they fought back through the massive RABIS organization, the All-Soviet Professional Union of Arts Workers, which accused her of dictatorial, anticommunist conduct. The chorus, opera, and ballet joined in the attacks. She was forced to form a commission devoted exclusively to the resolution of conflicts, but the commission itself became embattled. Malinovskaya rallied her backers within the commissariat, who sent a letter to Stalin (head of the organizational bureau of the Central Committee at the time) to defend her honor and prevent her arrest. "Accusing comrade Malinovskaya of forsaking communist principles, being patronized by bourgeois elements, protectionism, and other terrible crimes is senseless and baseless," they wrote.[52]

Comrade Malinovskaya survived, but she was pressed, now for her own sake, to provide ideological justification for the Bolshoi's continued operation. And so on September 2, 1923, as part of her presentation to the council of artists, Malinovskaya outlined the task before them all. "New topics and scripts for the opera and ballet repertoire," she said, should be "formulated in consonance with contemporary ideological objectives, broadly understood. Libretti from the old repertoire to be rewritten, with attention to literary form, in a manner that responds to current needs and new production concepts; the latter, along with the new vision for the repertoire to come, to be rendered with similar attention to verbal form."[53] Goleyzovsky's tamer projects might have been part of this new vision had the rhetoric been anything but rhetoric and practice met intention.

Malinovskaya's emphasis on the texts—the scenarios and libretti of the ballets and operas under her control—has idiosyncratic explanations. Lunacharsky's ideological arbiters tended to be writers whose careers stretched back to the Silver Age, the quarter century before the revolution. They themselves had been forced to renounce their own pasts and adapt, chameleon-like, to new political conditions. (Those who did not evolve either put down their pens or packed their bags for Paris.) Some of these writers nurtured dreams of world transformation and thus found it possible, even while queuing for rations, to interpret the events of 1917 in eschatological terms, as the striving for a realm beyond. Alcohol lubricated some of these conjectures, along with narcotics and bouts of psychosis.

The most notable of the converts was a figure of Mephistophelian countenance named Valeriy Bryusov. He endorsed the revolution, the Bolsheviks, and Lunacharsky, serving the cause from 1917 to his death in 1924. A writer who rose to prominence during the Silver Age, Bryusov produced hackwork for the Central Control Commission (Tsentral'naya kontrol'naya komissiya), which was responsible for ideological discipline within the communist ranks. In this capacity he drafted an aesthetically radical resolution on the state of affairs of the Bolshoi Theater, pointing out that, despite endless promises of reform, little had changed. Dissent in the ranks persisted, and the ideological retooling of the repertoire had yet to begin. "Ideology, in the sense of social and political ideology, as envisioned by the directorate of the Bolshoi Theater," he lamented, "has manifested itself only weakly in the past three years, chiefly through the elimination of those plays from the repertoire that were obviously contrary to the communist world outlook." *A Life for the Tsar* was swept off the stage (though it would return), but most everything else remained. The Bolshoi was "academic" rather than "experimental," Bryusov continued, and had not contributed to the aesthetic innovations in proletarian cultural venues, which nurtured constructivism, biomechanics, ballet-circus hybrids, and experiments in free movement. Bryusov endorsed the performance of dances by newer Russian artists, including expat Russian artists, who embraced the "simple" over "the imagined splendor of the past" and emphasized the need for synthesis. He believed gesture (*plastika*) could fuse with sound and image and imagined the corps de ballet leading a hypnotic round dance of the arts. Collective action, and through that action, collective transformation, now needed to be the focus. The theater's closure had been avoided for the moment, but Bryusov predicted the end if it failed to embrace the future.[54]

JUST AFTER BRYUSOV drafted his report, Lenin died of a massive cerebral hemorrhage. The news reached Stalin by telephone during the eleventh All-Russian Congress of Soviets on January 21, 1924, in the Bolshoi's chamber concert space. The meeting came to a halt; everyone began to cry. Stalin traveled to Lenin's home in Gorski to kiss the dead ruler's lips. The Bolshoi's orchestra provided accompaniment for the procession of Lenin's coffin to the Hall of Columns in central Moscow. To beat back the frost, the honor guard lit bonfires in the streets. Hundreds of thousands of mourners flowed past the coffin during the three-day viewing period. Lenin's remains were not interred, and never have been. His embalmed corpse is displayed on Red Square in a mausoleum designed by a constructivist artist.

On January 26, before two thousand delegates in the main hall of the Bolshoi, Stalin marked Lenin's demise by affirming, in vaguely menacing terms, the justness of Lenin's policies and pledging, in his high-pitched, measured cant, to continue the forced march to a socialist and then communist utopia. Having absorbed the paternalistic credo, delegates to the congress dispersed, and the artists of the Bolshoi went back to work, the first task for the orchestra and chorus being the preparation of a memorial concert for Lenin on February 10, 1924. Lunacharsky gave the preconcert lecture, drafting his speech several times on paper of different sizes with many other hands helping to edit. The music that evening, Lunacharsky explained at the podium, had no obvious connection to the revolution but had been written by Lenin's favorite composers. The pieces were heroic. The audience heard the Funeral March from Wagner's *Siegfried*, along with movements from Beethoven's Napoleonic *Eroica* Symphony and Tchaikovsky's *Pathétique* Symphony. Richard Strauss's *Death and Transfiguration* expressed the kind of "mystical beliefs and hopes" that Lenin the atheist despised, but Lunacharsky defended its inclusion on the program by asserting, limply, that its "pathos" could be felt even by those who did not believe in the afterlife.[55] The music was eternal, if not its message.

Just nine days after the memorial concert, the Bolshoi orchestra went on strike. Malinovskaya responded by disbanding it. The musicians could petition to get their jobs back, as long as the instigators were named. But they vowed not to return while she was in the job, and so on March 13, she submitted her resignation to Lunacharsky. The "battle that the union has waged over the last few years became intolerable for me last year and has achieved its goal—I can no longer work," she explained. "I ask you to relieve me of the directorship of the Bolshoi Theater."[56] She nominated an assistant as her replacement before retreating into the shadows in Lunacharsky's bureaucratic matrix. But it was not the end for her; indeed, Malinovskaya would return to the directorship in 1930, after Lunacharsky was gone and Stalin was in complete control of the Soviet Union.[57]

Ultimately, her achievement was negative, more about destruction than creation. Malinovskaya had culled the ranks, and she could argue that in so doing she had eliminated those employees of the theater who could not adapt to Bryusov's ideal of synthetic, collective action onstage. She had also, for this same purpose, culled the repertoire—again by ending things, not beginning them.

Imperial ballets and operas remained on the books, but decisions about which works would be performed were handled by Glavrepertkom, a censorship board that Malinovskaya co-chaired. Glavrepertkom decided the fates of new projects and those from the past, or from outside of Russia, that had hitherto been neglected by the Bolshoi. For a performance to be approved, it needed to be presented to the bureau in the form of a carefully nuanced write-up, an ideologically contextualized description that related the work, whenever it was written, to the present day. Mussorgsky's opera *Boris Godunov* was approved by Glavrepertkom because it described a corrupted tsar, but the bureau decided that in the crowd scenes the people had to do less kneeling. Tchaikovsky's opera *The Queen of Spades* received the nod, despite being set in the era of Catherine the Great. Glavrepertkom mandated that she be shown onstage—a pointed reversal of the convention during Tchaikovsky's time, when the empress, like imperial Russia's other rulers, could not be portrayed. Fokine's and Stravinsky's *The Firebird* and *Petrushka* received approval for performance given the "scarceness of balletic material responding to the times," but also in hopes of luring Fokine and Stravinsky back to Russia from France.[58]

Petrushka reached the Bolshoi stage in 1921, the grittiness of the opening and closing crowd scenes amplified with more "chatting" and "laughing" as the samovar hissed.[59] *The Firebird*, in contrast, was not performed. Strauss's gruesomely decadent opera *Salomé* raised hackles and was not, at first, approved by Glavrepertkom for the Bolshoi. The extremely dissonant harmonies were a problem, likewise the final scene of necrophilia. Boris Asafyev's revised orchestration of *La bayadère* also needed to pass through the censor, as did the decision to expand the title of *Esmeralda* to *Esmeralda, Daughter of the People*, with the plot now pitting the people against the Roman Catholic Church and the feudal order. Proposals for ballets about soldiers and soccer players were floated, line-edited, crumpled up, and, on second thought, smoothed out. As time went on, the fearsome censors imposed more radical changes on the standard repertoire, demanding life-affirming, folk-themed productions that focused on ensembles, not egos, and that expressed the ideals (as opposed to the realities) of the revolution. Even *Swan Lake* was reworked with a redemptive ending. The grimness of its original version, much like the neurosis and decadence evidenced in the Russian "mystic" symbolist dramas that the theaters could no longer perform, ended up in the tsarist dustbin. The Soviet version became much more profitable than the imperialist original.

The future of the Bolshoi Ballet, and the Bolshoi Opera, was to belong to the New Soviet Man, to the acrobatic, muscular builders of socialism. The heroes needed to be people of action, not witnesses to it (for this reason the artistic and political council of the theater rejected a proposed 1930 opera about John Reed).[60] The present also needed a New Soviet Woman, a heroine both onstage and off, who could perform the revised, female-driven repertoire of the imperial era but who was also committed to the bright future. "Russia's salvation lies with her women," claimed the ballerina Ekaterina Geltser

(1876–1962).[61] She embodied the revolution, having trained as an imperial dancer under the tsars to become, under Stalin, an icon of Soviet artistic power.

She also became an emblem of loss, being one of those dancers (and there was an alphabetic assortment of others) associated with the pitting out of the aristocratic inheritance of ballet. During her career the image of the art changed, recalling a revolution of another time: the French Napoleonic period, which the Bolsheviks embraced as a model in terms of the patriotic, defiant response of the masses to autocratic oppression. Exactly how the Bolshoi ballet master Adam Glushkovsky had inspired a new nationalism after the war of 1812 was lost to the Bolsheviks a century later, but he was remembered for adding folk fare to his creative arsenal. His embrace of the Russian people was important to the Soviets, but so too were the "important advances" of Parisian ballet masters under Napoleon—chiefly Pierre Gardel.[62]

In Paris, the demise of the social and political system of the Kingdom of France, the end of the ancien régime, influenced every aspect of early nineteenth-century ballet, from the choice of topic to décor to choreography. During the Napoleonic era ballet technique acquired a new brilliance, steps were redefined, legs came to be lifted above hip height, and bravura feats increased in frequency and velocity as ballet masters invoked ancient Greek and Roman notions of physical prowess. Defenders and disciples of the old *belle école* chafed. Something similar happened at the Bolshoi after 1917, sweeping away the Russian ancien régime represented by the Mariyinsky Theater and choreography of Marius Petipa. At least in terms of ballet, the Russian Revolution out-revolutionized (and in the opinion of conservative balletomanes, out-coarsened) the French Revolution and Napoleon. Dancers displayed even higher extensions and more daring acrobatics. Lines became less graceful, more graphic. Populist folk aspects of ballet were enhanced. Geltser did not author these developments, but, because she rose to fame during this period of radical rethinking, she ended up representing the newly muscular, assertive, revolutionary style. Much might not have been the result of her conscious intention, but one thing surely was: In her performances, even those from before the communist coup, she scrubbed small details from the ballets she danced, preferring simpler texts. She toughened up the classics.

AS A CHILD GELTSER trained at the Bolshoi. She danced under Petipa in St. Petersburg, and even appeared before Hitler at the 1936 Olympics. To bolster her imperial bona fides, she routinely fibbed that her father, the long-serving imperial dancer Vasiliy Geltser, had authored the scenario for *Swan Lake*. She lived through two tsars, two revolutions, and two wars, morphing from an "idol of pre-revolutionary millionaires and dapper officers of Moscow" into a judge in the "great accordion-playing contest" of 1928. She also danced to those accordions, "evoking frenzied delight in the popular audience which jammed the state experimental theater."[63] The first ballerina to be named a People's Artist of the RSFSR, Geltser received the Order of Lenin in 1937, and kept it pinned proudly to her fur coats and blouses (though sometimes, in old age, upside down). During the Soviet phase of the Second World War, she won a First Class Stalin Prize, and at her retirement in 1951, the Order of the Red Banner of Labor, which she affixed, aristocratically, to her hair. She sold off her collection of imperial diamonds to purchase portraits and landscape paintings, amassing a significant collection over the course of her life. She was an actress as much as a dancer, and was celebrated for her psychologically and emotionally nuanced performances. But she was conservative, the darling of the

Glavrepertkom censorship board. She avoided the riskier experiments of the choreographic avant-garde in the 1920s, and instead embraced the strictures of 1930s drambalet, the censor-approved storytelling ballet.

Her love life was bifurcated. She married her longtime mentor, the ballet master Vasiliy Tikhomirov, in 1900. The ambitious, self-aggrandizing ballerina needed a suseful partner, and the influential, methodical, thoughtful, and indeed loving Tikhomirov proved perfect for her. But she soon surrendered her heart to Carl Gustaf Mannerheim, a lieutenant general of Swedish-Finnish descent in the Russian imperial service. After the revolution Mannerheim became independent Finland's commander in chief, establishing a series of defensive fortifications, known as the Mannerheim line, to prevent Soviet invasion. The fortifications would stymy Stalin's troops at the start of the Soviet-Finnish war, in the winter of 1939–40. As early as 1901, a year after her marriage, Geltser and Mannerheim began an affair in St. Petersburg. He too was married at the time. Divorce never came up; Geltser did not once consider leaving her career with Tikhomirov to be with the uniformed Mannerheim as he roamed the Russian Empire. It was a sporadic passion, a hobby, and Tikhomirov turned a blind eye to it, allowing Geltser the dancer and Geltser the person to coexist in imagined harmony.

Geltser and Tikhomirov were both fêted for their Soviet service. Mannerheim, meanwhile, became persona non grata in the RSFSR, a scabrous white devil. Legend has him turning up in Moscow in January 1924 to see Geltser a final time. The illicit lovers exchanged symbolic vows before a priest in a Moscow church, then had pictures taken to preserve the moment. It was a frigid night; the ballerina wore a white shawl thrown over a chinchilla fur coat on top of a ball gown. They parted for good sometime during the official period of mourning for Lenin. Geltser fainted while standing in the line to view the catafalque, having contracted pneumonia in the frost.

When she was a child, in imperial Russia, she saw the Bogdanov ballet *The Delights of Hashish* at the Bolshoi. She remembered Lidiya Geyten in the lead role, the chandelier in the main hall, and the bouquets. Back at home she pirouetted in the mirror. Geltser dreamed of becoming an actress like Sarah Bernhardt or Eleonora Duse, but her father guided her into the dance division of the Imperial Theater College. She disliked being confined to the dorms and came across as disinterested and scatterbrained. But she found inspiration in her eventual principal teacher, José Méndez. He taught her to dance in an Italian manner, and in 1896 her father sent her with her mother to the imperial ballet school in St. Petersburg for refinement in the French style. Power and precision were to be blended with grace and lightness. Geltser trained with the octogenarian Christian Johansson and mocked the no less aged Petipa for his preposterous Russian and deteriorating French. Yet she fell under his spell. (He ridiculed her in turn for botching counts and missing tempo changes, and for the bunched muscles in her feet.) Her letters to Tikhomirov back in Moscow express her initial sense of disorientation: "It's horribly difficult for me, new *pas* every day, the likes of which I've never seen before. [Johansson] says that my biggest problem is lack of softness in my *pliés*, unfinished poses, and lack of softness in the hands and torso." She did not know the names of the movements Johansson taught, confused his precepts, and was told that she had to undo most of her habits. "It's amusing," she added, "how everyone scolds the Italian school."[64] The rapid *pas de basque* in *Mlada* flummoxed her, but she performed better than Johansson expected—a modest triumph.

Johansson continued to hector her over the next two months. Geltser sent Tikhomirov tedious lists, in a mishmash of French and Russian, of the lexicon she had absorbed in the studio with the other girls (the boys chiefly being in a separate studio with Enrico Cecchetti): "*assemblé, jeté, ballonné, brisé, glissade, entrechat six, sissonne-simple, sissonne fondue, saut de basque, cabriole fouettée, pas de basque.*" She fell ill from overexertion, worn down by the relentless criticism—"now for the fact that my arms have no life, as he says." But Geltser progressed, dazzlingly, her effort unbroken, her recall perfect. "Today, for example, included a very hard *coupé balloné, côté, pirouette en pointe à la seconde*, then from fourth position, and then two pirouettes en pointe, and on Saturdays there will be so-called steeplechase exercises, taxing but useful," she reported. "And they say my legs have gotten thinner."[65]

She danced the White Cat in *The Sleeping Beauty*, then each of the jewel fairies, and finally starred at the Bolshoi, with Petipa's blessing, as the heroine Aurora for a benefit for her uncle, a theater designer. Inspiration came from Pierina Legnani. Legnani was not the fairest princess of Russian ballet, in Geltser's opinion, but the pure verticality of her pirouettes had made an unforgettable impression. Geltser left St. Petersburg in 1898, bringing her refined Franco-Italian steps back to Moscow with her, determined to make a name for herself. She interacted with Anna Pavlova, Johansson's greatest student before her, to whom she would on occasion be compared, negatively. Tikhomirov mentored and partnered her throughout the transition to soloist. The last tsar entrenched the privileges that allowed her, for example, to recover from a leg sprain amid the flora and the fauna of the Crimea, tanning her injured limb in between massages and swims.

Gorsky came to Moscow in 1900, but he and Geltser did not get along. She was investigated in 1906 when it was determined that she had simplified her variations in Gorsky ballet's *The Golden Fish* (Zolotaya rïbka) and, much more egregious, had swapped out the harder numbers for dances from other ballets. Geltser claimed illness but made no secret of her dislike of Gorsky's dances. They would clash again over Gorsky's decision to assign the part of Odette/Odile in *Swan Lake* to two separate dancers; she wanted to take both parts herself. Gorsky scolded her, then flattered her, and then grew exhausted and indifferent. He found an alternative muse in Vera Karalli, a ballerina extolled in the reviews more for her radiance, her glowing skin, than her technique. She partnered with Mikhaíl Mordkin, an exhibitionist dancer who left the Bolshoi for the circus. (His engagement as director of the Bolshoi Ballet in 1922 lasted all of twelve days.) Karalli took the melodramatic overacting that she learned from both of the men in her creative life to the silent screen. Her films are transpositions of ballets, set in another language, calibrated to the rhythms and meters of celluloid.

Geltser took a pass on film but absorbed Gorsky's flair for the overdramatic as well. He cared about the emotions behind the moves and considered symmetrical movement overrated. She did too. Geltser's opinion of Gorsky changed over the course of her career but settled, as she put it to a group of students in 1937, in the belief that he was a "talented innovator" with a weakness: getting carried away with "the new, and sometimes forgetting about the old classical heritage."[66] Her eyes glowed, however, as she recalled his ballet *Salammbô* (1910). It was perhaps his greatest achievement, lost to posterity after a warehouse fire destroyed the sumptuous costumes. She took the lead role as the daughter of Hamilcar I, king of Carthage, and priestess of a city's moon goddess, to whom children are sacrificed. The handsomest mercenaries in pursuit of the king's head fall in love with her. The ballet abandoned conventional syntax in favor of orgiastic mayhem. Geltser found her true, heroic, *demi-caractère* self in the mix. "I absorbed each movement, each gesture, each turn of the head of the greatest ballerinas of the past:

Zambelli, Brianzzo [Carlotta Brianza], Bessoner [Emma Bessone]. And having mastered the art, I understood that only a gesture that is inspired by feeling, lives. If a movement lacks feeling, then it is a dead copy instead of being a living creation; a caricature instead of an artist's invention."[67]

Dancing with such passion came at a cost. She accrued an impressive list of injuries as an imperial dancer: one from an accidental pirate pistol-whipping in *Le corsaire*, another from slipping under a horse in *Schubertiade*. Photographs show her indulging the Hellenic dancing popularized by Isadora Duncan and adopted by Michel Fokine for the Mariyinsky and later the Ballets Russes. Before the revolution, Duncan's bare feet, loose-fitting tunics, fevers, and furies became "a symbol of freedom" on the imperial stage.[68] She opened a school for dance in Moscow in 1921, encouraging the children of workers to express themselves freely, helping them to realize their dreams of flight. The school existed for three years, and Duncan fed the children and kept them warm using some of the income she earned on tour. In her absence from Moscow the enrollment increased to five hundred pupils, who greeted her with hurrahs, red kerchiefs, and an outdoor performance on the grounds of a stadium when she returned. The influence of her teaching outlasted her presence in Moscow, and likewise outlasted the private dance studios in the city. These taught Free Movement and improvisation to proletarian children. Mossovet ordered them closed in 1924 owing to their "unhygienic and unsanitary conditions," "amoral atmosphere," and appeal to "crass" sensibilities.[69]

On the professional front, Duncan's "authentic classicism" was seen as a potential means of inoculating the Bolshoi Ballet from the feudalism, the "inauthentic classicism," of the court style.[70] Geltser embraced the Hellenic trend, but she never forgot her imperial training, "the seven exercises which I must take every day of my life."[71] One of the first ballet films ever made shows her and Tikhomirov in one of Schubert's *Moments musicaux*. The selection was choreographed by Gorsky, as influenced by Isadora Duncan, to music by Chopin and Schubert as orchestrated by Anton Arensky.[72] It gives a sense of Geltser's unsettled acting skills, not to mention her partner's generous proportions. The thin thighs, slim calves, sharp knees, and swollen foot muscles of dancers of later generations would have been thought unnatural at the time. Tikhomirov represented the übermasculine norm. Geltser, no stick figure herself, performed with the Ballets Russes in Paris in *Les orientales* (1910). She also appeared in Brussels, London, and New York City. Cultural-exchange initiatives took her to Harbin, China, where she collected antiquities. She dallied with diplomats and Russian émigré artists, and even, in Berlin, arched to a violin played by the physicist Einstein, but her thoughts, she reassured Tikhomirov during her seasick journey to the United States, remained of home. Her reception abroad was mixed. She triumphed in Great Britain, but was found lacking in the "finish and refinement" of Pavlova in the United States, though Herbert Corey of the *Times-Star* newspaper bureau conceded Geltser's auburn good looks—she was a "pretty little trick"—and her "spirited, startling" manner.[73]

In Moscow in 1914, the critic Vlas Doroshevich sent her a tender letter after seeing her perform Gorsky's *The March of Freedom* (Marsh svobodï) outside in the cold in support of Russian soldiers. She rallied the troops to battle against unspeakable horrors, high-stepping in her tunic and helmet to the music of three brass bands and pretend-blowing a bugle. "You are a God; you danced amazingly!" Doroshevich gushed. "You are a Canova statue come to life! . . . But to dance outdoors when it was seven degrees! This is the height of madness!"[74] She had conquered the classical repertoire, but she also connected with the public on the street, becoming "a hero of socialist labor" even before the phrase was coined.

She missed the revolution while on vacation in southern Russia. Soon after, on tour in Ukraine, she declared her allegiance to the Bolsheviks. When the Germans invaded Kiev during World War I, she traveled back to Moscow in a cattle car with Russian troops. Thereafter Geltser became everything that the Soviets needed her to be, and they to her as well: obliging, benign, useful. She performed for peasants, soldiers, and laborers, donating the proceeds from benefits to political causes. The *Swan Lake* "Russian" dance she had learned from Anna Sobeshchanskaya became a hit with the proletarian public. In 1921, Lunacharsky honored her quarter-century of service, noting the Soviet people's love of dance and, crucially, pledging the preservation of the Russian balletic tradition.

Geltser had saved Russian ballet, or so thought no lesser a light than Konstantin Stanislavsky, the pioneer of method acting, whose influences ranged from constructivism to yoga. "It seems we can be assured that Russian ballet has escaped deadly danger," he wrote. "Its salvation is greatly indebted to you, to your keen devotion to art, the enormousness of your achievement, your tirelessness, your sparkling technique, and that fire within that has enabled you to create enduring, living characters and maintain ballet's high standards."[75] Geltser was the model of a Soviet diva, humbly surrendering without fuss her luxurious living quarters in an artists' building in the center of Moscow for a smaller space. She did not miss the en-suite bath, because, she said, she was "aquaphobic."[76] She willed her 100 paintings and portraits to the Tretyakov Gallery for the people to see.

Geltser's artistry made a case for the survival of the Bolshoi Ballet. Her body demonstrated that service to the Bolsheviks and to classical ballet might not be incompatible. Her aspiration to become the lodestar for the integration of the two enjoyed the obvious support of Soviet critics, especially those allergic to the decadence of the Silver Age and the experiments of the 1920s. "After the winds and storms of sexual passion, after the extensive flood of all manner of eroticism onstage, with all its ruinous hypnoticization," the critic Akim Volynsky wrote in 1923, "a new and fresh historical dawn will arise. . . . Everything will be explained and justified in the rays of Apollonian sunlight: the toes, turnout, the hidden wisdom of the human body itself, which has awakened to prophetic speech after a long, lethargic sleep."[77] His article was titled "What Will Ballet Live By?" The answer was Geltser, possessed of talent, malleable technique, and great political savvy.

A year later, the government decided that ballet would "live" by taking on modern themes and privileging collective athletic movement. And so Geltser, the People's Artist, would in 1925 inspire the first ballet to be endorsed by the Soviet regime, *The Red Poppy* (Krasnïy mak). The Bolsheviks were desperate to impose order on chaos, to put the past in service of the present and the imagined future. Here was a ballet that, at least in terms of its plot, represented the triumph of "new" civilization over "old" barbarism. The dance and music, however, actually imposed imperial-era constraints on the messiness of proletarian artistic experiments.

THE CONCEPT BEHIND the ballet, if not the ballet itself, dates from the year that the Soviets decreed to be the centennial of the founding of the Bolshoi Theater. Developing a new repertoire for the Bolshoi became a priority. A contest was held for a new ballet to be staged in celebration. Among the entries was *The Daughter of the Port* (Doch' porta). The overarching concept, desire for personal and national independence, was unproblematic. Yet setting it in eighteenth-century Spain proved a nonstarter. It was deemed insufficiently "dynamic," too dull, too archaic, to stage.[78]

Just then the Bolshoi designer Mikhaíl Kurilko supposedly retrieved from his pocket a copy of the newspaper *Pravda* with a story about Port Arthur (Hankou) in China, which had links to tsarist Russia. The Soviet steamer *Lenin* had been detained at the port by the English imperialist exploiters of Chinese workers, preventing food from reaching them. Kurilko pitched the idea of a ballet on the subject. It had everything a Soviet spectacle needed: exotica, politics, clear heroes and Western villains. Kurilko was a charismatic intellectual who wore an eye patch (he lost his left eye as a student) and tucked his well-pressed trousers into black lacquer boots—a look that would find its way into the ballet. Geltser had a eureka moment and helped Kurilko fashion the libretto, conceiving the lead role so idiosyncratically that no understudy would think to learn it. Reinhold Glière earned the commission as reward for his improvements to the scores of nineteenth-century ballets, including *Esmeralda*. He studied Chinese folk music, he claimed, in an eastern communist college, but if so, he did not learn much. The cutesy pentatonic tunes in the score, floating atop otherwise conventional chords, are so generically oriental as to make a mockery of themselves. Glière's music for the imperial overlords is likewise formulaic but somewhat more varied, involving chromaticism, whole-tone clusters, and flaccid Western "jazz." The audience-pleasing sailors' dance, titled "Little Apple" (Yablochko), derives, according to the official record, from a limerick sung by sailors in the Russian Black Sea fleet. Geltser's husband, Tikhomirov, created the dances for the second act, a mixed-up orientalist version of a traditional vision/dream scene, and his student Lev Lashchilin, a gifted pantomimist, set the framing acts. The Bolshoi Theater administration second-guessed the political content of the ballet, but because tickets had been distributed in advance to workers, it reached the stage and became an official sensation, receiving 100 performances in its first year.

In truth, Kurilko came up with the idea for the new project based on two unrelated articles in *Pravda* that happened to be published in the same page and column on January 9, 1926. The first article told of a "new phase in the struggle in China," a struggle that pitted Soviet-armed Chinese nationalists against Japanese-backed warlords; the second, much shorter article reported the detention of the Soviet steamer *Ilyich* (Lenin's middle name) in England. Police searched the vessel for "communist literature" yet found nothing.[79] Kurilko must have merged the details, placing the boat and the English police in China at the start of the civil war, and pitched the concoction to the Bolshoi Theater as a possible subject for a ballet. Enough interest was shown for the idea to be handed to the scenarist of *The Daughter of the Port* for fleshing out, since both he and Glière were under contract with the Bolshoi.

Glière wrote the music in isolation while everyone else involved in the ballet quarreled, in person or by telegram, over the scenario. (The composer was not one to argue, having played it safe throughout his career, never resorting to extremes, and maintaining, in his stout middle age, "the glossy air of a well-nourished cat.")[80] The scenarist, Mikhaíl Galperin, mishandled the new project, centering the action less on the ship than on a secret trade deal meant to ensure the eternal exploitation of Chinese laborers. A Soviet steamer arrived at port to support nationalist forces only at the very end; even worse, the heroine was French, a hopelessly démodé ballerina in the Petipa style, as opposed to a Soviet Madame Butterfly. Glière passed on Galperin's scenario, which left the project back in the hands of Kurilko, who would receive official credit as the author of the script. He was tasked with designing a ballet that would capture the political moment: Stalin's support of Chinese nationalists in their struggle against foreign-backed warlords, and his fantasy of an eventual alliance between Chinese nationalists and Chinese communists. Soviet involvement in China was covert, but the anti-imperialist rhetoric in *Pravda* extreme, leading the charge of international revolution.

Kurilko did not work alone on the script, nor did he work in peace. Other cooks came into the kitchen, including, at the start of the rehearsals, the Moscow Jewish Theater actor and director Alexei Dikiy, who would be feted for playing the role of Stalin in Soviet films; before then, he spent four years in prison, branded a traitor for his political satires. He animated the scenario, filling it with fisticuffs, but fell out with the ballet master Tikhomirov over the second act. Dikiy wanted the act simplified; Tikhomirov insisted on complicating it. Dikiy was removed from the project and his name scrubbed from the playbill. Thereafter *The Red Poppy* fell under the control of the husband-and-wife team of Tikhomirov and Geltser, with the pantomime specialist Lashchilin heeding their whims. The solo dancing was conceived in the summer of 1926 in Kislovodsk, the realistic plot discarded in the second act to allow Geltser to dwell in an unrealistic, astral plane.

Before and after it reached the Bolshoi stage, *The Red Poppy* was tested, presented to audiences of workers to ensure it made its point. Kurilko mentioned going with Geltser, Tikhomirov, Lashchilin, and Glière to factories for show-and-tell sessions. The composer played selections from the first act at the piano, including the Boston waltz that ended up in act 3. Geltser demonstrated some of the pantomime, seeking to show that the ballet's heroine is "Chinese on the outside, but with a spirit common to all humankind. Neither her feelings nor moods are foreign."[81] The workers enjoyed the sailors' dance but suggested changes elsewhere. Once the creative team complied, the factories "bought [tickets to] a series of performances."[82]

Glière knew that he would have to make changes and wrote his music accordingly. His relationship with the other participants in the ballet was not one of "trust," as he claimed, but the opposite: he worked from the vaguest of outlines, a sense of the beginnings and endings of scenes but no knowledge of their middles.[83] During the rehearsals, the exotic-rustic dances were shifted around, reversed, fast-forwarded, interrupted, and augmented. The second act was to have included distorted American dances (the Boston waltz, plus a foxtrot and a Charleston) followed by a Chinese opera episode, but these ended up being abbreviated and repositioned in favor of an elaboration of the vision scene.

All in all, *The Red Poppy* is a pageant, a spectacle for the senses requiring no sustained engagement. The political message is obvious, fixed in place before the curtain rises. It is the opposite, in short, of an abstract, "symphonic" ballet, and the sailors' dance, though popular with metal- and steelworkers, met with fierce resistance from Bolshoi Theater musicians, who found it demeaning to play, an insult to their training. In time it became a concert favorite, thanks less to the composer Glière than to its other creators. Glière had wanted to end the first act with a rousing folk dance, "Uzh tï Van'ka nachis' / uzhe tï Vanyushka prichnis'."[84] He was voted down and had to write, or rather arrange, music that Kurilko and his comrades demanded of him. The sailors' dance lacks the infectiousness of "Uzh tï Van'ka," especially since the choreographer slowed it down to the point of sabotaging its likelihood of success. But the music has endured.

Rehearsals continued into the spring of 1927, at which point Lunacharsky unexpectedly bumped *The Red Poppy* from the stage in favor of an opera by Sergey Prokofiev, *The Love for Three Oranges*. Prokofiev, a modernist wunderkind born near present-day Donetsk, Ukraine, had left Russia in 1918 for the United States and Europe.

Lunacharsky wanted him back. Staging *The Love for Three Oranges*, which had found limited success abroad, was part of the courtship, and Lunacharsky instructed the Bolshoi to make room for it in the season. Geltser had other ideas, however, and insisted that rehearsals for *The Red Poppy* continue in the ballet school. She found support for her cause thanks to political developments that no one at the Bolshoi could have anticipated: crowds attacking the Soviet embassy in Beijing on April 6, 1927, and metropolitan police rummaging through the offices in search of proof of Soviet meddling in Chinese affairs. Meantime in Shanghai, the nationalists organized the slaughter of communists. Stalin worsened the crisis by instructing the Red Chinese to mobilize against both the nationalists and the imperialists, and the Comintern to "concentrate on providing support" to Red Chinese fighters.[85] *The Red Poppy* had found its moment. The ballet was an innocent affair, light in style from start to finish, but it resonated with the current political situation and thus received approval for performance.

The plot changed before and after reaching the stage. Geltser took the part of an exotic dancer named Táo-Huā, a combination of orientalist clichés at constant risk of sexual assault. Her name translates as "peach blossom" in this spelling, but it has other transliterations from the Mandarin, and the creators of the ballet rendered it as "red poppy." Flowers are symbols of beauty, splendor, and youth; red is the color of love, also of revolution and communism. Thus both the title of the ballet and the name of the heroine are positive. Somewhere lost in translation is the negative association of poppies with narcotics, specifically the enslavement and exploitation of Chinese laborers in the international opium trade. As scholar Edward Tyerman has written, one of the greatest tragedies in Chinese history became, on the Soviet stage, a parable about "solidarity and liberation," even as it hinted that the Soviets might be just like the tsars, just like Western imperialists when it came to China. They were colonizers.[86]

The audience attending the June 14, 1927, premiere first heard the music of repression: A listless theme wanders aimlessly in the low strings, punctuated by gongs. Glière marked the passage "lifeless China" in his manuscript. A soaring, searching Russian tune follows, associated with the appearance of the Soviet ship as a symbol of new ideas and attitudes.[87] The curtain rises to show the ship being unloaded and Táo-Huā entertaining Englishmen in a restaurant near the dock. The unskilled southern Chinese laborers lift crates onto their backs and trudge barefoot down the gangplank three steps apart, the thud of the loads being dropped represented by accents in the score. They are the heroes of the ballet, but they are given the racist name "coolies" in the scenario. The oldest one collapses, having been worked to death by the evil dock master, the Englishman Sir Hips. The Soviet captain puts a stop to the constant beating of the laborers and joins his crew in completing the unloading. Táo-Huā, moved by his kindness, flutters her fan at the captain and gives him a poppy. Her master, Li Shan-Fu, menaces her, yanking her to her knees from a fragile position (one leg en pointe, another in *demi-attitude*). The captain intercedes once more, allowing the scene to conclude in casual merriment, with the laborers joining the Soviets and the crews from other boats: Australian, Japanese, Malaysian, Negro, and (not to be confused with Negro) American. The next scene unfolds in an opium den (or, depending on the staging, a teahouse), where the captain has been invited as a guest. Sir Hips plots his murder, but just as the knives are drawn on the captain by his henchmen, the captain whistles for his sailors. Undeterred, Sir Hips comes up with a plan to poison the Soviet captain.

Distressed, Táo-Huā falls asleep in a cloud of opium. Her vision scene features fantastic geometrical shapes that shimmer behind a scrim, followed by fairy-tale fish and birds. All manner of generic ballet fictions appear: the temple dancer, the pharaoh's daughter, even the children of Gorsky's *Ever-Fresh Flowers*. The Golden Buddha makes an appearance, along with a procession in the shape of a dragon and a quartet of bare-chested saber-rattlers. "Here flowers, butterflies, and birds come to life to dance," according to one of the scenarios. "Moving among them in her dreamscape, Táo-Huā seeks the [ideological] truth."[88] Táo-Huā sees herself in flight only to wake up back in the port, back in the grip of Li Shan-Fu. The stage becomes a casino. Chinese guest workers look on as the English perform a Charleston. A banker is entertained by a striptease in the form of a tango; the dancer disrobes atop a giant platter carried on the shoulders of Chinese lackeys. Táo-Huā performs her umbrella dance. The showcase ribbon dance ensues, the invention of the acrobatic Asaf Messerer, who remembered pitching the idea of the dance to the creative team on the eve of the dress rehearsal. He imagined a battle of the gendered props, "female" umbrella against "male" ribbon. Inspiration, he said, came from childhood recollections of "traveling Chinese magicians," but the hoop dance in *The Nutcracker* must have influenced the ribbon dance as well. Messerer remembered taking several "turns and pirouettes in a tight circle while manipulating the ribbon, which wrapped around me like a ring, then coiled around me like the body of a snake, and then transformed into an enormous hairband, through which I jumped. Lashchilin suggested something for it; then I did. Kurilko watched while we made it up and liked it. And so, in an hour or an hour and a half we came up with the dance."[89] The costume came from gold silk cloth, a pink leotard, and flower decals. Later a snake was stenciled onto the leotard.

Next came the Boston waltz, staged with forty-eight dancers, the women in black gowns, black jewels, and black heels, the men all in white. Li Shan-Fu orders Táo-Huā to perform for the Soviet captain and serve him a cup of poisoned tea. She instead declares her love for him in stilted, "semiliterate" pantomime: "Come, hero from land of happiness, I have to tell you something big important. Little Táo-Huā want to protect you. Táo-Huā love you; you are her one and only in the world; take Táo-Huā with you. If you leave Táo-Huā die a cruel death because of you." But the captain serves a cause higher than mere human love, and he struggles to explain that the same cause must be hers. "Fight for the red banner; it is the happiness of China and all humankind," he benevolently gestures.[90] Li Shan-Fu trains his revolver on the captain but misses. His next bullet reaches the kneeling Táo-Huā. In the paradisiacal apotheosis, the fantastic imagining of act 2 comes true. Táo-Huā is draped with a red banner by children. Poppies rain down on the Chinese workers, now liberated by Soviet partisans. The cast breaks out of the muteness of ballet into song, the inevitable "Marseillaise," with organ and orchestra accompaniment.

Reviews were poor. The act 2 vision scene predictably flopped with the critics, those writing for both political and non-political publications. *Pravda*, the most political publication of all, disputed the references to ancient religious symbols in the "naïve" second act. Geltser earned praise for her evocation of the heroine's search for freedom, but she problematically recalled, in her dress and demeanor, "the fairy-tale princesses beloved in the far east."[91]

Even critics writing for theater journals found that the formula— Marxist-Leninist agitprop on the outside, a mash-up of decadent imperial vignettes in the middle—did not work. Sergey Gorodetsky loathed the "marmalade" of effects in the vision scene, finding it altogether inappropriate "in 1927! In Moscow!" for the dancers of the Bolshoi to be dressed as flowers.[92] An even harsher verdict came from Vladimir Blyum, who was both a critic and a censor, writing in the evenings for *Zhizn' iskusstva* and toiling by day at Glavrep-ertkom. He savaged *The Red Poppy* as the product of the Bolshoi's imperial-era hangers-on, its "ruling class." He overheard a patron calling Tikhomirov a "pregnant cherub" onstage, and described Geltser's acting as "all 'on one note': a frozen expression that tells us she feels lost, and a tedious 'shivering' gesture—look, it's our old friend 'the dying swan,' stretched out over several hours and this time representing revolutionary China!"[93]

Even so, owing to the currency of its subject matter and the endorsement from the Kremlin, *The Red Poppy* racked up more than two hundred performances at the Bolshoi in its first years, and some three thousand throughout the USSR—an astonishing success that silenced the naysayers.[94] It faded from the Bolshoi stage in the 1930s, but reappeared in the 1940s, in celebration of the Chinese communist revolution. In the 1950s, the ballet was revived again at the Bolshoi, as *The Red Flower* (Krasniy tsvetok). The new title made clear, in belated response to complaints from Chinese diplomats, that the ballet was not about the opium trade. The poet Emi Xiao, a former classmate of Chinese Communist Party chairman Mao Zedong, had in 1951 expressed his unhappiness with the ballet to an employee of the Soviet cultural-exchange organization VOKS, noting that he and other visitors from China had avoided seeing the ballet at the Bolshoi because of its "essential inadequacies." The title needed to be changed, to something like *The Red Rose*, in recognition of the "Chinese hatred of poppies, the substance from which opium is made." Other problems included having one of the male characters wear a pigtail, a look banned in China back in 1912, and portraying the heroine as a dancer, a profession associated with prostitution. "Even the dancer's death does not eliminate our negative attitude to the fact that the main character in the ballet is presented as a prostitute," Xiao remarked.[95] So the name was changed, the pigtail cut, and the heroine recast as a freedom fighter. When Chairman Mao began to denounce the Soviet government of Nikita Khrushchev, however, the original title was restored.

As THE WAY FORWARD to the imagined communist utopia detoured and narrowed, growing more prescriptive, so too did the route of Soviet ballet. But the art mattered, in a way that, arguably, ballet has never mattered anywhere else. Choosing suitable subject matter was a high-stakes game—even when games were actually the topic, case in point being a modest "first attempt" by the Bolshoi to stage a ballet on the theme of sports to include a *pas de deux* between a soccer player and a sweeper.[96] Brilliant Soviet composers would be censored, their careers threatened along with their lives, in their efforts to create the right kind of music for the right kind of dance as determined by thugs at the helm of the ship of state. Many ballets from the years after the 1927 premiere of *The Red Poppy* never saw the light of day, and some that did ended up suffocated by didacticism. For the sake of the people, whose wants and needs the elite claimed to know, folk dance and music were stuffed into ballets, shoving aside any joy. As the censors turned the screws, the performers tightened up.

Among those arrested was Fyodor Fyodorovsky, the brilliant designer for Gorsky's children's ballet *Ever-Fresh Flowers* and *The Red Poppy*, plus several ballets and operas in a grand Soviet style. He also designed the hammer-and-sickle-embroidered curtain of the Bolshoi—first imagined in 1919, then realized in no-expense-spared gold and crimson silk in the first half of the 1950s. His fate reveals the extent to which the Bolshoi and the police state had become inextricably entangled, although the theater always inhabited its own strange world. Art cannot be reduced to politics, but that does not mean it escapes it.

In 1928, Fyodorovsky found himself embroiled in scandal. He was imprisoned on allegations, made from within the Bolshoi, first for plagiarism (supposedly violating Article 141 of the penal code) and then for his suspected involvement in the suicides of two women, Natalie Aksenova and Agnessa Koreleva, at the Bolshoi.[97] "I cannot be likened to a criminal and answer for the gossip, psychopathic hysteria, and suicides happening in the theater," he pleaded, after explaining that the twenty-year-old "girls" in question were untalented artists who had insinuated themselves into his atelier, pestering Geltser, Tikhomirov, and his own staff. "I want to create, to work, not to sit in prisons," he added to his self-defense.[98] The case was described in a pair of articles in the *New York Times*, which provided the shocking details of the double suicide during, not by chance, a performance of *The Red Poppy*. The girls were identified as dancers as well as "students of theatrical decoration," and the subject of their compact was not Fyodorovsky but the refined, roguish Kurilko. "Devoted to each other and yet both desperately in love with the painter, it was thought that the dancers preferred a common death as the best way out of the situation." They "plunged to death from the uppermost flies of the stage in full view of the public and just as the curtain was about to fall." The reports added that they had bound themselves together with a silk scarf and timed their fatal seventy-foot jump to coincide with the fictional death of the ballet's heroine (danced by Geltser) and the performance of "La Marseillaise." Some in the audience considered it a garish special effect. "To the corps de ballet, however, who at that moment came from the wings advancing to midstage in a dance of revolutionary triumph, the tragedy was only too apparent in all its gruesome aspects. Before their eyes lay the two girlfriends, the one dead and the other just breathing." Geltser breathlessly shared the details of the "awful crunching sound," "gasps of horror," and "suppressed scream." "I felt that something tragic had occurred, but I knew that I must play out my role. Then the curtain fell and I rushed to the corner where the two bodies lay bleeding and broken. One was motionless; the other was writhing in agony."[99]

Kurilko pointed the finger of blame at Fyodorovsky, whom he resented for being promoted above him in 1927, and Fyodorovsky was interrogated and imprisoned. He pled his case from his cell to Avel Enukidze, the secretary of the government's executive committee. Enukidze had a soft spot for the ballet and had defended the Bolshoi against its antagonists in the government. But he had an unpleasant reputation for pouncing upon ballerinas, some under-age, after wooing them with boxes of sweets and other gifts. For this reason he took the deaths of two of the Bolshoi's beautiful young dancers personally. Once the details of the suicides became clearer, however, Fyodorovsky was released. Kurilko took his place in the dock before also being freed. His future lay in Siberia and the design of the opera and ballet house in Novosibirsk. Meantime, the newspapers reported the arrests of "two unnamed young men" in the matter of the double suicide.[100] Enukidze continued his unhealthy patronage of the ballet until 1935, the year he was removed from his posts after a political power struggle with his old friend from Georgia, Stalin. The times were obviously hedonistic, even lethal.

AFTER THE DRAMA, and trauma, of the initial run of *The Red Poppy*, Ekaterina Geltser retired from the Bolshoi to dance in galas and concerts throughout the Soviet Union, displaying her oft-mended ballet slippers "before the workers of Magnitogorsk and Stalingrad, before the miners of the Donbas and Kuznets," and "in the taiga."[101] She achieved fame, she said, during a period of endless possibilities in Russian culture; she ended it, she did not say, during a period of impossibilities—of censorship, repression, the perpetual anxiety of not knowing the rules that were always changing anyway. Life and art coalesced in her old age; confused memories washed up at Táo-Huä's port and onto the streets of Moscow, where Geltser could be seen strolling in *chinoiserie* and other fashions from days long gone. The delights of hashish and of the opium den were one and the same in her mind. The prima ballerina assoluta, as the press in the West had dubbed her back in 1910, fought physical decline and overindulged in lipstick, powder, and eau de cologne. Her vision began to fail, and she died blind, having spent her final two years "sitting too close" to a television that she pretended to hate.[102]

Her heart remained with Mannerheim, but her career belonged to Tikhomirov, who doted on her until he died, six years before her. She wrote to him in 1939 from a booking in Krasnodar. She had pushed her tired limbs through the mazurka from *A Life for the Tsar* (renamed *Ivan Susanin*) and, on special request, something from *Swan Lake*. It was the worst of times in terms of arrests, confiscations, disappearances, and ideological thought control. She retreated, describing the evening as would a little girl. The bouquets were lovely, the stage nice and clean, her room was warm, and the linens fresh.

From Krasnodar, she went to Stalingrad, formerly Tsaritsïn, to perform in another concert in another House of the Red Army. Her apartment was searched when she returned, and the letters from Mannerheim confiscated, likewise two portraits of him by Silver Age painters. The Soviet-Finnish war had begun, and Geltser had been caught staring at pictures of a Soviet people's enemy. Fame saved her from arrest. Fifty-seven years later, in 1997, a nephew of hers living abroad sent a letter to the Bolshoi Theater Museum in which he brought to light both the search and Geltser's subsequent efforts to liquidate her personal archive. He added, perhaps in the form of a complaint, that the location of the "fifteen hundred letters" Geltser received over the course of her life is unknown.[103]

She had no students to define her career for her, and so had to define it herself. In 1949, she reminded Tikhomirov of their mutual joys and sorrows, and how they both had "suffered" in defense of "pure" art.[104] That word—"pure"—finds Geltser rejecting Gorsky's violation of the Petipa tradition. It also has her rejecting that which is least pure, namely politics. She ended the letter with a reference to one of the biblical paintings in her collection, Vasiliy Polenov's *Christ Child*, which she had wanted to give to him but could not. It belonged to the state.

At the time of Tikhomirov's death, in June of 1956, Geltser wrote to him one last time, standing beside his coffin, in his apartment: "Thank you, my beloved, dearest friend, for everything—for the enormous work we did, for your classes, for your tolerance and patience with me, for your love of others and good wishes for the best for them. I bow to the ground to you. Farewell, I'll be there soon."[105]

A copy of the note was read at the Bolshoi Theater memorial service for Tikhomirov. The original went into his grave.

· 6 ·

CENSORSHIP

By the time Stalin had beaten back his rivals to consolidate power, there was as much real political drama at the Bolshoi as anything imagined in ballet or opera. Stalin delivered speeches onstage extolling the achievements of the Soviet people past, present, and future. The applause and hurrahs would crescendo, ebb, then begin anew. On one occasion the uniformed, pockmarked ruler poured himself a glass of cognac at the podium as a toast to the working class. More clapping. Another orgy of adulation ended with Stalin wiping the side of his face, slicing the top of his throat with the fingers and palm of his right hand, waving off the crowd in feigned humility, and finally saying, irritably, in his nasal, Georgian-accented voice, "Enough."[1]

The Bolshoi hosted several All-Russian Congresses of Soviets and several more All-Soviet Union Congresses. The very establishment of the USSR was celebrated on its stage with banners and speeches; the first Soviet constitutions were ratified there. Lenin had spoken dozens of times at the Bolshoi, as had members of the executive committee charged with determining the path to socialism and beyond to communism. The Communist International met in the theater, likewise the heads of the NKVD (Narodnïy komissariat vnutrennikh del), the People's Commissariat for Internal Affairs, which was established in 1934 as the replacement to the Cheka. Under the control of the Politburo, the inner circle of Stalin's inner circle, the NKVD targeted communist officials, members of the armed services, rank-and-file bureaucrats, perceived saboteurs, traitors, anyone among the intelligentsia suspected of resistance or subversion, and artists without the stature to make them indispensable to the regime. Those citizens of the police state whose names landed on arrest orders were taken into custody (often at night), tried publicly or secretly, and imprisoned in the labor camps that supported the Soviet economy. Or they were simply executed.

Stalin dreamed, as had the Russian tsars before him, of leading the huge swath of the planet under his control to dominate the rest and so demanded superhuman agricultural and industrial production. The Soviet Union would grow wheat and forge steel for the world while also exporting its values through the Communist International as well as more discreet espionage organizations, including one dedicated to the cause of cultural exchange. Among the consequences of Stalin's aims were a famine in Ukraine that killed millions, the construction of a vast labor-camp system known as the Gulag, and a literal decimation (it was reduced to a tenth of its size) of the Red Army officer corps that left the nation far more vulnerable to Nazi invasion. The trauma of Stalin's reign has not been much reckoned with in Russia, and the might and power he symbolized retains its noxious nationalist pull.

Long before these terrible events, long before the Imperial Theaters in St. Petersburg and Moscow came to be managed by a single
administration charged with "bringing theatrical performances to
perfection," the Bolshoi fell under the control of the military governor general of Moscow.[2] Under Stalin, the Bolshoi was milita-
rized again—both the building itself and the performances within.
The Soviet government exerted direct and indirect control over
every aspect of artistic life. Art was to be popular, people-minded,
and based on class struggle; it needed to celebrate love of the land,
love of the Communist Party, love of Stalin, and love of the surrendering of the self, in every sense, to the great collective being.
These were the ideals of socialist realism, the official artistic doctrine of the RSFSR and its satellites. By definition, the ideal cannot be realized, but the Soviet experiment, as it developed under
Stalin, ignored practicalities in pursuit of purist ideological principles, no compromises, no second-guessing, no vacillation. This is
the essential difference between Stalin and Soviet rulers before and
after him. The artists of the Bolshoi, and to a lesser extent those at
its neighboring "experimental" affiliate (the onetime home of the
Zimin Opera, a private enterprise abolished after the revolution),
were tasked with representing a freedom that was fundamentally
not free. Mature artists were turned back into submissive children,
awaiting their next instructions, radical external threats vanquished
by overcoming doubts from within. Censors dictated efforts to create the textbook socialist-realist artistic product, but eventually it
became easier, safer, to prohibit anything from reaching the stage.

Before and after the Soviet phase of the Second World War, few
ballets and operas on Soviet themes were produced; instead, *Swan
Lake* and *Boris Godunov* thrived, to the despair and relief of those
who performed them. Yet there were original efforts by three of the
most prominent Russian composers of the twentieth century, each

of whom suffered the consequences of the capriciously cruel regime. Their endless and unhappy encounters with government censors left them at a loss—at least in terms of composing music for the theater. Sergey Prokofiev suffered creative paralysis at the end of his life, as did Dmitri Shostakovich in the middle, before he turned away from the ballet altogether. Aram Khachaturian struggled in his early years. All worked in a genre known as *drambalet*, which privileged ideological storytelling, in simple terms, and which followed (or at least tried to follow) the aesthetic precepts of the Soviet regime. Socialist realism and *drambalet* preserved something of the classical tradition and strived to capture the new Soviet spirit of the age, but merriment was enforced, spontaneity scripted.

In the nineteenth century, dance evolved from a form of perfumed etiquette into a true art. It came to serve a dual purpose in the Russian imperial court, as an emblem of cultured enlightenment and of hierarchical, top-down government. Such would also be its use in the Soviet state theaters: the Bolshoi Theater in Moscow and the Mariyinsky Theater in Leningrad, which became known as the Kirov, in honor of the slain Leningrad Communist Party chief Sergey Kirov. Gorsky's antagonists accused him of wrecking the ballet classics through his embrace of realism, but he also helped prevent the Bolshoi from reverting to vaudeville, the fugitive vision of rabble-rousing proletarian factions after the revolution. Even as the Soviets drove the Russian Orthodox Church underground, as least until the Second World War, ballet endured—becoming just as sacred to devotees of the art. The Commissariat of Enlightenment under Lenin, the Committee on Arts Affairs under Stalin, and the Ministries of Culture under Khrushchev and Brezhnev pressed the Bolshoi into the service of their own particular dogma.

The earliest recognized example of *drambalet* was the 1934 Leningrad production of a harem tale titled *The Fountain of Bakhchisa-rai* (Bakhchisarayskiy fontan). It dazzled, but the politics behind it and its successors deadened. As the repatriated Prokofiev learned the hard way, and as Shostakovich and Khachaturian already knew, censorship was unpredictable, taking different forms and coming from different places, not just Glavrepertkom. The path from scenario to production was treacherous throughout the entire Soviet experience.

Censorship had existed during the imperial era too, but it had focused then on the sources for scenarios—usually the stories behind the plots. During the Soviet era, government control went several steps further, making the challenge of getting a ballet onto the stage no less onerous than being admitted into the ballet schools of Moscow or Leningrad. The daunting auditions of Soviet legend—teachers scrutinizing pre-adolescents for the slightest physical imperfection—found an ideological parallel in the required inspections by censorship boards at the Bolshoi and the Mariyinsky–Kirov Theaters. First the subject of a prospective ballet was adjudicated in terms of its fulfillment of the demands for people-mindedness; the music and the dance would be likewise assessed. There would follow a provisional closed-door run-through to decide if the completed ballet could be presented to the public, after which it would either be scrapped or sent back to the creative workshop for repairs. Dress rehearsals were subsequently assessed by administrators, cognoscenti, politicians, representatives from agricultural and industrial unions, and relatives of the performers. Even then, after all of the technical kinks had been worked out, an ideological defect could lead to the sudden collapse of the entire project.

Bodies as well as plots were changed by politics. The traditional *emploi* that defined *danseurs noble* and *demi-caractère* endured, but emphasis was placed on bigger builds and altogether less softness in the curves. In sculpture, "Soviet man" became like a Greek or Roman demigod, the muscles stronger than steel. So too he became in ballet.

In 1927, Prokofiev and the choreographer Leonid Massine tried to make exactly this point about the heroic Soviet man to audiences in Paris. Their ballet *Le pas d'acier*, or *The Dance of Steel*, was brought to the Bolshoi Theater two years later for a show-and-tell session, igniting a bonfire of communist apparatchik vanities. Resentful mediocrities from the Russian Association of Proletarian Musicians (RAPM) attacked the composer, who found himself in a terra incognita of unlettered sarcasm, baseless paranoia, and pointless rhetorical argument. The ballet had been seen in Paris, London, and Monte Carlo, but it would never reach the Bolshoi stage.

Beyond voicing covetous disdain for Prokofiev's coddled lifestyle in the capitalist West, critics expressed resentment that the composer should dare to represent the Soviet experience without having firsthand knowledge of it. Indeed Prokofiev had watched the revolution from abroad, touring as a pianist and composer through Europe and the United States. He returned to the Soviet Union first in 1927, at Anatoliy Lunacharsky's behest and with much fanfare, then again in 1929, to a less glorious reception. Had Prokofiev composed an allegorical drama, he might have succeeded, but since he had not himself sold cigarettes (as the worker-girl heroine of the ballet does) or worn an anchor around his neck (as the sailor hero does), he got it all wrong. Plus, it was said, the hammer heavers in the steel plant onstage looked less like the ecstatic fulfillment of one of Stalin's five-year plans for industrial development than oiled-up slaves.

Le pas d'acier was drafted to depict the aftermath of the revolution, but the first half of the scenario was rewritten by the émigré impresario Sergey Diaghilev, who turned the tale into a series of scenes from folklore for the entertainment of French audiences. Diaghilev added a witch and a crocodile into the middle of a drama unfolding on and around a rural railroad platform, rendering the events of the second half—the metamorphosis of the hero and heroine into model urban workers, and the sacrifice of their individual desires for the benefit of the collective—ambiguous at best. Prokofiev hoped that the Bolshoi staging would restore the original plot and clean up the ending: the steel mill was to be shut down by the bankrollers of the New Economic Plan for failing to turn a profit but subsequently reopened by the workers themselves, with the owner of the steel mill tossed into the clink. Thus the ballet was meant to depict the chaos under Lenin's coup in the first half, with the swindlers on the streets having no time for political speeches, but in the second half, portray the order of the Stalin era. Grotesquerie morphs into something beautiful. But it was not altogether about factories, communist or capitalist. It was about the kinetics, the mechanical parts, of the body, which are more sublime in their communal operation than anything that could ever be forged, smelted, or tempered.

RAPM would have none of it, and Prokofiev was left to joke, ruefully, that he had been pitched from the theater along with his principal supporter, the deputy administrative director Boris Gusman, a force for change who believed that the old repertoire needed to go. "The salvation of the Bolshoi Theater would to a large extent be achieved by a big—*bol'shoy*— bonfire," Gusman told a repertoire commission a month before Prokofiev's appearance, "so long as it burned all those things, so long as it pushed the Bolshoi Theater onto new rails."[3] Those rails were part of the stage design for *Le pas d'acier*.

In his diary, Prokofiev used the Russian word for "purge" to

describe his conflict with RAPM, albeit long before NKVD interrogators extracted another meaning from it. He described playing
through the score and then sitting behind a table on the stage to
answer several dozen questions from the audience in the presence of
the director, Vsevolod Meyerhold, who proposed redoing the ballet
for Bolshoi audiences in collaboration with Asaf Messerer, and "a
boilerman or fitter who was acting as presiding officer and who was
in fact quite competent in the role."[4] Prokofiev glowered when told
he needed political reeducation, and after the following unpleasant
exchange about the accelerated machine rhythms of the ballet's end:
"Is the factory capitalist, where the workers are slaves, or Soviet,
where they are the masters, and if it is Soviet, then when and where
did you have the opportunity to study any factory here, since you
have been living abroad since 1918 and only came back for the first
time in 1927, for just two weeks?" "That is a political question, not
a musical one, so I don't intend to answer it."[5] The consequence of
his silence became evident at the January 23, 1930, meeting of the
Bolshoi's artistic and political council. The meeting, chaired by
Gusman, concerned the repertoire for the season. Shostakovich's
raucous first opera, *The Nose*, was listed as "doubtful" for a Bolshoi
staging, and Prokofiev's dance of steel—"canceled."[6]

UNLIKE PROKOFIEV, SHOSTAKOVICH came from inside Soviet
culture and had an artistic and political support network that ensured
his embittered survival of, and triumph over, the politics of several
Soviet leaders. He cut his teeth as a composer during the revolution
and civil war and embodied the aesthetics of the 1920s. As he completed his conservatoire education, he became a fellow traveler of proletarian arts organizations, which increased in prominence through
the 1920s, thriving in the cultural badlands before the Great Gar-

dener (one of Stalin's many sobriquets) weeded them out of existence. He dabbled in the burlesque and the sleazier sides of American popular culture, and he worshipped the German modernist Alban Berg, whose short career came to a sudden end in 1935, leaving unfinished an expressionist nightmare of an opera about a prostitute whose last john turns out to be Jack the Ripper. A prodigious pianist, Shostakovich earned an income improvising into existence the accompaniments to silent films and theatrical revues bearing weirdly untranslatable titles like Uslovno ubitïy (Conditionally [?] killed). His macabrely comic first opera from 1928, The Nose, finds the hero "gargling at his sink" instead of singing a cavatina.7 Both the plot and the cast are battered into submission by drums and cymbals.

In short, Shostakovich liked being all over the map, privileging nothing and everything, pinching from the classics and smashing the purloined goods into the songs and dances of the Communist League Movement. "Tea for Two" too. RAPM respected his iconoclastic approach to the imperial era, but could not abide the neurosis, psychosis, and anti-agitprop, anti-Marxist/Leninist content of his scores. Up to a point, his music sounded like he looked: it stammered, pontificated, protested, lacked sentiment and seriousness, but also twinkled with erudition. Shostakovich was an old-fashioned vaudevillian in modernist threads. Those who did not enjoy the fun, including the RAPM veterans who would bring him low in the mid-1930s, failed to understand that the revolution, for all the suffering it induced, was a free-for-all for creative experiment. He would be forced to repent, but not before deprecating the solemn rituals that once occasioned the coronations of the tsars, and also out of the maturing revolution.

For the fifteenth anniversary of the Bolshevik coup, in 1932, he began work, for the Bolshoi, on an opera about a human-primate hybrid, Orango, who rises and falls in the French business world only to end up caged in a Moscow zoo. The project, which never had any chance of reaching the stage, was meant as a satire of the bourgeois capitalist West, though it was convoluted and opaque enough as to invite all manner of interpretation. Charles Darwin appears; Bertolt Brecht too. The leading Shostakovich scholar Olga Digonskaya considers it a meta-satire, an example of a work that mocks itself: "laughter at Orango is turned around by the author's laughter at their ridicule."[8] Since the protagonist is a radical hybrid, it is fitting that the opera, at least the concept behind it, privileges doubleness. The tragic and the comic are swapped around as symbols of the protagonist's split consciousness, his fear that those around him regard him as pitiable despite, or because of, his constant efforts to ennoble himself.

The characters include an emcee, a chorus that celebrates the liberation of Soviet man from serfdom, a Bolshoi ballerina, soldiers, and sailors. There is a touch of pathos: Orango complains to his keeper about the "suffocating" animal costume into which he has been stuffed.[9] The prologue lasts thirty-two minutes—too long, the emcee tells us, for its performers, and too long for Shostakovich, who, seeing the writing on the wall, abandoned the opera after less than a month of work.

By the late 1920s, the aesthetic and political ground had shifted, and artists as well as bureaucrats struggled to keep their footing. Lenin's cultural commissar, Lunacharsky, was elbowed into retirement in September of 1929, having left the "golden rattle" of the Bolshoi Ballet in rougher hands than his—hands capable of smashing a lot of toys.[10] He was put out to pasture as a Soviet diplomat and died three years later. Elena Malinovskaya resigned (for the second time) from the Bolshoi in 1935. She had just turned sixty and needed a cane to get around. The proletarian organizations of the 1920s were liquidated and replaced by artists' unions under the eventual control of the Committee on Arts Affairs. Few fantasies were given wings.

During this period, Stalin began to take an intense interest in the affairs of the Bolshoi Theater, creating a "state within the state" with special perks for the chosen few. Cafeterias opened inside the theater; dancers were awarded apartments, dachas, and vacations at the spa; children of employees found places in pioneer camps.[11] Stalin allocated (or specified, as he tended to do, that he "did not object" to allocating) hard currency to injured stars of the Bolshoi so they could seek medical treatment abroad.

There were also prizes named for Lenin and Stalin, the Red Banner of Labor, and awards for service of distinction, for defending Moscow during the war, for dancing on sprained ankles, for not defecting on tour, or, in the case of ballerina Olga Lepeshinskaya, for having the shoplifting charges brought against her in Brussels in 1958 dropped.[12] These all came with pendants, ribbons, and up to 100,000 rubles. Lobbying was intense, decorum intricate. Awards ceremonies were another kind of performance, with harsher consequences for any miscues. How a winner (or loser) reacted would be recorded in his or her file. Among the janitorial staff, makeup and wig artists, stagehands, and performers themselves lurked agents of the Sekretno-politicheskiy otdel, the clandestine political department of the NKVD tasked with reporting on their fellows. Yet it was not, in fact, secret. Everyone knew and played along.

Thus in 1937 Lepeshinskaya knowingly uttered within earshot of an NKVD scribe that she credited her prize to her country. Only "in the USSR," she dutifully declared, could such an award come to an artist of her age. (She was twenty-one at the time.) Dancer Mikhaíl Gabovich also announced his joy at being named a "merited artist" on the same day he became a member of the Communist Party—membership being another form of honorific. Those

denied prizes and membership, moreover, could whisper their dis-
satisfaction to the eavesdroppers in hopes of reconsideration. Soloist
Sulamith Messerer was not one to hold back: "I've been working
in the theater for eleven years, dancing lead roles the entire time.
When word of the presentation of awards reached me I had no
doubt that I'd somehow be recognized. Such bitter disenchant-
ment. Lepeshinskaya, performing for just a few years, receives an
Order, but I am denied. I can't show my face in the theater."[13] Her
wounded pride was not allowed to fester. As soon as word reached
the Politburo, she received her prize.

Such was the remaking of Moscow's grand ballet and opera
house, which had fallen into a disgraceful physical state after the
revolution, and which, during the tumultuous 1920s, had lost a
lot of talent. Stalin did not offer a return to the imperial era but
instead struck a devil's political bargain. The government privileged
the artists of the Bolshoi, but in exchange they had to commit to
the cultivation of a strictly defined Soviet repertoire and maintain a
properly joyful communist attitude. More than prizes or trips to the
spa hung in the balance: personal safety could be won or lost.

The first Soviet ballet, the Janus-faced *The Red Poppy*, anchored
the new repertoire, but its politics no longer suited the times and
had to be reworked. That was step one. Step two involved putting the triumphs of the five-year plans on the stage. The Bolshoi
floorboards were reinforced to accommodate industrial equipment
that was to appear in ballets and operas about dams, crops, trac-
tors, power plants, and collective farms. Yet Glavrepertkom would
approve few of these new works. Among the bigger fiascos was a
hydroelectric-themed ballet called *Native Fields* (Rodnïye polya,
1953), "an outright failure from the beginning," Christina Ezrahi
comments, "synonymous with the shortcomings of *drambalet*."[14]
Lenin himself became a character in many works—not seen or

heard from, but constantly invoked, as though he were lurking just around the corner. He would have a cameo in a socialist-realist opera called *Into the Storm* (V buryu, 1939), by Tikhon Khrennikov. Lenin speaks instead of sings, typically a symbol of deformity in opera, but here a mark of divine otherness.

The artistic challenge for composers and choreographers increased even as their creative options narrowed. By the time the ideological transformation of the Bolshoi was complete, at the height of the Great Terror, there could be no expression of autonomous will within the public sphere. The experience of the willful Shostakovich marked the beginning of the cataclysm. Hindsight sees in his ballets a Soviet culture that might have been, could have been, had Leninism not ceded to Stalinism.

In the short-lived 1930 production of *The Soccer Player* (Futbolist) at the Bolshoi Theater, Lev Lashchilin and Igor Moiseyev sought to invigorate classical variations and ensembles with goal-scoring headers and penalty kicks—although the action, in truth, unfolded in a department store. It was supposed to delight but instead garnered mean-spirited reviews. The critic for the proletarian publication *Rabochiy i teatr* (Worker and theater) mocked its attempt at fusing real life with "pure classicism, founded on adagios and the simplest classical variations."[15] The dancers were also accused of failing to capture the seriousness of purpose with which Soviet sportsmen conducted themselves. Even some of the performers found fault with the ballet. "I leapt over a group of girls," soloist Asaf Messerer recalled of a dance called "The Waterfall." "I leapt over one group, then another. I just showed off my leaps, that's all."[16] Not to be excluded, the Bolshoi condemned itself for allowing the ballet to be performed, in the form of a "briefing" to the director on the "painful phenomena" afflicting the rehearsals.[17] That *The Soccer Player* lacked a plot was one problem—but hardly a serious one, since it was conceived less as an action-filled spectacle than as a criticism of contemporary culture. It surveyed socialism under Lenin and found it wanting. A more serious concern was that the second and third acts were hastily set to hastily composed music. The composer of *The Soccer Player*, Viktor Oransky, had taken ill with scarlet fever and missed the rehearsal deadline, leaving much of the ballet to be staged at the last minute, leaving no time for nuance—hence Messerer's deadpan description of his leaping, again and again.

Shostakovich loved soccer and was an ardent fan of his local Leningrad teams. Naturally he was drawn to the idea of writing music for a ballet about soccer and other sports that would be at once more artful and more realistic than *The Soccer Player*. The resulting ballet, his first, involved three sports-minded choreographers, one for each act. In the second, choreographer Leonid Yakobson turned his dancers into athletes and their equipment; the "high jumpers" became the "high jump."[18] Scholar Janice Ross quotes a thirteen-year-old dancer, Natalya Sheremetyevskaya, recalling how she and her balletic teammates "had to recreate precisely the moves of a volleyball game, the teams were next to each other, and there was an imaginary net separating them." Yakobson's insistence on precision—his refusal to permit improvisation—made the rehearsals "painful and tortuous." Ross further describes a photograph of the emerging superstar ballerina Galina Ulanova in the role of a Komsomol (Communist Movement of Youth) girl, one of the positive Soviet characters in the ballet. Her partner, Konstantin Sergeyev, lies on the floor as she balances "with one foot" on his stomach, articulating "a deep and beautifully arched backbend."[19]

The ballet's original title was *Dinamiada*, after the actual Soviet soccer team Dinamo, but ended up being renamed *The Golden Age* (Zolotoy vek). The title in Russian rhymes with that of *The Red Poppy* (Krasnïy mak), and the echo is not accidental. As the distinguished editor of the Shostakovich complete edition notes, there are numerous similarities in the plots of the two ballets: "The main character in *The Red Poppy*, Chinese dancer Táo-Huā, who falls in love with the captain of a Soviet ship, can be likened to the dancer Diva who is infatuated with the Leader of the Soviet football team (also a symbolic figure without a name)."[20] But Shostakovich was not simply out to embarrass Glière; he was hunting bigger game. *The Golden Age* transplants upstanding Soviet soccer players into a netherworld of fascist sports, racism, sexual licentiousness, boxing-match-rigging, and "mass hysteria." The action takes place in the none-too-subtly named realm of *Faschland*, also known as "a large capitalist city in the West." The chaos of the years surrounding the revolution is impishly referenced when a raised soccer ball is perceived as a bomb (Bolshevik terrorism!) and the Soviet sportsmen pestered by provocateurs (anti-Soviet infiltrators!). The music enhances the zaniness of the plot but is relentlessly unserious and intended to offend tender sensibilities. "The Touching Coming-Together of the Classes with a Certain Degree of Fakeness" is a cancan; the divertissement that precedes it a racist assemblage of a tap dance titled "Shoe Polish of the Highest Grade," a polka, and a tango. American blues makes an appearance in the form of a weird banjo-and-sax combo in the episode with the black man and the Komsomol girl. Warhorses of the nineteenth-century ballet and opera repertoire are quoted, along with a few orchestral bonbons like Tchaikovsky's Italian Capriccio. Shostakovich invokes *Swan Lake* but vandalizes the great tunes, stripping them of passion and interrupting beautiful melodies with trite xylophone licks.

Reviews of *The Golden Age* shifted from positive to negative as the ballet found itself caught in a cultural war that pitted the advocates of avant-garde experimentation against the extreme proletarian factions who favored didactic storytelling. Thus the ideological encounter, or collision, represented in the plot had its real-life counterpart. Shostakovich's own loyalties lay with the experimental camp in the cultural war. He and his allies dug their trenches and settled in for the long fight against conservative political factions, but they were destined to lose. RAPM and other organizations of its ilk morphed into official cultural organs, and the kinds of criticism in *Rabochiy i teatr* found a home in *Pravda*, the official newspaper of the All-Union Communist Party of Bolsheviks, which was published in a building named after Stalin. *The Golden Age* would be prohibited from production under Stalin and would not be revived until 1982, albeit with a different plot and a bowdlerized score.

The plot of Shostakovich's next ballet, a second front in the cultural war, took up the topical theme of industrial sabotage. Titled *The Bolt* (Bolt), it tells of a "lazy idler" who jams and shortcircuits a machine with the help of a naïf from the streets. For this act, the "lazy idler" must be punished by the Communist Union of Youth. The urchin who helped him, and who later outs him for his crime, must be converted—turned from a breaker into a fixer, given a job and girlfriend. "Comrade Smirnov" assembled the scenario, Shostakovich recalled in a letter, and the composer made it seem that he himself considered the project trifling, with the action confined to the third act and the rest unfolding as but a series of divertissements: an exercise class, a civil defense drill, a drunken priest and dancing church, and the cacophony of the plant.[21] Critics agreed, though perhaps the scenarist Viktor Smirnov, who had a jumbled career in the Communist Party, the Red Army, the Moscow Arts Theater, the cinema (he loved Disney), and the VOKS cultural exchange organization, took it all more seriously. He had padded the plot only at the choreographer's insistence and had been sincere in his representation of industrial sabotage. Smirnov claimed to have found inspiration in a visit to the factory Red Hercules, where he saw the objects that had been mangled in the machines, and a banner threatening severe punishment for bad conduct.

Choreographer Fyodor Lopukhov thought of the project in nostalgic terms, in the spirit of the factory dramas staged by the Theater of Worker Youth in the 1920s. Lopukhov pioneered a phenomenon nowadays known, derisively, as "mickey-mousing." His *Dance Symphony: The Magnificence of the Universe,* for example, sets music by Beethoven to movements that trace harmonic shifts, phrases, and larger formal divisions. For *The Bolt,* Lopukhov thought in geometric terms, stacking and leaning together his lankier dancers, making two-story trapezoids and trapeziums out of them. He included a "multi-bodied pyramid formation" like that of the stars that used to top the corner towers of the Kremlin.[22] He also thought in binaries, soft *plié* landings versus hard ones, *relevés* versus circus highwire acts. But what was needed, according to the critics, was not a divide but a synthesis. Ivan Sollertinsky presented the challenge in a seminal article for *Zhizn' iskusstva* (Life of art). Ballet had to avoid the abstract gesture—formalism—and choreographers needed to realize that new subjects demanded new "content." Making the captain of the boat in *The Red Poppy* look and move like the handsome prince in *The Sleeping Beauty* was a mistake. And the floor of a metal shop was no place for the "pirouette" or "entrechat."[23]

Lopukhov mined athletics for ideas and studied the labor production model developed by Frederick Winslow Taylor, known as Taylorism. He also drew from folklore and the burlesque, making the dancers look like the figures on the propaganda posters that hung in the windows of the Russian Telegraph Agency. The workers in *The Bolt,* his detractors claimed, were two-dimensional cardboard cutouts, with nothing in their heads, no class-based consciousness. Lopukhov conceded the point, declaring that Soviet ballet could not live by the grotesque alone. The first performance of *The Bolt,* on

April 8, 1931, at the Leningrad State Academic Theater of Opera and Ballet, was also its last. The criticism directed at Shostakovich centered on his multitasking (he was trying to do too much too quickly, and in too many genres) and his lack of seriousness. No one thought to consider that his approach to the score of *The Bolt* might exist in a realm beyond farce. The title of the "Dance of the Machines" is a grim joke, the stuff of urban nightmares everywhere. People dance, not machines, unless the machines in question have been made into people or people into machines, with tin skin and spark-plug sinew. The apotheosis of the ballet is a climax to nothing, and the brass and strings double, triple, and quadruple themselves like the demonic brooms in Goethe's (or Mickey Mouse's) *The Sorcerer's Apprentice*.

Ultimately, *The Bolt* is about a machine being broken by a villain who does not understand the world in which he lives. It is fixed by those in the know. Ballet was a machine of a different sort, an old imperial machine in need of a Soviet upgrade. Shostakovich and Lopukhov, possessed of sufficient ego and genius, imagined themselves as the repairmen, and so the plot of *The Bolt* focuses on the boy caught in the middle. Their hero is the one who does bad in order to do good and the one with emotional and psychological appeal. But instead of being praised, even hesitantly, for their effort, the ballet's creators read that "*The Bolt* is a flop and should serve as a last warning to the composer."[24] Smirnov alone escaped the flack, fleeing to New York to head the Amkino Corporation, which distributed Soviet films in the United States, while Shostakovich and Lopukhov went back to work in Leningrad.

They teamed up once again to create *The Bright Stream* (Svetlïy ruchey) for the State Malïy Opera Theater (the former and present Mikhaílovsky Theater), which, backed by regional communist officials, had formed a comic ballet troupe in 1933. If they feared another flop, *The Bright Stream* betrayed none of it except insofar as its creators made sure to exclude negative characters from the script. The grotesque still had a place, likewise satire. The composer and choreographer knew the names of their enemies and the position on the political spectrum from which they were writing, but the bad boys of modern ballet welcomed any attention—even in the form of bad press. Judging from Shostakovich's correspondence and Lopukhov's recollections, fear did not yet hang in the air.

Shostakovich's letters to the erudite ballet critic Sollertinsky, his close friend from school as well as an adviser and champion, ironized the politics of the moment, including the hysteria surrounding a speech that Stalin delivered, in November 1935, to the "shocked" laborers who had exceeded a five-year plan for economic development. "Today," Shostakovich wrote, "I had the enormous happiness of attending the concluding session of the congress of Stakhanovites," as though pleased to have a break from the monotony of composing the classics of the Soviet repertoire. "I listened to the introduction of comrades Stalin, Voroshilov, and Shvernik. I was captivated by Voroshilov's speech, but after hearing Stalin I could not hold back and shouted 'Hurrah' with the entire hall and applauded without end. You will read his historic speech in the newspapers so I won't expound on it here. Today, of course, was the happiest of my life: I saw and heard Stalin."[25] He concluded his lampoon with a reference to the work at hand. "The meeting began at 1. In light of this I left the Bolshoi Theater rehearsal early," referring to rehearsals for the Moscow premiere of *The Bright Stream*, which followed the reasonably successful Leningrad premiere by some five months.

Attitudes remained positive in advance of the November 30, 1935, Bolshoi Theater production. Machinists from a suburban plant (SVARZ) that specialized in the manufacture of trolley buses were invited to a rehearsal, likewise ball-bearing makers and a group from a plant (DINAMO) that produced locomotive engines. This might not have been the ideal audience for a preview of a ballet about life on a collective farm, but the industrial workers enjoyed themselves, despite being baffled by the intrigues of the second act. Later, during the actual run at the Bolshoi, "a group of Don Cossacks" took in the show; having won dancing and singing contests in their local collective farms, they had earned the privilege of being "shown the wonders of the Soviet capital."[26] (Whether these were true farmers remains unknown, and in fact most of those forced onto Stalin's collective farms lacked basic skills, which resulted, as Stalin's braver aides suggested it might, in disaster.) Besides the Bolshoi, the tour of the Don Cossack "farmers" around town included a ride on the Moscow Metro, the first line of which had just been completed, the circus, the planetarium, the zoo, and the state stores for manicures, coats, boots, and gifts for people back home. The expenses were charged by Malinovskaya's replacement, Vladimir Ivanovich Mutnïkh (1895–1937), to the Bolshoi account. His guests sent him a thank-you note printed in big, childlike letters in crayon: "We would ask you personally, Vladimir Ivanovich, when comrade Stalin next comes to the Bolshoi Theater, to tell him that we, the collective farmers of Veshensk, will never forget December 3, 1935, when we saw on that happy day our dearest friend, our great leader comrade Stalin."[27]

The scenario of *The Bright Stream* pits people from the city (in this case professional dancers) against country bumpkins in the form of workers on the "bright stream" collective farm and endearing cottage-dwelling retirees who have seen and done it all. The visitors bring along red communist banners to decorate the farm, but the peasants prove indifferent, even hostile to the communist court—as they had been to the imperial court. The banner-waving urban ballerina finds her double in Zina, a local entertainer. They had been friends in childhood and even attended the same ballet school together. The rest of the tale consists of amorous intrigues reminiscent of Shakespeare's *A Midsummer Night's Dream*, which the scenarist, Adrian Piotrovsky, adored. Lopukhov underscored the two-world nature of the drama by matching the phrases of the female leads, formalizing and abstracting the gestures of the former while making the latter freer, looser, much more approachable. The ballet is for and about pantomime and character dances, with which all three acts are chockablock. Of course the unprepossessing rubes from the "small wayside halt," as the setting is described in the scenario, emerge as superior in heart and mind to the sophisticates. Ultimately, too, "the festival ends with a general dance in which all, young and old, take part, together with the guest artistes."[28]

There were grumbles from other workers in the audience about the absence of North Caucasus flavor in the music; the collective farmers' constant partying; the squandering of state produce in the apple-fight scene; and women being excluded from the "national" dances. Plus nothing in the ballet indicated "the role of Party organizers, Party leadership in the farm." To gauge the ballet's accessibility, after a performance, the workers in attendance were given a quiz: "Who is Zina?" Answers: "1/She came to the collective farm from the theater for charity work. 2/A boss, a city woman temporarily living on the farm. 3/Someone on a business trip from a factory to the farm. 4/A Komsomol representative. 5/A recreational activities organizer. 6/The leader of a shock brigade of collective farmers. 7/Someone who married a farmer and so lives on the farm." There were other quizzes, about the other characters, the results a mixed bag. In surveys conducted after the test runs, "Comrade Postnikova" reported that she "had understood the ballet correctly." Likewise "Comrade Kireyeva" thought it all easy to follow and, as if a student seeking a gold star, filled in answers about the plot that her colleague could not recall. The process was beautifully sincere, and everyone was grateful to be part of it.[29]

The new Bolshoi Theater general director, Vladimir Mutnïkh, energetically supported the production throughout, but, as Shostakovich informed Sollertinsky, Mutnïkh's assistant Boris Arkanov wanted it struck from the repertoire for lack of seriousness. And Arkanov, Shostakovich knew, had Kremlin connections. Given that Sollertinsky also found much to dislike in *The Bright Stream*, Shostakovich felt the need to ask his friend's forgiveness. He described the ballet as his personal Waterloo, a "shameful failing," adding that he himself would not object to its cancellation.[30]

And when the noose tightened on artistic expression, Shostakovich was turned into just that—a shameful failure—in front of his colleagues, both those who had nurtured his precocious talent and those who resented him for it. The criticism that came from RAPM centered on the notion that he had spread himself too thin, flitting between film, young people's theater, and the major ballet and opera houses. Once the criticism sharpened to suggest a lack of political seriousness, his support network shrank, and he was even compelled by the top cultural official in the land, Platon Kerzhentsev, to distance himself from Sollertinsky.

In January and February 1936, Shostakovich was the subject of two damning critiques published in *Pravda*. Their appearance followed the successful run of *The Bright Stream* at the Bolshoi Theater, including a performance on December 21, 1935, Stalin's fifty-sixth birthday. The Soviet ruler had taken in an earlier performance from his concrete-reinforced loge, and he had not, it seems, disapproved of what he saw—at least not at first. The newspapers endorsed both the Leningrad and Moscow versions of the ballet, emphasizing the tenderness of the adagios and the simple charm of the waltz. The cast, a gathering of sylphs on the steppe, was outstanding, and of tremendous significance to the future of ballet, Russian and otherwise. Among the coryphées were Pyotr Gusev, future founder of the Beijing Ballet Academy, as well as Sulamith Messerer, who as a ballerina "had technique and pushiness (in life, she was pushy too) and could take a lot; she danced almost the entire repertoire of the Bolshoi." The quoted words, along with the put-down that Messerer "had no sense of line," from her niece, the illustrious, all-conquering ballerina Maya Plisetskaya, whom Messerer fostered after the arrest of Plisetskaya's parents in the late 1930s.[31]

The lone complaint launched against *The Bright Stream* in the Soviet capital concerned the "naïve and primitive" libretto, though that was Piotrovsky and Lopukhov's fault, not Shostakovich's.[32] Things turned sour for the composer, however, when his second opera, *The Lady Macbeth of the Mtsensk District*, began to be performed, simultaneous with the ballet, at the Bolshoi Theater's experimental affiliate. The opera, from 1934, had been performed almost two hundred times, in Leningrad, Moscow, Paris, London, Copenhagen, and Prague, and had become an international sensation, one of two such hits in Shostakovich's career (the other being his wartime *Leningrad* Symphony). There were also performances in Cleveland and New York, conducted by Artur Rodzinski in a high-stakes deal brokered through the offices of the American Communist newspaper *Daily Worker*, which published glowing reviews, and the cultural-exchange organization VOKS.

The plot is a nightmare, but a politically correct one, being set in the depraved imperial era, when the lives of the working class were dreadful, services inadequate. The title character, Katerina Izmaílova, is the childless, uneducated wife of a tradesman. The source short story, published in 1865 by Nikolay Leskov, describes her as "only twenty-three years old; not tall, but shapely, with a neck as if carved from marble, rounded shoulders, a firm bosom, a fine, straight little nose, lively black eyes, a high and white brow, and very black, almost blue-black hair."[33] She semi-exists in the blandest part of the bland interior of Russia, a fate she sought to escape. She also wanted to exact revenge on her besotted, cheating husband.

Thus Katerina takes an office clerk, Sergey, as a lover. Her loathsome father-in-law finds out about the affair and takes off his belt to beat her. She retreats to the larder, returns, and feeds him poisoned mushrooms. When her husband, arriving home from a business trip, discovers the rancid corpse of his father, he is strangled by Katerina and Sergey. The heroine now has two deaths to her credit, and she will have two more. Katerina and Sergey are sent to prison for their crimes, having been reported by a local drunk to the corrupt local police chief. En route to Siberia, Sergey becomes involved with another woman, the callous, selfish Sonyetka. Katerina sings a shattering lament before drowning Sonyetka and herself in the Volga River. Things could have been worse: the source text for the opera also includes the murder of a child, but Shostakovich excluded that.

Shostakovich takes Katerina's side in these terrible events, pushing his opera beyond the bounds of theatrical convention, and good taste, to assert a greater moral message. His heroine's behavior might accord with certain vulgar Marxist-Leninist precepts about feminist liberation, but it is hard to defend a killing spree.[34] It is a lurid entertainment, and seems, like Shostakovich's ballet scores, meant to poke and prod, though one expects that the gentle workers who conscientiously vetted *The Bright Stream* would have fled for the exits. Forget folksiness. Shostakovich represents Katerina's depraved, rubbish-filled existence with musical rubbish: paraphrases of lowbrow, popular musical genres such as the cancan, the polka, the gallop, and the kind of saccharine ditties that Shostakovich composed for silent films, music-hall revues, and his three ballets. His aesthetic was materialist, not idealist, but he assigned Katerina some of the most heart-wrenching passages ever conceived for coloratura soprano. The eminent Galina Vishnevskaya built her career on the role.

Katerina is an unusual heroine, but also a great one: She avenges not only what she has suffered, but also what all the sopranos of the past have had to put up with, in the Russian, French, German, and Italian repertoires. Her predecessors achieved grace through their martyrdoms, but Katerina gets payback.

STALIN LIKED PAYBACK, and opera, but he did not enjoy *The Lady Macbeth of the Mtsensk District*. On January 26, 1936, Stalin attended a performance led by the seasoned Armenian conductor Alexander Melik-Pashayev, whom Shostakovich accused, in racist fashion, of overzealousness at the podium. Details of the evening come from the memoirs of the composer's helper Levon Atovmyan. A dashing, roguish figure, Atovmyan survived a stint in a Stalinist prison camp in the Northern Urals in 1938–39 and would later, in 1948–49, be at the center of a financial and political scandal in the Union of Soviet Composers.

> Shostakovich stayed at the time [1935–36] in a rented room on Petrovka. On the day he was due to leave for Arkhangelsk, his opera *The Lady Macbeth of the Mtsensk District* was being performed at the Bolshoi affiliate. I fetched him for the train station; by telephone, however, he said he'd been instructed without fail to attend the performance. Shostakovich protested that he could hardly be there since he was heading to Arkhangelsk to perform a concert. "You

know," he implored, "I sense something unpleasant in this telephone call and the director's invitation to the performance. Would you please go to the theater and call me to let me know what's going on there?" I promised to stop by the affiliate but also said that I'd return to take him to the station. Shostakovich objected: "There's no need for you to come to the station. Why rush about? Spare the tears for future goodbyes."

When I arrived at the affiliate I learned that members of the Politburo, including Stalin, would be present at the performance. It went smoothly, but in the entr'acte before the scene of Katerina's wedding the orchestra (especially the brass section) became overzealous and played extremely loudly (I think that the brass section had been increased that day). I looked by chance at the director's loge and saw Shostakovich entering it. He was called to the stage after the third act: he was as pale as a sheet and left the stage after a quick bow. I met him back in the loge: he was no less pale than before and said: "Come on, Levon, let's go quickly. I should be at the station by now."

On the way he couldn't calm himself down and irritably asked: "Tell me, why did the volume of the 'band' need to be increased so egregiously? Why did Melik-Pashayev over-pepper the entr'acte and the entire scene—is this his excessive, Armenian, shish-kabob-house way? The din from the brass group must have made those sitting in the officials' loge deaf; I feel in my heart that this year, like other leap years, will bear new misfortune for me."[35]

Indeed it did. Shostakovich had been set up, and he knew it, so it is no wonder that he spent the night after his concert in

Arkhangelsk in the company of vodka. The Kremlin dropped the hammer on the composer in the form of two articles in *Pravda*. They were unsigned, signaling that they had received top-level approval, but came from the typewriter of a timorous journalist named David Zaslavsky on the instruction of the newly formed Committee on Arts Affairs (Komitet po delam iskusstv). This "mega-administration" was established on January 17, 1936, by decree of the Central Committee and Council of Peoples Commissars of the USSR.[36] Its chairman, Platon Kerzhentsev, was a fifty-four-year-old career propagandist, censor, and Lenin hagiographer.[37] He took on the task of eradicating formalism in the arts with extreme prejudice and launched smear campaigns against convicted "enemies of the people," the victims of the purges.

On Kerzhentsev's instruction, Zaslavsky denounced Shostakovich's opera *The Lady Macbeth of the Mtsensk District* and his ballet *The Bright Stream*, the former a source of pride for the composer, the latter a lesser love and pretext for self-ridicule. The denunciation of the opera was dated January 28, and appeared on page three of *Pravda* under the title "Sumbur vmesto muzïki," or, as it is frequently translated, "Muddle instead of music." The prose is imaginative, a departure from *Pravda*'s stultifying homogeneousness, and focused on Shostakovich's desire to titillate the "perverted tastes of bourgeois audiences with twitching, bawling, neurasthenic music." Little is said about the plot of *Lady Macbeth* or the impulse behind the chaotic "gnashing and squealing," because the editorial was meant to frighten. The composer was indulging "abstruseness," playing a game that "might end badly."[38]

The denunciation of the ballet appeared on February 6, also on page three, under the title "Baletnaya fal'sh'" (Balletic falsehood). It targeted Lopukhov more than Shostakovich, with devastating consequences for the choreographer's career. It was also the beginning of the end for Mutnïkh, who had appointed Lopukhov to the position of artistic director of the Bolshoi Ballet. In *The Bright Stream*, Lopukhov had attempted to hybridize classical and amateur (folk) dances, inserting several sequences with characters from the city and characters from the farm performing the same steps in different styles. The effort was ignored in the *Pravda* editorial, likewise the entertaining plot—which includes a dancing harvester machine, a man dressed as a dog on a bicycle, and an entire lexicon of sight gags. Zaslavsky first focused on the art of ballet itself, declaring it an outmoded art. It featured "dolls" as opposed to dramatically convincing actors, and dolls, for all their prettiness, could not hope to represent the miracle of forced collectivization. The Stakhanovite Shostakovich was accused of laziness. He should have gone to the Krasnodar region to see for himself the achievement of the crop growers and herd tenders. And both he and Lopukhov should have ennobled the merriment in the scenario, as opposed to trivializing it. "A serious theme demands a serious attitude, conscientiousness in the execution. The rich sources of creativity in the people's songs, dances, and games should have unfolded before the authors of the ballet, before the composer."[39]

Shostakovich interpreted the censure of these works in *Pravda* as a grave threat to his livelihood and, through Kerzhentsev, reached out to Stalin for advice on how to mend his ways, how to engage in a personal "perestroika," but the meeting did not happen.[40] The fix was in. Shostakovich had been targeted for ideological reeducation by the Central Committee and had to find a path to rehabilitation without the benefit of an audience with the Great Gardener, the Great Leader and Teacher, the Great Everything. He wrote to Sollertinsky on February 29, 1936, "Desperately sitting at home. I'm expecting a call."[41] But the summons to Stalin's office did not come.

He recovered, but the moment must have been dreadful. The

Bolshoi dancers remembered him playing through the score of *The Bright Stream*, laughing like a child, the merriment in his eyes shining through the thick lenses of his glasses. Following the "newspaper inquisition," he turned up at the theater again, looking for something in a panic. "His voice trembled, he stammered, his hands were shaking," and he pledged to be serious, responsive, to do "everything they want me to," no more fooling around.[42] He was frightened, but he also seemed to be offended, for himself and for Russia, hurt that his art had now to be somehow like *Pravda* itself—that ballet, opera, and the other arts had to read in black and white.

For Stalin, who caged Soviet artists inside his fantasies of ideological purification, "Muddle instead of music" served its purpose. "Yes, I remember the article in *Pravda*," he reportedly remarked. It set the correct policy."[43] These words were transcribed by the cinema-affairs official Boris Shumyatsky, who met with Stalin at night on January 29 to record the fallout from "Muddle instead of music." Shumyatsky affirmed Stalin's opinion that "Shostakovich, like most composers, can write good realistic music, provided, however, that they're led."[44] "That's the nail," Stalin answered, before opining at length on the subject in a virtual paraphrase of "Muddle instead of music."

> But they are not led. People toss whatever weirdness they like into the mix. And for this they are praised, glorified. But now that *Pravda* has clarified things our composers should begin writing clear and comprehensible music, not riddles and puzzles where the meaning of the work dies. And people need melodic skills. Some films, for example, can make you deaf. The orchestra jabbers, squeals, something whistles, something rattles—you can't follow

the visual images. Why is leftism so persistent in music? There's only one answer. Nobody is keeping track, nobody is giving composers and conductors specific requirements for mass art. The Arts Committee should adopt the *Pravda* article as a program for music. Otherwise the result will be bad. The experience of film should be taken into account in this regard.[45]

Henceforth, Shostakovich knew, the fruits of his labors would be inspected, like produce from a collective farm, for any blemishes. But government scrutiny was as inconsistent as the policies it tried to reinforce, placing his career in a state of flux even as his value to the regime increased. The fates of his ballet *The Bright Stream*, his opera *The Lady Macbeth of the Mtsensk District*, and the less aberrant fare that followed were determined, indeed overdetermined, by bureaucrats and bureaucracies. The stock price of his scores rose and fell as the Kremlin set it, in accord with what the regime needed from its leading artists at any given moment. Shostakovich absorbed political blows, created symphonic and string-quartet masterpieces, and provided service to the regime when called upon, even joining the Communist Party in 1960. Under Stalin, Khrushchev, and Brezhnev, he lived an elite but cautious life. After the damage inflicted on him in the purge era, he never composed a ballet or an opera again.

ALONGSIDE THE POSITIVE-THEN-NEGATIVE *Pravda* articles on *The Bright Stream*, there appeared excited notices of a forthcoming Bolshoi premiere of a ballet by Prokofiev, *Romeo and Juliet*. But it was not performed as scheduled, owing to politics; several members of the composer's inner circle were arrested. Prokofiev's *Romeo and Juliet* became a true tale of woe.

The ballet was to be a homecoming of sorts, meant to mark the triumphant conclusion of a multiyear effort, backed by the Central Committee, to repatriate Prokofiev after eighteen years in the United States and Europe. In 1918, Prokofiev had packed his steamer trunk and left Russia with Lunacharsky's blessing. During his years abroad, he stayed in touch with the commissar and proved reliable in matters of cultural exchange. But the shellacking he received at the Bolshoi for *Le pas d'acier*, and his knowledge—from colleagues, his exiled cousins, tapped telephones—of the shift to barbarism in matters of law and order, kept the modernist superstar out of the clutches of the regime. Dull-eyed but vulpine diplomats from "Bolshevizia," as he termed it, turned up at his Paris doorstep with requests for music about the revolution.[46] But meeting young, energetic Soviet artists also evoked, within Prokofiev, nostalgia for a Russia he thought still existed. In his diary, he expressed his longing to see his small circle of Russian friends in Moscow; he missed seeing Cyrillic letters on street signs, missed the magical landscape of his spoiled childhood in Ukraine.

He hesitated to return, however, until 1935, when the Mariyinsky–Kirov Theater dangled a commission that he could not refuse for an opera or ballet on the subject of his choice. Prokofiev prided himself as a dramatist, but to bourgeois, imperialist impresarios, he seemed at once too radical and not radical enough, and he never achieved the triumph in the West that he craved. So he took the bait, half thinking that he could simply travel back and forth between Russia and France and so continue to fulfill his international concert engagements.

The regime, as represented by the Bolshoi director Mutnïkh, had other plans and scripted a bucolic summer for him in Pole-

The Maddox theater, predecessor of the Bolshoi, circa 1800

Side view of the Bolshoi Theater, with Russian imperial soldiers on parade, undated

Ekaterina Sankovskaya, "as fleet as lightning" in the ballet Le corsaire

Illustration of the appearance of the swan maidens for the original 1877 production of Swan Lake

Playbill for the original 1869 production of Don Quixote, *a benefit for Anna Sobeshchanskaya*

Anna Sobeshchanskaya as Odette in Swan Lake

Ballerina and silent movie actress Vera Karalli as Odette in 1906

Studio image for Ivan Clustine's ballet Stars *(1898), to a scenario by Karl Valts, showing Clustine, as Castro, holding a lightning bolt*

One of Gorsky's "choreographic photo etudes," 1907–09

Alexander Gorsky

Gorsky's Children's ballet Ever-Fresh Flowers, *1922*

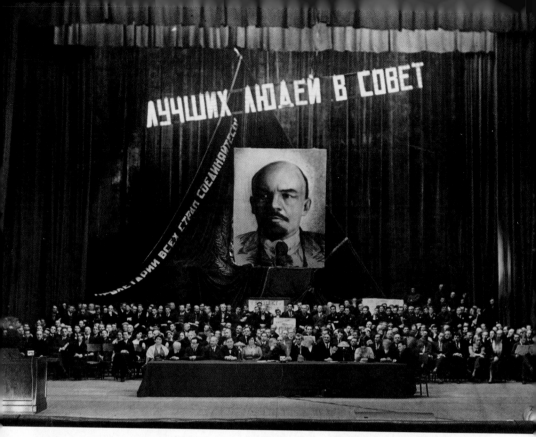

A portrait of Lenin looms over the Bolshoi Theater stage, beneath an electric sign directing "the best people to the Soviet"

Caricature of Elena Malinovskaya, Bolshoi Theater general director under Lenin and Lunacharsky, in a foul mood

Malinovskaya at her desk

Employee registration form for Vladimir Mutnikh, Bolshoi Theater general director, who was arrested and executed in 1937

Stalin with members of the government in a Bolshoi Theater loge in the mid-1930s

Postcard image of Ekaterina Geltser in La bayadère

The Soviet steamer arrives in the Chinese port in The Red Poppy

Asaf and Sulamith Messerer in The Bright Stream, *1935*

Ekaterina Geltser as Tăo-Huā in The Red Poppy, *"the first Soviet ballet"*

Leonid Lavrovsky rehearses The Tale of the Stone Flower, *1953*

Mother Earth swallows
the villain of The Tale of
the Stone Flower, *1954,*
by command of the mistress
of Copper Mountain

Yuriy Grigorovich

Khachaturian at the piano in the Bolshoi Theater in 1957, with Yuriy Fayer, Leonid Lavrovsky, and Igor Moiseyev listening in

Maya Plisetskaya and her brother Alik in childhood

Alicia Alonso, minister of culture Ekaterina Furtseva, Plisetskaya, and Grigorovich at the first international ballet competition in Moscow, 1969

Plisetskaya in The Dying Swan, *1940s*

Elizaveta Gerdt rehearsing Plisetskaya and Vladimir Preobrazhensky, 1947

Grigorovich's long-time set designer Simon Virsaladze, Alexander Lavrenyuk, and Plisetskaya, Legend of Love, *1972*

Vladimir Vasiliev and Natalya Bessmertnova in Spartacus

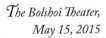

The Bolshoi Theater, May 15, 2015

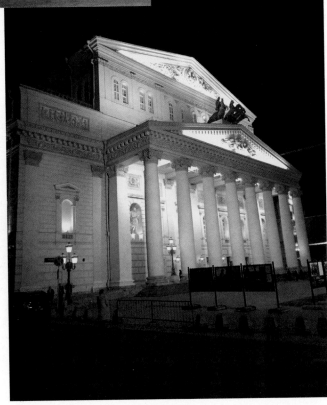

novo, a Soviet artists' retreat south of Moscow. Prokofiev settled in a cabin by the Oka River; he swam and played volleyball and composed, a lot, in the heat of motherland-fueled inspiration. In fewer than four months, he produced an annotated piano score for a ballet "on motives" from Shakespeare's *Romeo and Juliet*.[47]

Prokofiev chose this subject in consultation with the dramatist Piotrovsky, whom he knew from an earlier Soviet film project. They settled on Shakespeare's tale of tragic love as their subject, and ballet as the genre. Input also came from the theater-turned-ballet director Sergey Radlov, who had mounted a street-level, vernacular version of *Romeo and Juliet* with young actors at his Studio Theater in Leningrad. Prokofiev had seen it and liked it, inspiring him and his team to think that it might be possible to push dance and pantomime to the background of the ballet and instead have real life in the foreground.

But the contract never materialized, the unspoken reason being Radlov's firing from the Mariyinsky–Kirov in a nasty internal fight. Mutnïkh swooped in to acquire the ballet for the Bolshoi, allowing Piotrovsky to remain involved as scenarist, Radlov as scenarist and director. The Bolshoi director visited Prokofiev in Polenovo to see how he was getting along, and everyone involved, including the dancers who were also spending their summer at the retreat, had great hopes for it. These increased when Mutnïkh invited Prokofiev's wife to attend the Bolshoi premiere of Shostakovich's *The Bright Stream*, which did not impress her. "A cheerful show, in general," she declared, "but I have a lot of buts and I was disenchanted with the music . . . listening in on the chatter around me it seemed everyone expected more from Shostakovich." The dancing was a success only insofar as it was "pulled by the hair," in her opinion, and compromised by the absence of the injured ballerina Marina Semyonova. Mutnïkh took her under the arm during the

entr'actes, fed her tea, and said "no worries, we'll have a big celebration when Sergey Sergeyevich's ballet is done."[48] Two months
later, when Shostakovich was denounced in *Pravda*, that celebration
seemed all but certain, and Prokofiev deluded himself into thinking
that he would be welcomed to permanent residency in the Soviet
Union as a savior.

The key to success for *Romeo and Juliet* resided in *drambalet* as
defined by the orientalist extravaganza *The Fountain of Bakhchisa-
rai* as well as *The Flames of Paris* (Plamya Parizha), premiered in
Leningrad in 1932 for the fifteenth anniversary of the revolution.
The latter, a primitively allegorical ballet on the subject of the
French Revolution, became a staple of the Soviet repertoire, trav-
eling from Leningrad to Moscow and then throughout the Soviet
Union and eastern Europe. It also received a Stalin Prize. Radlov
had been involved in the original production, with music by Boris
Asafyev pinched from French sources. Prokofiev had supplied the
French melodies to Asafyev from Paris as a favor, and he was not
impressed with the plagiarized result. "General rehearsal of *The
Flames of Paris* in the Bolshoi with Semyonova and Chabukiani,"
Prokofiev recorded in his diary. "I told Asafyev it was high time he
did a proper job of composing this ballet."[49] But Asafyev had done
the proper job, in the sense of surrendering his own creative urges
to the diktat of Soviet aesthetics. Prokofiev's fate, in contrast, would
be one of trying but failing to sublimate his individual artistry.

Still, he recognized that Asafyev had a pair of successes on his
hands. Prokofiev weighed the artistic pros and cons of *The Fountain of Bakhchisarai* and *The Flames of Paris*, took the political temperature, and, in collaboration with Piotrovsky and Radlov, came
up with what he thought would be a safe plan for *Romeo and Juliet*.
The ballet would respect Shakespeare to a point, but it would also
have room for exotica—its own version of the waltz in the harem in

The Fountain of Bakhchisarai. (The choreographer of that waltz, Rostislav Zakharov, was enlisted to set *Romeo and Juliet.*) The greater
stretch, but the essential one, was to include, within the familiar
tale of star-crossed love, intimations of revolution. Here the trio of
scenario writers came up with the perverse but ingenious idea of
shifting the focus of the plot from the struggle between the Montague and Capulet clans, with the teenage hero and heroine caught
in the middle, into a broader struggle between representatives of the
old and new political orders. The move away from feudal thinking
and behavior would become the shift from the imperial era to the
Soviet one. And the ending of the ballet would be happy, or at least
bittersweet, for reasons that were pragmatic for Prokofiev—"living
people can dance, the dying cannot"—but political for Piotrovsky
and Radlov.[50] Mid-1930s aesthetics mandated optimistic tragedies:
as Soviet citizens, Romeo and Juliet could not die in so pointless
and accidental a fashion as a double suicide.

The drama comes to a close before the ending itself. Friar Laurence stays Romeo's hand by telling him that the sleeping potion
that Juliet has taken to feign death is just that. As the towns-
people gather to celebrate her awakening, Romeo bears Juliet from
the stage. The couple takes leave of the story. Depending on the
design budget, the production might have included a cloud bed for
the lovers, or perhaps the happy pair would float free in the stars—
an Orphic apotheosis, in essence, in which the consonant C-major
music of the cosmos, if not the unstable sonorities of first love, conquers all.

Prokofiev performed the piano score for adjudication at the Bolshoi Theater, receiving criticism from the conductor Yuriy Fayer
about the nettlesome musical syntax. Radlov insisted on keeping the
unusual ending intact, but Prokofiev signaled a willingness to compromise, to traditionalize the ballet if it would help to get it onto

the stage. In January of 1936, Shostakovich's fateful month, Prokofiev played through the first three acts of the piano score before a group that included Mutnïkh and the litterateur Sergey Dinamov, a member of the Bolshoi's artistic and political council. Dinamov, a Shakespeare expert, cautiously supported the happy ending. So too did one of the composers in attendance, Alexander Ostretsov, but he also felt that "the life-enhancing tone of Prokofiev's entire piece, clearly manifest in the culmination, will not be weakened if he follows in Shakespeare's footsteps in the denouement."[51]

But the ballet was doomed. Kerzhentsev, the chairman of the newly formed Committee on Arts Affairs, initiated a cull of the Bolshoi Theater administration as part of an ideological campaign against anti-democratic, "formalist" experimentation in Soviet art. He submitted a memorandum to Stalin reporting his intention to dismiss the conductor Nikolay Golovanov from the Bolshoi Theater and reevaluate the repertoire. The memorandum listed *Romeo and Juliet* as a prospective production for the 1936–37 season, but preparations were suspended pending the "assessment" of the repertoire "by the theater's new leadership."[52] Despite Prokofiev's best efforts to calibrate *Romeo and Juliet* according to what had already found favor at the Bolshoi, the original version of his ballet went unperformed. It became the first painful lesson for Prokofiev that his careerist decision to relocate to the Soviet Union had been a massive mistake.

The administrative review of the Bolshoi led, on April 20, 1937, to Mutnïkh's arrest. Three months later, on July 13, he was "deregistered," officially removed from his posts.[53] He was sentenced to death on September 15 and executed on November 11. He was forty-one.

Mutnïkh was gentle-faced, with a fetching mop of brown hair, but he embodied the militarization of culture under Stalin. He came to the directorship of the Bolshoi in 1935 from the Central House of the Red Army, currently known as the Cultural Center of the Armed Forces of the Russian Federation, and he had championed *Romeo and Juliet*. Mutnïkh was arrested at almost the same time as Leonid Lyadov, the director of the Malïy Theater next door to the Bolshoi. NKVD agents dragged Lyadov to the Lubyanka prison on suspicion of his planning to blow up the government's loge at the Malïy Theater when Stalin or another member of the Politburo was in the audience. The Soviet newswire TASS relayed the rumor of the discovery of "several incendiary devices that were supposed to be exploded when the right time presented itself."[54] Stalin declared the story a "ludicrous fabrication" but allowed it to be spread, since the reason for the arrest was irrelevant: the NKVD was filling an arrest quota.[55] Lyadov's liquidation ended any thought of staging Prokofiev's happy-ending ballet that year, since the reigning practice was to consider everything related to an arrested cultural official contaminated, including unrealized commissions and ballets, films, operas, and plays in progress. Tainted by its association with a disappeared enemy of the people, the plot of *Romeo and Juliet*, which involved a potion thought to be poison, a stabbing, class conflict, and subversive historical references, could not possibly be produced in 1937, the eve of the Great Terror, and the twentieth anniversary of the Great October Socialist Revolution.

The scenarist Piotrovsky landed on an arrest order in July of 1937, denounced for his lack of enthusiasm for the new creative strictures. He was convicted of treason and died in prison. The Shakespeare scholar Dinamov, Prokofiev's advocate to the Central Committee, was sentenced to death in the spring of 1939 for fraternizing with a counterrevolutionary terrorist organization.

The trauma was not confined to the arts, ballet, and the Bolshoi, of course, but affected millions of people. Supposed spies and

industrial saboteurs were put to death, likewise pre-1917 landown-
ers (*kulaks*), Trotskyites, and those disliked enough to be reported
on by coworkers, relatives, or neighbors. To furnish their squalid
rooms, agents of communal apartments stole tables and chairs,
pots and pans from the flats of those who had been arrested; they
also had license to stalk the coveted wives and girlfriends of the
disappeared, lending petty bourgeois pathos to the communist
purges. The cleansing expanded to include entire classes of people: gypsies, homosexuals, Jews, the disabled, the left-handed,
and, en masse, the restive folk of the restive towns at the edge
of the empire. Second- and third-tier artists suffered much more
than elite talents, as Piotrovsky's arrest confirms, but there were
shocking exceptions, the most notable being the detention, torture,
and murder by firing squad of the eminent theater director Vsevolod
Meyerhold and the killing of his actress wife, Zinaída Raykh. She
was stabbed multiple times, even through her eyes, by unidentified
assailants. Her death on July 15, 1939, shocked the Moscow theater
world, but was ignored by state media, as was Meyerhold's death on
February 2, 1940. The ballerina Marina Semyonova lost her second
husband, a diplomat, to the terror. He perished in the Gulag.

The purges—great and small, local and national—were managed by Nikolay Yezhov, the diminutive head of the Peoples Commissariat for Internal Affairs (NKVD). Each cycle of biological and
ideological purification begat another, until those responsible for
fulfilling the arrest quotas began to turn against themselves. Yezhov
would be beaten and dragged, weeping, on February 4, 1940, into
an execution chamber that he himself had designed. The balding,
bespectacled Lavrentiy Beria replaced him; he would be eliminated
too. During their tenures as head of the NKVD, the arrest sweeps
were concentrated in the elite north-central neighborhoods of Mos-

cow. Interrogations occurred at the Lubyanka, the nexus of the police state, and such notorious prisons as Butïrskaya and Lefortovo. The Memorial Society of Moscow created a database showing the names and addresses of the more than eleven thousand people confirmed to have been purged, but it is no longer accessible.[56] The House of Composers at 8/10 Bryusov Side-Street was spared; the building at 51 Bolshoy Karetnïy Side-Street, where Shostakovich rented an apartment before his marriage to Nina Varzar, was the site of numerous arrests; four tenants of the Zemlyanoy Val apartment building, where Prokofiev took up residence in 1936, disappeared.

Prokofiev survived, though the trauma damaged his health and warped the psyches of his children. His wife recalled hearing talk around their kitchen tables of class warfare, fascist menace, the capitalist encirclement of the USSR—in other words, ideas straight from the pages of *Pravda*. She did not want to join the discussion and suffered a nervous breakdown when Prokofiev told her that the Soviets would not allow them to return to Paris. Their marriage fell apart in 1941. Seven years later she was arrested on trumped-up charges of low-level espionage, tortured for months, and sentenced to twenty years' hard labor. She served eight, winning early release thanks in part to efforts on her behalf by Shostakovich.[57]

A PRODUCT OF the tsarist era, Prokofiev maintained the snobbish air of the noblesse, and condescended to the Soviets, which made them all the more committed to breaking his spirit, inveigling him into compromise, frightening him if need be. Kerzhentsev made this point clear in a 1937 memorandum to Stalin regarding Soviet musical affairs. Referring to *Romeo and Juliet*, he remarked that Prokofiev now recognized that he had to change his tune in order "to overcome formalism and approach realism."[58] Kerzhentsev had in mind two orchestral suites arranged from the ballet, which were all that could be performed of the grand 1935 score—pending its refashioning as a proper Soviet ballet.

A premiere of sorts took place in a provincial theater in Brno, Czechoslovakia, on December 30, 1938, a gesture of Soviet cultural support for the nation on the eve of its fall to the Nazis. Ivo Váňa-Psota choreographed the ballet and took the part of Romeo. Zora Šemberová partnered him as a winsome Juliet. In her memoirs, titled *Na šťastné planetě* (On a happy planet), Šemberová confirms that it was a partial presentation, not the full score, and that the choreographer sought in the dancing to reflect the lean modernism of the music, though the novelties of the original scenario did not make it to Brno. The interruption of the quarrel between Montague and Capulet factions by a Soviet May Day parade never left its page in Prokofiev's manuscript, and neither did the bizarrely retrospective exotic divertissement (involving bejeweled Syrian girls, moors, and pirates with contraband) that is seen just after Juliet imbibes the "death" potion prepared for her by Friar Laurence. In Brno, a chorus recited the end of Shakespeare's play after Váňa-Psota had run out of music for dancing. "Desolate Romeo, convinced that Juliet is indeed dead, finishes his suffering by drinking poison. Juliet awakes, sees her beloved, and leaves the world that had begrudged them their love. Did their love have to die in order that the hatred between the Montagues and Capulets would also expire?"[59]

So no happy ending, and no Prokofiev: By the end of 1938 he was barred from travel outside of the Soviet Union. The Commissariat of Foreign Affairs declined to issue him a passport: his status had been changed from *vïyezdnoy* (allowed to travel) to *nevïyezdnoy* (disallowed). He missed the production of *Romeo and Juliet* in Brno, which closed after seven performances on May 5, 1939, a victim of the Nazi German occupation of Czechoslovakia.

Yet the premiere foretold a change in fortune for the ballet. In August of 1938 Prokofiev received a telegram from the Mariyinsky–Kirov Theater in Leningrad expressing interest in staging *Romeo and Juliet* during the 1939–40 season. The invitation came from the choreographer Leonid Lavrovsky, who had earlier proposed performing the ballet with students. In his hands, *Romeo and Juliet* became a *drambalet*, a naturalistic production that blurred the line between acting and dancing even as the division between good and evil hardened. To be a heroine or a hero in Lavrovsky's universe was to submit, to soften, to meld ballet and melodramatic acting. To be a villain was to remain trapped in the realm of stiff-boned caricature, the bland world of obvious political lessons. Prokofiev had no choice but to accept Lavrovsky as the choreographer of the Soviet premiere, but he resented it—especially after he learned that his score would be overhauled to be made more tragic, more Soviet. He had learned to compose ballet in Paris under the tutelage of Diaghilev and the Ballets Russes. Diaghilev loved scandal; Kerzhentsev and the Committee on Arts Affairs did not. The filigreed textures of *Romeo and Juliet* were thickened and slowed in revision until the music seemed to petrify.

Even after the required changes were made, some without Prokofiev's permission, the dancers still struggled with the score. Galina Ulanova, the passionate ballerina who would forever define the role of Juliet, echoed various official complaints about Prokofiev's clotted harmonies and tangled rhythms. "To tell the truth we were not accustomed to such music, in fact we were a little afraid of it," she parroted. "It seemed to us that in rehearsing the Adagio from Act I, for example, we were following some melodic pattern of our own, something nearer to our own conception of how the love of Romeo and Juliet should be expressed than that contained in Prokofiev's 'strange' music. For I must confess that we did not hear that love in his music then."[60]

Ulanova's complaints reflected both official opinion and her own—there was no separation between the two—and Prokofiev had to accommodate her. He dismissed her "hysterics," as he quipped condescendingly, but lambasted Lavrovsky and the conductor Isay Sherman.[61] Despite the discontent on all sides, Ulanova ensured that *Romeo and Juliet* was a success at its premiere in Leningrad during the dark days of the Soviet-Finnish War. She filled Prokofiev's acerbic brass and string lines with feeling while enlivening the cartoonish didacticism of *drambalet*. Ulanova donned the air of a pensive innocent onstage and was occasionally criticized for appearing too submissive as she ran toward Romeo, nightgown fluttering, or too obligingly offering her breast to a knife in the Bakhchisarai seraglio. Yet her earnestness lent classical ballet a common touch. Her arabesques seemed unstudied but communicated passion between the lines. She was a prima ballerina, an actress inspired by silent movies, but also a real person. "Her steps appeared to contain her deepest thoughts and to unfold spontaneously, as if she too were just discovering them," the ballet historian Jennifer Homans writes, then finds in her dancing a political force. Ulanova "stood both for and against: for the socialist state and its accomplishments but against its empty, canned slogans, its deceptions and lies," Homans claims.[62]

Perhaps. But Ulanova also lobbied for state awards and ended up with a greater collection of them, before the Soviet Union collapsed, than her peers. She was treasured enough by the regime to be transferred from Leningrad to Moscow, removed from the theater of the tsars and brought to the theater of the Soviets, now the more officially prominent venue of the two. With Moscow now the seat of political power, the Bolshoi could claim cultural command both at home and abroad. Stalin saw Ulanova dance on its stage, more than once, and she received a Stalin Prize in 1947 for her outstanding interpretation of the lead role in *Romeo and Juliet.* The other performers in the production were not so recognized, a detail that the ballet master Lavrovsky timidly protested in a letter to the ruler. First, of course, he expressed his deepest gratitude to Stalin for granting him his wonderful life, and pledged in return to continue sacrificing his health and strength for "our beloved Soviet art, which you so broadly protect." He admitted that he had no business writing to the living god, but willed himself to mention that the wonderful Ulanova was the lone member of the cast of *Romeo and Juliet* to have a Stalin Prize pinned to her chest. It seemed, perhaps, that other deserving dancers had been "forgotten" by the Committee on Arts Affairs, including veterans of the iconic Soviet ballet *The Flames of Paris*, which, Lavrovsky knew, was Stalin's favorite. Lavrovsky ended his terrified request for a review of the prizes, and for the ruler to "defend" the other dancers, with the words "forgive me."[63]

The special treatment for Ulanova continued even after Stalin's death. She all but awarded herself the Lenin Prize in 1957, promoting her candidacy in a speech to the nominating committee. The director of the culture division of the Central Committee, Dmitri Polikarpov, demurred, asserting, in a February 9, 1957, memorandum, that the award should go to new work rather than "for past services," but she received it nonetheless.[64]

As a student of Agrippina Vaganova, Ulanova was the product of a pedagogical method that emphasized *épaulement* and thus the simultaneous coordination and harmonization of the head, torso, feet, and hands. The goal of this coordination was to align not only all the parts of the body but also to connect the body to the mind and heart; such perfect coordination was meant to open a line of communication with the audience. Vaganova dedicated a chapter of her 1934 treatise on Russian ballet to the proper support for jumps, and she devoted several pages to the poetics of the wrists, how they should flex, for example, to represent the ebbing into stillness of the wings of a dying swan. Vaganova placed a premium on tradition, by which she meant Russian tradition, as defined by a drawing, in her 1934 treatise, of three ballerinas from three different places in *attitude effacée*. The ballerina on the left-hand side, labeled "French," tilts obsequiously forward; the ballerina on the right-hand-side, labeled "Italian," stands rigid and upright, as if on a trampoline. The "Russian" ballerina in the middle tilts less severely in attitude and showcases an elongated back leg.[65] That dancer is Ulanova, and, with even greater elongation, the great Soviet ballerinas who followed her.

Ulanova embraced *Romeo and Juliet* after Prokofiev disowned it. He had run into a wall of Soviet artistic and political resistance from Vaganova, Lavrovsky, and Ulanova, together with designers, instructors, and scenarists, all of whom believed, because they had to believe, that the salvation of their craft resided in *drambalet*. Prokofiev was instructed to embrace naturalism and reject the incoherence of experimental productions like *The Bright Stream*. He tried, losing his dignity and sacrificing his health in the effort, but never quite absorbed the lesson the censors set for him. His second Soviet ballet, *Cinderella*, likewise had a rough start before eventually earning accolades in a postwar Bolshoi Theater production. But his music was once more changed without his permission, and even nastier clashes with the censors lay ahead.

• • •

Where Shostakovich and Prokofiev failed from an official standpoint, composer and conductor Aram Khachaturian succeeded. He was a colonial subject, a migrant from the distant Soviet republics, and he behaved as one. He conformed to the dictates of Moscow, wearing, when called upon, the ethnic costume of the Georgia of his birth and the Armenia of his ancestors. The son of a bookbinder, Khachaturian was raised in a simple house on a bleached Tbilisi mountainside; his humble proletarian origins appealed to Soviet sensibilities. He ended up becoming intricately involved in the Soviet musical administration, holding senior positions in the Union of Soviet Composers, though he would, in 1948, be sacked from the union in a political and financial scandal centering on excessive payouts and perks, including interest-free loans, to his colleagues. Khachaturian was eventually denounced for failing to uphold socialist principles in his music and dabbling in anti-populist experiments. But he and his assistant in the union, Levon Atovmyan, had really just been looking after their friends.

Khachaturian's first ballet was a modest success, and his second, which knowingly derived from the first, a greater one. The third and most famous, *Spartacus* (Spartak), had a tough time reaching the stage, but the composer was not to blame, and ultimately *Spartacus* won international fame. Indeed, it survives to the present day in the Bolshoi repertoire. Khachaturian received his first Bolshoi contract in 1939, the year officialdom blandly deemed him a "talented young composer."[66] That talent rested less in his melodic and harmonic inventiveness than in his selection of sources, his ability to find what he needed in the nineteenth-century repertoire. Insofar as he could compose with more than two lines of motion, he far surpassed the hampered Asafyev. His orchestral imagination, moreover, eclipsed that of Glière, a composer who contentedly sat in the fat middle of the bell curve of Soviet music.

Khachaturian got his start in the theater collaborating with the Armenian scenarist Gevork Ovanesyan and the Armenian choreographer Ilya Arbatov. Backing came from an Armenian politician, Anastas Mikoyan, one of Stalin's most devoted servants during the purges, a charmer and a monster. "It was hard to dislike him," Valerie Hemingway, the author's daughter-in-law recalled of a meeting with Mikoyan in Havana, but "he had the roundest, blackest eyes I have ever seen."[67] Mikoyan heaped praise on Stalin at a celebration of the NKVD on December 21, 1937, at the Bolshoi Theater; he was on hand for the culling of the Armenian communist ranks; and he signed the order for the 1940 massacre of more than 22,000 Polish officers and others at Katyn, a long-denied act of barbarism that haunts Russian-Polish relations to the present day. These activities fell outside Mikoyan's official duties as Soviet minister of trade. In his own memoirs, Mikoyan rinsed the blood from his hands. Such were the times, he protested, and besides, he had children to protect. "I had no choice except complete submission," he claimed.[68]

Although proud of his birthplace (the Armenian village of Sanahin) and often disdainful of Russians, Mikoyan capitulated to Stalin's vision of a Soviet Union whose republics had but fictional control over their destinies. The RSFSR defined the USSR; Russians dominated the friendship of the peoples. The thick-haired, thick-lipped composer with whom Mikoyan shared a common heritage adapted accordingly. Some of Khachaturian's music pretends to be 100 percent Armenian but actually derives from age-old Russian compositional practices. Just as Stalin once treated his rheumatism by leaving Moscow with Mikoyan to take in the thermal waters of the Caucasus, so too Khachaturian dipped his toes into original folk sources from the region. Atop a traditional Russian foundation, he erected elaborate musical structures of bright exotic colors, though paradoxically, even while privileging orientalism, he resented the trivializing labels that came with it. Khachaturian grumbled to his colleagues during the war about being stuck "within the boundaries of national music."[69] Such was his fate, but it kept him out of the classroom, in the spotlight.

Khachaturian developed a formula for the festive parts of his ballets, scenes much beloved by corps de ballets for their garish ease of comprehension. The adjectives accumulate when it comes to the music he created for all-male groups. It is potent, precise, pungent, and above all else wild, the perfect partner for physical virtuosity. Khachaturian's recipe included up-tempo ostinato patterns; original tunes in the brasses and woodwinds offset by "folk" melodies in the strings; occasional pentatonic scales; even more occasional chromatic clusters. Semitonal displacements between the upper and lower lines are matched by misplaced accents in the rhythms. Such are the elements from which Khachaturian fashioned his famously raucous "Saber Dance." The bends and turns in his slower pieces for dance match those of the torsos and arms of dancers in beaded costumes. Much of his contrapuntal writing has the texture of over-cooked pasta in pots boiling over with emotion. The shared adagio music of his first and second ballets expressed the anxieties of a collective farm on the eve of the Nazi invasion. But it could also, as the filmmaker Stanley Kubrick demonstrated in *2001: A Space Odyssey*, evoke the frigid solitude of outer space.

In 1939, Khachaturian composed music for a ballet on an Armenian theme. It was created on a tight schedule in the spring and summer, premiered by a relatively new company in Yerevan, then re-premiered at the Bolshoi Theater on October 24, 1939. This second performance was part of a ten-day festival, or *dekada*, dedicated to Armenian folk traditions—at least as defined by Moscow. Stalin welcomed the participants at a Kremlin reception, where Mikoyan was praised for having "motivated all of us, the Armenian workers, to raise our culture and art to the highest level."[70] At the peak was the ballet they had brought to town. Titled *Happiness* (Schast'ye), it was an obvious winner at the Bolshoi. Positive reviews overflowed the columns of newspapers otherwise committed to reporting on the war in Europe. The *Pravda* review opened with a reference to the French fairy-tale writer Countess d'Aulnoy—"This is not the blue bird fairy tale, about happiness being stolen away from the people"—but also took a veiled swipe at Lopukhov and his tippy-toed formalism. *Happiness* was considered "an authentic dance symphony," depicting "the people's happiness in their work, in love, in giving their all to glorify the Soviet homeland."[71]

The ballet consists of montages of toil and rest plus depictions of soldiers packing up and trudging off. The most important event occurs offstage, out of sight, at the end. After a cluster of stylized folk dances to abstracted folk themes, the ballet suggests the presence of foes who, if not checked, will devastate the grape gatherers of the Ararat Valley, Armenia's Garden of Eden. The symbolic national hero, Armen, must decide if he will forgo his own pleasures—in this instance, dating the heroine, Karine—to join his Red Army comrades at the frontier.

As a Soviet man, Armen is not one to cower, so he enters into unseen battle and returns home in bandages. On the way, he crosses paths with Karine, giving her a chance to dance out her dread that he might have been killed, but the two of them are destined to be together. Their wedding party expands into a broader celebration of the friendship of the peoples and their leader. The point is made explicit in the final lines of the scenario: "The act concludes in an apotheosis, a hymn to the leader of the peoples, to the great Stalin. The border guards join the collective farmworkers in a song about Stalin."

Khachaturian emphasized that his entire score bears the intonations of Armenian folk material, which he learned not firsthand, as Soviet writers asserted on his behalf, but from listening to recordings and performances of the Armenian Philharmonic and its chorus. Nine folk tunes are used in *Happiness*, although one of them—the music for a gopak dance—was actually Ukrainian, and another was lifted from a Russian limerick. Fittingly, it serves as the basis of a comical crane dance, or *zhuravl'*. The Armenian material includes "Duy-Duy," a staple of Azeri musicians often performed as flamenco; "Ashtarak," a tune named after a town that expresses romantic longing; and the popular wedding tune "Shalakho," which involves two men courting the favor of the same woman in adagio gestures.

The ending of the score was, as everyone involved pointed out, a paean to Stalin: "Our happiness," Khachaturian explained in his remarks on the ballet, "is inextricable from the name of the person who gave us this life, from the name of great Stalin." The choreographer Arbatov repeated the points about love for the land and its leader, offering no specifics about his dances other than his avoidance of the angular, agitprop poster style that had been popular in the Lunacharsky era. He shunned abstract gestures in favor of "national folk elements," these being integrated into classical balletic syntax. Arbatov repeated the wooden refrain about the happiness of the characters in this, the first Soviet-Armenian ballet, again emphasized the broader friendship of the peoples, and described the ending as a "cantata in honor of the great Stalin. Hence the name of our ballet: *Happiness*."[72]

THAT *HAPPINESS* WAS so well received meant that a sequel would be commissioned for professional dancers. Scenarist Konstantin Derzhavin in Leningrad was charged with preserving the best of *Happiness* while replacing the worst. The obvious problem in the original was its lack of drama: life in the utopian domain of Khachaturian's first ballet is plot-free, except offstage. In the follow-up version, Armen is given a sister, Gayané, after whom the ballet is named. The setting remains an Armenian kolkhoz, this one devoted to cotton picking and carpet weaving, but life is now much less paradisiacal. Gayané's husband, Giko, is an abusive alcoholic who colludes with unnamed criminals to torch the crops, setting the surrounding hills demonically aglow. Things end back in contentment, though: Gayané escapes her husband and finds new love with a dashing young Russian officer, Kazakov, and Armen meets his Kurdish sweetheart toward the end. The infectious "Saber Dance" is performed as part of a grandiose trans-Caucasian divertissement. Khachaturian completed the ballet in 1942, and it was premiered at the end of that year.

Details were added and subtracted from the plot during the initial run as well as the 1952 and 1957 revivals, for purely political reasons. The immediate context for both *Happiness* and *Gayané* was the signing of the Molotov–Ribbentrop Non-Aggression Pact between the Soviet Union and Germany on August 23, 1939. The Soviet foreign minister, Vyacheslav Molotov, and his German counterpart, Joachim von Ribbentrop, devised a secret protocol that aimed to define the Soviet and German spheres of influence for a decade. They split Poland, the three Baltic states, and the enclave of Bessarabia between them. For the two years that the pact remained in force, the Committee on Arts Affairs curtailed the creation of anti-Nazi plays, films, operas, and ballets. Hence the reason the border infiltrators in *Happiness* go unidentified; hence the emphasis on threats within the Soviet sphere, as opposed to foreign enemies, in the draft scenario of *Gayané*. And hence, when the pact ended, further revisions to the scenario adding explicit references to the Nazi invasion, including air-raid alerts.

Khachaturian decried the ravages to his nation—and to his ballet, which the censors left in a mess of "confused notation, confused libretti, everywhere the same arrogance and distortion."[73] But as the shredded pages of the conductor's scores to his third ballet, *Spartacus*, attest, his complaints went unheeded. Little had changed for ballet composers since the time of Pugni and Minkus; their music still belonged to choreographers, even if it had become more sophisticated, the scores integrated, representational, the melodic details of individual numbers resonating across the wholes. Politics accounts for some but not all of the distortion, as Khachaturian's experience in 1967 with the dictatorial Bolshoi Theater ballet master Yuriy Grigorovich would attest. Experience, fame, and state prizes, including the Lenin Prize for *Spartacus* in 1959, perversely gave him less rather than more control over his music.

THE SOVIET-GERMAN PACT was shattered on June 22, 1941, when Hitler double-crossed Stalin by invading the Soviet Union in a three-pronged assault known as Operation Barbarossa. That December, the Japanese bombed Pearl Harbor, bringing the United States, now allied with the Soviet Union, into the night and fog of Hitler's madness. Humiliated, Stalin disappeared from public view for a week and a half as the Wehrmacht, unopposed, scorched the fields and cities of his empire. He had received reports of Germans taking down the barbed wire along the immense Soviet border, but he had hesitated to respond, seeking to prevent all-out invasion, even after the Germans swarmed into Soviet terrain from points north, south, and west, "from the muddy lagoons of the Danube Delta to the tidy sand dunes of the Baltics." "Some waded," Constantine Pleshakov reports, "some rowed, some ran, some walked, some rode in tanks and trucks."[74] It fell to Molotov to broadcast the news of the invasion to the terrified masses, and to signal to Stalin that lack of readiness had caused the loss of hundreds of aircraft, thousands of tanks, and hundreds of thousands of soldiers arrayed at the front. The Soviet Information Bureau invoked the *Otechestvennaya voyna*, the Patriotic War of 1812 against Napoleon, to mobilize the populace in the *Velikaya Otechestvennaya voyna*, the Great Patriotic War against Hitler.

In October 1941, government ministries, the Communist Party, diplomatic missions, and cultural agencies evacuated Moscow for Kuybïshev (present-day Samara), an industrial center on the Volga River. Those who refused the order to leave Moscow, or did not receive one, recalled a lawless and hedonistic atmosphere as the last trains left. Stalin reemerged as a mega-mind war strategist to direct the generals of the Soviet armed forces (those senior officers who had survived the purges) into ill-equipped battle against the mechanized Nazis. Hitler studied the Napoleonic campaigns before plotting his invasion of the Soviet Union and dreamed of Moscow in flames again, its 4 million citizens subjugated. His war would take a much ghastlier toll on the former Russian capital than the new one. Hitler blockaded Leningrad for 872 days, starving the populace into acts of cannibalism before food and fuel could be conveyed into the city across the ice of the Gulf of Finland.

The Luftwaffe dropped five-hundred-pound explosives on Moscow's factories, and clusters of cruder, smaller firebombs on the buildings, adjacent to the factories, where people lived. The planes whined across the skies in half-hour waves, five or more hours a night. The Red Army and the *trud* (labor) front—including men who had connived deferments, critical officials, prisoners, the aged—manned the cannons and the spotlights, hacked at the mud with pickaxes to make trenches and tank traps, erected barricades, planted mines, and chased sparks on the rooftops, dousing them with buckets of water tugged up the sides of the buildings. During the raids, mothers took shelter with their children in the cavernous metro stations, bedding down on the platforms or in the tunnels.

The State Academic Bolshoi Theater had been closed two months before the invasion for repairs to the ventilation and an expansion of the backstage area. It was not in use on the day of the attack. The leading artists received the order to evacuate with the government to Kuybïshev; others boarded trains loaded with tsarist treasures bound for Sverdlovsk; still others joined the fight. The Bolshoi Ballet soloist Alexei Varlamov received his "war christening" driving a T-34 tank through the brick dust and oil smoke of the Battle of Stalingrad; he was discharged a hero after a shell tore through his left leg, and yet managed to return to the stage.[75] Vasiliy Tikhomirov, choreographer of *The Red Poppy*, had taken ill and could not leave. The ballerina Olga Lepeshinskaya, star of the post-Geltser version of that ballet, showed her mettle during the war. She was a committed communist from her teen years and a member, from the first year of the war, of Mossovet, the Moscow city government. Her patriotism, obvious talent, and the example she set as a hardworking, self-sacrificing Soviet artist granted her access to political power from age twenty-five. Her colleagues feared her connections, but she too had her moments of panic. Lepeshinskaya's first husband served as senior interrogator for the NKVD. He was twice imprisoned, which forced her to twice divorce him, the second time for a general. In the tumult, the head of the secret police called into question Lepeshinskaya's loyalty, inviting her for a chat in his book-lined study. "I've heard rumors that you don't trust Soviet authority," he said. She replied, robustly, "Let's talk like communists. If he's guilty, punish him. If not, let him go." Earlier, Stalin—a "bad man, vindictive and malicious"—had laid his piercing eyes on her, and she wore revealing clothing when dancing at Kremlin receptions in his presence.[76] Lepeshinskaya was no less proud of her marksmanship and service to Soviet anti-fascist causes than her ecstatic physical exertions on the stage; she resented being evacuated in 1941 and did not particularly enjoy entertaining the populations of the provinces in social clubs and other make-do spaces. She took a pass, at least at first, on the ballet *Crimson Sails* (Alïye parusa), which tells the tale of a motherless girl, her sea-faring father, the toy boat he gives her, and her dream-come-true of escaping across the waves with a prince. A pastel-colored ballet of pleasant dances and innocent comic roles, it was created, in difficult conditions, by three young choreographers to music by a young composer, Vladimir Yurovsky, with a young dancer, Nina Chornokhova, making it special. *Crimson Sails* premiered in the Kuybïshev House of Culture (Dom kul'turï) on December 30, 1942, and had fifteen performances. Lepeshinskaya danced in the revival at the Bolshoi.

"This was in truth the first and last time in my life when I threw my ballet shoes into the cupboard," she recalled of her march to the Sverdlovsk regional Komsomol command "to demand, not request," that she and two other patriot-dancers be sent to the front.[77] That did not happen, for the sake of her safety. Instead, Lepeshinskaya returned to Moscow to guard the rooftop of her building. Anecdote has her practicing her ballet poses in one of the turrets. After the Germans were repulsed from Moscow, Lepeshinskaya joined a crack ballet brigade that did, in fact, make it to the front to boost morale; she also performed in concerts in hospitals and munitions factories. The ballet historian Elizabeth Souritz distinctly remembers Lepeshinskaya performing in concert with Pyotr Gusev in Kuybïshev on August 31, 1942, and the ballerina playing games of bridge with her parents, who had also been evacuated to Kuybïshev during the war (Souritz's father was an ambassador for the Soviet Union.)[78]

The experience of the war became part of Lepeshinskaya's dancing afterward. She shed the flirtatious, happy-go-lucky comic roles of her youth to become a serious Soviet heroine: formidable, indomitable, unhesitating. In 1953, Lepeshinskaya broke her leg in the first act of a performance of *The Red Poppy* but continued performing until the entr'acte, fracturing it in two more places and losing consciousness when the curtain came down.[79] She eventually retired with an unprecedented four Stalin Prizes.

THE ART ENDURED. During the war, the evacuated students of the Theater College toured hospitals, schools, work settlements, and orphanages around the Volga with a ballet about the Slavic Santa Claus, Grandfather Frost. A wartime photograph captures an outdoor ballet class in a ruined Russian town. Girls stand in third position on planks thrown across the mud, with a thin log serving as handrail. Tots in kerchiefs, their torsos folded around another log, gaze openly at them, as does a worker in soft cap and peasant blouse.[80] Those dance pupils who remained in Moscow, and who had not effectively replaced their parents as medics and machinists, fell into the care of the dancer Mikhaíl Gabovich, one of the acclaimed Romeos to Galina Ulanova's Juliet.

Gabovich had joined the fight, operating a spotlight during the worst of the Luftwaffe attacks. In the fall of 1941, however, the Committee on Arts Affairs made him the artistic director of what remained of the Bolshoi Theater ballet and opera. Gabovich was ordered to stage classic ballets and operas in a classic style—nothing Marxist, nothing done from the perspective of dialectical materialism. He had nowhere near the number of professional dancers required, however, and so placed a frantic telephone call to the Theater College: "Natalya Sergeyevna, come immediately to the

Bolshoi!" "Why, what's happened?" "Performances are being revived, and we need children for the ballet, those that weren't evacuated to Vasilsursk." "What's with you, Misha! What ballets, we're at war, the Germans are close to Moscow . . ." "The Germans won't last. The people of Moscow need us at the theater—for a rest, to distract themselves, to forget about war for a few hours. We have to support them. Our fighters will come. They will gather their strength, feel better, become stronger in beating the enemy."[81]

And so, according to this breathless anecdote, a fifteen-year-old ballerina named Maya Plisetskaya was given two of the adult roles in *Swan Lake*, with one of her rehearsals conducted under sirens and bombs. For performances of *Boris Godunov*, the ushers, stagehands, and tutors of the Bolshoi were dressed up as sixteenth-century peasants in the crowd scenes before a packed hall of conscripts holding weapons. Unlike the factory workers and peasants who had been trucked to Moscow to assess Shostakovich's last ballet, *The Bright Stream*, the soldiers were agreeably uncritical.

These and other performances occurred in the affiliate of the Bolshoi, not the historic building. In the first months of the siege, firebombs and the casings of antiaircraft shells routinely fell onto and through the roof. The Bolshoi was under constant threat and so was placed under the protection of Moscow civil defense commander Alexei Ribin. To him, protection meant stamping out cinders; it also meant preventing the theater from being occupied by fascists. Ribin ordered his subordinates to mine the first floor with "several tons of explosives of tremendous destructive power."[82] The Metropole and National Hotels were also defended from invasion in this fashion. From the air, meantime, the Luftwaffe targeted the building of the Central Committee, which was located in the neighborhood between the theater, the river, and the Kremlin. At four in the afternoon of October 22, 1941, eighteen minutes after sirens began chasing the public toward the shelter of Okhotnïy ryad metro station, a huge bomb landed in front of the Bolshoi. The blast slammed Rïbin into a wall as the theater rocked back and forth on its ancient pilings "like a suspended cradle."[83] The bomb killed the soldier standing on guard at the front, bloodied and fractured the faces and limbs of those who had not made it to the metro on time, and collapsed the floors and walls of the foyer, crushing a janitor. The sculpted columns buckled along with the thick oak doors, the underground water pipes burst, and the asphalt all around sank. Had Rïbin's mines gone off, he would have died, and the entire building and the surrounding streets would have been razed. But they did not, and he ordered them removed.

Resolve met defiance. Repairs to the theater began in the winter, and the gala agitprop concert celebrating the twenty-fourth anniversary of the Great October Socialist Revolution went ahead as scheduled, on the platform of Mayakovskaya metro station.

THOSE ARTISTS WHO declined to use the spotlight to spread nationalist propaganda during the war watched their commissions disappear. Defeating Hitler was the focus, on all fronts. Even after the Soviet triumph, the sacrifice and suffering of the people remained a sacred touchstone of the Soviet experience. Efforts by artists to turn the page in the spirit of rebirth, to create new ballets, operas, films, and plays about current events often came to ruin, subject to ridicule by the cultural police of Glavrepertkom. Of a doomed postwar ballet called *Love Poem* (Poema lyubvi), one of the censors wrote, "The pursuits of the characters are amorous," such that "one might think that this is the sole pursuit of our youth." The plot seemed to lack the requisite heroic deeds and moral lessons. "Meanwhile one of the heroes is writing a dissertation," the censor lamented, although "he might as well not be writing it for all it affects the plot." The ballroom scene, set under a disco ball, also did not impress. Even in "the glow of life's sunrise," Soviet youth were supposed to have more on their minds than sex.[84] Razed towns and cities needed rebuilding, farms re-collectivizing, and repurposed factories restarting, and meanwhile all that had to be shown onstage.

Love tended to fail; historical subjects involving merciless rebel defenders of the people did not. As he had been before the war, the Cossack leader Stepan Razin (1630–1671) remained a Soviet hero in ballets and operas. Under the tsars, he had topped the Russian equivalent of the most-wanted list, but in the Bolshoi Theater, he was imagined to be a "knight of the great Russian people," the "poetic" embodiment of the "Day of Judgment" for the feudal boyars he battled.[85] The 1939 ballet version of his adventures was performed in an amusement park before its successful premiere at the Bolshoi Theater.

Still, certain romances from the past endured—as long as the productions privileged realism. Myths, legends, and bedtime tales likewise passed muster if the content could acquire the correct political resonance. Tchaikovsky's ballets remained in the repertoire, and even for Stalin, hardly a romantic, *Swan Lake* was a touchstone of Russian/Soviet ballet. The legend of him seeing it "perhaps for the thirtieth time on the eve of his stroke in 1953" seems quite farfetched, though; his taste in ballet was largely limited to *The Flames of Paris*.[86]

THE BLACK AND WHITE SWANS, Sleeping Beauty, and the Nutcracker were soon joined on the stage by a fairy-tale newcomer: Cinderella. Coming from the lower classes, Cinderella posed less of an ideological threat than did her peers. She was beaten but not broken; she lived in a dirt-filled, gruesome world while her abusers hoarded consumer goods. These material possessions attracted Cinderella until such time as her consciousness was reshaped. The prince's too.

So the story could work. The sole problem in getting her foot into the glass slipper seemed merely practical: she needed a choreographer, and the choreographer needed music.

Prokofiev had been approached in 1940 to write a ballet for Ulanova based on the legend of the Snow Maiden, but he rejected the idea along with the dreadful scenario that came with it. When the vintage seventeenth-century fairy-tale *Cinderella* was proposed instead, again with Ulanova's backing, he made it clear that he wanted to avoid a repeat of the fiasco of *Romeo and Juliet.* The new ballet was to be *dansante,* but not in the Tchaikovskian mode. He insisted that if he had to submit to composing waltzes, polkas, and variations for a traditional *grand pas de deux,* the musical syntax would at least be more modern, spikier, and harder-edged. The familiar pathos of the plot did not, to his musical mind, require similarly comforting, romantic music.

When Prokofiev spoke of the project in interviews for the Soviet press, however, the ventriloquist's hand snaked up his back. His Cinderella would be a "true-life Russian maiden with true-life experiences, not the stuff of fairy tales," he explained, though he gave his heroine music that would allow her spirit to travel anywhere in the cosmos it desired.[87] In his party-line comments about true-life experiences, he had in mind Soviet films like *The Shining Path* (Svetlïy put', 1940), which begins like the old fairy tale (indeed, the working title was *Cinderella*) but ends in a textile plant, where the heroine receives the Order of Lenin. She proves so good at her job, in fact, that she is allowed to leave it altogether for the Supreme Soviet. The film was a musical, although with a different contour from the resplendent Disney *Cinderella* film of 1950. Instead of "Bippity Boppity Boo," the big number in *Shining Path* involves the magical manipulation, to song, of more than 150 spinning looms. The big number in Prokofiev's ballet centers on the doomsday clock.

Prokofiev's scenarist was the well-regarded Nikolay Volkov, who submitted an exquisite twelve-page scenario to Glavrepertkom for assessment on April 1, 1941. The censors found nothing to complain about. Volkov had, in their opinion, successfully refashioned his source material and provided the ballet master everything necessary to create a "generous mixing together of classical pantomimic principles and character dancing."[88] In his typescript, Volkov considered how the ballet should look, how the décor should represent Cinderella's traumatic past: her mother's death, her father's betrayal. "She stopped, became pensive," Volkov writes, after Cinderella appears onstage. She pulls back taffeta coverings from portraits of her mother and father and loosens her limbs to suggest getting lost in "memories of a children's game." The ghost of her father rushes in to conceal the portraits again. "Father, father, what have you done?" Cinderella mimes. Her mother is gone, replaced by her stepmother and the two menacing girls "peering over her shoulder."[89] The censor also praised Volkov for having collapsed together the public and the private, for having Cinderella fulfill her individual desires within a communal context.

In keeping with the fairy godmother's paradoxical mantra that even miracles take time, *Cinderella*'s path to the stage was fraught. As required, Volkov recalled the evolution of the ballet in cheerful terms, outlining for readers of the newspaper of the Mariyinsky–Kirov Theater, *Za sovetskoye iskusstvo* (For Soviet art), his initial conception, though by the time the article came out, in 1946, it had been radically altered. The "gilded philistinism" of the step-mother's manor and the "palace's prim world" was to have been presented in a grotesque light; the opposing world of childhood bliss, of Cinderella's memories, was to have faded in and out of view in warm hues. The tick-tock briskness of the climax was to have ceded to a song about the "eternal springtime of the heart."[90] Elsewhere, Volkov recalled Prokofiev devising the harmonies for that love song in his head while playing the card game solitaire on the lid of his piano.[91]

The collaboration ended once the war began, and the dramatic structure changed. Sight gags, which Prokofiev paired with musical pantomime, became important. In a nod to the pantheism of the rejected Snow Maiden project, the spirits of the seasons dance along with grasshoppers and dragonflies. Volkov had imagined the prince touring the world of folklore in search of the foot to fit the lost slipper. Along the way, he was to encounter "The Queen of Shaman, the Russian Swan Princess, and the fantastic Firebird." They headed for the exits long before rehearsals began, so to speak, and were replaced by the prince scouring the globe, "from North to South, East and West," like a heroic Soviet explorer—or even the Allied military forces themselves.[92] The prince experienced Africa in a dance that never made it into the final score. During World War II, the heroine was the USSR herself, the Stalinist Motherland; her stepmother the Third Reich; and her stepsisters the countries that Hitler had occupied and turned against Russia.

Yet even as the scenario was rewritten, Prokofiev insisted that his score would not be tampered with, not a single note, and would be composed independent of the dance. This left the choreographer Vakhtang Chabukiani, a celebrated *drambalet* dancer at the Mariyinsky–Kirov, in the awkward position of having to show the composer what he thought he might do without having heard the music. Chabukiani marked the movements for the composer, the silence in the studio broken by the ominous ticking of a metronome.[93]

As war reached the USSR, composer, choreographer, and dancers were evacuated to Chabukiani's native Tbilisi, Georgia, where their collaboration fell apart. Chabukiani took sick and petitioned to remain in place when everyone was ordered to evacuate farther from the fighting, to Perm. The upheaval left the choreography in the hands of Konstantin Sergeyev. He was the original Romeo, dancing opposite Ulanova for the premiere of Prokofiev's first Soviet ballet, and soon becoming a dominant force as choreographer, artistic director, and pedagogue under Stalin and Khrushchev. His aesthetic never developed past his 1930s youth, and to his disciples both he and Lavrovsky defined *drambalet*. Sergeyev became a fossil and took out his bitterness about his calcified condition on the stars of the next generation. His career at the Mariyinsky–Kirov came to an ignominious end when Rudolf Nureyev and then Natalya Makarova defected to the West. He was blamed.

In Perm, under evacuation, rehearsals for *Cinderella* began in the makeshift leaky studio of the House of the Red Army. Just half of the ballet was set when the Mariyinsky–Kirov dancers returned to Leningrad in 1944. The city endured unfathomable hardship during the nearly nine-hundred-day German siege. Cut off entirely, without food, medical supplies, or even warm winter clothing, people went insane from hunger and collapsed on the streets. Aid convoys arrived erratically over the Lake Ladoga ice road, but it was used chiefly for evacuations, and accidents were frequent. Convoys sank through the ice and soldiers drowned. The siege ended at the start of 1944, allowing evacuees to return, and with it a semblance of life. Performances in 1946 of first *Swan Lake*, and soon after *Cinderella*, symbolized the city's resilience.

The premiere of *Cinderella* had happened at the Bolshoi The-ater a few months earlier, on November 21, 1945. The choreography was created anew by Rostislav Zakharov, for whom *Romeo and Juliet* had been intended before the purges destroyed the creative team. A subdivision of the Committee on Arts Affairs, the "artistic council for theater and drama," assessed the gauchely opulent staging at the rehearsal stage, vetting details as trifling as the toothache suffered by one of the cobblers with whom the prince interacts, and fretting about the Russian content of the visual designs, which seemed less Russian to the auditors than French. The crown worn by the prince was likewise a sticking point; it looked monastic to some, fantastic to others, but all agreed it had no place in a Russian Soviet *Cinder-ella*. Zakharov, who had just been elevated to the position of chief ballet master by the committee, made clear that he respected the richness of the classical traditions but would never allow his dances to drift into abstraction. He explained to the committee that his first task was to listen closely to the music; then fill the ballet with action; and then ensure that the dancing, including the *fouetté* turns he had in mind for his heroine, elucidated the central concept of triumph over adversity. The committee approved of the approach he had taken and then got down to specifics, recommending, after seeing the ballet rehearsed, the removal of one of the mazurkas and the shortening of the variations for the stepsisters.

The committee deemed Ulanova a better poetess, and better at expressing love, than Lepeshinskaya, with whom she alternated in the lead role. But neither of them was to be reproached, except by the composers on the panel, who believed that the dancers had colluded with the choreographer and strangely tin-eared conductor Yuriy Fayer to change the music. It was amplified, bolstered, the dreamlike textures eliminated, the brasses made more triumphant. With the composer himself too ill from a heart attack to protest,

Shostakovich joined Khachaturian to complain about the changes in his stead. Shostakovich used the word "offensive" to describe them; Khachaturian found the instrumentation "too cumbersome," too monumental, in certain passages.[94] The Bolshoi Theater percussionist Boris Pogrebov had been tasked with the orchestration and had tried to make everything audible from the stage. But after years in the pit, his hearing might not have been the best: he replaced a flute line with three trumpets and a bass drum.

The end of the otherwise positive discussion of the ballet took a negative turn: the dramatist Nikolay Okhlopkov declared Prokofiev's music the product of an artist of little feeling and said that Zakharov had had to depend on Ulanova to provide her own internal music to create the role of Cinderella. "There's more music in Ulanova than in Prokofiev," Okhlopkov emphasized. "It's the truth so it needs to be said." Shostakovich bristled, recalling the criticism he had received for the same lack of feeling in the forgotten ballets of his youth: "It's not true, so you didn't have to say it."[95]

Changes to the scenario, score, and even the décor drained the magic from *Cinderella*. The unprincely prince, a man of the people not of the palace, finds his beloved living under his nose not far from the court. She is a real girl, salt of the earth: pure and honest and gracious, not needing heels to define her virtue. Whereas the slipper was imagined to be the tangible, visible evidence of her stunning inner beauty, in the Bolshoi production, Cinderella might as well have been dressed in fatigues for all that Charles Perrault's footwear mattered. The ballet had become a morality play about a working-class victim who overcomes her upper-class oppressors. Soviet ballet was by that time old enough to somehow be about itself. The effort to make ballet both approachable and aspirational was embodied in the figure of Cinderella. Emphasis fell on her pureness inside and her external metamorphosis from coal dust into diamonds, with the aid of Mother Earth (the third of the three mothers who appear in the tale). She is like glass herself, gleaming but fragile, enslaved by her stepmother and, in a sense, by the worst aspects of *drambalet*. The stepmother lives only in pantomime; likewise the banal, lumpy stepsisters are unable to dance. Cinderella's triumph comes in the court dances of the ballroom scene, which, in their general appeal, capture the best elements of the genre.

A spectacular command performance on December 23, arranged for two thousand foreign diplomats and hosted by Stalin's inner circle amid negotiations over the postwar world order, secured official awards for its creators. Zakharov maintained proper Soviet humility in this, his finest hour, noting the "inspired labor" of his colleagues Lavrovsky and Sergeyev in a newspaper article, but not mentioning his own.[96]

HE KNEW, PERHAPS, that awards did not protect artists from censure. Indeed, they exposed them to more. So too did the ailing composer of *Cinderella*, who was denounced together with Khachaturian and Shostakovich in an odious 1948 Central Committee resolution, charged with subverting the precepts of socialist realism in his compositions, including even those that pre-dated the invention of socialist realism. Various works were banned, the list being generic and random enough to signal to theaters and concert spaces that nothing by Prokofiev should be performed.

Losing performances meant losing income, and Prokofiev was left near destitute, with no means to settle the interest-free loan that he had taken out from the Union of Soviet Composers for a dacha far from the political mayhem of Moscow. The Central Committee allowed him to return to the fold in 1949, contingent on evidence of his ideological reeducation in the form of musical pabulum—

especially scores for or about Soviet youth. These were hard to compose, even with help from his communist-born and -bred second wife, Mira Mendelson, a librettist, and from musical assistants like Levon Atovmyan, himself a victim of the 1948 scandal. Tossed out of the union, Atovmyan needed the work as an arranger and orchestrator that Prokofiev offered to him.

In 1949, the three of them began work on a new ballet for Leonid Lavrovsky and the Bolshoi, *The Tale of the Stone Flower* (Skaz o kamennom tsvetke). The story was drawn from a prize-winning collection of stories native to the Ural Mountains, as collected by Pavel Bazhov and published in Russian in 1939 under the title *Malakhitovaya shkatulka* and, in English in 1944, as *The Malachite Box*. The attractively illustrated tale had already appeared on the big screen in 1947: *The Tale of the Stone Flower* was the first-ever Soviet movie in color, and it was deemed enough of a success, regional dialect and all, for transposition to the grand theater.

The mistress of Copper Mountain guards a cache of fabulous jewels and stones buried beneath the rugged terrain. The hero is a stonecutter, an artist-laborer obsessed with chiseling a dazzlingly lifelike flower out of malachite for his betrothed; the villain is a corrupt bailiff doomed to be swallowed up by the mountain on the mistress's command. The symbolism might seem opaque—Mother Earth subdues the lawless outback within the dark, deep context of the mining folklore of the nineteenth-century Russian interior—but it comes down to good versus evil and, at a stretch, art versus life. Together with the wild trio of gypsies who take over the central market scene, the death of the people's enemy would become, over time, a tremendous *coup de theatre* accompanied by the copper instruments of the orchestra and illuminated in glistening malachite green. In concept and realization, *The Stone Flower* suggests an alchemical project, with everyone involved, from its rocky start to its polished 1959 realization, seeking a magical artistic and political formula to make ballet an exciting adventure again.

The original version was anything but exciting. Ideologues imposed changes on the plot, the music, and the choreography, with the aim of pulling the ballet into the ideological center of socialist realism. Forget the hero's love of his bride and fear of the bailiff who would snatch her away: the ballet needed to refer to Marx and Lenin and communism too. Lavrovsky recalled his miseries with the censors at the start of the 1950s: "Prokofiev and I brought our libretto to Glavrepertkom over and over again, endlessly, and they told us: yours is a love triangle; please make it about labor. We rewrote it fifteen times, pared the romance, making it about real life, showing labor. We put it on the stage. But during this time attitudes began to change, and even our own interpretation of the subject. And they said: we don't need this."[97] There followed the familiar complaints about the music from the artistic and political council: it was bleak; it lacked emotion; the rhythms tripped up the dancers. To help get the notes into their feet, Lavrovsky added eight-measure repeats and removed trickier sixteen-measure extensions. Actually, however, the dancers praised the score for sounding so much like Tchaikovsky. Prokofiev took solace in not being likened to Minkus.

The Union of Soviet Composers harassed him about the music, repeatedly sending him back to the piano to reorder and reshape. He recycled children's pieces and folksong settings into his revisions. Lavrovsky arranged for the Bolshoi's concertmaster to improvise some examples of gypsy music at the composer's own piano, to convey a sense of the sound they wanted—an insult Prokofiev could not bear.

Prokofiev died of a cerebral hemorrhage on March 5, 1953, the same evening, at perhaps the same hour, as Stalin. The coincidence chilled the hearts of those who cared about him. The news about Stalin shook the world.

The wayward son of a drunk and a washerwoman, Stalin had fought his way up through the ranks of a political crime syndicate to command a significant share of the globe. But he had been unable to shape the world as he desired, and in his paranoid old age, when even the suggestion that he replace his stump of a toothbrush seemed suspicious, he appeared less frequently in public, preferring the celluloid company of Charlie Chaplin, John Wayne, and the stars of American film. He suffered a massive heart attack with his daughter, Svetlana, at his side, in a fortified dacha guarded by three hundred officers. "The death agony was horrible," Svetlana recalled. "He literally choked to death as we watched. At what seemed the very last moment, he suddenly opened his eyes and cast a glance over everyone in the room. It was a terrible glance, insane or perhaps angry, and full of the fear of death."[98]

So great was the ensuing panic on the streets of Moscow that few beyond Prokofiev's sons, second wife, and inveterate hangers-on learned of the composer's own passing. The Bolshoi's ballet master marked the event in the studio with his dancers, and briefly noted the funeral in his diary. On Saturday, March 7, Lavrovsky wrote: "S. S. Prokofiev buried." On Monday, March 9: "I went to Red Square. Burial of I. V. Stalin." Tuesday, March 10, found him back at work in the studio with Ulanova, setting *The Stone Flower:* "I set Katerina's dance in the cottage. I think it turned out well."[99]

Lavrovsky brought *The Stone Flower* to the stage on February 12, 1954, only to be scolded, gently but firmly, in reviews published throughout the season. *Pravda* suggested that he should enliven the ensembles and enrich the adagios. The ballet seemed to commentators a hesitant draft of something, an illustration of allegorical conceits yet to be made plain. Prokofiev might have been chided as well, but he could finally rest at peace in the grave. Thus it was Lavrovsky's responsibility "to find choreographic expression of the central concept: the people's spirit as manifested in their work and their constant striving towards beauty and perfection."[100]

Foreign reporters found some good in the ballet beyond Prokofiev's score. For Harrison E. Salisbury, Moscow bureau chief of the *New York Times*, Ulanova was a "dream fairy," impressionistically contrasting the "sinister glimpses of chained workers heaving precious stones in subterranean chambers"; the "flashing and sparkling stones and stalactites" of the mistress's cavern; and "the strange surrealistic green stone toads along with asbestos-like gnomes who might have come from another planet."[101] *The Stone Flower* was Lavrovsky's last major work.

AFTER STALIN'S DEATH, and with Nikita Khrushchev's elevation as supreme leader, the Soviet Union entered a period known as the "Thaw." It was marked by a reassessment, even a rejection, of Stalinism and the "cult of personality." Once again as the political winds shifted, so too did aesthetic diktats. Lavrovsky struggled to shed the constraints of *drambalet* and failed to impress the decidedly second-tier composer Mikhaíl Chulaki, who served as general director of the Bolshoi after Stalin's death, from 1955 to 1959, and then again, after a forced "time-out" from the theater, from 1963 to 1970.[102] In Chulaki's opinion, Lavrovsky was squandering his talent in "strange experiments," such as an attempted production of Béla Bartók's expressionist ballet, *The Miraculous Mandarin*. "He completely destroyed the integrity of that ballet," Chulaki fumed, "turning romantic mountain robbers into Parisian gangsters."[103] In fact, Lavrovsky had done no such thing: Bartók's ballet has no mountain robbers. Chulaki confused Bartók's ballet with a merrier one by Karol Szymanowski called *Harnasie*, about the robber bands of the Tatra Mountains.

Regardless, *The Miraculous Mandarin* was an unusual project for the Bolshoi, and provoked the ire of the Central Committee, which in 1961 chastised Lavrovsky for his cynical attempts to "propagandize from the stage of the Bolshoi Theater anti-realistic compositions alien to the spirit of our art."[104] Even by the more fluid cultural standards of the Thaw, he had gone too far, and he needed to be reined in again. The censure went down the chain of command from the Central Committee to the Ministry of Culture (which had replaced the Committee on Arts Affairs under Khrushchev) to the Bolshoi and Lavrovsky's studio. Chulaki took part in the drubbing, in part because he had never much liked Bartók, insulting his music as "formalist" and "bourgeois" during a 1949 visit to Budapest.[105] He repeated the Central Committee's talking points about Lavrovsky's fondness for "pathological experiences," thus demonstrating his own trustworthiness as a party loyalist.[106] The Thaw, Chulaki knew, did not melt everything.

Lavrovsky's time had passed—politically as well as artistically. In 1963, Chulaki prevented Lavrovsky from joining the ballet on its second London tour, despite pleas from the dancers. Ulanova claimed that the choreographer needed to be on-site to stage his chef d'oeuvre from 1940, *Romeo and Juliet*, but she did not protest too loudly, perhaps because she nurtured an ambition to take over his duties. The following season, Chulaki packed Lavrovsky off to the Theater College and replaced him at the Bolshoi with the handsome, chiseled face of the future: a thirty-seven-year-old choreographer from Leningrad named Yuriy Grigorovich.

Lavrovsky knew his successor well, since, in Leningrad, Grigorovich had exploited the grumblings about *The Stone Flower* to stage his own version of the ballet with dancers from the Komsomol. He faced resistance at first from his supervisors (he was an assistant ballet master at the time) but eventually won their support. Grigorovich took the best features of Lavrovsky's staging while tossing out the enervating pantomime along with its music. Dance suites, some premade, replaced it. Grigorovich opened up the hero's heart, and softened the heroine's backward leans. He deployed fewer gestures than can be counted on the hands, and despite being credited with restoring a long-lost symphonism to the ballet, he struggled to build meaningful choreographic phrases.

Grigorovich's adapted version of *The Stone Flower* took five years to reach the Bolshoi stage, but audiences at its premiere, on March 7, 1959, embraced the ballet and its young choreographer. The newly arrived Moscow correspondent for the *New York Times* made the obvious connection between the production and the tentative reforms of the Thaw. "A grand evening," Osgood Caruthers concluded, having been in attendance at the Bolshoi with Shostakovich and the US ambassador to Russia, Llewellyn E. Thompson, "and if not exactly a forward-looking one from where we stand, undoubtedly an adventure in the development of the Bolshoi's particular progress." The first act had its stumbles, and the phrases lacked the qualities of growth and change needed for richly expressive narration, but the chain dances of the second act represented "one of the marvels of the repertory. The scene is a market, and every conceivable Russian type is there, dancing his (and her!) head off. In contrast to the vehemence of most of it, there is a gypsy ensemble done in terms of exaggerated relaxation, and this theme is topped by a gypsy threesome of fantastic brilliance."[107]

If the Americans liked it, then something must be wrong with it. Or so concluded the Kremlin. Enthusiastic telegrams sent to the United States by correspondents for United Press International and the Associated Press were intercepted and translated into Russian for the Central Committee. The director of the culture division, Polikarpov, came to this conclusion about the 1959 version of Prokofiev's *The Stone Flower*, as now set by Grigorovich: "The mistress of Copper Mountain comes across in the production not as a symbol of the might of Ural Mountain Russians, not as a fetchingly half-fantastic depiction of Russian woman, but as an 'enigmatic' image of a female serpent whose dancing is much beholden to Western artistic fashion. . . . The movements and costuming of those dances depart from the Russian and Soviet classical ballet traditions."[108] The Central Committee reported the ballet's flaws to the minister of culture, Nikolay Mikhaílov, and asked him to make it a teachable moment, so to speak, by arranging a critique to be published in *Pravda*. Mikhaílov and the newspaper complied, as did, in his own way, Grigorovich.

ONCE UPON A TIME, ballet was a private art, an entertainment for the few, hardly the pretext for geopolitical intrigue. Imperial censors awoke to its powers during the second half of the nineteenth century, when ballet, no longer the plaything of Catherine the Great, was cast out of the royal garden and into the public theaters. The moment the art was freed from the government and let loose in the theaters of Moscow and St. Petersburg, it was enslaved by the imperial censors; scenarios were vetted and critiqued. Alexei Bogdanov's *Svetlana, the Slavic Princess*, for example, had to be reviewed by the print censor at the Ministry of Internal Affairs just in case the heroine came too close to impersonating an actual royal figure, even though the princess in question is completely fictional, an early nineteenth-century invention. What was kept inside the realm of the court could be trusted as elite entertainment, but as a public performance, ballet required oversight.

Stalinism all but collapsed the distinction between public and private, government and art, performances at the court at the Kremlin and those for audiences at the theater. The Bolshoi was bound up with the government both physically and politically, and censorship intensified to the point where almost nothing new could be approved for performance—despite best efforts from all involved, including the censors themselves. The tsars were gone, and fear reigned; the political uncertainty and creative anxiety could be seen and heard in those few new performances that made it through the filter. The oversight increased through the revolution and the civil war, hung over the killing fields of the purges, the Second World War, and the height of Stalinism. It relaxed but never relented, and it persists to the present day with the hand-in-glove involvement of politicians and priests, even though top-down government meddling in the arts is prohibited by the constitution of the Russian Federation. In 2015, while in Beijing staging his version of *Romeo and Juliet*, Grigorovich himself remarked, with a tired shrug, "there was censorship; there still is."[109]

· 7 ·

I, MAYA PLISETSKAYA

Maya Plisetskaya emblematized the power and might
of the Bolshoi Ballet in the mid-twentieth century. This decorated,
Moscow-trained ballerina had the essential elements of the Bolshoi
style: vigor, luster, fearlessness, and a showiness that admittedly
appealed to Soviet audiences more than sober-minded adjudicators
of her performances in the West. She also possessed, at her peak,
complete command of the big Bolshoi roles, boasted a packed international touring schedule, and indulged endless curtain calls before
her obsessed fans.

Born on November 20, 1925, she was the daughter of a silent-film
actress and a Soviet businessman. Maya's mother, Rakhil Messerer,
found herself tied to the tracks on screen and once, as the little girl
recalled, "trampled by horses."[1] From her father, Mikhaíl Plisetsky,
Maya inherited her facial features and brook-no-fools temperament.

He worked for the commissariat of foreign affairs and trade before becoming the director of the Soviet mining concession Arktikugol (Arctic Coal). Maya's erudite, polyglot grandfather, a Lithuanian Jew, made his living as a dentist. Her parents, grandfather, some of her aunts, uncles, and cousins, plus a pianist of no relation lived together in a large, fourth-floor apartment on Sretenska Street, a historic market district tucked inside the Garden Ring Road in central Moscow. Her uncle Asaf and aunt Sulamith danced with the Bolshoi.

Nature endowed Maya with red hair, lissome arms and legs, a long neck, over-gesticulating hands, a pliant spine, and a restless mind. Her athleticism would exceed even that of the daredevil Asaf. Maya danced before she could walk, her mother claimed, and as a toddler liked to balance on her father's extended hands, stretching herself upward and outward in delight. Once, when she was twenty-one months old, she climbed out a window of her apartment. She stood outside on the brick ledge and perched four floors above a cluttered courtyard with one arm hooked around the handle, calling to her mother for help. An uncle rescued her from a potentially fatal fall. On another occasion, "Mayechka" disappeared into the traffic-filled streets, prompting a frantic search. Her mother guessed that she might be lost within an enormous crowd that had gathered on the boulevard, between tramcar lines. "I thought that there might be a bear on show and that she might be here," her mother recalled. But Maya herself was the star attraction. "I fought through the crowd, looked, and saw Mayechka dancing, with everyone gasping about how good she was."[2] Plisetskaya recalled the anecdote similarly: "I naively loved Delibes's waltz from *Coppélia*. On holidays a cadet band played it on Sretensky Boulevard—out of tune but with feeling. . . . I pulled my hand from Nanny's tight hold and unexpectedly—even for me—started to dance. Improvising. A crowd gathered; a few loafers."[3]

She was admitted into the Bolshoi ballet school without debate. It had been a part of the Theater College during the imperial era, but dancers aspiring to the stage of the Bolshoi no longer studied alongside the actors of the Malïy Theater. Plisetskaya trained at the barre under the patient guidance of Yevgeniya Dolinskaya, whom she remembered setting part of Tchaikovsky's *Serenade for Strings* on her and three other little girls: "We danced in the kingdom of an abstract pastoral as graceful, mythological shepherdesses bathed in the sun and sky, catching floating butterflies."[4] Such was both the beginning and end of her interest in dancing delicate, Arcadian roles. Her regal appearance and impulsiveness ruled them out.

Plisetskaya spent less than a year at the school before her family moved to Spitzbergen, the island of permanent winter that crowns Norway. Her father had been appointed the general counsel and director of the Soviet mining complex there. "Suitcase, trains, Berlin, German lawns, ferry, seasickness, high waves, snow, plank stairs, albatrosses, cold, and wind," Plisetskaya wrote of her miserable trip to and life on the island.[5] Her mother also remembered skiing, bears, and frostbite. In the spring of 1935, Maya's father arranged for his daughter to travel back to Moscow, by icebreaker and then train, in the care of an Arktikugol accountant, who arrived at death's door, suffering from the cold and coal dust. Thus Plisetskaya returned to the ballet school, now under the direction of Elizaveta Gerdt. The broader curriculum included reading, writing, and arithmetic, along with French (which she failed to grasp) and piano (which she mastered). Stardom seemed destined.

Later in life she would rail against the Soviet system that she believed compromised her career. Yet that same system—with its instabilities, its traumas, the artists it ruined—cleared the path for her ascent. Plisetskaya joined the Bolshoi Ballet in 1943 at the nadir of the Second World War, and after less than a season in the corps de ballet she became a soloist. She said no to Giselle but yes to the frolicsome free-spirited Kitri, a girl of the streets, much like her beloved Carmen. Maya was impatient, paradoxical, and according to a devotee, a "Futurist" capable of expressing the most extreme of emotions in the coolest of manners.[6] Her beautiful back, the merriment and sauciness of her acting (she danced Juliet like a teenager who had just rolled out of bed with her boyfriend, as opposed to a naïf falling in love), the ease of her overextended splits, and her incautious attitude inspired the choreographer Yuriy Grigorovich to create demanding, even dangerous roles for her that she herself rejected. Once cordial and mutually supportive, their relationship eventually deteriorated, turning hostile.

From her aunt, Plisetskaya learned the solo miniature that would become her signature role: Michel Fokine's *The Dying Swan*, set to music from *Le carnaval des animaux* by Camille Saint-Saëns. Her interpretation swept aside the traditional sense of quiet surrender to assert an unexpected defiance. The swan is a cruel, harsh creature, she suggests in footage from the 1950s. Her range became bigger and motion faster in the 1970s, her arms and neck more refined, the torso longer and leaner. French choreographer Maurice Béjart found in her performance a "sweetness" and "joie de vivre."[7] But Plisetskaya was one of his muses and he was biased, not to mention inaccurate. Critics outside of Russia mocked the dance as a crowd-pleasing cliché, an unsubtle exercise in zoological mimesis.[8]

She performed *The Dying Swan* as late as her seventieth birthday, turning her back to the audience for her metamorphosis. She did it two or more times in a row—undyingly, yielding to public demand. "It's not a question of whether I personally like 'the dying swan,'" she told the Moscow-based British journalist George Feifer after enthralling an enormous crowd of villagers brought to the Kremlin to see her. "I dance for *them* not myself; to give *them* aesthetic pleasure," she said. "Of course I like the ballet, but I could live without it, *I* get no dazzling joy from it. But the public expects something from me, and I have no right to let them down."[9]

Feifer had fought hard to get access to the ballerina—to the point of being told by a midlevel foreign-affairs official to cease and desist. But he persisted, and so attended both the performance of *The Dying Swan* and a Bolshoi Ballet class, where she was the lone female dancer in the room, "in striking black practice dress, cream mohair leggings and full kit of makeup."[10] The gorgeous men in the studio were all straight, Feifer underscored, insisting that the culture of the Soviet Bolshoi Ballet was entirely heterosexual. (It was, at least in terms of appearances and mixed-orientation, or lavender, marriages, such as that between Vyacheslav Gordeyev and Nadezhda Pavlova.)[11] He extolled Plisetskaya's musicianship and—noting the leaps she made but fairer, gentler dancers might not attempt—he identified one of the secrets of her success: intense self-love. "After the round of exercises she moves to an inch from the mirror and stares at herself with the same penetration and lack of affectation as she stares at others. This dazzling narcissism, her total absorption with herself goes beyond egotism to an honest leveling with herself—the perception of Plisetskaya as an object which is essential to her approach to art."[12]

She owned her roles, among them Odette/Odile in *Swan Lake*, which she performed, according to her own generous estimate, eight hundred times—including, for the fifty-fifth time, on the evening of February 28, 1953, just a week before Stalin's death. Legend has it that Stalin was in the audience that night, but Plisetskaya actually denied this, pointing out, in an otherwise inconsequential 2008 sequel to her 1994 memoir, that she would have been warned about Stalin's attendance in advance. Whenever the supreme leader of the Soviet Union came to the Bolshoi, "dim-witted but vigilant spies" swarmed the theater, setting everyone's nerves on edge. She only wished that the "demonic charm" of her Odile had actually occasioned the fatal stroke of "the best friend of the working man." And she regretted the fear she felt on those occasions when she had danced for Stalin. "We were all slaves then of totalitarian terror."[13]

She told this tale in her own words, having decided against collaborating with a professional biographer. Her 1994 memoir is a brash, score-settling performance, toughest on artists who kow-towed to the regime, bleakest about the fate of her father; she remembers him sinking into depression at the start of the purges while still indulging the hope that he might be welcomed back into Stalin's good graces after months of fear and trembling. He had sat in the Bolshoi on December 5, 1936, for the formal proclamation of the new Soviet constitution, with Stalin himself presiding, but sub-sequently, unexpectedly, lost favor with the ruler. His sin? He had insisted on keeping in touch with a Trotskyite older brother who had emigrated to the United States. In the spring of 1937, a pardon seemed to come in the form of a prestigious invitation to the May Day celebrations on Red Square. Eleven-year-old Maya planned to put on a new dress and walk hand in hand with her daddy to the parade. But just before dawn that day, "the stairs creaked beneath the leaden weight of sudden steps." The apartment was searched while her pregnant mother sobbed, her little brother wailed, and Maya watched. "The last thing I heard my father say before the door shut behind him forever was 'Thank God, they'll settle this at last.'"[14] His family was told that while in prison, he had been deprived of the right to write letters for a decade. That meant he had been shot.

Plisetskaya's mother was herself jailed, with her newborn, the following March, though she would be spared execution. She sang lullabies to her baby in a prison cell in Moscow before being shipped by cattle car to Kazakhstan and condemned to a labor camp with the other wives of supposed traitors. In 1939, she earned a sort of reprieve by being exiled to the south, where she taught dances in clubs. Plisetskaya was taken in by her aunt, the dancer Sulamith Messerer. Custody was at first temporary, since the Stalinist system deemed the children of "enemies of the people" to be wards of the state. Thus the Soviets had their own version of the Imperial Foundling Home, which, back in Michael Maddox's time, had tutored the unwanted children of philandering noblemen in dance, drama, and Enlightenment values. Rather than receiving a basic education, however, now the orphans of the purges were subject to psychological rehabilitation according to Soviet dogma.

The night Maya's mother disappeared, Sulamith was performing *Sleeping Beauty* at the Bolshoi. Somehow (neither she nor her aunt were clear about the details) Maya made her way to the theater with her little brother Alik. The bad-tempered director of the production made the children wait in Sulamith's dressing room until the entr'acte. "Mayechka, where's your mama?" her aunt asked, bursting backstage. "She said she's been urgently summoned to our father in Spitsbergen," the girl answered. "She told us to come see you in the theater."[15] Sulamith took the children home to her communal apartment. Plisetskaya promised to be good; her brother cried inconsolably, not knowing why his mother had taken his baby brother away but left him behind. Their uncle, Asaf Messerer, gave him shelter while Plisetskaya remained in the communal apartment with Sulamith, who received legal guardianship of her against the wishes of the menacing matriarchs of the orphanage system. Her aunt (known to family and friends as Mita) housed Plisetskaya until 1941, when her mother was released and moved into the same communal flat, sleeping on a cot beside her now adolescent child. "I was saved by Mita," Maya recalled. "I did not end up in [the labor and death camps of] Vorkuta, Auschwitz, or Magadan. They tormented me, but they didn't kill me. Didn't burn me in Dachau." Instead, "my knowledge of the ballet grew."[16]

Plisetskaya enrolled in the Communist Movement of Youth, as required, and its newspaper announced the professional debut of the "*komsomolka-solistka*" on April 6, 1944. She was eighteen, center stage in *The Nutcracker*. "Plisetskaya joined the Bolshoi Ballet during the war," the newspaper reported, noting her instant promotion to the rank of soloist in a trio in *Swan Lake*, a "leaping variation" in *Don Quixote*, and the *Chopiniana* mazurka. She "seems to live in the elements of dance and speaks through its poetic language: she embodies themes of sadness, rumination, love, pleasure, and merriment to great effect."[17] The accompanying photograph shows her flinging herself through the air with more style than technique. Ovations followed in the pages of *Sovetskoye iskusstvo*, the mouthpiece of the Committee on Arts Affairs, and, after Plisetskaya began to tour the Soviet Union with her longtime partner Nikolay Fadeyechev, similar accolades appeared in the regional newspapers of Kazakhstan, Ukraine, the Baltic States, and the Russian interior.

Stalin made Plisetskaya an Honored Artist of the RSFSR in 1951 and kept her confined in the Soviet Union, apart from allowing her to perform in youth festivals in eastern Europe. Her first trip abroad as a professional came in response to a November 28, 1953, directive from the Central Committee to "prepare a group of Soviet artists, 30 people, for a concert tour to India."[18] The concerts mixed ballet and opera excerpts, and Plisetskaya was slated to dance *The Dying Swan* and a *pas de deux* from *Don Quixote*. She was required to gather character references and sit for interviews meant to gauge her trustworthiness. Although the most notable (and, for the regime, embarrassing) defections came about only in the 1960s and 1970s, traveling out of the Soviet Union had always been a special perk reserved for a chosen few. Permission was granted for Plisetskaya to go on tour in 1954.

During the trip, she had to put up with Yuriy Shcherbakov, the deputy director of the Department of External Relations of the Ministry of Culture or, as Plisetskaya described him, a "sweaty" NKVD/KGB agent with "bad breath."[19] The Russian delegation also received an invitation to perform in Rome, since the artists were traveling through that city to and from Karachi and Delhi. The request was rejected, owing to the risk of the performers getting "tired"—never mind the six days of travel, by train and plane, to get to India from the USSR.[20] The same excuse, tiredness, served to keep the artists out of Egypt and Pakistan.

Under Khrushchev, Plisetskaya was named a People's Artist. Her talent continued to stun audiences, critics, and bureaucrats alike. In June 1956, she danced the lead role in the Bolshoi's production of *Laurencia*, a ballet choreographed by Vakhtang Chabukiani to music by Alexander Kreyn, first performed in Leningrad in 1939.[21] The plot concerns the revenge of Spanish villagers on a Lothario-like prince who ravishes a maiden at her wedding. Khrushchev brought the Yugoslav president, Marshal Tito, to the show, a "high-voltage" display of technical bravura. Plisetskaya, as Laurencia, was "lithe and slender and as much at home in the air as on the ground," in the opinion of critic John Martin, who left the Bolshoi Theater stunned. She tore up the stage, concluding sequences of springing leaps by brushing the back of her head with her foot. It was a statement, a riposte to the recoiling pitter-patter, the heels-on-the-ground *blinchiki* of the other dancers. "Not until my eyes have returned to their sockets and my jaw has resumed its natural position can analytical judgment be attempted," Martin concluded.[22]

The Soviet regime would continue to exploit her talents, marketing her on tour to the West as one of the wonders of the socialist-communist system—once, that is, she was cleared to travel, and once the Kremlin allowed the Bolshoi to compete on the stages of supposedly hostile imperialist capitalist nations. The Russian repertoire of the Bolshoi ballet might not appeal to audiences elsewhere, but the dancers themselves were the real draw, out-hustling and -muscling their counterparts in modernist ballet companies as part of the larger battle for cultural and ideological dominance. Ballet would join chess and rocket science in the effort to prove, on the world stage, that Russian political and nationalist might was right. Such were the conceits of the Cold War, which continue to haunt ballet's global present.

Plisetskaya was prime flesh for the Kremlin to flaunt, but she was a problem. Ever since India and since she had begun fraternizing with foreigners, the government had declared her unexportable. She had her enemies, including the perspiring KGB operative Shcherbakov, a French-horn player charged with enforcing communist discipline at the Bolshoi, and the hardline communist ballerina Olga Lepeshinskaya, who battled rumors that she had slept with Stalin.[23] Mocking her government minders had done her no favors; nor, despite Khrushchev's denunciation of the crimes of Stalin, had the arrest of her father during the purges; nor her being Jewish. Yet when the government sanctioned a cultural exchange between the Bolshoi Ballet and the Royal Ballet, "Covent Garden," in the fall of 1956, Plisetskaya was slated to go to London. Of course, she and her fellow artists would be closely minded by "KGB workers" who served as their tour guides.[24]

The Kremlin made politics and nationalist ambitions seem the prime motivation for the London tour and those that followed in the 1950s and 1960s. But the actual motivation was financial: touring was intended to turn a profit. Stalin had left the Soviet budget in a catastrophic state, the industrial and military complex so dilapidated as to allow US spy planes to fly unimpeded over Soviet terrain. USSR cultural exchange and international friendship organizations (VOKS, SSOD) made the crucial point that other ballets in other places, like the Sadler's Wells Ballet in England, had made up for lean times with lucrative tours; the Bolshoi Ballet could compete with these companies across the globe. It became a product to be sold—like the silver deposits of Transbaikalia or pearls fished from the rivers of the Kola Peninsula. Fearing defections, the KGB did not want to sanction the trip, but the financial argument won out. Exploiting the commercial potential of the Bolshoi meant dispensing with the amateurish ideologues of the friendship organizations in favor of professional entrepreneurs like Sol Hurok in the United States. The ministers of culture under Khrushchev talked a good game about disseminating Soviet values abroad, but for the Central Committee the point was to bring in much-needed foreign funds. Thus the Cold War was allowed to thaw for the sake of the bottom line—at least until, under Brezhnev, oil profits rose, leading to a political refreezing, the arms race, and a reprise of hyperconservatism.

Plisetskaya would certainly be a box-office draw in London, but likely an unreliable representative of the Soviet Union. Two months before the tour, she was struck from the roster, angering the English. The threat of Soviet tanks rolling into Budapest encumbered negotiations, as did an absurd London shoplifting scandal involving the Soviet discus thrower Nina Ponomarena and five hats. For British balletomanes, however, Plisetskaya's absence was the focus. "I must protest the withdrawal of one of your leading dancers without explanation and ask you to re-consider this decision," the Royal Opera House beseeched an assistant to the minister of culture, on behalf of a public expecting to see the ballerina of the future.[25]

The ballerina of the past, Lepeshinskaya, was ruled out as a substitute. Never popular with her colleagues, she had fallen out of favor with the Central Committee as well, despite continuing to make a case for herself as an artist and ideologue. Her association with Stalin and promotion of the Stalinist cult of personality ended her career under Khrushchev. Others were removed from the list owing to problems at home (recent divorces, no children or relatives to compel them to return after the tour), a record of conduct unbecoming of a Soviet citizen, even insufficiently Slavic looks. Julia May Scott (Zhilko), a dancer with a Russian mother and an African American father, learned that she would not be traveling owing to her heritage: she was a "half-breed," according to the commission on foreign travel.[26] Thus the spotlight turned on Galina Ulanova. She had to dance on tour, even though she was long past her peak.

Four ballets were to be performed: *The Fountain of Bakhchisarai*, *Giselle* (or the altogether unrelated *Gayané*), *Romeo and Juliet* (or *Don Quixote*), and *Swan Lake*. A contract was also worked out with the British Broadcasting Corporation to televise the second act of *Swan Lake*, starring Ulanova, for a fee of 1,250 pounds sterling, with 1,000 pounds sterling more for a rebroadcast. The rehearsal plan for London, dated May 24, 1956, had Plisetskaya scheduled for eleven appearances and Ulanova twelve. The cancellation of Plisetskaya's performances added to the burden on the forty-five-year-old Ulanova, whose health was already in question before the tour. (Plisetskaya, in contrast, was in top form at just thirty-one.)

Ulanova strained a calf muscle midway through the tour and collapsed in exhaustion at its end, but her performances that fall radiated reclaimed youth. The critic for *The Observer* geared up to malign *Romeo and Juliet* for its baleful Stalinist monumentalism, which he dismissed as "a lumbering three-decker-pageant, moving at opera pace against pillars and brocade," and acting that should have been left in the era of silent film.[27] The atmosphere in the theater was tense. "You could hear a fly fly" as the curtain rose, Ulanova commented, long after the fact, in 1986.[28] She took the stage and won over the audience. "Peaky and wan," she enchanted the critic with her "pale hair and pale eyes . . . as transparent as a drop of water." Her performance showcased "the art of interpretative movement carried to the nth degree."[29] Her naturalness won the day, and "stunned" the English prima ballerina Margot Fonteyn, who recalled being transformed by Ulanova's performances in 1956. "Her dancing had exactly the smooth perfection of thick cream poured from a jug, with never a harsh movement anywhere. Her beautiful legs were steely and lithe."[30]

A recent graduate of the ballet school, Nina Timofeyeva, substituted for Plisetskaya in a version of *Swan Lake* that combined the first and second acts into one. She overcame the pressure to deliver "an astoundingly complete rendering," according to *The Spectator*, "slighted only here and there by placing faults due only—observably—to her nervousness."[31] The Bolshoi Ballet received standing ovations, and its principals "saw rose petals strewn by admirers on the path from the theater to the hotel," despite the disgraceful absence of Plisetskaya.[32]

No one forgot that insult; she made sure of it.

PLISETSKAYA REMAINED BEHIND in Moscow during the London tour but participated in a spiteful, look-I-told-you-so experiment initiated by the dancer and choreographer Anatoliy Kuznetsov. He was happy to exploit the fact that the Bolshoi's superstar had not been able to take her ebullient head-kicks to London and buck the Bolshoi tradition. The habit for the Bolshoi Ballet on tour is for those dancers left behind in Moscow to perform smaller, simpler ballets. That did not happen in 1956. Plisetskaya took the part of Odette/Odile in a revival of a four-act 1937 version of *Swan Lake*. Her uncle, Asaf Messerer, staged the climax of this version, a duel between Rothbart and Siegfried. Siegfried slashes Rothbart's wings, the source of his power, thus freeing the maidens from his spell. Kuznetsov choreographed the "masculine" first and third acts of the revival, and Marina Semyonova, who danced the lead role in 1937, the "feminine" second and fourth acts. Conceived with Plisetskaya's explosiveness in mind, the production became the talk of the town, with the stalls mobbed and foreign journalists scrambling to obtain passes. Plisetskaya remembered taking six curtain calls after the adagio and four after the variations. She exited the second act with her back to the audience to exhibit the *plastique* of her arms, and generations of ballerinas have followed her example. But her overseers disapproved. Plisetskaya was summoned to speak with Ekaterina Furtseva, future minister of culture, at her Central Committee office, and the police interrogated her claque. Kuznetsov, the mastermind of Plisetskaya's triumph, expected an award from the Bolshoi for his initiative and got one. But it was for his contribution to the production as a dancer, not as director. Offended, he refused the award.

Plisetskaya chafed against her Soviet confinement. Denied permission to go to Paris with a group of Bolshoi soloists in 1958, she flashed steel, writing to Khrushchev to remind him that she was the star. "The government performances," those meant to showcase Soviet culture to foreign dignitaries, had been "entrusted" to her, she insisted.[33] But arguing did not help: she had been kept from London, and now Paris, and was likely to be left behind when the company went on tour to New York in 1959. She was left begging Khrushchev to forgive her loose tongue, apologizing for not respecting the constant KGB surveillance of her activities and the mistakes that "remained an obstacle" in her "joining the Bolshoi Theater" abroad.[34] "In the last few years, I have behaved unspeakably badly, without realizing the responsibility that rests on me as an actress with the Bolshoi Theater," she wrote to the leader of the USSR. "I allowed myself to be irresponsible; it is inadmissible to speak about our Soviet reality and the people leading our art without bearing in mind that my words have resonance." Her openhearted plea to Khrushchev, a socialist-realist caricature of a politician, continued with the admission that she had "often been tactless and behaved provocatively at parties, mostly talking with foreigners. I am very sorry that I allowed myself to invite the British Embassy Secretary Morgan to my home, without consulting with anyone first. There was also the time I did not go to a reception at the Embassy of Israel, saying that I had not received an invitation that had in fact been extended to me by employees with the Ministry of Foreign Affairs. For all of my indiscretions, believe me, I am sincerely repentant today." The self-debasement continued with mention of the fact that she had just gotten married, to the composer Rodion Shchedrin, and that "things will be different now," "no one will be embarrassed by me."[35] With a husband to come home to, she advertised, there was no chance of her defecting. That helped her case; she received permission to travel to the United States.

Plisetskaya wrote again to Khrushchev as she packed her bags on April 9, 1959, to express her gratitude for his "trusting" her. "I'm endlessly happy. Never have I felt so good and calm inside," she gushed.[36] She might have been baffled to learn that one of the people who recommended that the travel ban be lifted was Olga Lepeshinskaya. Plisetskaya had little positive to say about Lepeshinskaya in her memoir, for reasons both personal and professional, but in 1959 Lepeshinskaya did her a good turn by speaking to the Communist Party organization within the Bolshoi Theater "about the need to include Plisetskaya on the tour to the USA," since American audiences demanded it.[37] Plisetskaya's husband, Shchedrin, also promised in the offices of the KGB director that she would not defect, which, despite the anguish she had suffered in childhood at the hands of the state, she did not think to do—both out of fear for herself and love for him.

The announcement that she would be joining her comrades on tour came as a surprise. The program for the performances at the Metropolitan Opera did not even include Plisetskaya's name; inserts had to be printed. On April 20, 1959, Plisetskaya appeared on the cover of *Newsweek*, dressed as the mistress of Copper Mountain in *The Stone Flower*. The blurb writer speculated that the Kremlin had "turned her loose" in order to "attach the upmost propaganda value to her appearance here."[38] Yet for the Kremlin, filling coffers remained paramount, above even the health and well-being of the dancers. Plisetskaya offered a long and bitter description of the meager rations she and the rest of the Bolshoi Ballet survived on during their American tour.

Thanks to Plisetskaya's "triumph," the Ministry of Culture was able to report to the Central Committee that the foreign funds equivalent of "3.5 million rubles" had been injected into the "USSR state budget."[39] A second tour in 1962 was planned. Plisetskaya was now less of a concern to the KGB. For holding her tongue in the presence of foreign reporters, for dancing, as it were, with her mouth shut, she earned permission to travel again to North America, which in turn earned her limited freedom of movement elsewhere.

The 1962 tour was the most elaborate one to date, part of an exchange that brought the New York City Ballet to the Soviet Union, a homecoming of sorts for the illustrious émigré choreographer George Balanchine.[40] The KGB had more influence on the planning than Plisetskaya or the other participants would have known at the time, weighing in on who would be allowed to go as well as what might be performed. The "measures" put in place to protect the "interests" of the USSR included assessing the repertoire to be performed, changing that repertoire if necessary, and presenting it in the proper perspective.[41] The KGB, competing for control of Soviet affairs with the Central Committee, worked to ensure that the cultural product sold abroad conformed to official artistic policies. Hence the report prepared for the Central Committee by the director of the KGB, Vladimir Semichastnïy, decrying "the serious inadequacies in the preparation of the Bolshoi Ballet's tour abroad in 1962." Of special concern was the ballet *Spartacus*, as choreographed in Leningrad by the iconoclastic, temperamental Leonid Yakobson. "Several leading performers are concerned about the repertoire scheduled for the US and Canada," Semichastnïy began. "They object in particular to the inclusion of the ballet *Spartacus*," which "has big drawbacks: the absence of dancing, first of all, but also inaccurate interpretation of the characters, and the presence of sex scenes adopted from Western art." He added that staffers with the US embassy in Moscow sensed trouble for *Spartacus* in America, but did not say why. "It would be wiser to include *Cinderella* and *The Fountain of Bakhchisarai* in the repertoire rather than *Spartacus*," he wrote. It was also essential "to take urgent measures to upgrade the concert program, to include numbers that reflect Soviet life."[42] Semichastnïy meant, of course, the exoticized life of imagination, what art alone could create. Soviet life as such was not to be staged. *Spartacus* was eventually allowed to make the trip, once the ballet had been reworked and American audiences properly primed for its size.

Meantime there was the all-important task of checking and rechecking personnel. Semichastnïy laid out the pluses and minuses of each person scheduled to tour. He agonized the most about sending the Bolshoi ballet master Lavrovsky. His colleagues "characterize him as conservative and biased," the KGB director wrote. "He has not paid the required attention to the tour's success, being more concerned with promoting himself and the productions he has staged, while at the same time ignoring other ballets, for example, *The Stone Flower,* during the 1959 tour to the U.S. In previous trips abroad Lavrovsky made extensive contacts with Russian emigrants and other foreigners without approval from the leadership of the delegation." This made him a traitor. Having analyzed the intelligence gathered, Semichastnïy proposed a coup: Lavrovsky would be replaced by Ulanova, who "conducts herself abroad with utmost dignity and modesty."[43] The Central Committee objected to the plan, however, and Lavrovsky remained in his job for another year.

Of particular concern was Māris Liepa, the dancer cast as Spartacus. Semichastnïy worried that Liepa might follow the example of Rudolf Nureyev, who turned himself in to Paris airport police in 1961, betraying the Soviet people on whose bread and salt he had been raised. To assuage the "doubts" about Liepa's trustworthiness, the "leadership" of the Bolshoi Theater argued that, despite his bulging muscles (he had bulked up for the part of Spartacus), he was "exceptionally loving," wholly devoted to his "young son, mother, father, and his sister, who lives in Riga."[44] His family, effectively held hostage by the state, would ensure his return. Liepa received permission to take the tour and came back as promised.

Like the theater itself, Plisetskaya had by the time of her second American tour become a trusted Soviet brand, a marketable commodity at home as well as abroad. During her ascent, jingoistic articles appeared in the Soviet press under her name, some short and sweet, like the January 1, 1960, New Year's proclamation, "Proshchay, stariy god!" (Farewell, old year!) in *Sovetskaya kul'tura*, and a March 23, 1965, piece titled "Iskusstvo shagayet v kosmos" (Art steps into the cosmos), extolling the first spacewalk. "As a Soviet person, I'm inspired by this latest victory of our science and technology. As a ballerina, I envy Lieutenant Leonov; I'd so like to experience the feeling of freedom and lightness that must come from weightlessness."[45] Of freedom and lightness Plisetskaya knew more than the cosmonauts: Leonov's spacewalk lasted just over twelve minutes, and he had a hard time squashing himself back into the hatch, since his spacesuit had puffed up in the vacuum.

Also bearing Plisetskaya's name was a half-page gloss in *Izvestiya* of the 1962 US tour under the title "Russkaya terpsikhora pokorila Ameriku" (Russian Terpsichore conquers America). It describes how President John F. Kennedy and Jacqueline Kennedy Onassis congratulated her for her performance in *Swan Lake*, and reports that average Americans commended the "wise" leadership of the Soviet Union for bringing the Cuban Missile Crisis to an end, thus preventing the US government from blowing everyone to smithereens.[46] Most of these articles were command performances, commissions, typed up by journalists in house agitprop style and presented to Plisetskaya for her signature. Other celebrities exploited by the state, including Shostakovich, tended to ignore the prayers for peace and fanfares for the common man published under their names in the Soviet press, but Plisetskaya was a bit more attentive. She clipped them and might even have read them. She countered the blandness of her official pronouncements by granting interviews in which she spoke in no-nonsense terms about the future of her art.

In 1966, she was interviewed for *Vogue* about, of all things, her favorite recipes. The reporter traveled to Moscow from the haute cuisine capital of Paris to learn about the "rustic, stick-to-your-ribs" fare that the ballerina prepared at home. The expectation had less been peasant beef stew, which Plisetskaya indeed fed to the reporter, than lighter-than-air angel food: "the yolk of an egg and two rose petals."[47] The British journalist George Feifer, who also enjoyed some of this nosh, added that she and her husband lived in a two-bedroom apartment with "Canadian" wallpaper and "American" telephones. Their personal surroundings were "sumptuous" by Soviet standards, the art collection rivaling that amassed by Ekaterina Geltser during her life. The apartment had two grand pianos; piles of coffee-table books; and a "collection of paintings, drawings and lithographs" from Braque and Chagall, among others; an "early Picasso dish"; and a "superb Léger rug." Plisetskaya harvested these items on tour, which somewhat compensated for the confiscation of her earnings. Her home also included "Woolworth-like portraits of herself in oil and watercolor" and tacky souvenirs, "the casual mixture of masterpiece and carnival doll" lending "an air of artlessness to the flat, a lack of pretension, even order, which is characteristic of many poorer Russian homes."[48]

Her activities abroad were carefully monitored, her conversations with foreigners transcribed and translated throughout the administrations of Khrushchev and Brezhnev, the fleeting Andropov and Chernenko interregna, the twilight era of Gorbachev, up to the end of the Soviet Union altogether. But her keepers so often let her out of the keep that the impulse to defect, never that strong, faded to null. She found her escape on the stage, making the once-chic act of defecting déclassé while increasing her Cold War mystique. She played the role of cultural diplomat abroad, charming foreign heads of state and serving as muse to Parisian fashion designers and filmmakers along with choreographers. Pierre Cardin fetishized the minimalist, black-on-black aesthetic she cultivated on the Soviet runway.

Plisetskaya's oft-stated reasons for remaining in Russia included her husband, a prominent composer who made the case for artistic experimentation in speeches delivered at the Union of Soviet Composers. He was her best friend; their love proved steadfast, their marriage rock-solid. Plisetskaya also claimed that her "conscience" prevented her defection, knowing the anguish she would have felt about breaking her promises, even those made to the besotted, bumbling politicians. She recalled pleasure beaming from Khrushchev's "pancake face" after she came back to the USSR from America in 1959; he called her a "good girl" for not making a "fool" of him. And there was always the Bolshoi, her true home and the source of her strength. The Bolshoi granted license, freedom, for her semi-improvised, dangerous-looking recalibration of newer and older roles. Such freedom did not require an exit visa. "There was no stage so comfortable, the most comfortable in the entire solar system, in the entire universe, as the Bolshoi!" she rhapsodized.[49] The theater had endured tragedy and triumph. Maintenance was haphazard, the budget for upkeep inadequate. The Bolshoi had survived attacks from inside, outside, and—owing to the concealed tributaries of the Moscow River that flowed under the foundations—from below. But its big stage and excellent sightlines remained. It maintained its neoclassical composure even as it fell into ruin at the end of the Soviet era. Perhaps the theater's past mattered to Plisetskaya. Certainly its future did.

FOR A TIME, that future resided with a dancer and choreographer from Leningrad, Yuriy Grigorovich, a disciple of Fyodor Lopukhov's who represented an exciting break from convention, a muscular retort to Zakharov, Lavrovsky, and the stagnant strictures of *drambalet*. Ulanova endorsed his appointment as Bolshoi ballet mas-

ter in formulaic terms, ticking, as it were, the right boxes on the rec-
ommendation form. Grigorovich sought "new rhythmic and figural
language" but resisted the "cold, formalist" experiments of European and American choreographers, she wrote. Tick. He was a dramatist, interested in "conflict" and its resolution, and he cared about
the "inner world," the emotions and thoughts of his characters.[50]
Tick tick. And so forth. Ulanova would find little in his muscular,
alpha-male ballets to suit dancers of her modest, serene disposition.
But Plisetskaya could power through them, and she performed the
parts assigned to her as though her very life depended on it—which,
for a time, it did.

A showman, Grigorovich organized mass forces for mass entertainment, geared toward seemingly superhuman dancers of astonishing physical strength. He made use of folk dance but excluded
character dance, a sin that Moscow balletomanes will perhaps never
forgive, given its importance to the Bolshoi tradition. His inspiration, he claimed, came from Marius Petipa, but he also found
artistic stimulus on the streets, in the behavior of people at bars,
brothels, gyms, and on battlefields. His choreography possessed
a hard-angled grit unknown to the ballets of the past—the pret-
tier, blurrier spectacles after which Soviet hair salons were named:
Giselle, *Paquita*, and *Raymonda*. The sex and violence irritated the
censors, but still his works set forth the proper lessons about good
and evil, patriots and traitors, oppressors and liberators. Politically,
he largely had his way; clashes with officialdom never lasted more
than a few days. "She loved me," Grigorovich said of Ekaterina
Furtseva, the minister of culture from 1960 to 1974.[51]

He came to the Bolshoi in 1964 with two notable successes
under his belt. He had turned *The Stone Flower* from a work of
late-Stalinist paralysis into an international box office success, and
although his *Legend of Love* (Legenda o lyubvi, 1961) ran enough

fingers down enough thighs to provoke howls of protest from Soviet ballet hardliners, Plisetskaya enthusiastically embraced the work. Even less ardent supporters like Ulanova considered *Legend of Love* a revelation for its "symphonic construction," in which dance and music coalesced to push the plot forward and add depth to the characterizations. Everything counted; there were no pointless "concert numbers."[52] And Grigorovich had managed to solve the problem that had brought woe to his teacher, Lopukhov: He had figured out how to make his dances musical without making them abstract.

Legend of Love takes its plot from a 1948 poem by the Turkish poet Nâzım Hikmet, with décor by a Georgian designer, Simon Virsaladze, and music by an Azeri composer, Arif Melikov. The multiethnic collaboration, guided by a Russian ballet master, offered a clinic in the friendship of the peoples. It is an angst-ridden nocturne. Hearts are exposed, swords drawn, breasts and chests angled to the ground, and love trampled on in a tale of a queen's sacrificing of her beauty and a court painter's impossible heroism; he vows to chip through a mountain to a secret water source, thus ending a fierce drought. The movement is ritualistic, somber and austere, but there is also the sultriness of the Orient.

For the sake of symmetry, if not symphonism, Grigorovich altered the music. The composer pretended to go along, but had little say in the matter, since he had returned to his native Baku for a political appointment during a crucial phase in the rehearsals. In his absence, the ballet achieved balance. Grigorovich added repeats and excised transitions to keep the action flowing in the allegorical mass movements. The scenes of farewell and prayer, the people's dances, and the court dances recur in variation, as does the figural language in the gut-baring monologues. The conductor's score for the 1965 Bolshoi Theater premiere records Plisetskaya's cues: the arabesque and finger point that chase the courtiers into the wings; the twirling, leaping explosion of emotion; the hard landings on Melikov's chords of doom. Everyone understood what everything meant—the public, the politicians, and Grigorovich's allies among the critics. As one of the reviewers determined, the opening court tableau symbolized "powerless servitude," the procession of soldiers "terrible, blind, and soulless despotism," and the shower of gold coins that the queen pledges to a dervish "deceptive and transparent vainness."[53]

Legend of Love is bleak and spare. The movement is "anti-mime" without being "pro-dance," to quote Arlene Croce, one of Grigorovich's sternest critics outside of Russia. Croce concedes that "simplified and serious is not a bad thing to be" in ballet, but "simplified and mediocre is."[54] Moscow dance critic Tatyana Kuznetsova agrees, arguing that the storytelling in *Legend of Love* is blunt to the point of obtuseness, the syntax barren, ballet's Sahara Desert. Certain gestures became terrible tics for Grigorovich: "falling to the knees" in supplication, for example, or standing split patterns and crazed dashes from one corner of the stage to another. They recur in this long, three-act ballet, and in all of the long, three-act Grigorovich ballets created after it, regardless of where the action is set—the Near East, the Rus of Ivan the Terrible, the ancient Rome of Crassus and Spartacus, or Shostakovich's Soviet Russia. Most galling is that Grigorovich's preferred movements occupied the grand stage for "almost forty years."[55] *Legend of Love* remains in the repertoire, with Plisetskaya's role taken by Svetlana Zakharova in the most recent Bolshoi Theater production, from 2014.

IN 1966, GRIGOROVICH ascended to the position of ballet master in chief. That same year he received the assignment for his third major ballet, *Spartacus*. The score by Khachaturian had twice been choreographed for the Bolshoi, in 1958 and 1962, but the ballet had failed at home and on tour. Grigorovich had himself danced the part of a gladiator in an earlier setting, and joked about being the "first one killed" in the ballet—which suited him fine, since he was then first in line at the buffet backstage.[56] Yet when the general director of the Bolshoi, Mikhaíl Chulaki, handed over the scenario and the score to Grigorovich to set anew, there was nothing to laugh about. Spartacus had long been an irresistible subject for the Soviets, and Grigorovich's new ballet was slated to premiere on an important date, the fiftieth anniversary of the revolution.[57]

Spartacus projects had been planned, replanned, and unplanned since close to the founding of the Soviet Union, and ballets, operas, and films on the topic of the Spartacus-led slave uprising timed for the fifteenth and fortieth anniversaries of the revolution. A who's who of greater and lesser Soviet talents had tackled the subject. An elaborate silent movie treatment was released in 1926 by the Turkish-Soviet director Muhsin Ertuğrul, and the proletarian composer Georgiy Dudkevich completed a Spartacus opera in 1928. Dudkevich received permission from Glavrepertkom for a production, but only if it happened outside of Moscow and Leningrad, his music having been deemed too amateurish for the "general worker-peasant public."[58] It was heavy on choral singing, light on action—a passable historical epic, in short, but not an especially compelling one. The opera house in Perm staged it. Petipa's niece Kseniya took a stab at the story as scenarist, and the composer Boris Asafyev pounced on the subject in 1934 when he thought the political moment apt. In 1935, however, he retreated hotfoot when he realized that the music would have to come from his imagination, there being no ancient Roman musical sources to base it on.

The saga of the great slave-rebel also attracted Kasyan Goleyzovsky, the choreographer of the biblical parable *Joseph the Beautiful*. He relied on friends to outline the scenario: an expert on ancient Greek theater named Nilender Ottonovich, as well as the writer Vasiliy Yanchevetsky, who had earlier published a Spartacus novella. He entered the resulting concoction into a 1934 contest for ballets and operas on Soviet themes, but it did not receive the votes needed for a staging, even a prospective staging, at the Bolshoi. Goleyzovsky persisted with the project, nonetheless, thinking it through to the end in a precise ratio of "55% dancing and 45% pantomime."[59] He brought other cooks into the kitchen, and the bill of fare changed from Russian to Georgian as prospects for the ballet moved from Moscow to Tbilisi. The Georgian composer Tamara Vakhvakhishvili composed the music at the insistence of the ballet-obsessed Georgian communist bureaucrat Avel Enukidze. The result was beyond eclectic, bearing the influence of the Middle East, the Spanish composer Isaac Albéniz, with "gongs, tambourines, rattles, horns, little bells, drone horns," marches for the Roman legions, and a chorus tasked with making sense of it all.[60] But it was not to be: Tbilisi did not have the dancers the ballet needed, and Goleyzovsky, an experimenter, lacked the political support to recruit them.

He made enough noise about his efforts to attract the attention of Nikolay Volkov, author of the scenarios for the successful *Flames of Paris* and *The Fountain of Bakhchisarai*. Volkov thought that he had the clout, when he signed the contract in December of 1934, to muscle the ballet onto the Bolshoi stage by himself. The general director at the time, Mutnïkh, had other ideas and rejected the first draft. The plot needed to be thinned out, the tale simplified. There was too much moralizing and confusing behavior, and, perhaps worst of all, Volkov was acting as if he had a monopoly on the theater. The sprint to a premiere that Volkov imagined turned into a marathon as the project bounced back and forth between the Bolshoi and the Kirov for two decades. It was also handed off from one composer, the mediocre Asafyev, to another: the sought-after, overcommitted Khachaturian. Before *Spartacus* could be finished, Mutnïkh was purged, the Soviet Union defeated Hitler, Stalin died from a stroke, and an entire generation of dancers came and went.

The events of 1917 were much on Volkov's mind as he started writing his scenario in 1934—both the combination of fact and fiction in the representation of the revolution to the masses and its dialectical-materialist interpretation by Marxist historians. Volkov claimed to have been inspired by Lenin, and Lenin himself claimed inspiration in the actual historical figure of Spartacus. In 1919 at Smolensk University, the instigator of the Bolshevik coup gave a speech about statehood in which he declared Spartacus "one of the most prominent heroes of one of the greatest revolts of slaves, which took place about two thousand years ago." He professed admiration for the unlikely hero and his just cause. "For many years the seemingly omnipotent Roman Empire, which rested entirely on slavery, experienced the shocks and blows of a widespread uprising of slaves who armed and united to form a vast army under the leadership of Spartacus."[61] Thus the slave had thrown off his chains, sparking a revolution taken up again by the Bolsheviks nearly two thousand years later. Spartacus's uprising was quashed. Lenin's was not. Thesis and antithesis, with the ballet as synthesis.

In crafting his scenario, Volkov relied on an 1874 novel about Spartacus by Raffaello Giovagnoli. But, averse to its melodrama, he also mined a text by Plutarch of Chaeronea, *The Life of Crassus*, and another by Appian of Alexandria, *The Civil Wars*, which had likewise entered the communist canon, having been quoted by Marx and Engels. From these romantic-historical sources, the socioeconomic consideration of the Spartacus insurrection that rolled off the Soviet presses in 1936, ballet and opera projects of the recent past, and from his own imagination, Volkov blocked out a scenario in three parts: (1) Spartacus as an armor-clad gladiator in the arena, battling giants; (2) Spartacus as stripped-down leader of a revolt, commanding slaves, gladiators, and peasants against the supreme Roman commander Crassus; (3) Spartacus as hero for the ages, fighting to the death, his corpse never found. This last detail was theatrically intolerable; a funeral march would be introduced, the hero's crucified body held aloft. His name would prove "immortal," his feat "eternal," and his tragic demise paradoxically "optimistic."[62] The plot stayed true to the ideal of Spartacus the insurrectionist hero, a symbol of freedom from oppression in any era—from the Russian Revolution to World War II, and even beyond to Korea and Vietnam. Volkov padded his scenario with impossible-to-choreograph historical minutiae, and Khachaturian, in composing his score, matched his music to the excessive scenario without fretting over the difficulties it might present to choreographers.

The first of these, Igor Moiseyev, tried his best. He choreographed *Spartacus* for the Bolshoi in 1958, lavishing huge sums on costumes and sets. Act 1, scene 2, for example, featured "a wide rectangular square surrounded by porticos. Under the canopy are a lot of shops. Here all races and tribes are presented, from Gauls to Africans. Each of the slaves wears a plate around their neck indicating their age, origin, advantages and disadvantages."[63] The arena and road scenes included allegorical dances called "The Fisherman and the Fish" and "The Wolf and the Sheep." In act 2, scene 6, Aegina, the emperor's lover, rises up from the bottom of a fountain—just like the ballerina in the "Water Nymph Ballet" choreographed by Balanchine for the 1938 Hollywood film *The Goldwyn Follies*.

And folly it was. For its excesses, which diluted the action at the center of the plot, Moiseyev's *Spartacus* was removed from the repertoire of the Bolshoi after just two performances and pulled from the 1959 tour, even though it had been advertised in *LIFE* magazine, among other large-circulation US publications.[64] "No one under-stood it," Grigorovich noted with a shrug, "so it was cancelled."[65]

Such also happened, he claimed, to *Spartacus* as choreographed by Yakobson. It was staged at the Kirov in 1956 before being revised for the Bolshoi in 1962 and brought to the United States on tour. It was even more extravagant, and even harder to understand. As Janice Ross notes in her biography of the choreographer, Yakob-son drew inspiration for his version of *Spartacus* from the "physically kinetic" but "politically ambiguous" reliefs on the ancient Perga-mon Altar (180–86 BCE), then hidden in the Hermitage museum as war booty. He hoped his ballet would incite an aesthetic rebel-lion against the strictures of Soviet ballet under Stalin.[66] Yakob-son excluded pointe shoes (as one might expect in a ballet of blood and sand), avoided blocklike, unison movements, and exposed a fair bit of flesh—all in a search for a new choreographic and expressive freedom. As Ross writes of the final farewell between Spartacus and his wife, "there is no divide between acting and dancing; all of the action is naturalistically in character."[67] Even crowd scenes were meant to depict not a mass but a gathering of individuals; the tech-nique of "choreographic recitatives" rendered each dancer unique.[68] These made the crowd scenes vibrant, but the non-imitative texture exposed Yakobson to accusations of sloppiness, because the lack of coordination could be misinterpreted as the result of hasty improvi-sation. Moreover, the realism pushed too far for the censors, and the sexiness of his production eclipsed the ideological message. Depic-tions of sordid Romans distracted from what should have been an emphasis on the struggle for freedom, whether in ancient Rome, the Holy Roman Empire, or Moscow as the Third Rome.

Yakobson had created a better ballet than Moiseyev but suf-fered greater and meaner abuse for it, first from peers and officials in Leningrad, then from peers and officials in Moscow, and finally, when his *Spartacus* went on tour in 1962, the American press. Here was the strange case of a ballet that the bureaucrats disliked, but became enough of a hot ticket, in Leningrad at least, to justify the expense of shipping it abroad.[69] Pyotr Gusev, an unabashed traditionalist, was the first to excoriate Yakobson in Leningrad, though he pretended to do so with his interests at heart, out of deep collegial respect for his talent, and with greetings sent, at the end of the sixteen-page screed, to Yakobson's wife. "The worst part of the production," Gusev huffed on the back of page three, was the camp scene. "This was the place to show Spartacus attracting slaves, shepherds, and peasants from everywhere around. Bonfires, dancing, the people's joy in being freed, their pure souls. But there's none of that, and it's more than annoying."[70] The slave-market scene had its problems too, as did the feast scene, since Yakobson had lodged himself in the ruts of the scenario, pantomiming interpersonal quarrels and tests of loyalties instead of depicting Spartacus's chest-beating awesomeness. Instead, Spartacus seemed "calm," "humble," even when told by heralds that the Romans are upon him. "His oath—'to death!!!'—should be here, and certainly not a puppet-like battle to relieve all of the tragic significance of the moment," Gusev added on page five.[71] His lexicon of invective eventually failed, and he was left describing things he did not like as simply "stupid." But he found the words to address the occasional rhythmic mismatches between dance and music, to deride the costumes (fewer belts and straps, please, more exposed backs), and to shove the choreographer back into the studio in hopes that, despite all of the problems, *Spartacus* might become for Yakobson what *Romeo and Juliet* became for Lavrovsky: not exactly classical, but a repertoire staple. "I do wish success and recognition for you but I'm very afraid that you'll squander it by ending work on the ballet, deciding, good enough, it's a success, [Party] secretaries praise it even if the critics understand nothing. Fear this!!"[72]

Yakobson did, in fact, fear it, and he made some changes, though never enough to satisfy Gusev and the guardians of the *drambalet* tradition. He had supporters, and they praised him for his "mass of extremely successful discoveries, innovations," but, before and after the Kirov premiere, he was at the center of a storm, alienated even from his collaborators.[73] He "disagreed" with Volkov's scenario and squabbled with Khachaturian about the "score's obvious deficiencies: its dramaturgical incompleteness." He never said what he meant, but Yakobson seems to have been recalling the criticism directed at Khachaturian by the composers and theorists of the Union of Soviet Composers, who first heard the music in the summer of 1954, almost five years after Khachaturian signed the contract for it. His colleagues enjoyed the extravagantly ludicrous score (its author was "the Rubens of Russian music"), but felt that the music given to Spartacus needed further development. His theme evolved heroically between the first and fourth scenes into a grand hymn to freedom, but it did not change much after that, with five scenes left to go. Yakobson also complained about the "absence of integration and wholeness in the development of the action."[74] Here too he was echoing Khachaturian's peers. After hearing the score played through on the piano, one of them said, "I can't decide which of the scenes is the center, the one where the development of the drama is concentrated, where everything comes together."[75]

He had a point, as did Yakobson. Khachaturian's music is nothing if not a curio cabinet, or slave galley, of Romantic and Orientalist references. *Swan Lake* makes a guest appearance, likewise Rimsky-Korsakov's *Mlada* and *Scheherazade*, Stravinsky's *Firebird*, the *dies irae* funeral chant, and various thumps and melodramatic swells that come straight from Hollywood—as in, to quote one of Khachaturian's future naysayers, "Drum, drum: Kill that guy! Violin, violin: Wrap that girl around your neck!"[76] Khachaturian made some of the changes suggested by his colleagues in 1954, pruning the number of repetitions and digressions, but by 1956 considered his work on *Spartacus* done. He told Yakobson that he did not want a single pitch changed. Christina Ezrahi describes what happened next, based on the recollections of the choreographer's wife. Upon learning that his score had, in fact, been severely molested, during an argument with Yakobson in the middle of Leningrad, Khachaturian flew into a rage, waving his arms in the air and "accidentally" belting Yakobson in the face. Yakobson hit him back, with more serious intent, causing a rift that, unsurprisingly, lasted "many years."[77]

Street brawls aside, there were just enough compromises to leave everyone dissatisfied. The Bolshoi premiere of Yakobson's *Spartacus* on April 4, 1962, disappointed the bureaucrats, floundering, according to Ezrahi, when it came to establishing "the desired balance between heroism and entertainment."[78] Too much luridness in Rome, not enough bravura on the battlefield. The New York premiere on September 12, 1962, was an embarrassment. Critic Allen Hughes, writing for the *New York Times*, declared the work "one of the most preposterous theatrical exercises" he had ever seen. "The fact that one of the greatest ballet companies in the world would invest so much talent, time, money, and, presumably, belief in the staging of a dull pageant is simply beyond understanding."[79] Plisetskaya was poorly cast "in a part that contains very little dancing of any kind, and none . . . that she does best." The score was "in the style of Hollywood soundtracks," the fighting (and body count onstage) excessive, the storyline opaque. The myriad failings prompted Hughes to posit a Cold War aesthetic divide: "Are we to think that Soviet and American artistic tastes are so different that this 'Spartacus' says something profound to the Soviet citizenry?" Indeed, in a follow-up article, Hughes concluded that although *Spartacus* "is not for us," perhaps Russians "have their reasons" for liking it as "a necessary if faltering forward step of Russian dance on a winding path toward real modernism."[80] The reviewer for the *Herald Tribune*, Walter Terry, summed up *Spartacus* as "wildly extravagant" and likewise compared the ballet to a Hollywood production, with "the eye-battings, lurchings, and gesticulations of silent movies."[81] The lavish production had "out-DeMilled" the famous screen epics of Cecil B. DeMille.[82] The choreography may be "silly" but offered thrills and chills. "For every fabulous leap by a Bolshoi male star or a magnificently staged sword fight, there are arm-wavings (all hail!), arm-writhings (ah, sex!), arm-foldings (oh, woe!), arm-bulgings (don't you dare touch this virgin!)" along with "thigh-strokings (essential to any bacchanal)." So much acting and action, urged on by Khachaturian's "silent movie stuff" score, reportedly led one member of the audience to exclaim: "Look, Ma, no dancing!" The second performance was better received thanks to the alternate cast, featuring Liepa as Spartacus.[83] Terry indolently concluded that "it is all marvelous if you go for this sort of thing."[84] Even so, such gleeful mockery may have proved too much; three scheduled showings of *Spartacus* the week following its premiere were pulled, and the ballet would not return to the repertoire.[85] Logistics offered a convenient excuse. According to a report in the *Los Angeles Times*, *Spartacus* was removed owing to "the difficulties of transporting huge settings and other complicated trappings by air to the west."[86]

The extreme rhetoric not only reflects Cold War tensions but also a decision, in advance of its New York run, to discredit any attempt by the Bolshoi at innovation. The Russians were allowed to keep their classics, their kings in castles, but modernism belonged to the Americans. The American critics had an agenda, and their rhetoric ended up being no less heated than Soviet-style denunciations, had they the wit to see it. Perhaps Yakobson did.

Plisetskaya admired his ballet, but she could not console Yakobson after the *Herald Tribune* mopped the floor with him and KGB handlers on the tour told him that he had gotten what he deserved. "Large, heavy tears dropped from his blue eyes" as he expressed his gratitude to Plisetskaya for her "brilliant" performance in the role of Spartacus's lover, Phrygia.[87] The duet she danced with Dmitri Begak (the alternate to Liepa in the part of Spartacus) was "singular," according to Ross, in "its condensation of the flickering emotions of grief, resolve, and the anguish of parting."[88] But this description comes from a biographer who never saw the ballet; critics of the time did not recognize the achievement. Yakobson's *Spartacus* would not be seen in the United States again. The Bolshoi too rejected it.

So *SPARTACUS* ENDED UP in Grigorovich's hands. It became the first ballet that he created for Moscow, and the first ballet intended to cement the relationship between the Bolshoi Theater and the Kremlin, since it was assigned to the Kremlin Palace of Congresses, a newly built space that served, from 1962, as the Bolshoi's second stage. Here were the classics at discount ticket prices, the public racing up the escalators between acts before the food ran out in the top-floor canteen. The palace hosted the congresses of Soviet People's Deputies until the collapse of the Soviet Union, and the plush red chairs could hold more than five thousand delegates, ethnic Russian bureaucrats mixing with laborers, artists, and the occasional astronaut from the fifteen republics. Leonid Brezhnev would mumble through his congress keynotes, mispronouncing words even in his healthier years at the helm, but otherwise sat impassive as others lauded his titanic labors and the rightness of the communist path, as evidenced by the summer fruits and vegetables that would appear, like a Christmas miracle, in the kiosks just before the deputies came to town. The mosaic banners of the republics still grace the marble atrium of the Palace, even though the congresses and the Soviet Union are long gone. Now the place hosts ballet galas, ancient crooners, and musicals like Disney's *Beauty and the Beast*.

Grigorovich's new setting, *Spartacus* No. 3, was to be a ballet that even a people's deputy could understand—a ballet, Chulaki pledged, that would not replicate the mistakes of *Spartacus* Nos. 1 and 2. "All excess is discarded. Everything is done to highlight Spartacus's and the rebels' struggle against Crassus and his adherents," the director of the Bolshoi insisted. Chulaki spoke of its ostentatious "militaristic spirit" and the modern approach to the subject. It was "not an academic re-creation of events from the far-distant cold past," he insisted.[89] Volkov's scenario had been reduced to the barest of outlines: three acts of four scenes each with marches, battles, and fights to the finish. The sinuous monologues offer generous doses of anguish and passion. Pantomime disappears, and along with it narrative storytelling. This *Spartacus* is a Passion set in a world of decay. And at the end, the hero is left slung over the tops of spears.

The music was shorn to fit the mold. Most who knew it thought the score about an hour too long. Moiseyev had encouraged Khachaturian to compress the ending, and Yakobson had tossed out the chorus and sliced through the bacchanalia, reducing the whole from some four hours long to just over three and forcing Khachaturian to appeal to the artistic council of the Bolshoi Theater to defend his music. "I wrote the crosses," the music of the slave crucifixion, "with my blood."[90] Yet even with the cuts, the music maintained its colorfully episodic character; Khachaturian could at least recognize it, and the dancers sitting at the meeting, including Lepeshinskaya and Ulanova, found as much good as bad in Yakobson's changes—and their concerns had more to do with the loss of pointe work and the posing that substituted for action.

When Grigorovich sat down at the piano with the dancer in the role of the rebel-slave, he decided that perhaps a tiny bit, *chut'-chut'*, of Khachaturian's score needed revising. *Chut'-chut'* became a complete overhaul, initiated without the composer's knowledge and using the harshest of means: Grigorovich literally tore out thick handfuls of the score, pasted over passages that he no longer needed, and scribbled in inserts. When Khachaturian heard about the evisceration of his Lenin Prize–winning masterpiece and saw the patched-together rehearsal score, he turned apoplectic. He could not appeal to Chulaki, who had staked his reputation on Grigorovich succeeding. "I have a suggestion," the director of the Bolshoi Theater said to his colleagues on the artistic council. "Show your trust in Yuriy Nikolayevich. Based on his past accomplishments, and his bold approach to his work." "Of course!" said a voice in the crowd.[91] Grigorovich tried to ease the composer's pain with Armenian vodka, but the fuss continued until the principal conductor of the Bolshoi Theater at the time, Gennadiy Rozhdestvensky, convinced Khachaturian to trust Grigorovich.[92]

Once *Spartacus* was in rehearsal, even more changes were made, as evidenced by the big pencil question mark scrawled on one of the blank paste-overs. Chulaki warned Khachaturian that there would be major alterations but made clear that the composer had no choice but to accept them. Still, the extent of the rearrangement was shocking: the ethnic dances performed by people of color were deracinated, used less to stereotype the captives from the Mediterranean and Middle East than to represent extreme emotional states. Other changes included moving the music for the "Requiem" from the end of the score to the second scene, under the new title "Spartacus's monologue," and recasting the music originally written for the gladiators' procession as accompaniment to a sale in the slave market.

Grigorovich tried to explain his conception to the composer. The dancing would be musical, structured by repeated themes and episodes as in a fugue, but it would not be "philharmonic," since the goal was to communicate the overarching idea of the story rather than matching each pitch in the score to a particular movement. There were general correlations between music and dance, as in the closing sections that paired compositional and choreographic climaxes. At the height of Spartacus and Phrygia's *pas de deux* in the camp, Grigorovich has her leap into his arms, and Spartacus carries her by her leg accompanied by full string section and trumpet— pure Hollywood. The parade of passages nicked from other scores is matched by the parade of dances on the stage and parades of characters enacting the plot—excess that reaches a climax with the hero's grisly martyrdom. The processions replaced the messier crowd scenes that Moiseyev and Yakobson had come up with for the ballet.

Khachaturian was unimpressed: "Where are the women?" he asked, after Grigorovich described the opening scene and the décor that Simon Virsaladze, his longtime collaborator, had devised. The curtain would rise to show a wall made out of the shields of the Roman soldiers; Crassus would stand like a statue at the top; the wall collapses; the Roman Empire is reduced to rubble. The future. Grigorovich went on to describe the second scene, featuring Spartacus's monologue. "But where are the women?" Khachaturian asked again.[93] Aegina and Phrygia turned up soon enough, with thighs exposed rather than swords drawn.

Here Grigorovich takes the low road, bypassing Eros to pursue sexual exhibitionism. "There's no eroticism in the erotic scenes," the ballet historian Vadim Gayevsky wrote in 1981, as part of a critique of Grigorovich's craft that infuriated the choreographer so much that he arranged for the book, titled *Divertisment* (Divertissement), to disappear from print. "Proud patricians and enticing courtesans are not to be found in Grigorovich's Rome," a "dead city" of drunkenness without merriment. "Is this Aegina supposed to be a courtesan?" he asked. "She's a soldier's girl, scraped up from the bottom."[94] Gayevsky doubtless had in mind the middle of the third act, where Aegina performs a strip-club dance (for the sake of period realism, a Bacchic pinecone staff, a sexual symbol, serves as the pole). It confirms, in case her solos in the first and second acts had not, that women are objects to be ogled.

Plisetskaya danced the part in later years, but the muscles in her back flinched. "In the adagio with Crassus I had to grab my toe with my hand and pull away in attitude from my partner, who held me in counterbalance," she protested. "The muscles of my spine were twisted like laundry being wrung out."[95] Risks aside, the part remained central to the ballet. As critic Marina Harss wrote of a 2014 performance, "Aegina shows off her legs incessantly, running her hand down a thigh, holding one leg up to her head as she turns, or, more obviously, raising her crotch like a weapon while she lies provocatively on the floor. Not much is left to the imagination."[96] Phrygia too is objectified by Grigorovich, hoisted by Spartacus above his head, then dangled downward as a submissive burden to be tossed around. The suggestiveness can be dialed up or down depending on the performer. In tamer presentations, the fate of nations is reduced—or, if the perspective is right, elevated—to the level of a marital quarrel.

The dancer in the title role, Vladimir Vasiliev, was neither gigantic nor muscle-bound, but proved such a compelling stage presence that Grigorovich made the decision, shrewd in retrospect, to reassign Liepa, Yakobson's Spartacus, to the role of Crassus. In Grigorovich's revision, the scenes featuring Spartacus are mirrored by those featuring Crassus, an ancient Roman leader with Imperial Russian cravings for opulence in his personal surroundings. He and Spartacus look and sometimes act the same, yet Spartacus wears rags and chains, an obvious source of resentment. Liepa had the expressive range to fill out the part of Crassus, adding fear and self-doubt to the Roman despot's strutting sadism, while Vasiliev brought unexpected conviction to the role of Spartacus. The new hero gave Grigorovich ideas when the ballet master ran out of them. Vasiliev added tricks of his own, including his patented one-handed lift of Phrygia and turns in the air in attitude. (He benefited from the fact that his longtime partner and wife, the wonderful lyric ballerina Ekaterina Maksimova, was slight.) He also devised the choreographic equivalent of stentorian speech: he would run and leap downstage on the diagonal from right to left, pause, loop back upstage in the wings, then run and leap on the diagonal from left to right. Liepa, as Crassus, did the same thing, exhaustingly, but Vasiliev turned it into a call to arms and cri de coeur. *Look,* his crisscrossing seemed to say, *I may not be as awesomely musclebound as you, you consider me merely irritating, but I represent the aspirations of an entire populace.* Through his performance, the pianissimo presence of one became the fortissimo presence of the multitude.

Rome stagnates, Crassus feasts, Spartacus rallies his forces, there are traitors on both sides, and someone might be having an affair. The uprising threatens chaos. The audience is left to mull the dialectical relationship of subjugator and subjugated. Is insurrection worth the price? The answer is no; there is nothing subversive in the ballet, which ultimately suffers from a lack of integration

between the ensemble dances and the soloists' monologues. Grigorovich imagined the contrast between the collective and the individual in symphonic terms, but fashioned his ballets more like
Baroque-era concertos, in which two or three solo instruments inter-
act loosely between repetitions of a refrain played in unison by the
full ensemble. There are other musical analogies, many made dis-
paragingly. Gayevsky, the critic Grigorovich most despised, claims
that the choreographer (like the Soviet leadership) had an allergic
reaction to American jazz but might have benefited from listening
to it, given the stiffness of his rhythms. The ensemble dances were
too "mechanical," governed by the metronome, with each of the
slaves raising one of their feet to the knee, stepping forward, and
then sinking to the ground in sync. Spartacus stepped further forward, and the men and women sunk down in counterpoint, but,
for Gayevsky, the "motor-like movement" made effective transitions
to the poetic monologues difficult. "The procession moves, and the
soul is silent," Gayevsky lamented, evidently presuming that the soul
has a rather impoverished choreographic lexicon. "The soul speaks,
and the procession stops."[97]

Decades later, and at a safer distance from Stalin, the Thaw,
and Russia itself, Joan Acocella referred back to the crisscrossing
diagonals in *Spartacus* to articulate what she considered to be the
central problem with his method: "Practically every time Spartacus
comes onstage he does so in leaps on the diagonal. Then he runs
into the wings, scoots upstage, and leaps down the space on the
opposite diagonal. Then his enemy Crassus comes in, leaping on the
diagonal, and all you want is to go home."[98] But in Soviet Russia,
home—cramped, sometimes communal prefab apartments—was
not especially desirable. The dancing had broad escapist appeal for
Soviet audiences, the cheap athletic thrills repeated on the other
side of the scrim that descended for the first of the monologues, and

the politics did not matter once the ballet was cleared for production. It entertained despite its ideological content, which was indeed something new.

Grigorovich's *Spartacus* succeeded because of its iron-jawed heroics, its unabashed sexiness, and because audience members could congratulate themselves on teasing out what seemed to be a subtext, but which had been calculatedly laid out on the surface. The moral of the story is that suffering in defeat proves nobler than exulting in triumph. Such is what it meant to be a Soviet Man, and what the transformation of Spartacus into a flying machine, hurtling across the stage with limbs thrown back and heart open, was meant to represent.

MISSING FROM THE cast was Plisetskaya, who was on tour when work began on the ballet and enmeshed in a project of her own, one that, to be successful, required her to exploit her fame. In 1964, she received the Lenin Prize, performed at La Scala, and became the subject of a documentary film. The official imprimatur emboldened her to approach Shostakovich, Khachaturian, and then her own husband for a balletic treatment of *Carmen*. The sexual subject matter called for a woman's legs to be wound around not a staff, but a man's hips, along the lines of Balanchine's 1929 ballet *The Prodigal Son*, which the New York City Ballet brought to Moscow in the Cold War cultural exchange of 1962. So this particular provocation had choreographic precedent. Still, to perform as Carmen, Plisetskaya had to argue her way through a thicket of nastiness involving the beautiful but unsexy minister of culture and her no less prudish aides. *Carmen Suite* was her cardinal obsession, and getting it onto the Bolshoi Theater stage and into the touring repertoire became the fight of her career.

The ballet is based on Georges Bizet's opera titled for its tragic heroine. Carmen, a Spanish gypsy, has a tryst with a soldier, Don José, whom she rejects in turn for a toreador, Escamillo. Seeking revenge, Don José sticks a knife in her heart, and she perishes as crowds cheer Escamillo's triumph in the bullring. Plisetskaya was inspired to pursue the role in 1966 after seeing Cuban choreographer Alberto Alonso on tour in Moscow. The dancing of the Cubans was a revelation—"Spanish" without the clichés of Spanish character dancing, performed en pointe in a non-classical manner. Their visit was part of an international cultural exchange prompted by the increasingly friendly relationship between the Soviet Union and Cuba after the socialist revolution in 1959, led by Fidel Castro, and the establishment of communist rule in 1965. There followed a dialogue between the Bolshoi Theater and the Ministry of Culture concerning the possible participation of Plisetskaya, along with Maximova and Vasiliev, in the international dance festivals in Havana in 1966 and 1967.[99] The retired Ulanova was invited along as a guest. Nothing came of the invitations in 1966, and the trip in 1967 also proved impossible to arrange: Maximova and Vasiliev had committed to *Spartacus*, Ulanova was ambivalent, and Plisetskaya was scheduled to be in Czechoslovakia, another important front in the cultural Cold War.

To mark Moscow and Havana's alliance, Alonso was invited to serve as a resident choreographer at the Bolshoi from December 17, 1966, to May 4, 1967.[100] When Plisetskaya pitched Carmen to Alonso, he immediately said *"Da!"* and received 1,082 rubles to create *Carmen Suite*.[101] He became the first choreographer to create a ballet specifically for the ballerina, exploiting the physical intensity that so exceeded that of the other dancers, female and male, in the troupe. Left unsaid was the fact that the choreographer's sister was prima ballerina assoluta of the Ballet Nacional de Cuba. She also took to the idea of Carmen, and she had the perfect dark eyes and copper skin for the role. Thus the Moscow premiere starring Plisetskaya would be followed by the Havana premiere starring Alicia Alonso.

In realizing Carmen's tale of seduction and betrayal, Plisetskaya drew on the real sexual tension between her and the male dancers at the Bolshoi. She taught classes for men that demanded "far more sheer physical output" than those for women.[102] The segregation also served her artistic purposes. She did not want to dilute the testosterone-fueled atmosphere by adding other women to the mix. The physical intensity was superabundant in *Carmen Suite*— and controversial. Ekaterina Furtseva, the minister of culture, approved the project believing that it would be a one-act version of *Don Quixote* or *Laurencia* or perhaps an audience-pleasing admixture of both. After the first performance at the Bolshoi Theater on April 20, 1967, however, Furtseva and the inspectors from the other Soviet agencies involved in the arts complained that the ballet was trafficking in "smoldering emotion and Latin sexual appetites."[103] She ordered Plisetskaya to cover up for the second performance of *Carmen Suite* and demanded that the erotic adagio, wherein, thighs exposed, she coiled herself around Don José and kissed him hungrily, be cut. Had the order been refused, *The Nutcracker* would have been performed in its place. Plisetskaya would never forget Furtseva's unlettered declaration that she and her collaborators had "turned a heroine of the Spanish people into a whore."[104] Rodion Shchedrin, who assembled the score from a montage of melodies taken from Bizet's opera, was accused of plagiarism.

Later, Furtseva stepped in to prevent *Carmen Suite* from being performed in Montreal as part of Expo 67, a half-year-long international exhibition that marked Canada's bicentennial. More than 50 million people paid the $2.50 entrance fee. Along with *Swan Lake,* the Red Army Chorus, and a Ukrainian folk ensemble, *Carmen Suite* was to have been part of an elaborate Soviet demonstration of achievements in culture, engineering, and science. Interested in space? Come into the Soviet pavilion to experience the simulated moon trip! Never tried caviar? Eight tons have been shipped! Even during this period of detente, however, a relaxing of the intense international arms race, Furtseva did not ease up on Plisetskaya. Chulaki recalled the minister of culture scrambling to block the sets and costumes of *Carmen Suite* from being shipped overseas out of Leningrad.

It became clear to me that Furtseva's nervousness stemmed from the fact that she had been asked to explain just why *Carmen Suite* had been included in the USA tour [*sic*, Expo 67]. As was her habit, she blamed it all on the willfulness of the theater's administration. And it was of no use saying that the repertoire for the tour had been set long before the criticism, and that no official or "permanent member" [of the Central Committee] had contested the decision-making process for the American tour. None of my arguments were accepted by the exasperated Minister. She demanded that the sets of *Carmen Suite* not be sent to Leningrad! I answered that they'd already been sent. Then she ordered that they not be loaded onto the cargo ship! I told her that they'd been loaded some time ago. Then she ordered that they be unloaded from the ship at the dock! I reported that the ship had already left the port. Then she said that the ship had to be detained in the open sea (!) and the sets transferred onto whatever vessel was available (a tugboat?) and brought back to port!

Obviously she couldn't wait to report to those "higher up" that all measures had been taken to prevent the undesirable *Carmen Suite* from touring to America.

When I firmly stated that the operation she proposed was completely unrealistic, she raged and raged, and only calmed down somewhat when I assured her that the sets would not be unloaded at the port of arrival, but would be separated out and put in the brig, returning unused to the USSR.[105]

Furtseva did not appreciate Chulaki's condescending tone. He was an imposing, bald-headed, bespectacled bear of a man, but she was the boss. After the sets of *Carmen Suite* returned to the USSR unused, Chulaki was fired.

Nevertheless, *Carmen Suite* returned to the Bolshoi Theater stage. The chairman of the Supreme Soviet, Alexei Kosïgin, took in a performance and, by saying he liked it, instantly turned it into a Soviet classic. Thereafter Furtseva was required to sing its praises just as loudly as she had raged against its flaws on the telephone to Chulaki, and Plisetskaya would coil her legs even more tightly around Fadeyechev as Don José. She no longer brooked any criticism of the concept behind the ballet or her performance. She jettisoned friends who considered the dancing too piquant and disparaged critics outside of Russia who thought it, to the contrary, not heated enough—a sincere effort to sexually liberate Soviet ballet, perhaps, but still a Soviet ballet. The Bolshoi was "five minutes short of becoming a museum," in her opinion, and so she dismissed the suggestion that what she considered brazenly sultry could not compete with the offerings on Broadway.[106] To that end, she eventually performed her "good-bad" ballet as part of a "Stars of the Bolshoi Ballet" gala in New York. "Flaunting and grinning," she was "vividly feline" and, like the other members of the cast, "larger than life," a law unto herself. [107]

PLISETSKAYA DERIDED GRIGOROVICH for losing his edge in the 1960s, and for rejecting progress by affixing his name to modest revisions of the classics. The worlds before and after the revolution were worlds apart, but, like other choreographers of his time, Soviet and otherwise, he reverted to the narrative ballets of the past. It was not, as Plisetskaya doubtlessly recognized, entirely a matter of creative impoverishment. Soviet audiences liked the classics, and in most instances preferred them, even in bowdlerized versions, to ballets about insurgencies and five-year plans. So Grigorovich put his personal stamp on the canon. Other choreographers, East and West, do the same, which makes authorship a fraught matter. Additions, subtractions, augmentations, diminutions: who is to tell who did what?

The question was raised at the Bolshoi in 1969 about the most classic ballet of all, *Swan Lake*. Grigorovich wanted to restore to Tchaikovsky, the machinist Karl Valts, and the Bolshoi Theater of 1877 the dark, grim ballet they had conceived. It was not a research project, more an effort to return *Swan Lake* to the Romantic era, which for Grigorovich meant E.T.A. Hoffmann. He restructured it to make the sorcerer Rothbart the Hoffmannesque double of Prince Siegfried—his shadow, dancing together with him in unison, peering over his shoulder, pulling his emotional and psychological strings. (Gayevsky claims that the problem faced by Siegfried is typical of Grigorovich's heroes: They seem to be free, but they are in fact "prisoners, hostages, and also somewhat like marionettes," beholden to ideals that sow confusion in their heads.)[108] Had the sorcerer been given some mime he might have cast spells, but mime was, for Grigorovich, taboo, along with earthiness in the national dances, which are performed en pointe in the ball scene.

The prince does not see what is happening. He imagines escaping his pseudo-aristocratic knightliness for a future with Odette in a realm of pure divine love, but the evil spirit offers him destructive Romantic passion in the form of Odile. He succumbs, and then everything is eradicated in a restoration of the 1877 storm scene. Siegfried is left alone after Odette/Odile and all of the white swans are washed from the black stage "like chalk from a chalkboard."[109] Whereas the Stalinist conclusion had the prince finding redemption through his love for Odette, in Grigorovich's conception there is no saving the prince or his would-be princess, no triumphant conquest over Rothbart in a sword fight. Fate leaves him on the shore alone, possessed of nothing but the knowledge of his own delusions.

"Everyone dances," one of the in-house assessors of the new production declared, and all of the dancing mattered, since Grigorovich had excluded "the window-dressing of the old production." The act 1 waltz was "festive," a guileless celebration; the polonaise served as the balletic equivalent of a ballad, introducing intrigue, trouble, into the proceedings: "As the goblets are clinked in the middle of the polonaise, it becomes mysterious, magical. Using this effect Grigorovich reveals his hero's internal aspirations, exposes the split between his world and external events."[110] Act 2 came from Ivanov, and parts of the framing acts from Gorsky and Petipa, but the borrowings were neither criticized nor challenged, since Grigorovich got out front to defend them. He had kept the best of the past, he said, in the service of the new. The absence of specialist national dancers doing the Hungarian czardas along with the Spanish, Italian, and Polish dances in the ball scene, however, became a point of contention in the closed-door discussions of *Swan Lake*.

Grigorovich opted for a "pathetic imitation of Balanchine" in his "illogical" and "monotonous" ballet, in the brutal assessment of the critic Elena Lutskaya.[111]

But a larger group in Grigorovich's camp, including the dancer Māris Liepa, predictably defended the production from the first step to the last. Grigorovich had established himself as a choreographer by rejecting realism and the silent-movie-acting style of *drambalet;* his ballets were meant to occupy a higher plane, and his version of *Swan Lake* put a stake through the heart of the Lavrovsky realist tradition. The ethnic dances, he decided, needed to be poeticized, classicalized, which meant eliminating the heeled shoes and commedia dell'arte shenanigans. Grigorovich's teacher, Fyodor Lopukhov, further defended the production on the grounds that his prize pupil had been "exceptionally attentive to Tchaikovsky's music," restoring, for example, the Russian dance that had been tossed even before Gorsky (by Petipa and Ivanov in 1895). And just what was so "Polish" about Gorsky's *Swan Lake* mazurka anyway?[112] Nothing. Plus it was profoundly unmusical, attaching a male national dance pair to a national princess.

The minister of culture attended the dress rehearsal on December 18, 1969, after which a discussion of the pluses and minuses of the Hoffmannesque production was to be held. But it did not happen. Furtseva appeared to inform the group who had packed themselves into the tiny waiting room outside the director's office that everything was understood, everything was "clear."[113] She smiled left and right but refused to comment further, offering only to deliver her verdict in the morning, since, in accord with the Russian proverb, morning is wiser than evening. Grigorovich met with her the next day and learned that *Swan Lake* had been canceled, despite being slated to open a New Year festival. He must have been devastated, but he remembered defending himself. He did not invent

Romanticism, he told Furtseva, and insisted that his version of *Swan Lake* remained faithful to Tchaikovsky's great score and to something that the composer understood very well: an ideal is a cruel, evil thing. To pursue an ideal is to invite ruin, and the ballet reckoned with this truth. Furtseva said, "All right, all right, stage it."[114]

But that "all right, all right" was contingent on the ending being changed to a sunrise and light, and Odette remaining a princess, as opposed to turning back into a swan, in that glow. Grigorovich headed back into the studio and came up with the required alternate. The discussion that followed the second general rehearsal, on December 23, 1969, reflected the tensions. The final act "moves the entire struggle into the spiritual realm. It speaks of devotion and the triumph of love," one of Grigorovich's lieutenants commented, before hinting at the drama behind the scenes. "I want to add that another concept was planned and realized as an alternate. It was a profound one, but it did not get to be fully expressed. Two paths led from it: one with a tragic finale, and the other path Grigorovich took to preserve and complete it as conceived."[115] So in this convoluted formulation, the radiant central conceit of the ballet did not find its true expression in the tragic ending but instead found its proper realization through the merciful intervention of the minister of culture.

Grigorovich assigned the role of the sorcerer Rothbart to Spartacus—that is, to the soloist Boris Akimov, who alternated with Vasiliev in the role of the slave-rebel.[116] Akimov cavorted and gamboled in a manner that some in the Bolshoi Theater audience found "hard to take" once the ballet was allowed to be publicly performed, on December 25, 1969.[117] It trafficked in an implausible contrivance. Rothbart ran circles around Siegfried, mocking his knightly affectations and throwing the royal ball into chaos, only to be "crushed by the spiritual force of the love of the Prince for

Odette."[118] That is the metaphorical interpretation of the happy ending. Onstage, Siegfried prevents the sorcerer from slaying the swan-maiden by blocking his path to her and covering her with his own body. The sorcerer collapses dead at the lovers' feet. The opposite of this ending, the tragic finale, was never shown to the Soviet public.

THE ROMANTIC INTERPRETATION of Grigorovich's career marks *Swan Lake* as both the end and a beginning: the end of an experimental and explorative phase, and the beginning of a period of frustration, when the creative well (never especially full) began to run dry. Plisetskaya began to distance herself from Grigorovich, hand over her roles in his ballets to younger dancers, and suggest that, having shifted from the acquisition of power in the theater to the protection of it, he had become boring. In her memoirs, she avoided mentioning his name as much as she could but, close to the end, settled the score that, in her creative life, most needed settling. "I have not changed my opinion of *Stone Flower* and *Legend of Love*," she wrote long after the fact. "They are the peak of his work. All his subsequent works—this is my opinion—went downhill. Fast."[119] She twisted the dagger, describing Grigorovich as a dictator, a Stalin in the Bolshoi Theater, who shaped the entire Russian ballet tradition in his image. "He changed the good old classical ballets, adding just a slight retouching but not forgetting to add his name. And then he took on Petipa, Perrot, Ivanov, Gorsky. In the last ten years he didn't even bother making changes."[120] In truth, he did make some changes, but Plisetskaya was not to be dissuaded from her assessment—a vile tale that had Grigorovich, notoriously repetitive at the start of his career, repeating himself long into his dotage.

Grigorovich still relied in his ballets on classical steps circa 1910, kept the women in pointe shoes, and preserved the traditional architecture of ballet. His setting of *The Stone Flower*, for example, retains the familiar balance between soloists, coryphées, and the corps de ballet. As a dramatist, however, he was more of a modernist, stripping plots down to bullet points. About *Spartacus* he said simply, "This production is conceived as a tragedy of personality."[121] The hero chooses his own fate (he errs by sparing Crassus's life, a mistake that Crassus does not replicate when the tables are turned). To stage that conceit, Grigorovich could not count on soloists and the corps de ballet alone. Paradoxically, then, as he stripped down the story he filled up the stage. His *Legend of Love* adds a pair of youths and a buffoon; *Spartacus* features a mix of shepherds and profligates; his 1975 ballet *Ivan the Terrible*, also known as *Age of Fire* (Ognennïy vek) includes heralds, bell ringers, and both male and female boyars. In his version of *The Golden Age* from 1982 there are gangsters, robbers, and fishermen. Like everything else in Grigorovich's ballets, however, the characterizations are compressed, reduced to one or two defining features, outlines. And compression leaves little room for error.

Thus in the 1970s, the Bolshoi Ballet, like the Soviet political structure itself, failed to combat inertia. Faith in the Soviet cause flagged. Everyone under Brezhnev, and indeed Brezhnev himself, contented themselves by going through the motions, and even as Grigorovich tightened his fist around the reins of power within the theater he seemed to be playing a part too long rehearsed. For Plisetskaya and his other critics this was the truth of Grigorovich's career: having remade the classics in his own symphonic choreographic image, having laid to rest plot and pantomime and the traumas of the *drambalet* years, Grigorovich ended up, after a scintillating start, marking time, moving bodies across stage without much inspiration.

• • •

PLISETSKAYA, HOWEVER, HAD a vision. The seasoned dancer became an unseasoned choreographer who brashly imagined herself, her husband, and their allies establishing an alternate repertoire. They believed that the old classics of the ballet stage needed to be replaced by new classics: the sacred masterpieces of Russian literature that had resisted adaptation through traditional means and had not been reinterpreted by the Soviets along socialist-realist lines. Thus she based a ballet on a masterpiece that no choreographer had hitherto dared to touch, Tolstoy's *Anna Karenina*.

To consider the choice imprudent would be an understatement, but Plisetskaya maintained, as did her husband, that the capacious novel could be contained. His music and her dance were meant to capture a specific aspect of the deep and rich internal life of Tolstoy's heroine: her increasing inability to distinguish the real from the imagined. The ballet was conceived in 1967 with the help of Plisetskaya's trusted colleagues, Natalya Ryzhenko and Victor Smirnov, who co-choreographed the ballet with her. Some of the dancers were, like her, veterans of Grigorovich's ballets eager to try something new; others were untested.

The first script, by Natalya Kasatkina and Vladimir Vasilyov (not to be confused with Vasiliev), reduced the novel to eleven scenes with a prologue. Each of the discrete plot points would be "depicted, as it were, through the feelings and imaginations of the characters."[122] The ballet was to have opened with a blizzard, the howling wind becoming the sound of a bell becoming the light of a candle that illuminates Karenina and three other characters at the heart of the story. Shaking the stage-set snow globe in the first scene revealed the sparkling interior of a St. Petersburg ballroom. Karenina and Count Vronsky, who will indulge in a scandalous high-society affair, collide with each other at the end to music that suggests, according to the script, the screeching brakes of a train—the harbinger of Anna's suicide when faced with the impossible choice between her lover in exile or the son she has had in St. Petersburg with a Russian imperial minister. That scream of the brakes resonates throughout the score such that Karenina dies continually in her imagination before the train actually arrives.

Plisetskaya rejected this extremely compact original scenario. The treatment was too terse, and as such too harsh. In search of something more literal, she passed the project along to Boris Lvov-Anokhin, an experienced theater director who came with strong recommendations. Lvov-Anokhin preserved the opening snowstorm and claustrophobic concept of the first script but expanded it into a full-evening production of three acts. His scenario opens with Karenina alone in the drifts, then moves to the silent crowd, which makes the heroine seem all the more alone. The train wheels running over her body is presaged by the death, also under a train, of a holy fool-like figure. At the end of the ball, Karenina runs into her future lover, and their relationship is carried out discreetly until the pivotal episode at a racetrack. The din from the orchestra pit, representing the heroine's innermost feelings and thoughts, is joined by the racket of an onstage band: the real world. Shchedrin's score is a brooding, throbbing affair that privileges the low registers of the instruments and tritone-based, dissonant harmonies. Karenina is assigned a cluster of melodies that depict the conditions imposed on her, by her, and outside her as others witness her disintegration.

The steeplechase race ends in mild embarrassment for Vronsky, who slips from his saddle after his horse loses its footing. For Karenina, it is a catastrophe. She gasps in shock, instantly exposing the affair to the public and severing all relations with her husband. Cue the train music. The epilogue finds the tragic heroine alone in the murk as the light of the locomotive comes into view. Afterward, everyone involved in the production would breathe a sigh of relief that the ballet had not turned out to be the train wreck its detractors joked it would.

Among the skeptics were the two general directors of the Bolshoi Theater between 1967 and 1972. Plisetskaya faced resistance first from Chulaki and then from Yuriy Muromtsev, who served as head of the Bolshoi from September 1970 to December 1972 as the ballet crawled toward the stage. In her memoirs, Plisetskaya cast the story of her ballet's tortured path from page to stage as a bleak comedy, describing locked doors, bad lighting, unfinished Pierre Cardin costumes, and missing dancers. It was finally produced thanks to Shchedrin's political savvy during the initial planning stages and a fortuitously timed attack on the Bolshoi repertoire.

On April 5, 1968, Shchedrin announced in the pages of *Pravda* his and his wife's ardent desire to create a ballet on *Anna Karenina*. In an article titled "Uznayem li mï Annu?" (Will Anna be recognizable?), Shchedrin vowed that the ballet would not be a "profanation of the novel" because "we have taken a different approach."[123] It would be a distillation, not a wholesale adaptation. The minister of culture knew nothing of Shchedrin's and Plisetskaya's intention and did not appreciate learning about their plans from the newspaper. Furtseva called Chulaki to demand that he issue a denial. He refused, and Furtseva's anger was enough to shelve the project until 1972.

By that time—and in that year—the lack of innovation in the repertoire, the Bolshoi's stagnation, had become a serious concern to the government. The Central Committee signaled its concern publically in *Pravda*. A long-retired dancer and a prominent journalist, Viktorina Kriger, was either asked or moved to rebuke the Bolshoi Ballet, and by extension Grigorovich, for the predictable performance schedule. The *New York Times* picked up the report and summarized it from top to bottom, embarrassing the theater internationally. "The posters of the Bolshoi Ballet cannot exactly be called diverse," Kriger deadpanned. "Today is *Swan Lake*, tomorrow *Giselle*." Then *Swan Lake* would be performed again. And then *Giselle* again. Grigorovich's *Legend and Love* and *Spartacus* appeared now and again, along with *Romeo and Juliet* and a couple of other lesser-known ballets. But the offerings truly did exceed the dull. The sameness of the repertoire had begun to affect the box office and impede the development of young talent.[124]

Desperately seeking something new, the government gave the green light to Plisetskaya and Shchedrin to stage *Anna Karenina*. It premiered on June 10, 1972, just before the season ended. Their "profanation" of Tolstoy had little of the shock effect of *Carmen Suite*; letters to the editors of the Soviet culture desks reiterated now-familiar complaints about Plisetskaya's affront to grace. Her "suffering is not profound," objected one writer. "It is not affecting. Tolstoy's aristocratic Anna is missing from her character." And although "skirts flounced in the air," another observer failed to "see any other emotions expressed."[125]

The ballet received support in learned circles, before and after its premiere, and Plisetskaya tried to prepare the audience of the Bolshoi for a different experience, explaining, in her essay for the program booklet, that "ballet these days is without a doubt strongly influenced by gymnastics, acrobatics, and figure skating. If earlier an abundance of pantomimic gestures obscured the meaning of the drama, then the current emphasis on sophisticated virtuoso technique also distances the viewer from understanding the events on the stage." Her choreography strove for the middle ground in its representation of Anna as "the supreme symbol of femininity." Her anguish exposes "the 'total' lie of high society, its hypocritical claims to morality and decency."[126] Such was the ideological justification for bringing Tolstoy's novel to the Bolshoi. The cost? When Plisetskaya, her co-choreographers, and her husband created *Anna Karenina*, they melodramatized the heroine's death but left out the release of the spirit that Tolstoy describes in the final pages of his novel. Here Konstantin Levin, the character with whom the author identifies and whose trajectory in the novel is the opposite of Karenina's, has an epiphany. He looks up into the cosmos and feels it opening up, enveloping him, bathing him in radiance, truth, and inner peace. This apotheosis could not be represented on the Soviet stage.

Anna Karenina proved too austere for the old guard, the *Carmen Suite* too inflamed, and a third dance, called *Bach Prelude*, too spiritual.[127] Didacticism and nationalism remained the moribund emphasis in the repertoire, not Plisetskaya's decadent deviation from this static thralldom. In the *Bach Prelude*, Plisetskaya performs steps of Eastern derivation and some basic ballet moves, *bourrées en couru*, *piqués en arabesque*. She seems to be tasked with communicating that these positions contain the spirit, entrap it. The performance begins as a solo before her romantic partner turns up—another form of containment. A striking passage has Plisetskaya moving perpendicular to the floor, legs split in a manner that seems to negate the pull of the Earth. Her leg rises in the other direction and then to a *grand battement en rond*. Then she repositions her body and moves her traveling leg in the opposite direction, in seamless fashion. Space becomes fluid, likewise time as she appears to be moving in slow motion against the flow of the music.

WORRIES ABOUT THE repertoire of the Bolshoi had been made public, but opposition to Grigorovich's rule within the theater remained hidden behind the scenes. It was real, and it involved dancers young and old, conservative and progressive. Some of them protested, anonymously, to the Central Committee of the

Communist Party of the Soviet Union. On April 3, 1973, its chief ideologue, Mikhaíl Suslov, received an unsigned letter advocating that Grigorovich be deposed—or at least demoted. He had been removed from his previous post at the Kirov Theater in Leningrad, the letter began, owing to his mistreatment of the talented dancers there, and since his appointment to the Bolshoi in 1964 had not staged an original ballet. "He is occupied with redoing, 'perfecting' old productions," even though the productions in question, by Ivanov, Petipa, Gorsky, and others, held a place of distinction in their original form, praised both at home and abroad. Such was Grigorovich's artistic "credo," his raison d'être as a choreographer. Meantime, the denunciation continued, efforts by talented newcomers to create ballets on Soviet themes had been suppressed.

The subject turned to Grigorovich's quest for power: "For completely inexplicable reasons Grigorovich simultaneously occupies two different positions: artistic director and ballet master in chief, even though our collective includes other capable, talented people who have devoted their entire lives to the art of ballet." He had become a "dictator," aided by the minister of culture, which had allowed him to handpick the Bolshoi's artistic council, even though Grigorovich was not a member of the Communist Party and "had declared, insolently, that the criticism he received from the party organization interfered with his work." (The decorated ballerina Marina Kondratyeva held the post of Communist Party secretary for the Bolshoi Ballet during the period in question.) Grigorovich further "allows himself to be rude, tactless, callous, and creates a tense atmosphere," the hostilities fueled by the division within the ballet between those dancers who belong to the troupe that travels abroad, and the troupe that stays at home. The letter included an invidious suggestion, meant to cement the case against the ballet master: "Since Grigorovich's arrival homosexual activities have been promoted within our collective, despite being illegal in our society. On tour in Paris in 1971 Grigorovich informed our younger members about his meetings with the homosexuals Jean Marais, Lifar, Roland Petit, and Béjart."

The cure for the malaise included elections for a new artistic council by secret ballot and the naming of a new artistic director, a "Communist, an honest, objective individual, someone as clean as crystal, an ideal citizen of the Soviet Union." The minister of culture needed to make some corrections.

The complaint—both the parts that had merit as well as the homophobic prattle about Grigorovich's meetings with France's leading artists—ended up being ignored. Grigorovich was called in for tea and a chat with the assistant minister of culture, Vasiliy Kukharsky, who reported the substance of the conversation to the minister of culture herself, Furtseva.[128] The Bolshoi had achieved remarkable things despite the strife, and perhaps even because of the strife, and so, Furtseva concluded, perhaps nothing needed to be done. She had engineered a confrontation with Grigorovich over *Swan Lake*, less because of the substance of the ballet than a need to remind him that she controlled him, not the opposite. "She would dismiss directors, rebuke critics and ban productions in a peremptory manner of the 'Off with his head' of Alice's Queen of Hearts," her biographer observed.[129] He had been checked, and so there was no need to use his problems with his dancers to check him further.

FURTSEVA HAD TRAINED as a textile worker in a town near the village of her birth. She married a pilot, and they had a daughter. After he flew away for good, she found support in the greater family of the Communist Party. She moved to Moscow and rose through the political ranks to a position not unlike that of a big-city mayor. Malicious tongues wagged about her relationship with Khrushchev after he promoted her to the Presidium of the Central Committee, though she did not last long in the post. Her phone was tapped by the KGB, as was everyone's, and in 1961 she was overheard criticizing Khrushchev's muddleheaded pseudo-liberalism. She knew she was in trouble. Sensing the loss of everything she had worked to achieve, she "opened her veins in her bath," according to her biographer.[130] She was found alive, and Khrushchev, who had the suicide of another official on his hands, granted her a pardon in the form of a demotion from the Central Committee to the position of minister of culture. She remained the most powerful woman in the Soviet government, an elegantly attired and modishly coiffured figure in a sea of dull pinstripe suits.

Those who knew her well, including Grigorovich and Plisetskaya, described Furtseva as seemingly confident but deeply insecure, aware of her limited knowledge of the arts and hostile to those who reminded her of it. When Chulaki did just that, his tenure as general director of the Bolshoi abruptly ended. At least so too did his shouting matches with her over the appointment of a chief conductor, his choice of repertoire, and personnel for foreign tours. The soprano Galina Vishnevskaya recalled the men of the Bolshoi, including Chulaki, being pulled into Furtseva's office to explain why they had spoiled Vishnevskaya's tour to America by denouncing her to the KGB. Lined up against a wall, they sputtered apologies like badly behaved schoolboys in front of a headmistress. Vishnevskaya received permission to tour, but the singer first had to meet, on Furtseva's insistence, with a "vile, grey creature" of the Central Committee.[131]

Furtseva's misogynist male detractors claimed that she used her feminine wiles to get her way and staged spectacular "temper tantrums" in her office when she did not.[132] She was also an inconsistent enforcer of official artistic policies. Furtseva had her pet peeves and indulgences, according to this same critique, and maintained a stable of handsome aides and advisers. She liked receiving expensive gifts from her petitioners but was capable of turning on her supplicants for thinking that she could be bribed. Shchedrin gave her a diamond; she accused him of purloining Bizet's music.

Furtseva was known as "Catherine the Third," as if she were the rightful heir to Catherine the Great and her enlightened reign.[133] A truer assessment of her administrative style finds her struggling to reconcile competing interests and achieve some kind of balance within the theater. Thus both Grigorovich and Plisetskaya could claim her support as well as the lack of it. At times her favor turned to dogmatic hostility. She did not referee their dispute, recognizing that the conflict between the two weakened each against her.

In 1974, Furtseva came under political attack, charged with abuse of power by the Party Control Commission of the Central Committee. Her daughter and son-in-law had been caught stealing from party coffers to build "the family's palatial dacha."[134] Furtseva accepted blame and pawned her jewels to settle the bill, but Brezhnev, with whom she had clashed, denied her a pardon. He had built an even gaudier dacha for himself from the state coffers, but he wanted her out and so had her family's petty corruption exposed. She drank; she lost her bid to be elected to the Supreme Soviet, and she was told, on the day before she died, that someone else would read the speech she was supposed to give at the Maliy Theater.

These events precipitated a fatal heart attack on October 24, 1974, according to the official account. Either that or Furtseva had opened her veins again, successfully this time. She was sixty-three. The joke went around Moscow that she turned up at the pearly gates for admission to heaven just after Pablo Picasso had arrived. Having forgotten her passport, she could not prove her identity. So Saint Peter gave her a quiz. Who was Pablo Picasso? he asked. She did not know, and her ignorance was proof enough that she was indeed the Soviet minister of culture. Saint Peter opened the gates and welcomed her inside the clouds, with Pyotr Demichev assuming her former role on Earth.[135]

For Grigorovich, Demichev seemed better than Furtseva, who had given him grief over his monopolization of his position, and he turned out to be right. For Plisetskaya, he also seemed an improvement, for he had earlier, as a member of the Central Committee, granted her permission to stage *Anna Karenina*. But as minister of culture he wanted to avoid the drama that had engulfed Furtseva, and thus he trusted Grigorovich to enrich the repertoire on his own terms, muzzle dissenters, and keep the dirty laundry in the hamper.

The conflicts inside the theater persisted, and the repertoire did not receive the enrichment it needed. To Plisetskaya's disgust, Grigorovich blamed the absence of new offerings not on himself, but on his powerless dancers, accusing them of dragging their feet in the studio. "It's the opposition in the ballet that's keeping me from working," she remembers him grumbling on Soviet television.[136] She rejected his claims, thought his bellyaching feeble. The resistance he claimed he faced was just an excuse for his own failings, according to Plisetskaya. How could he feel so aggrieved, she wondered, when he had at his disposal more than "two hundred" dancers, the support of the Soviet government (even its "missiles, tanks, and aircraft carriers," she claimed), and the time and space to do as he liked?[137] She contrasted his situation with that of repressed Soviet geniuses like Shostakovich, who kept working, creating, kicking against the pricks, trying to maneuver around the censors—all of which only made things worse, drove the thorns in further.

Plisetskaya knew Shostakovich and had once hoped that he would collaborate with her on *Carmen Suite*, but, tired of being pricked, he declined her invitation. Grigorovich also knew Shostakovich; his mentor Fyodor Lopukhov had collaborated with the composer on *The Bright Stream*, the ballet that ended Shostakovich's career in ballet. Same hopes for a collaboration, same result. The all-powerful Grigorovich imagined another of the neglected scores from Shostakovich's experimental youth coming to his creative rescue. That did not happen until 1982, seven years after the martyred composer had died. Plisetskaya sarcastically noted Grigorovich's effort to get a new ballet, any new ballet, onstage earlier: "He would announce one work, then another. Then silence. Quiet. As if people had misheard him."[138]

GRIGOROVICH MOOTED SEVERAL possible projects. Of special interest was a ballet to be based on Mikhaíl Bulgakov's *The Master and Margarita*, a dense, scary novel begun in 1928 and almost finished in 1940, the year Bulgakov died. It was never published during Stalin's rule and only made it into print in the late 1960s. It was *the* book of the Thaw: demonic, religious, psychiatric (the Master of the title takes residence in a madhouse to write a book about Pontius Pilate), and rich with subtext. Life is difficult for the artists in the novel, likewise for the bureaucrats who abuse them, and the layers of political pragmatics offered Grigorovich the opportunity to stage particular scenes from competing perspectives or perhaps have the corps de ballet switch allegiances in curious fashion. The novel also featured sex, magic, jazz, and an outrageous party inspired by a lavish ball held at the Moscow residence of the American ambassador in 1935. The obvious composer for such a riotous romp was Shostakovich, but he would not—could not—take it on. He remained "spooked," Grigorovich explained, by previous experiences in the Bolshoi Theater and preferred composing symphonies and string quartets.[139]

Another possible subject from fiction was the Soviet classic *The Quiet Don* (or, at it is commonly translated, *And Quiet Flows the Don*), by Mikhaíl Sholokhov, a sprawling saga in four parts that won the Stalin Prize in 1941 and did much to win for its author the Nobel Prize in Literature in 1965. It involves a love triangle with a hero who switches sides between the Reds and the Whites during the civil war that followed the revolution—a theatrically viable topic. But the novel has a massive number of characters, including the brooding Don River of the title and the black Russian earth. Grigorovich claimed that Shostakovich took to the idea of a partial adaptation and even played through some sketched-out musical ideas. But these might actually have been written for a potential opera based on the novel rather than a ballet, or perhaps he merely plinked out some of the folksongs referenced by Sholokhov. Author and composer had met in May of 1964, but besides a great affection for vodka, they had little in common, Grigorovich claimed. Even if Shostakovich's imagination had been inflamed, and even if the idea for the opera had morphed into a ballet, Grigorovich might have had a hard time selling *The Quiet Don* to the artistic council of the Bolshoi Theater. He laughingly recalled the wry response to his initial pitch: "Too many Dons," since *Don Quixote*, *Don Carlos*, and *Don Giovanni* were already in the repertoire.[140]

Still seeking a new subject, and heeding the advice of the conductor and composer Abram Stasevich, Grigorovich listened to the music Prokofiev had composed for Sergey Eisenstein's two-part film *Ivan the Terrible* (1944–46). Here at last was a suitable topic and workable score, at least after Chulaki shaped it to suit Grigorovich's needs by nipping, tucking, and threading in passages from other Prokofiev scores. Copyright was not a consideration—Soviet art belonged to the Soviet state—so they had license to do as they liked. Prokofiev was long dead anyway and could not defend his work. Perhaps in his stead, Shostakovich blanched at some of the cuts and additions after seeing the ballet in rehearsal. Yet he believed that Prokofiev ultimately would have wanted his music to be heard no matter the context, so he stuttered faint praise to Grigorovich. Perhaps bowdlerizing the soundtrack for a ballet might not have infuriated Prokofiev after all.

The project was first called *Age of Fire* before reverting to the title of the film that inspired it, *Ivan the Terrible*. The ballet defends the violence of Ivan's reign in keeping with Soviet historical accounts of the origins of the tsardom of Russia and the Russian Empire. Looking back on the sixteenth century from the middle of the twentieth, Ivan was said to have taken the throne as a teenager and thereafter (in a blending of fact and fiction) consolidated the Russian state by first liquidating the Tatar inhabitants of the important trading center of Kazan. That ended the exterior threat to his rule. He then subdued the boyars of Moscow, the interior threat. The corps de ballet, in the role of the People, defend the tsar, even when he establishes a cruel personal guard, the *oprichniki*, to menace them into submission.

Grigorovich made sure that the *oprichniki* recalled the KGB, even as he sidestepped the troubling features of Ivan's psychology that had obsessed Eisenstein. The dancers in the lead role did not. Yuriy Vladimirov exposed Ivan's barbarousness in a performance of disturbing contortions, after which dark-eyed Tatar dancer Irek Mukhamedov took the part, bringing greater introspection, according to the consensus of Moscow balletomanes. The tsar's doomed bride Anastasia bears the emotional burden of *Ivan the Terrible*, its pathos, but at its core the ballet is about fire, blood, swords, and the pursuit of power in Russia. As Grigorovich put it, "To be in power is to have unclean hands."[141] Those hands caress Anastasia, strangle a traitor, and become tangled in the ropes of the bells that rang in his coronation. That final image, intended as a *coup de théâtre*, took time to perfect.

AFTER SHOSTAKOVICH'S DEATH in August 1975, Grigorovich decided to revive one of his ballets, something the composer himself had not endorsed. "I don't want them reconstituted," Shostakovich insisted.[142] In his later years, he had been plagued by nervous tics, seemingly tormented by something dark and deep— the sheer terror of the 1930s, Grigorovich surmised. He decided to overcome the fear that the composer himself could not by staging the first of Shostakovich's ballets, *The Golden Age*. Progress was sluggish; creating the dances meant changing the music, which meant changing the dances again. The plot too. *The Golden Age* did not reach the stage until November 4, 1982. It was Grigorovich's last original work.

The period in between the conception and the completion of the ballet was acrimonious. Tensions increased between Grigorovich and the Bolshoi Ballet's stars, including the emblematic Moscow virtuoso Vasiliev, who would, in 1995, replace Grigorovich as artistic director, lasting five years in the job before being removed by presidential decree; Vasiliev's partner, Ekaterina Maksimova, a glamorous student of Ulanova and darling of the foreign press; and Plisetskaya, who overambitiously aspired, despite her international commitments, to create a de facto troupe of her own within the Bolshoi. Rancor led to schism, a split between those who supported the status quo, the larger "Bolshevik" faction, and those who did not. The latter, the smaller "Menshevik" faction, faced the wrath of the ballet master in chief, whose consumption of Ararat cognac increased along with his invective against Plisetskaya, the brightest of the stars. He punished the dancers who gravitated toward her, excluding them from productions of his own ballets and denying opportunities to perform on tour. Since the dancers worked without the protection of legal contracts, Grigorovich did not need to threaten to dismiss them. He could just do so.

Plisetskaya deliberately added to the strife by speaking her mind to the foreign press. While on tour in the summer of 1977, she revealed to newspaper and magazine reporters in France that she wanted to escape the theater's tedium. Her comments were relayed by the Soviet embassy in Paris to the Kremlin, which had been tracking the reception of the Bolshoi Ballet abroad. For "bourgeois propagandists," the interviews were a gold mine, and Plisetskaya had the audacity to stand by them. Stepan Chervonenko, the ambassador of the Soviet Union to France, reported on her activities to the Central Committee.

> Firstly, M. M. Plisetskaya expressed her thoughts about the stagnation in our ballet art, its alleged dullness and conservatism ("in Russia freedom must be earned"; young Soviet ballet dancers "are not given sufficient opportunities to travel outside of Russia"; "the Russian public also wants to see something new"; "Are there choreographers in Russia who reach beyond the outdated rules?—I (M. M. Plisetskaya) don't know of any. —Then what's to be hoped for?— Little if anything"). Secondly, M. M. Plisetskaya criticized the Bolshoi Theater, its repertoire, "which today under the influence of Yuriy Grigorovich has become deadly dull. Think about it, not one of the Bolshoi Theater choreographers has created a ballet for me!"[143]

Upon returning to Moscow in July of 1977, Plisetskaya was invited to the Central Committee for tea and a chat with its director of cultural affairs, Vasiliy Shauro. The exchange is not recorded, but she apparently stood her ground, boasting of upsetting "ballet Moscow" and incensing the bureaucrats by bringing word to Russian ballet-goers that Maurice Béjart had discovered "new worlds" in dance.[144] In attendance, besides Shauro, was Mikhaíl Zimyanin, the editor in chief of *Pravda* under Brezhnev and the Central Committee's ideological watchdog. Plisetskaya had to go around him to bring one of Béjart's worlds, a planet conjured into being through sexual fantasy, to the Bolshoi stage, and had to plead for Brezhnev's approval through one of his assistants.

Grigorovich had also shown an interest in Béjart, and dispossessed Bolshoi Ballet dancers slandered him for it, ending what might have been a revolution at the top. For Plisetskaya, however, Béjart seemed the antipode to Grigorovich, a messianic iconoclast at once down and dirty and intensely cerebral, the escape valve for her aspirations. He claimed Plisetskaya as a kindred spirit, a "liberated" artist like himself, albeit one fluent in "the grand Soviet tradition."[145] For Bolshoi Ballet observers outside of Russia, this was not much of a compliment. Arlene Croce lampooned Béjart's pretentiousness, describing his choreographies as once-fun nightclub acts masquerading as serious philosophical treatises. She suffered them, then swept them into the dustpan with a one-liner: "Béjart's ballets are like serious parodies of things that are no longer taken seriously."[146]

Plisetskaya began to collaborate with Béjart, and he with her, in Brussels in 1975. There she starred in a revival of Béjart's 1961 *Bolero*, standing on a blood-red table with a group of dancers seated in a half circle behind her, and another group in the background. The scenario derives from an earlier 1928 script by Ida Rubinstein and Bronislava Nijinskaya, in which an exotic gypsy maiden dances atop a table in an auberge in Spain, enticing and exciting the loins of the male spectators, the threat of gang rape made plain. When Maurice Ravel's Basque-themed score began, Plisetskaya initiated a seduction rite. She learned the part in a week, having obsessed about doing it for a year (she had seen it in 1974 in Dubrovnik and claims that her letter to Béjart expressing her desperate desire to perform the dance disappeared, like most mail bearing foreign addresses, in the Soviet postal service). The movements "came hard" to her, owing to the diluted Southeast Asian aspects of Béjart's art and the cross-rhythms—with four counts in the dance rubbing up against three in the music; in truth, the surrounding men in the cast had trickier rhythmic misalignments to navigate.[147]

The effort showed, and her performance evinces a studied, self-conscious coolness. It was not definitive—the American ballerina Suzanne Farrell, and Béjart's own dancers, both male and female, also gave the role its soft-porn sizzle—but it was nonetheless a statement, a declaration of intent. Béjart sang Plisetskaya's praises in a filmed recollection of their collaboration, folding his arm around her shoulder paternalistically as she looks away from the camera, suddenly the shy, retiring Soviet citizen. But she fought hard to bring his "striptease," as it was derided in the Central Committee, to Moscow, using her official awards and several decades of service to the Bolshoi as leverage.[148] *Bolero* received grudging last-minute permission for a performance in Moscow in 1977, along with a dance about Isadora Duncan that Béjart created especially for Plisetskaya.

Objections from defenders of Russian-Soviet tradition poured in, as they had for *Carmen Suite* and even Grigorovich's *Ivan the Terrible*. Both the outspoken red-haired diva and the ballet master with the no-nonsense buzz cut were heckled by ballet-going puritans. Grigorovich seemed to be going in for shock value and titillation—"shame on you!"[149] The defenders of Soviet moral values feared that his next ballet, *The Golden Age*, would traffic further in tawdriness. It included, after all, gangsters and shooting, cabaret dancing, musclemen, and musclewomen.

The result was tamer than expected. Grigorovich's version of *The Golden Age* updated the Yakobson-Shostakovich ballet from 1930. Some of the brash original score was tossed, with the rest rearranged and supplemented to make the music more lyrical. Shostakovich's two piano concertos and an interlude he composed for a drama by Honoré de Balzac provided music for the adagios, which are given out, like meals on a ration card, to the hero and heroine, Boris and Rita. Boris (danced in the premiere and on subsequent tours by Irek Mukhamedov) is a fisherman in a Russian seaside town, who must rescue Rita (danced first by Natalya Bessmertnova, then by Alla Mikhalchenko) from her demeaning job in a cabaret. She escapes his clutches and ends up dressed in white just like Boris, the stain of her days in the cabaret bleached out. The moon and the stars bless their love, before individual desires are necessarily sublimated in the collective. The seaside folk festival that opened the ballet resumes, as Boris and Rita disappear into the crowd.

Grigorovich coauthored an illustrated book about the ballet to explain his transformation of the original 1930 version, and his collaborators likewise attempted to justify the ballet in articles and reviews.[150] They argued that the cluttered original scenario, by Alexander Ivanovsky, prevented Shostakovich from expressing his true musical self—at least as defined by his later years. Had he composed *The Golden Age* in a mature voice, the argument continued, the ballet would have had the same lyrical content that Grigorovich brought to it—never mind that the lyrical content dates not from the late 1970s, when the ballet was restaged, but rather from the 1930s and 1950s. Thus references to the original ballet's stylizations are highlighted as stylizations; the past appears in quotation marks.

But the plot of the ballet is no less hackneyed, no less a caricature, than the divertissements, and so it proved a difficult product for the actual flesh-and-blood dancers of the Bolshoi to perform with zest. Still, they did so, at home in the Bolshoi Theater in 1982, for the Soviet television broadcast in 1983, and on international tour in 1987. "The Bolshoi dancers defy us not to adore them and their vehicle," the *Los Angeles Times* concluded. "They are very competent high-pressure salespersons." Then some acidic remarks about the actual dancing: "The corps struts, gesticulates, preens, twirls and contorts with an irresistible combination of Rockette precision and pristine Muscovite fervor. The secondary dancers—most notably Stanislav Chasov as the frenetic nightclub emcee—perform as if lives were at stake. The youthful principals manage to convey savoir-faire and conviction under fatuous, demeaning pressure."[151]

The ballet marked the end of an era, not just for Grigorovich but for the Soviet Union. Six days after the premiere, Brezhnev died, and with him the softer, gentler edition of Stalinism that had defined his regime. The supreme leader had covered his chest in medals in his final years, hiding behind the emblems of power as the USSR lurched along, living standards low but stable, health care and pensions guaranteed, dissent squashed, the past and the future replaced by an eternal present. "Until," to quote the title of a book on the Brezhnevite stagnation, "it was no more."[152]

PLISETSKAYA TOOK A PASS on stagnation, and on "fatuous, demeaning pressure," devoting her final years at the Bolshoi to her own creative initiatives. She created two chamber ballets to music by her husband that did not require massive resources or a large number of performers; both set texts by Anton Chekhov, bringing that writer to the ballet stage for the first time. The process was predictably arduous, since Grigorovich had effectively blackballed her. Chulaki and the general directors of the Bolshoi Theater who succeeded him (including, between 1976 and 1979, Georgiy Ivanov) upheld the de facto ban. Plisetskaya either had to stage her dances at another venue or plead her case to the minister of culture, Pyotr Demichev.

She did, and he supported her. Doubtless her husband, Shchedrin, used his own influence as chairman of the Union of Russian Composers. Thus her ballets were staged at the Bolshoi in 1980 and 1985.

The first, *The Seagull* (Chayka), is metatheatrical. The cast includes an actor, an actress, and two writers—one an aesthete, the other an anaesthete. The action includes a play within the play, and the staging references the scandalous 1896 premiere of Chekhov's original. Plisetskaya's sequel, *Lady with the Lapdog* (Dama so sobachkoy), is of more modest proportions. Premiered in celebration of the ballerina's sixtieth birthday, it is a dialogue between a modest, provincial woman at a seaside resort and a Muscovite who surprises himself by developing genuine feelings for her. The ballet is a Don Juan tale of sorts, but without its erotic and exotic aspects. Yet the staging was still "naturalistic" enough to offend crustier Soviet TV watchers, who thought it inappropriate for their children to see Plisetskaya partnering with a male less than half her age.[153] Their duet imagines the affair that might have happened, each escaping seemingly unfulfilling marriages for the delight of a new lover, had forbearance not prevailed. He gazes into the sunset, bleak and jaded; she looks into the light, the emotional equivalent of an iceberg.

Nothing more opposite to *Spartacus* can be imagined. Her adaptations of Chekhov appealed to non-ballet audiences, to lovers of serious drama and music. The drama unfolds in gestures, the ballet steps compressed, as it were, from octave leaps to half steps. The reduced technical demands suited not only the restrained qualities of Chekhov's bourgeois tragedy, but obviously also Plisetskaya's own inevitable decline as a dancer. She could no longer perform the parts of fancy-free girls or cursed princesses, but her own ballets kept her on the stage after she was pensioned. In her youth, it seemed that she could go anywhere in the universe she liked, conquering time and space. As the years advanced, her universe shrank to a point of abstraction.

She was accused of hubristic overreach in her ballets (much as Vasiliev would be accused of hubristic overreach for taking on Shakespeare's *Macbeth* in 1980), and they could not in truth survive without her name in the cast. Russian ballet observers outside of the USSR expected more of her self-declared love of "formalism" than "guts and stamina." Alastair Macaulay tut-tutted about *Anna Karenina* in a piece in *The New Yorker* and, critiquing a BBC program on the Bolshoi, said of *The Seagull* and *Lady with the Lapdog*: "Chunks of her Chekhov choreographies were then shown, and there descended between the television screen and this viewer a thick fog of incomprehension."[154] In her well-publicized eagerness to distance herself from Grigorovich's hyper-obvious narratives and the crudities of the "mimeless mime," in which the same arm or hand gesture is made dozens of times in variation without the meaning ever changing, she had forgotten that dance in and of itself, pure dance, is not automatically meaningful.[155]

Grigorovich shunned her, as did the artists under his control, the communists, and the "bitch goddess" known as Mother Russia.[156] In her sixties, Plisetskaya concentrated her energies elsewhere. She directed and coached, held master classes, and adjudicated competitions throughout the world. She brought Carmen along with her on most of her trips, Anna Karenina and the lady with her dog much less often. In the late 1960s, she had told the journalist George Feifer that she had as much chance of taking vacation in Italy as "flying to Mars on a broom."[157] Eventually she got her broom. From 1983 to 1985, Plisetskaya held the position of artistic director of the ballet of the Rome Opera; during the last three years of the decade she served as head of the Spanish National Ballet in Madrid. *The Seagull* was tolerated in Boston in 1988, as part of a Soviet-American cultural exchange. After the show, Plisetskaya released a dove, Soviet symbol of peace, into the rafters of the theater.[158] She remained a Soviet citizen until the end of the Soviet Union, but by the 1980s she could accept the foreign offers she liked without resistance from the authorities. Frustrated by her failed attempts to depose Grigorovich, she left—as had Stravinsky; Diaghilev; the defected dancers Baryshnikov, Makarova, and Nureyev; plus countless other members of the Russian-Soviet artistic intelligentsia before her. In 1991, after the collapse of the Soviet Union, she moved with her husband to Vilnius, Lithuania, the birthplace of her mother, and then to Munich. Beloved in every theater except the one she loved the most, she retired as a prima ballerina of the world stage even as she still longed for the Bolshoi.[159]

She had fought for, not against, Russia throughout her life and considered it her home from the distance she maintained as a global citizen. Even those who never saw her dance felt her absence from the international stage. Her last Russian state honor (she compiled an impressive list of them from other nations) came from President Vladimir Putin in 2000; she declined to comment on his administration and kept essentially silent about the Bolshoi in her final years, letting prying researchers know that she had said all she wanted to say in her memoir.

• • •

GRIGOROVICH AGED IN place, with no thought of retiring, pulling back, or letting go. He remained the eternal overlord. After finishing *Ivan the Terrible*, he presided over the bicentennial of the Bolshoi in 1976. He and Ivanov lobbied for funds to repaint and repair the cracks in the walls before the official celebrations began. Tributes poured in from the Kremlin, artists, and even the boss of the machine-building plant Kommunar, whose House of Culture hosted Maksimova, Vasiliev, and Plisetskaya for performances. The cosmetic repairs were completed, and *Pravda* found the Bolshoi looking "young" again.[160]

As part of the bicentennial celebrations, Grigorovich created dances for the Siberian melodrama *Angara*, set to music by a young composer, Andrey Eshlay, and based on an exceedingly popular play that had made the rounds of Soviet theaters and been filmed for movies and television. It concerns a simple Soviet woman destined for psychological transformation. Her husband drowns in the Angara River, leaving her alone to care for their two children. She is also called upon to replace her husband in his job. She faces obstacles but ultimately makes it all look easy. *Angara* lasted in the Bolshoi Theater repertoire for eight years; its sentiments presaged those of the iconic Soviet movie of 1979, *Moscow Does Not Believe in Tears.*

After *The Golden Age* was staged in 1982, Grigorovich slowed further as a choreographer. The Supreme Soviet offered him a golden handshake in the form of the Hero of Soviet Labor award on the last day of 1986, but Grigorovich did not retire. The following spring, *Sovetskaya kul'tura* announced the "capital renovation" of the Bolshoi, everything from the foundations to the plasterwork. It was to begin in the summer, Grigorovich explained, then pause for three months of performances, then resume. During the planned shutdown, for an extremely underestimated "2–3 years," ballets and operas were to be performed in the Kremlin Palace and on another stage, known as the New Stage, located just across from the Bolshoi.[161]

After years of extreme economic stagnation, the Soviet Union began to undergo an overhaul initiated by the last Soviet leader, Mikhail Gorbachev. He had ascended to the highest ranks of the Communist *nomenklatura* from the humblest of places: the collective farms of the North Caucasus, where, as a teenager, he drove combine harvesters. He worked for local, regional, and national Communist Party offices as the USSR weakened; his tinkering with broken-down industries and the discredited constitution merely hastened the collapse. His provincialism was obvious to those who heard him speak on television and radio in the Soviet Union, but Gorbachev proved a capable statesman. *Perestroika* (rebuilding) failed as an economic initiative, but the liberalization known as *glasnost'* (openness) succeeded, albeit too much so for the regime to survive. The Chernobyl nuclear disaster of 1986 could not be covered up as radiation spread from Ukraine through Europe. Gorbachev failed to put down the ethnic strife in Azerbaijan. The end of the Soviet empire was nigh.

His essentially bankrupt government did not have the resources to commit to the renovation of ballet and opera houses. To survive, the artists of the Bolshoi needed more than ever to tour. The public abroad continued to take to them, as did the critics, since the performers demonstrated such astonishing technique and commitment. As in the past, reaching back to the Sankovskaya era, the principal dancers had famous Bolshoi retirees as personal coaches, and these luminaries (Ulanova, Kondratyeva) passed along their wisdom. The coaching system could have its downsides in the form of overpolished, unspontaneous performances, but it helped to preserve the old-time aura. It was felt in 1986 in London, despite concerns about the "bad wigs and fondness for turquoise eyeshadow."[162] Ticket lines were long, and the flamboyance missed after the dancers and their props had left town.

Grigorovich's ballets lost their Cold War sheen, however, and the new political imperative of openness left the choreographer facing tough questions, during a subsequent North American tour, about Plisetskaya's, Vasiliev's, and Maksimova's invective against him and the loss of morale in general at the Bolshoi. In July of 1990, the *New York Times* dance critic Anna Kisselgoff put his feet to the fire by asking about a one-day hunger strike the previous month. "Yes, everything is going downhill," Grigorovich acknowledged. "What is happening in the theater reflects what is happening in the entire country."[163]

In August of 1991, there followed a failed coup d'état and a showing of *Swan Lake* on state television. Plisetskaya had danced in Grigorovich's version of the ballet for the first time on April 18, 1970. Her performance was recorded, and from then on, it was broadcast during holidays and after the deaths of Soviet leaders. To turn on the television and see Plisetskaya in Grigorovich's *Swan Lake* meant something big was happening.

The ballet was shown repeatedly on every channel as tanks rolled into Moscow on Monday, August 19. The coup attempt, led by Gennadiy Yanayev, was organized against Gorbachev by the KGB and Communist Party hardliners who were threatened by his liberal policies. Boris Yeltsin, the reform-minded, recently elected president of the RSFSR, stood on a tank in the rain to protest the putsch in front of the Russian parliament building. If the coup succeeded, he knew, one of the quarter million pairs of handcuffs that had been sent to Moscow from a factory in Pskov would be on his wrists. That did not happen. The coup was a botch, the plotters inept and inebriated, and it unraveled before the rain ended, hastening the event that the plotters feared the most: the curtain coming down on the Soviet Union, the exposure of all the corruption, lies, and repressions that had held it together for seven decades.

The successful putsch of 1917 did not have a sequel. Yeltsin, who fashioned himself a populist strongman, defeated the trembling Yanayev in a battle of wills; Gorbachev was released from house arrest in the Crimea; soldiers returned to their bases. The clouds cleared, and the sun rose over the motherland, just as it does at the end of *Swan Lake*, which some older Russians find hard to watch nowadays, owing to its unpleasant associations with these events.

The Soviet Union had officially collapsed, and Russia had not yet recovered as a functional state. With no cash on hand, the Bolshoi had become a sagging, buckling firetrap, and what appeared onstage seemed just as dilapidated. Grigorovich's dispiriting production of *Don Quixote* comprised a handful of recycled steps, devoid of caprice. Those dancers who had not found work abroad wanted contracts and an end to the political favoritism that promoted lesser talents over greater ones; serfdom had long been abolished, except, it was said, at the Bolshoi and in the labor camps. The general director at the time, Vladimir Kokonin, recognized the need for changes and agitated for the naming of a board of directors. Grigorovich resigned in response to threatened strikes, but not before prodding his supporters to organize a strike of their own. On March 10, 1995, the dancers refused to take the stage— something that had never happened before—and forced the cancellation of a performance of *Romeo and Juliet*. The surviving communist newspapers, voices of doom in the 1990s, excoriated the striking dancers, one-quarter of the cast, for stripping Russia of its cultural pride. *Izvestiya* published a chronicle of the events that had "pushed the Bolshoi to the edge of the precipice." The predicted collapse would be "a crime against Russian culture."[164] Forced out under a cloud, Grigorovich remains on the books as the sole ballet master of the theater.

A series of artistic directors took the helm during the 1990s, their tenures all undistinguished save for that of Alexei Ratmansky, who mounted new productions on other stages during the protracted renovations to the theater. Having been announced in 1987, the New Stage finally opened on November 29, 2002, replacing a run-down set of apartment buildings on the site. Alexander Gorsky had lived in one of those apartments; all that is left of it now is a memorial plaque. The restoration, indeed resuscitation, of the Bolshoi began just under three years later, at the urging of Dmitri Medvedev, the stand-in Russian president between the first and second Putin administrations. Grigorovich was not involved in the massive repair. Ratmansky is at present the most fecund and most in-demand choreographer in the world, but he quit the Bolshoi in 2008. He now lives and works eight time zones away in New York City.

GRIGOROVICH NOW SPENDS much of his time in his dacha, imported cognac on the table when his Georgian housekeeper permits, relaxed in jeans and plaid flannel shirts. Photographs and posters from productions of his ballets around the world line the staircases and the landings, along with models of stage sets and a miniature regimental costume once worn by Marius Petipa. There is less from the Bolshoi than one would expect from his decades in charge, the spectacles of power displaced by charming drawings of children in foreign performances of his *Nutcracker.* His home is a shrine—not to his career but to the life of ballerina Natalya Bessmertnova, his muse and his second wife. She died of cancer in 2008; a replica of her headstone hangs in his sitting room. She enriched the roles he created for women, staying truest to her temperament as Giselle, the role that defined her career. In *Ivan the Terrible*, she assumed the haunted and haunting look of a Byzantine icon, but she also possessed great acrobatic skill, blazing across the stage at the end of *The Golden Age*. Grigorovich may have fashioned tendentious ballets at the expense of the Romantic tradition, but his ivory-skinned, raven-haired leading lady recalled the Russian imperial era of Ekaterina Sankovskaya.

His *Spartacus* continues to be performed in Moscow and abroad, an artifact of a time when Marxist-Leninist dogma tried to disguise itself as dance. For highbrow ballet devotees, it is more like a dinosaur that somehow survived the end of the Mesozoic Soviet Union. Grigorovich's *Legend of Love* returned to the Bolshoi in 2014, the silver jubilee of its Moscow premiere. And for the 2012–13 season, *Ivan the Terrible* was revived after a twenty-two-year hiatus. In the opinion of the reviewer for the business newspaper *Kommersant*, it should have been marketed exclusively to tourists as a "souvenir" of "Russian-Soviet exoticism," together with Russian nesting dolls, fur hats with hammer and sickle pins, vodka, and dark chocolates wrapped in pictures of the Kremlin steeples.[165] The run of *Ivan the Terrible* ended in disaster, however, when the dancer in the lead role, Pavel Dmitrichenko, was arrested on suspicion of planning the attack on artistic director Sergey Filin. The perfect villain in life and in art, he spent three years in prison. Folklore has the real Ivan the Terrible putting out the eyes of the architects of Saint Basil's Cathedral on Red Square in the sixteenth century to ensure that they never built anything as beautiful ever again. There is no factual record of such a horror, but Dmitrichenko and his accomplices, as the world learned in 2013, almost blinded Filin.

Grigorovich had no public comment about the scandal. Nothing of the sort happened on his watch, for he alone meted out the punishments, and the jealous, obsessive, sadomasochistic world of Russian ballet was less known (and, excluding Plisetskaya, less glamorized) than the jealous, obsessive, sadomasochistic worlds of British and American ballet. Under his rule, the theater functioned reliably even as such control choked the life from the creative process. The freedom he offered his dancers was the freedom of little choice, and Plisetskaya balked, making it clear in her performances that there is a difference between dancing and being told to dance. She felt in charge of herself, but the institution—and the communist regime—insisted otherwise.

Tatyana Kuznetsova laid bare the realities of the age of Grigorovich in a tough-minded book translated, in English, as *Chronicles of the Bolshoi Ballet*. In Russian, the title has a second meaning that suggests chronic illness. Plisetskaya provided the foreword to the text, which dispatches four of the "myths" of Grigorovich's leadership of the theater, the first being that he had rescued it as a Soviet institution, observing that the most frequently performed Soviet ballet, *The Red Poppy*, and the most beloved, *Romeo and Juliet*, came from other choreographers. The success of the Bolshoi as a touring organization is also questioned, since the most famous tour—to London in 1956—pre-dated his tenure. His purported "charisma" is undercut by references to his coarse dressing down of his dancers, likewise his failure to nurture talent. In erasing the past, he left behind a power vacuum; thus even the fighting over contracts that followed his resignation is placed at his feet.[166] There is, however, context for her protracted complaint that goes beyond Grigorovich's dictatorial style. Kuznetsova settles her scores as a journalist and as a former character dancer with the Moiseyev folk ensemble. Her father and grandfather had also been character dancers, the latter repressed under Stalin, and her mother danced alongside Plisetskaya. She sees a different past from the one Grigorovich defends, bathed in sentiment, as the stable alternative to the unstable present. He is approachable, convivial, and garrulous on good days, still talking about *Master and Margarita*, but unreachable on others. After the death of his antipode, Plisetskaya, on May 2, 2015, he closed the door on reporters, and on his assistants, to be with his thoughts.

Maya Plisetskaya died at home with her husband in their apartment near the ballet and opera house in Munich. Shchedrin organized a private funeral for his wife of fifty-seven years; the Bolshoi Theater observed a minute of silence and recast the planned celebration of her ninetieth birthday on November 20, 2015, as a memorial tribute. Russia and the Bolshoi gave her the will to overcome all constraints by imposing so many on her. And so she would be truly free, if only at the end. Her last wish was to have her ashes scattered, from high in the air, over her homeland.

EPILOGUE

THE GALA CELEBRATION of the $680 million–plus restoration of the Bolshoi on October 28, 2011, marked a reinvention and reimagining of the theater. Work lasted six years—the last one busier on-site than the other five combined—and spanned the terms of two Russian presidents, Vladimir Putin and Dmitri Medvedev. When the Bolshoi reopened, the new Russian noble class basked in the stunning achievement of its largesse, never mind the resignations of people overseeing it (including the former mayor of Moscow, Yuriy Luzhkov) and the budget overruns. The fractiousness did not matter to those posing before the state media cameras at the gala. As Yuliya Bedyorova reported in a smart piece for *Moskovskiye novosti* (Moscow news) titled "Zerkalo parada" (The gala mirrored), the parliamentarians and show-business types in attendance seemed more interested in actress Monica Bellucci's gown than the historically accurate compound of ochre, umber, clay, and lime coating the new façade.[1] The culture channel tallied the glitterati in attendance, including Plisetskaya and Vishnevskaya, who sat in prominent boxes on opposite sides of the theater.

In the run-up to the gala, the federal agency in charge of the restoration dazzled journalists with exotic tales of miracle-working artisans. The craftsmanship was impressive, from first tier to sixth. De-mineralizing the limestone columns of the entrance had wiped away a century of city grime to uncover a matte, milky-white surface. The theater issued an account of the project chock-full of staggering statistics: 2,812 sheets of gold leaf were applied across the auditorium; 24,000 pieces of crystal were polished, refashioned, and rehung in the chandelier. The result is meant to stun, and it does. As Alastair Macaulay concluded in the *New York Times,* the new-old Bolshoi "may well now be the world's most splendid theater."[2]

No wonder the director of the high-pressure gala, Dmitri Chernyakov, chose to stage the Bolshoi itself by showcasing the process of the renovation along with its product. The curtain opened to reveal a noisy, dusty construction scene. Slowly workers gathered at the proscenium to form a chorus and sing the anthem "Be Glorious, Russia!" (Slav'sya, Rossiya!) to onstage brass accompaniment and the pealing of Orthodox bells. For those keeping score, no fewer than six works by Tchaikovsky were performed. Next in line came Prokofiev and Glinka, with two each. Medvedev, president of the Russian Federation at the time, applauded politely throughout, except after Natalie Dessay sang Rachmaninoff's setting of Pushkin's lyric "Sing Not, My Beauty" (Ne poy, krasavitsa). The song was affectingly performed, but the text refers to Georgia, whose government, like that of Ukraine, has not been a friend to Russia of late.

Invitations to the gala came from the Kremlin, though some purportedly appeared for sale online for 2,000,000 rubles ($66,500). Not everyone associated with the theater was invited. Before his retirement and relocation to St. Petersburg for the directorship of the Vaganova Ballet Academy, the dancer Nikolay Tsiskaridze complained a little too loudly about the low ceilings in the rehearsal studios. He was struck from the guest list.

A few days later, on November 2, conductor Vladimir Jurowski took the podium for the official opening of the regular season. For years everyone assumed that Glinka's opera *A Life for the Tsar* would be picked for this epochal evening; it is *the* Russian opera, having been blessed by nationalist ideologues even during the Soviet era. A resplendent new version seemed to be on the books for the Bolshoi Theater reopening. But circumstances changed. Somewhere along the chain of command from the Ministry of Culture and Mass Communications, to the Board of Trustees of the Bolshoi Theater, right down to its general director, Glinka's first opera was scratched in favor of his second, *Ruslan and Lyudmila*, a fairy tale for adults based on a lewd narrative poem by Pushkin. Perhaps its happy ending explains why it was selected over Glinka's aggressively anti-Polish first opera. Or perhaps offending Poland was not to be risked in the wake of the airplane crash outside Smolensk, in April 2010, that killed Polish president Lech Kaczynski.

Tickets were hard to come by, and some of those with tickets in hand worried they were fake. Yet the box office insisted they were authentic, especially those bought for huge sums from the scalper on the street. (The attendant took a cut of the proceeds.) Inside, Jurowski was relaxed, chatting in three languages with his aides, subsisting on regular infusions of caffeine. The director, Chernyakov, was less calm. He faced a daunting creative challenge, because Jurowski had decided to conduct the entire score—all five hours—without making any cuts. This *Ruslan and Lyudmila* was, like the theater itself, at once a restoration and a reimagining, a reaching back and projecting forward. The music was scrubbed of sanctimonious Soviet-era monumentalism to recover a lighter, antique texture more in keeping with the composer's original intent. Visually, the staging proved a technological marvel inconceivable in Glinka's time and unrealizable in any other opera house, anywhere.

Most of the critics loved it, but the public was divided, with cries of "*pozor*" (shame) raining down on the performers after the racy third and fourth acts. (Russian television had advertised that the heroine would be receiving an exotic Thai massage in the magical garden where she was imprisoned, so the crowd was primed to disapprove.) Conservative operagoers shook their heads in disgust at the sight of a muscle-bound masseuse dancing a Caucasian lezginka, a dance involving much foot stomping and arm splaying, in a theatrical nod to the garishness of the Azeri-operated Crocus City Mall on the edge of Moscow. There was whistling during the cinematic entr'actes from those who felt that 5,000 rubles ($165) was too steep a price for a trip to the multiplex. Some who left before the end expressed their disapproval by slamming the restored back doors of the restored loges. Three-quarters stayed and cheered.

Chernyakov not only anticipated the hostile public reaction but even built it into the staging. Elaborate, almost life-sized puppets lampooned a choral round dance in the first scene. The otherwise poignant death of a warrior took the form of an interrupted video transmission. The sorceress Naina mocked the hecklers in the crowd before exiting in a sable coat that concealed the cast on her arm. (She took a fall in act 1, and the bone was set during an especially lengthy intermission.)

There were two masterstrokes. The first was Jurowski's conducting, which highlighted, through delicate contrasts in tempo and timbre, the places where Glinka borrowed his supposedly "Russian" music from Italian composers like Rossini and Bellini. The second was the sumptuously stylized historical décor of acts 1 and 5. Here Chernyakov provided the audience with the exotic Russia of its own fantasies. Russian directors used to do this for foreign crowds. Now, evidently, it is desired at home.

Scarcely before the refinished floors of the new Bolshoi were scuffed, the terrible events of 2013 led to resignations, firings, imprisonments, much anxious contemplation, and true soul-searching. What had happened to the Bolshoi Ballet, that glorious troupe that had represented revolution and war in fatigues but had also, tucked back into clean white fabrics, embodied morals and ethics? Had it lost its soul? Detractors and supporters clashed over the state of the theater—and of the nation—as a sense of some sickness, a disease at the core, spread. But the essential nature of the disappeared soul went undefined, remaining an ephemeral and amorphous construct much like ballet itself. The Bolshoi came into being as the Bolshoi in the wake of the Napoleonic wars, and its art nationalized in response. That less animated its soul, however, than the personalities onstage who were powerful and colorful and removed from the muddiness of Moscow in the nineteenth century. Great art was conceived at the Bolshoi, but paradoxically Russian ballet did not realize its own greatness until it was exported elsewhere—to the Mariyinsky in St. Petersburg, to theaters in Paris, London, and New York. One imagines the theater weeping at the injustice of it all. In the twentieth century, the Bolshoi finally became the showcase stage, but the performers remained detached, this time from the ideological obviousness of the subject matter they were obliged to dance and sing. Then with the collapse of the Soviet Union and the ascent to power first of chaos, then of Putin, the special radiance associated with the Bolshoi style dimmed. The oddities of people who know nothing but the studio and the stage were exposed along with the infighting, the injustices, and the abuses backstage. Life on the streets leaned toward the lethal and so too, it seemed, did life in the theater.

ALMOST A CENTURY before Winston Churchill defined Russia as "a riddle wrapped in a mystery inside an enigma," the satirical novelist Nikolay Gogol wrote a parody of a satire of a lampoon about the country. In 1842 he published *Dead Souls*, wherein the spirits of serfs are bought and sold in the divine equivalent of a stock-market bubble; in his telling, landlords are brutal or grotesque, peasants wretched bumpkins. Positive values are hard to find, Gogol proposes. Baseness is the heart of the tale, concealed by a cloud of intrigue and spiritual ramblings. Narratives proliferate, interpretations of actual events substitute for the details, the facts. Russia has always been good at this: generating multiple meanings, conceiving competing realities, insinuating that we might never know the truth, that there might not be any truth at all.

At the end of part one of the novel a sleigh races along the winter steppe, and Gogol's narrator ponders the consequences of the wild ride. Will it end? Will it end well? Perhaps Sankovskaya and Ulanova and Plisetskaya asked and answered this same question in their own troubled times, in gestures rather than words as the sweat dripped down their backs. Recently an answer of sorts came from the bejeweled prima ballerina assoluta at the Bolshoi, Svetlana Zakharova. When asked about the future of her art in her country, she replied, "Only God knows what will happen to us."[3] Zakharova, a star who floats above the rank and file, nevertheless responded in the plural, considering "what will happen to *us*," the dancers. The thought is that the performers at the Bolshoi, who know to distrust the ballet masters and the administrators overseeing them all, depend only on one another. This interaction is one of the elements of their style. This is the collective soul. As Arlene Croce wrote about the Soviet incarnation of the Bolshoi Ballet, "With long experience and that theatrical instinct which Bolshoi dancers alone seem to possess, they took their support from each other. . . . No other resource was available."[4] Yet love for Mother Russia proves not enough to keep them home.

At the end of 2008, Alexei Ratmansky jumped off the sleigh, resigning from his position as artistic director at the Bolshoi. His innovations had met resistance from old-guard dancers like Tsiskaridze, which in turn motivated Ratmansky to promote up-and-coming dancers over established ones and weed out the naysayers. The nastiness that resulted included "phone calls in the night, threats."⁵ Ratmansky quit to escape the harassment, and accepted the position of visiting choreographer with American Ballet Theater in New York.

In both Moscow and New York, Ratmansky has made ballet, a mature art, seem fresh and young again. Recently the dance historian Jennifer Homans has proposed that ballet has not changed much since George Balanchine, that the art is dying. Our world has no patience for angels who want to teach us morals, she suggests, and if people want something ethereal, pixels seem better than pixies.⁶ But that might be too simple. Classical music has died a thousand deaths, likewise opera and likewise ballet. Yet all endure. Ratmansky has enriched the ballet repertoire by re-creating certain Russian works that either were censored or never had a chance, owing to the suffocating political constraints of the Stalinist era. He is a counterfactual choreographer, seeming to believe that if things had gone differently in history, then narrative ballets on present-day themes would have prevailed over the coolly modernist abstractions of Balanchine and Stravinsky. He loves the what-might-have-been in ballet history, the what-could-have-been, and he has dedicated himself to making that alternate history real. Working from a post-Soviet perspective, and working outside of Russia, Ratmansky takes the measure of the decades and of the century that followed the revolution.

Ratmansky seems also intent on liberating ballet from its own worst instincts. Interested in plot and character, he has put back the

character dancing that Grigorovich took out of the Bolshoi repertoire, increased the tempi, and overstuffed the balletic phrases to
increase by half or more the number of physical events per measure. Ratmansky finds his muse in the music of the Soviet composer Shostakovich, who was in his own youth (not his later years)
an insurrectionist iconoclast. The composer was mistreated by the
Soviet regime, as was Russian ballet in general. Ratmansky's ballets
to music by Shostakovich seem as though "created by some superhuman Methuselah," writer and journalist Wendy Lesser remarks,
"who enthusiastically participated in the Soviet Union's early revolutionary fervor, suffered through the harsh repression of Stalinism and its dreary aftermath, and then emerged into a cosmopolitan
twenty-first-century perspective from which he could view the
whole preceding era with a certain amount of rueful distance."[7] In
Ratmansky's mind, ballet is still like a child, unruly and exuberant,
who has yet to realize her full potential. His art has become more
rhythmic than it was at the Bolshoi, his dances newly playful.

And so in 2003, Ratmansky sought to restore the boisterous
spirit of *The Bright Stream*, banned in 1936, without erasing its history. Thus he staged both the ballet itself and its reception, high-
lighting the prohibition against the composer Shostakovich and
the choreographer Fyodor Lopukhov, staying true to their intent
while also realizing the possibilities of the work—and of dance—
for present-day audiences. An old couple pines for youth on the
stoop of their dacha. Shostakovich parodied their nostalgia, as did
Lopukhov, as does Ratmansky. Valerie Lawson glosses the resulting delights, including the performance of the old couple recalling
their vanished youths on the stoop of their dacha in a pathetic-
turned-sublime effort at a *pas de deux*. "She demands to be lifted
at the end and while he kneels to bear her weight she drapes herself around his shoulders," Lawson writes, "beaming with joy at the

final pose." The production, Lawson adds, brings to mind old-time, aw-shucks Broadway. Ratmansky includes "social dancing" in the mix, along with circus stunts. Amidst the games of dress-up and the congenial messing about, the characters somehow manage to harvest giant-sized vegetables from their collective farm, over-fulfilling Stalin's Five Year Plan for agricultural development. Making reference to the denunciation of the original ballet in *Pravda*, which criticized the doll- or marionette-like behavior of the dancers, Ratmansky made them jostle as if tangled in strings. The cleverest episode in *The Bright Stream* featured, in the original 2003 cast, Sergey Filin in drag as a ballerina. In the specific performance Lawson annotates, the part was taken by Ruslan Skvortsov, arms "held in a ludicrously twee interpretation of a soft romantic position," tulle billowing.[8] The wit lies in the radical unnaturalness of the episode—it is hard (and a bit unusual) for a male dancer to move like Anna Pavlova—and that a ballerina with a five o'clock shadow succeeds in seducing a geriatric at his cottage. His wife turns up. She has evidently seen her husband succumb before and, having no patience for it, slaps him in the face.

Ratmansky has also dusted off the agitprop spectacular *The Flames of Paris*, first choreographed in 1932 by Vasiliy Vaynonen. An excerpt from the revival was performed in 2011 at the gala performance celebrating the reopening of the Bolshoi Theater. *The Flames of Paris* is set in the third year of the French Revolution, which serves as a metaphor for the Russian Revolution. To the music of French revolutionary songs, quoted liberally and literally, the people storm the Tuileries Palace, oust their oppressors, and dance in triumph through the squares of Paris. The original choreographer was lauded for his crowd scenes, so the real revolution is converting ballet from its emphasis on the couple to an emphasis on the group—the essential communist principle. The essence of aesthetics under Stalin was people-mindedness, but Soviet chore-ographers like Lopukhov could never get the folk parts right. These always seemed strange, an anachronistic displacement of actual folk dances. Socialist realism was about the glorious existence to come, not the surrounding grayness. The doctrine was also premised on celebrated tales of yore, so that the directors of Russia saw less ruin in their wake, and more astonishing theatrical spectaculars.

Ratmansky embraces that problem by successfully stylizing the stylizations. He somehow turns the aesthetic dogma of the 1930s into sincere drama, taking precepts that seemed aesthetically impo-tent in their own time and showing how they might actually find force. There is caprice in his staging—with a morbid tinge, as Sarah Crompton claimed of a 2013 London performance starring Natalia Osipova and Ivan Vasiliev, two Russian dancers now living the high life in multiple time zones. The crowds waved their revolutionary hankies in blurry frenzy as Ratmansky privileged "great traversing jumps across the stage."[9] The glee ends with the thud of a guillo-tine; the celebration of agitprop turns into a kind of self-critique. The ideologies on which it is based, French turned Soviet, suddenly become dreadful. The dancers march in slow motion to the front of the stage looking like placards in a protest march, or the unblinking undead. This is Ratmansky's own ending, not found in the original scenario, one that stages history as simultaneity. All of these events are imagined to cause effects as yet not understood.

Ratmansky seems to want to tell us that he loves the Soviet aes-thetic, but not the politics behind it. Or that he wishes the politics were different, or that he wishes ballet were different. That last wish is something that he can grant himself as he reaches back in time, into the forsaken Soviet repertoire, to resurrect ballet's past and thus its future. In his more recent revivals of the three Tchaikovsky bal-lets, *The Nutcracker*, *The Sleeping Beauty*, and *Swan Lake*, a complicated relationship develops between archival artifact, familiar steps from favorite versions, and new inspiration. The wholes are more than sums of the parts, and look glorious, a mirage that pastes the present onto the past as a unified experience. In his most inspired moments, Ratmansky's ballets fold one layer of time onto another, sometimes in searing radiance, other times in calm glow. Great artists make simple claims: Aren't dancers beautiful? Ratmansky asks. Aren't people?

Meanwhile, the Bolshoi and the Kremlin across the square are left to quarrel not about the past and the present, but the future. There is no unified experience, of course, just the myths of nation and culture and art that arise from the imaginations of historians. President Vladimir Putin stands at the center of a small circle of associates, his motivations and intentions opaque by design or accident, as his administration, comprising the heads of the ministries and industries and the Federal Security Service, emulate Soviet and imperial Russian authoritarianism. The budget depends on oil, but the media reminds its audience of the spiritual and not material might locked within the black earth, the greatness, tapped and untapped, of the geographical landmass that stretches from the Baltic to the Pacific. Russia nurtures the impulse to expand even more, to reclaim the empire under Catherine the Great.

The outsized contribution to culture that began in the nineteenth century, cultivated in part on the Bolshoi stage, is central to the national narrative of Russia. Putin seems to fashion his rule after that of Tsar Nicholas I, which included imperial expansion, the crushing of an uprising, and the exploitation of the agitprop powers of the Russian Orthodox Church. Like Putin, Nicholas liked to depict himself as a strongman, unfettered by the rationalist materialism privileged in the West. Every nation lives in its own combination of realities, and truth and facts can seem overrated and old-fashioned. In Russia today, it is the task of the media to construct the illusions in support of Putin's imperial mission—and the task of the state-financed arts as well. The suppression of dissent and the promotion of traditional values by religious and cultural officials have left their mark, even as the government touts the legacies of victims of earlier periods of suppression and conservatism.[10] Perhaps there is an acknowledgment here that artists, even those badgered into compromise, lay true claim to the Russian soul.

THE BOLSHOI IS the most Russian of the nation's cultural institutions and ballet the most Russian of the arts. Since its founding in 1776, the government has regarded the theater as an emblem of power, whether ideological or commercial or both, and ballet at the Bolshoi—its muscular style, its bravura, and its self-conscious insistence on its own historical importance—likewise captures something emblematic. For Russianness (or Americanness or any kind of collective identification, for that matter) is a process, a performance. It is tied to place, perhaps, following the imperatives of empire, but dominion can encompass more than landmass. In much Russian philosophical thought, the spiritual and the rational unite under the premise that human experience is boundless, and desire uncontainable. Existence lies beyond the self, and the world is best understood not through closed cerebral processes but through intuition and the creative act; those acts should be grand, even at the risk of ruin. To burn down Moscow to defeat Napoleon is to make sacrifice the price of survival. This act was turned into art, but also seen as art.

Moscow has been rebuilt at regular intervals since 1612, and the Bolshoi repeatedly since the early nineteenth century. Preservationists decried the 2011 renovation, but like the city itself, the

Bolshoi as an institution, as an icon, sees the past in service of the present, which loops back to rewrite the past. Tradition is invented anew—inscribed on the bodies of dancers at the Bolshoi generation after generation, advertised to audiences at home and abroad, sometimes sold for profit, and otherwise hoarded as an inheritance, a birthright.

The history of the theater and of the ballet may be told in conventional, empirical fashion from then until now. Shocks and traumas duel with recalibrations and retrenchments. The narrative respects its own laws of storytelling; dancers live their lives loving their art; everyone strives. Thus the Bolshoi found a fresh start when Vladimir Urin was appointed general director in 2013, and now with Makhar Vaziev running the ballet as of 2016. They inherit the soul and the repertoire, the cliché and the truth behind it: Ballet is the cruelest and most wondrous of the arts, a discipline and a dream that asks people to aspire to the angelic in a demonic competitive process. The results of that process at the Bolshoi, time and time again, have proven artistically stupendous but personally, physically catastrophic. Yet the dancers keep dancing, hoping to escape the constraints of the here and now and grasp instead at something everlasting. There is no other choice. To dance, after all, is to condition the body, and with it the mind, to let go.

ACKNOWLEDGMENTS

THE DEBTS OF GRATITUDE I have accrued in researching and writing this book are immense, and I am proud to bear them. First and foremost, I bow low to my research assistant in St. Petersburg, Ilya Magin, a polyglot genius of encyclopedic knowledge and a wonderful interlocutor about politics, culture, and life in Russia during the nineteenth century. Ilya followed his intuition through the catalogs and collections of the historical archive (RGIA) in St. Petersburg to unearth crucial documents—especially about Michael Maddox and the Imperial Theaters. The donkey tale is his, as are the Bolshoi Theater incident reports. I thank him for meeting me in Moscow to discuss the project over pilsner, and for locating, in another historical archive (RGANI), the letters from Maya Plisetskaya to Nikita Khrushchev. Ilya's presence is felt on nearly every page in the opening chapters, and I consider the entire book as much his as it is mine, though I lay claim to all of its inadequacies.

I am also most grateful to Sergey Konayev, whose knowledge of Russian ballet and its archival sources is peerless. He answered numerous questions by email and in person, supplied essential sources, corrected my misrendered names and dates, and brought me into the precious rooms of the Bolshoi where the 1877 rehearsal score of *Swan Lake* is preserved on steel shelves in steel cabinets, along with other treasures. Sergey is in great demand in ballet circles, as he should be, lending his erudition to historically minded productions in Moscow, Paris, and New York. Thus I am ever the more grateful to him for his time and his counsel.

I rush as well to thank Alastair Macaulay, who has been the truest of friends to me this year and last. He has generously shared his profound knowledge of and love for ballet, which I consider to be the most complicated of the arts—in some ways as demanding of its admirers as its performers. He rises to meet the challenge like no other. His affectionate scoldings, which pointed out mistakes and misconstruals as well as infelicities, immeasurably improved the draft chapters. Always his advice is relentlessly correct, and I hope that I have incorporated it all into the final product with something nearing the grace and precision of his own prose.

My gratitude extends to Tatyana Kuznetsova for having educated me in Russian dance and opened the archive of her grandfather to me. Tatyana comes from a long line of ballet legends, and I was honored to receive her advice on the later chapters. Thanks as well to Nina Nikolayeva, for materials on Matilda Kshesinskaya; to Pilar Castro Kiltz, who researched Sergey Filin's career for me while also working at the New York Public Library to retrieve and annotate biographical materials on Plisetskaya; to Lisa Snyder, who accessed and assessed films of Plisetskaya's performances; to Darya Koltunyuk, for finding reviews in Helsinki, expressing enthusiasm for the book, and lending insight to chapter 7; and to the versatile Laura Ong, who gathered useful articles on the Bolshoi from historical newspapers. The eminent Slavist Boris Wolfson improved, and sometimes provided, the translations of numerous passages, and cast his erudition across the whole. Everything in the translations that reads properly, with archaisms intact, reflects his immense kindheartedness. Bruce Brown provided missing information and so rescued me from ruin in chapter 1, while Roland John Wiley, the leading English-language historian of Russian ballet, provided essential guidance in chapter 4. His book on Marius Petipa is eagerly awaited. As ever, I am deeply grateful to my beloved friend and colleague Caryl Emerson, who holds fast to high concepts that elude my grasp and motivates me to do better through the sheer impulse to follow her example.

I am also indebted to the esteemed Russian ballet historian Elizabeth Souritz. It was a pleasure to be welcomed into her home and hear her recollections of the Soviet-era Bolshoi Ballet, including the fracas over the Grigorovich production of *Swan Lake*. My thanks to Christina Ezrahi, for sharing her thoughts and advice on Khachaturian's ballet scores; to Elizabeth Stern, for information gathered from the St. Petersburg archives on *Flames of Paris* and *The Red Poppy*; to the dance critic Marina Harss, for reading through early drafts of two of the chapters; and to my ballet-devoted students for their insights, including Morgan Nelson on the intricacies of Russian ballet auditions, and Colby Hyland on the specifics of the Vaganova method. I am also grateful for questions answered, assistance provided, and therapies administered, to Ellen Barry, Anthony Cross, Tina Fehlandt, Gemma Farrell, Lynn Garafola, Leslie Getz, Robert Greskovic, Wendy Heller, Sandra Johnson, Vladimir Jurowski, Julia Khait, Nelly Kravetz, Stephen Kotkin, Natalya Parakhina, Dmitri Neustroyev, Serge Prokofieff Jr., Tim Scholl, Samuel Steward, Natalya Strizhkova, Raymond Stults, Richard Taruskin, Edward Tyerman, Suhua Xiao, Shaun Walker, and Jenn Zahrt.

My treasured friend Galina Zlobina provided the photographs and essential documents from the Russian Archive of Literature and Art. I owe Galina the bulk of my existence in print, and the contents of some Princeton theatrical performances as well. Mariya Chernova and Natalya Mashechkina of the Bakhrushin Museum offered their patience, kindness, and hotfoot, light-fingered retrieval of documents from the shelves; likewise Lyudmila Sidorenko of the Moscow Theater Union library-archive; and Lidiya Kharina along with her spirited staff at the Bolshoi Theater Museum. My gratitude as well to the effortlessly multitasking Katerina Novikova, whom the Bolshoi Theater is privileged to have in charge of public relations, and to the theater administrators and dancers whom Katerina arranged for me to meet. Of the dancers, I must thank in particular Svetlana Lunkina, who spread her prima ballerina magic across the Princeton campus during a visit in 2013.

My editor at Norton, Katie Adams, bucked me up with unwarranted praise and often explained to me what I actually meant to say. She possesses the power of alchemy, turning ore into malachite, and I will henceforth and evermore acknowledge the importance, in nonfiction, of chronological organization. Likewise I am grateful to Pamela Murray, of Knopf, for her comments on the draft, and to John Everett Branch Jr. and Rachelle Mandik for their proofreading and copyediting.

Will Lippincott convinced me that this book could be written, improved the proposal, taught me how to talk about it, and placed it under contract.

The heart and, indeed, soul of it all belongs to Elizabeth Bergman, who scrutinized the draft and revision, eliminating nonsense, improving transitions, teasing out new rhythms, and retrieving pages out of the hearth to convince me of their worth. She has done so much for me, for so long now, and we find the greatest meaning and purpose in the gift of our daughter, to whom this book is dedicated.

NOTES

INTRODUCTION

The description of the near-blinding of Sergey Filin comes in part from conversations with Katerina Novikova, Olga Smirnova, and Nikolay Tsiskaridze in March of 2013; earlier in February, I interviewed Svetlana Lunkina at Princeton University; later in November, I communicated with Dilyara Timergazina. For a fuller account of these exchanges than I provide here, see Simon Morrison, "More Tales from the Bolshoi," *London Review of Books*, July 4, 2013, 21–22; and "The Bolshoi's Spinning Dance of Power," *International New York Times*, November 25, 2013. The point about Balanchine and Ashton as inheritors of the Petipa tradition comes from Alexei Ratmansky, by way of Alastair Macaulay, in an as-yet-unpublished questionnaire concerning Ratmansky's 2015 staging of *The Sleeping Beauty*.

1   Karl Schlögel, *Moscow, 1937*, trans. Rodney Livingston (Cambridge, UK: Polity Press, 2011), 511.
2   Ibid., 514, 517.
3   Wendy Perron, "Inside Sergei Filin's Bolshoi Ballet (expanded version)," *Dance Magazine*, January 2013, dancemagazine.com/issues/January-2013/Inside-Sergei-Filins-Bolshoi-Ballet-expanded-version.
4   *Chyornïye lebedi. Noveyshaya istoriya Bol'shogo teatra*, ed. and comp. B. S. Aleksandrov (Moscow: Algoritm, 2013); *Bolshoi Babylon*, directed by Nick Read (New York: HBO Documentary Films, 2015).
5   Ellen Barry, "Harsh Light Falls on Bolshoi After Acid Attack," *New York Times*, January 18, 2013.
6   Ellen Barry, "Wild Applause, Secretly Choreographed," *New York Times*, August 14, 2013.
7   Shaun Walker, "Bolshoi Dancer Pavel Dmitrichenko Jailed for Six Years over Acid Attack," *The Guardian*, December 2, 2013.
8   Ismene Brown, "Opinion: How Can the Bolshoi Rise Again?," *thearts*

desk.com, December 4, 2013, http://www.theartsdesk.com/dance/opinion
-how-can-bolshoi-rise-again.

9   Kseniya Sobchak, "Nikolay i chudotvortsï," *snob.ru*, October 29, 2013,
http://www.snob.ru/profile/24691/blog/67131.

10 "Profile: Pavel Dmitrichenko," BBC, December 3, 2013, http://www
.bbc.com/news/world-europe-21697765.

11 Maya Plisetskaya, *I, Maya Plisetskaya*, trans. Antonina W. Bouis (New
Haven and London: Yale University Press, 2001), 158.

12 Ibid., 246.

13 Simon Morrison, "The Bolshoi's Latest Act," *NYRblog*, November 12, 2011,
http://www.nybooks.com/blogs/nyrblog/2011/nov/12/the-bolshois-latest
-act/.

14 Mark Monahan, "Olga Smirnova: Dancing in the Dark," *The Telegraph*,
March 25, 2013.

15 Sarah Crompton, "Mikhail Baryshnikov: 'Everything in Russia Is a
Damn Soap Opera,'" *The Telegraph*, July 3, 2013.

16 Jennifer Homans, *Apollo's Angels: A History of Ballet* (New York: Random
House, 2010), 382.

17 "Makhar Vaziev Appointed Bolshoi Ballet Head," *Ismene Brown Arts
Blog*, October 26, 2015, http://ismeneb.com/blogs-list/151026-makhar
-vaziev-appointed-bolshoi-ballet-head.html.

1: THE SWINDLING MAGICIAN

The largest holdings of material on Michael Maddox and the Petrovsky
Theater are in the Russian State Historical Archive (Rossiyskiy gosudar-
stvennïy istoricheskiy arkhiv/RGIA) in St. Petersburg and the Russian State
Archive of Ancient Acts (Rossiyskiy gosudarstvennïy arkhiv drevnikh aktov/
RGADA) in Moscow. Some of these materials are quoted in the 1927 monograph by Olga Chayanova that I reference below and relied on throughout
this chapter. A crucial document in RGADA, Maddox's 1802 petition to
Empress Consort Mariya Fyodorovna, is available in the original French in
M. P. Pryashnikova's article "Angliyskiy Predprinimatel' M. Medoks," also
referenced below. Additional sources for the chapter include D. Blagovo (Eli-
zaveta Petrovna Yan'kova), *Rasskazï babushki. Iz vospominaniy pyati pokole-
niy, zapisannïye i sobrannïye yeyo vnukom* (St. Petersburg: Tipografiya A. S.
Suvorina, 1885), 203–05; Gerald R. Seaman, "Michael Maddox: English
Impresario in Eighteenth-Century Russia," in *Slavic Themes: Papers from Two
Hemispheres*, ed. Boris Christa et al. (Neuried: Hieronymus, 1988), 321–26;
and Philip H. Highfill, Kalman A. Burnhim, and Edward A. Langhans, *A
Biographical Dictionary of Actors, Actresses, Musicians, Dancers, Managers &*

Other Stage Personnel in London, 1660–1800, 16 vols. (Carbondale : Southern Illinois University Press, 1973–1993), 10: 49. On Betskoy and life in the orphanage, I drew from David L. Ransel, *Mothers of Misery: Child Abandonment in Russia* (Princeton: Princeton University Press, 1988), 31–61. Petrovsky ticket information was obtained from the playbills reproduced in N. P. Arapov and Avgust Roppol't, *Dramaticheskiy al'bom s portretami russkikh artistov i snimkami s rukopisey* (Moscow: V Universitetskoy Tipografii i V. Got'ye, 1850), 417 and 419. Mention is made in a document dated February 21, 1782, in RGADA (f. 16, d. 575, ch. 1, l. 7) of Maddox wittingly or unwittingly including fifteen counterfeit rubles in the theater receipts. The detail about the buffet comes from RGIA 758, op. 5, d. 626 (the French caterer was obliged to pay the governing board 300 rubles a year from his receipts) and the Russian culinary dictionary: http://dic.academic.ru/contents.nsf/dic_culinary/. Information on the conflict between Maddox, Leopold Paradis, and the orphanage is from RGIA f. 758, op. 5, d. 314, 316, 441; Paradis's contract details, and those concerning the 250 rubles he was owed from the St. Petersburg court musician Bachman are contained in RGIA f. 757, op. 5, d. 441, f. 758, op. 3, d. 314, and f. 756, op. 5, d. 511, respectively. For details on the "travestied masquerade," I consulted Colleen McQuillen, *The Modernist Masquerade: Stylizing Life, Literature, and Costumes in Russia* (Madison: University of Wisconsin Press, 2013), 39–61. Alexander Ablesimov's *Dialog stranniki, na otkritiye novogo Petrovskogo Teatra* (Dialogue of the wanderers, on the occasion of the opening of the new Petrovsky Theater) was published in 1780 by N. I. Novikov; it can be accessed through Google Books. On the clock Maddox made for Catherine the Great, see http://kraeved1147.ru/chasyi-m-medoksa-hram-slavyi/. On Noverre, see Jennifer Homans, *Apollo's Angels: A History of Ballet* (New York: Random House, 2010), 68–97, esp. 73–74.

1   Rossiyskiy gosudarstvennïy arkhiv literaturï i iskusstva (RGALI), f. 2, op. 1, yed. khr. 329 (A Osipov, "Antreprener proshlogo veka"), l. 5.

2   This according to the undiplomatic Russian diplomat Filipp Vigel (1786–1856), one of the great dirt-dishers of the era; http://elcocheingles.com/Memories/Texts/Vigel/Vig_I_3.htm.

3   Quotations in this paragraph from Aleksandr Chayanov, "Venediktov," in *Red Spectres: Russian Gothic Tales from the Twentieth Century*, trans. Muireann Maguire (New York: The Overlook Press/Ardis, 2013), 69–70. Gothic fiction flourished in Russia during an anxious time of political transition, the interregnum between the eradication of the decaying imperial regime and the consolidation of Soviet power. Most

of the great tales in the genre were suppressed, along with their authors. Chayanov was shot for treason during the great terror of 1937, but not, however, for his writings. He was an agrarian by training, and branded a traitor for calling into question the wisdom of forced collectivization of the Russian, Ukrainian, and Kazakh farmlands. For that he was sentenced to five years in the Kazakhstan labor camps. He survived, only to be rearrested and executed by firing squad. The lives of his two sons were ruined owing to their blood relation to an anti-Soviet saboteur. His wife, Olga, a theater historian and expert on the Petrovsky Theater, was also arrested, in 1937, though she survived, granted release from the labor camps after Stalin's death.

4   Stanley Peerman Hutton, *Bristol and Its Famous Associations* (Bristol: J. W. Arrowsmith, 1907), 23.

5   Sybil Marion Rosenfeld, *Strolling Players & Drama in the Provinces, 1660–1765* (Cambridge: Cambridge University Press, 1939), 149.

6   Ibid., 196.

7   *Sanktpeterburgskiye vedomosti* no. 81, vo vtornik, oktyabrya 9 dnya, 1767 goda [Tuesday, October 9, 1767], 3. The advertisement is reprinted in the newspaper three days later.

8   M. P. Pryashnikova, "Angliyskiy predprinimatel' M. Medoks v Rossii," in *Pamyatniki kul'turï. Novïye otkrïtiya. Pis'mennost'. Iskusstvo. Arkheologiya. Yezhegodnik 2005*, ed. T. B. Knyazevskaya (Moscow: Nauka, 2013), 223.

9   Ol'ga Chayanova, *Teatr Maddoksa v Moskve, 1776–1805* (Moscow: Rabotnik prosveshcheniya, 1927), 23.

10 *Moskovskiye vedomosti* no. 77, v sredu, sentyabrya 23 dnya, 1780 goda [Wednesday, September 23, 1780], 477.

11 *Moskovskiye vedomosti* no. 79, v sredu, sentyabrya 30 dnya, 1780 goda [Wednesday, September 30, 1780], 642.

12 *Moskovskiye vedomosti* no. 24, v subbotu, marta 21 dnya, 1780 goda [Saturday, March 21, 1780], 185.

13 John T. Alexander, *Catherine the Great: Life and Legend* (Oxford and New York: Oxford University Press, 1989), 149.

14 *The Memoirs of the Empress, Catherine II, Written by Herself,* with a preface by A. Herzen (London: Trübner & Co., 1859), 346–47.

15 Ibid., 349.

16 L. M. Starikova, *Teatr v Rossii XVIII veka: Opït dokumental'nogo issledovaniya* (Moscow: Gos. in-t iskusstvoznaniya, 1997), 140.

17 RGALI f. 2, op. 1, yed. khr. 329, l. 2.

18 Carlo Brentano de Grianti, "Journal, 1795–1801," Princeton University Manuscripts Collection no. 649.

19   *Moskovskiye vedomosti* no. 18, v subbotu, fevralya 29 dnya, 1780 goda [Saturday, February 29, 1780], 137. The fire received front-page coverage.

20   *Moskovskiye vedomosti* no. 19, v sredu, marta 5 dnya, 1780 goda [Wednesday, March 5, 1780], 145.

21   Ibid.

22   A. Novitskiy, "Rozberg, Khristian," *Bol'shaya biograficheskaya entsiklopediya,* http://dic.academic.ru/dic.nsf/enc_biography/107194/.

23   RGALI f. 2, op. 1, yed. khr. 329, l. 4; Pryashnikova, "Angliyskiy predprinimatel' M. Medoks v Rossii," 219.

24   "Journal of Charles Hatchett's Journey to Russia, August 1790–November 1791"; quoted in Anthony Cross, *"By the Banks of the Neva": Chapters from the Lives and Careers of the British in Eighteenth-Century Russia* (Cambridge: Cambridge University Press, 1997), 42.

25   *Moskovskiye vedomosti* no. 76, v subbotu, sentyabrya 19 dnya, 1780 goda [Saturday, September 19, 1780], 618. The advertisement is reprinted in the newspaper four days later.

26   Richard Stites, *Serfdom, Society and the Arts in Imperial Russia: The Pleasure and the Power* (New Haven and London: Yale University Press, 2005), 131.

27   Michael Zagoskin, *Tales of Three Centuries*, trans. Jeremiah Curtin (Boston: Little, Brown, and Company, 1891), 99.

28   Ibid., 102.

29   Gotthold Ephraim Lessing, *Miss Sara Sampson,* 1755, in *World Drama: Italy, Spain, France, Germany, Denmark, Russia, and Norway,* ed. Barrett H. Clark (Mineola, NY: Dover, 1933), 467.

30   RGIA f. 787, op. 5, d. 441, l. 2. Paradis's original contract is dated November 23, 1778. According to documents preserved in the fond (No. 127) of the Imperial Foundling Home in the Central State Archive of Moscow, the contract was renewed on January 28, 1782, and once more on February 14, 1784. In between the renewals, Paradis lost some of his students to a public theater in St. Petersburg. An additional, somewhat more enigmatic, document finds him supporting the request of the Moscow major of artillery, F. N. Ladïzhensky, for the rescue by the orphanage of three children. Paradis retired with an imperial pension in 1797.

31   A Russian ambassador promised to pay the debts of the "poor devil" in exchange for service at the Russian court. Quotation provided by Helena Kazárová from a 1758 letter concerning Hilverding's financial troubles. It was sent by Prince Joseph Adam von Schwarzenberg to Maria Dominika Thürheim. Email communication, February 8, 2014.

32   S. Gardzonio, "Neizvestnïy russkiy baletnïy stsenariy XVIII veka,"

http://pushkinskijdom.ru/Portals/3/PDF/XVIII/21_tom_XVIII
/Gardzonio/Gardzonio.pdf.

33 RGALI f. 2, op. 1, yed. khr. 329, l. 11.

34 *Moskovskiye vedomosti* no. 23, v sredu, marta 18 dnya, 1780 goda [Wednesday, March 18, 1780], 177.

35 RGIA f. 758, op. 5, d. 58, l. 1.

36 RGIA f. 758, op. 5, d. 747, l. 1. The letter dates from 1784; Tanauer was the orphanage's bookkeeper.

37 Quotations in this paragraph from Lincolnshire Archives, Yarborough Collection, Worsley Manuscript 24, 188–89, 193–94.

38 RGIA f. 758, op. 5, d. 313.

39 RGIA f. 758, op. 5, d. 755.

40 Information and quotations in this paragraph from William Coxe, *Travels into Poland, Russia, Sweden, and Denmark, Interspersed with Historical Relations and Political Inquiries*, 3 vols. (Dublin: S. Price, 1784), 1: 416–20.

41 "Dvenadtsat' let iz zhizni Ya. B. Knyazhina (Po neizdannïm pis'mam G. Gogelyu 1779–1790 gg.)," ed. L. V. Krestova, http://az.lib.ru/k/knjazhnin _j_b/text_1790_pisma_gogelu.shtml.

42 Ibid.

43 RGALI f. 2, op. 1, yed. khr. 329, l. 16.

44 Ibid., l. 17; RGIA f. 758, op. 5, d. 755, l. 6.

45 RGALI f. 758, op. 5, d. 739, l. 24. The quoted words are Betskoy's, from a letter to Alexander Khrapovitsky, Catherine the Great's secretary, dated July 24, 1783.

46 This quotation and the remaining information in the paragraph from RGIA f. 758, op. 5, d. 748, ll. 5–6.

47 RGIA f. 758, op. 5, d. 748, l. 8. The complaint, dated October 2, 1784, was written by Mikhaíl Golitsïn for Georg Gogel.

48 RGIA f. 758, op. 5, d. 1063, l. 2.

49 RGALI f. 2, op. 1, yed. khr. 329, l. 23; also quoted in Chayanova, *Teatr Maddoksa v Moskve, 1776–1805*, 92.

50 RGALI f. 2, op. 1, yed. khr. 329, l. 26.

51 Chayanova, *Teatr Maddoksa v Moskve, 1776–1805*, 97.

52 Ibid., 97–98.

53 RGALI f. 2, op. 1, yed. khr. 329, l. 30.

54 Ibid., l. 31.

55 RGIA f. 13, op. 1, d. 92, l. 2.

56 Ibid., l. 3.

57 Ibid.

58 Ibid.

59 Chayanova, *Teatr Maddoksa v Moskve, 1776–1805*, 99.

60 RGIA f. 759, op. 94, d. 102 [1799–1800 g.], l. 2.

61 Ibid., l. 4.

62 S. P. Zhikharev, *Zapiski sovremennika*, 1890, quoted in Chayanova, *Teatr Maddoksa v Moskve, 1776–1805*, 220.

63 Ibid., 219.

64 RGIA f. 759, op. 94, d. 101, l. 14.

65 Hutton, *Bristol and Its Famous Associations*, 23.

66 Chayanova, *Teatr Maddoksa v Moskve, 1776–1805*, 20; the calumny is from the memoirs of Elizaveta Yankova (1768–1861).

2: NAPOLEON AND AFTER

I benefited throughout this chapter and the next from the foundational ballet scholarship of V. M. Krasovskaya, *Russkiy baletnïy teatr ot vozniknoveniya do seredinï XIX veka* (St. Petersburg: Lan', 2008). On Didelot, I relied on Mary Grace Swift, *A Loftier Flight: The Life and Accomplishments of Charles-Louis Didelot, Balletmaster* (Middletown, CT: Wesleyan University Press, 1974), 81–114 and 136–76. On the fire in Moscow and life in the city in general in 1812, including (via Tolstoy) the earnings of aristocrats, I used Alexander M. Martin, "Moscow in 1812: Myths and Realities," in *Tolstoy on War: Narrative Art and Historical Truth in "War and Peace,"* ed. Rick McPeak and Donna Tussing Orwin (Ithaca and London: Cornell University Press, 2012), 42–58. An excellent source on Napoleon's Russian fiasco is Adam Zamoyski, *Moscow 1812: Napoleon's Fatal March* (New York: HarperCollins, 2004), to which I referred for background information on Kutuzov, Borodino, and Napoleon's campaigns in general. Information on the Imperial Theater College comes from M. K. Leonova and Z. Kh. Lyashko, *Iz istorii Moskovskoy baletnoy shkolï (1773–1917). Chast' 1* (Moscow: MGAKh, 2013). (This publication lists the graduates of the college year by year and provides biographical information on all of the ballet masters and choreographers associated with the college and the Moscow Imperial Theaters from its foundation to the middle of the nineteenth century.) The construction of the Bolshoi Petrovsky Theater is chronicled in A. I. Kuznetsova and V. Ya. Libson, *Bol'shoy teatr: Istoriya sooruzheniya i rekonstruktsii zdaniya* (Moscow: Al'fa-Print, 1995), 35–63, 184–91.

Of the ballerina, Evdokya (Avdotya) Istomina, who took the lead role in *Prisoner of the Caucasus*, Pushkin urged his brother to "Write me about Didelot, about the Circassian girl Istomina, whom I once courted, like the Prisoner of the Caucasus"; Swift, *A Loftier Flight*, 171. Istomina, Didelot's longtime muse, is known as the first Russian dancer to perform en pointe.

For the details on Verstovsky's musical career I consulted Gerald Abraham, "The Operas of Alexei Verstovsky," *19th-Century Music* 7, no. 3 (1984): 326–35; the web page at http://www.greatwomen.com.ua/2008/05/07 /nadezhda-vasilevna-repina-verstovskaya/ tells the grim tale of the resignation of Nadezhda Repina from the Imperial Theaters. On Glinka's musical Russianness my sources were Richard Taruskin, *Defining Russia Musically* (Princeton: Princeton University Press, 1997), 25–47; and Marina Frolova-Walker, *Russian Music and Nationalism: From Glinka to Stalin* (New Haven and London: Yale University Press, 2007), passim.

A companion to this chronicle of Napoleon and Russian ballet is that of Napoleon and French ballet. On French ballet during the Revolution, Napoleonic era, and the Restoration, the finest source remains Ivor Guest, *Ballet Under Napoleon* (London: Dance Books, 2002). Valberg is mentioned in passing on page 119 and Didelot's fraught period in Paris discussed at length on pages 381–413.

1   A. P. Glushkovskiy, *Vospominaniya baletmeystera* (Leningrad and Moscow: Iskusstvo, 1940), 83.

2   Natal'ya Korol'kova, "Istoriya Teatral'nogo uchilishcha pri Malom teatre," http://www.maly.ru/pages.php?name=shepka_hist.

3   Ibid.

4   Ivan Val'berkh, *Iz arkhiva baletmeystera. Dnevniki. Perepiska. Stsenarii*, ed. Yu. I. Slonimsky (Leningrad and Moscow: Iskusstvo, 1948), 82 and 83 (letters from Ivan Ivanovich Val'berkh to Sof'ya Petrovna Val'berkh dated December 19 and December 21–22, 1807).

5   Leo Tolstoy, *War and Peace*, trans. Richard Pevear and Larissa Volokhonsky (New York: Vintage, 2007), 561. The Imperial Arbat Theater is reimagined by Sigizmund Krzhizhanovsky, "Postmark: Moscow," in *Autobiography of a Corpse*, introd. Adam Thirlwell; trans. Joanne Turnbull with Nikolai Formozov (New York: *New York Review of Books*, 2013), 186.

6   Swift, *A Loftier Flight*, 136.

7   Jennifer Homans, *Apollo's Angels: A History of Ballet* (New York: Random House, 2010), 255.

8   Ibid; Roland John Wiley, *A Century of Russian Ballet: Documents and Eyewitness Accounts, 1810–1910* (Alton: Dance Books, 2007), 6.

9   Yu. A. Bakhrushin, *Istoriya russkogo baleta* (Moscow: Sovetskaya Rossiya, 1965), 47.

10   Swift, *A Loftier Flight*, 112.

11   Val'berkh, *Iz arkhiva baletmeystera*, 166 (from the preface to the libretto

of Valberg's fantastic ballet *The Amazonians, or Destruction of the Magic Castle* [Amazonki, ili razrusheniye volshebnogo zamka, 1815]).

12 Ibid., 36.

13 Zamoyski, *Moscow 1812*, 229.

14 Tolstoy, *War and Peace*, 875.

15 Zamoyski, *Moscow 1812*, 241–42.

16 Glushkovskiy, *Vospominaniya baletmeystera*, 115–16.

17 Ibid., 121.

18 This quotation and the following from Glushkovskiy, *Vospominaniya baletmeystera*, 102–10, and RGALI f. 634, op. 1, yed. khr. 535, ll. 19–30.

19 Wiley, *A Century of Russian Ballet*, 20–21.

20 This quotation and the following from RGALI f. 659, op. 4, yed. khr. 879, ll. 1 ob., 19.

21 "Destruction of the Imperial Theatre, Moscow, by Fire," the *Illustrated London News*, July 2, 1853, 525.

22 This and the following quotations and information concerning the fire and its aftermath from *Moskovskiye vedomosti* no. 5, v subboty, yanvarya 17 dnya, 1825 goda [Saturday, January 17, 1825], 141. Besides general advertisements for upcoming productions, *Moskovskiye vedomosti* did not report at length on the Bolshoi Petrovsky Theater in the years ahead. Performances in the theater and elsewhere in Moscow by foreign artists received modest, sometimes hostile attention. An 1836 arrival of a Spanish dance troupe was denounced in advance by Prince Pyotr Shalikov, a dependably xenophobic contributor to the newspaper: "The 14th of this month features a benefit for the Iberian pupils of Terpsichore, who—alas!—are no longer content entertaining their compatriots, devotees of the goddess of discord" (*Moskovskiye vedomosti* no. 1, v sredy, yanvarya 1 dnya, 1836 goda [Wednesday, January 1, 1836], 22).

23 Mikhaíl Lermontov, "Panorama Moskvï," in *Sobraniye sochineniy v chetïryokh tomakh* (Moscow: Pravda, 1969), http://lib.ru/LITRA/LERM ONTOW/s_moscow.txt_with-big-pictures.html.

24 *Moskovskiye vedomosti* no. 5, v subbotu, yanvarya 3 dnya, 1825 [Saturday, January 3, 1825], 11. Tickets for the opening performance and masquerade ranged from 50 kopecks for the "second side gallery" to 15 rubles for a "loge in the stalls."

25 B. L. Modzalevskiy, "Avtobiografiya kompozitora Verstovskogo," *Biryuch Petrogradskikh gosudarstvennïkh akademicheskikh teatrov* 2 (1920): 231.

26 RGIA f. 652, op. 1, d. 64, l. 49. This letter, from September 21, 1838, and most of the other letters in the file are addressed to Nikita Vsevolozhsky

(1799–1862), a rich theatrical producer and the founder and host of the Green Lamp writers' club, which was frequented by Pushkin.

27 Ibid., l. 27 (received June 6, 1838).

28 Ibid., l. 19 (received March 8, 1838).

29 Ibid., l. 49.

30 Ibid., ll. 43–44 (received November 16, 1838).

31 Ibid., l. 42 (undated).

32 Ibid., l. 44.

33 Ibid., l. 8 (December 28, 1837).

34 This and the following quotations and information from RGIA f. 497, op. 1, d. 9191, ll. 1–10. Gedeonov's report is dated April 10, 1842; it incorporates the notes of the Imperial Theater College doctor, A. Ostrogozhsky, which are dated March 21, 1842.

35 K. F. Val'ts, *65 let v teatre* (Leningrad: Academia, 1928), 28.

36 RGALI f. 497, op. 1, d. 10996, l. 59 (November 16, 1846, letter from Ivan Naumov to Gedeonov).

37 Vl. V. Protopopov, "Stat'i muzïkal'nogo kritika 'N. Z.,'" in *Muzïkal'noye nasledstvo: Sborniki po istorii muzïkal'noy kul'turï SSSR*, vol. 1, ed. G. B. Bernardt, V. A. Kiselyov, M. S. Pekelis (Moscow: Gosudarstvennoye muzïkal'noye izdatel'stvo, 1962), 315 (letter from Verstovsky to the historian and publicist Mikhaíl Pogodin).

38 Val'ts, *65 let v teatre*, 26.

3: FLEET AS LIGHTNING

The statute of the Censorship Committee of the Ministry of Education is available at http://www.opentextnn.ru/censorship/russia/dorev/law/1804/. The tale of Tsar Nicholas I ordering the dancers of the St. Petersburg Imperial Theaters to be "taught to handle sabers" is told by Edvard Radzinsky in *Alexander II: The Last Great Tsar* (New York: Simon & Schuster, 2006), 38; on the imperial ballet being a harem, 239. The fact that the ballet in question, *The Revolt of the Harem*, is pro-feminist seems not to have made an impression, at least not a positive one, on the sovereign. See Joellen A. Meglin, "Feminism or Fetishism? *La Révolte des femmes* and Women's Liberation in France in the 1830s," in *Rethinking the Sylph: New Perspectives on the Romantic Ballet*, ed. Lynn Garafola (Middleton, CT: Wesleyan University Press, 1997), 69–90. For Marie Taglioni's and Fanny Elssler's reception in Russia I relied on Roland John Wiley, *A Century of Russian Ballet: Documents and Eyewitness Accounts, 1810–1910* (Alton: Dance Books, 2007), 81–89 and 173–77; the tale of her satin shoes being dined upon comes from K. A. Skal'kovskiy by way of Aleksander Pleshcheyev, *Nash balet (1673–1896): Balet v Rossii do nachala*

XIX stoletiya i balet v S.-Peterburge do 1896 goda (St. Petersburg: A. Benke, 1896), 109. Pages 130–31 of this book describe the excitement occasioned by Ekaterina Sankovskaya's September 16, 1846, performance in St. Petersburg of *La sylphide*. The details of her contracts, salaries, and health problems are from the *lichnoye delo* preserved in RGALI f. 659, op. 4, yed. khr. 1298. I also relied on D[mitriy] I[vanovich] Mukhin's chronicle of Sankovskaya's career in his "kniga o baleta," Muzey Bakhrushina f. 181, no. 1, ll. 118–78.

Luisa Weiss's 1845–47 engagements with the Moscow Imperial Theaters are described in RGIA f. 497, op. 1, d. 10616; RGIA f. 497, op. 1, d. 11478, l. 1, recounts the March 15, 1847, robbery in her apartment. The date of the installation of gas lighting in the theater is given in K. F. Val'ts, *65 let v teatre* (Leningrad: Academia, 1928), 36–37; the point about *Severnaya pchela* being the first newspaper permitted to publish reviews is from O. Petrov, *Russkaya baletnaya kritika kontsa XVIII—pervoy polovini XIX veka* (Moscow: Iskusstva, 1982), 66; RGIA f. 780, op. 2, d. 66, ll. 1–3, gives a sense of the rules governing review-writing, as of 1848. For the comparison of Andreyanova and Sankovskaya, I drew on a January 4, 1845, article in *Literaturnaya gazeta*, reproduced in *ibid.*, 226–28. Petrov also includes the November 26, 1949, article in *Moskovskiye vedomosti* that vaguely mentions Sankovskaya's foreign appearances: "Not only Moscow, but also Paris, Hamburg, and many other European cities were deafened with applause when she inspired them with her art, placing her in the company of famous ballerinas" (ibid., 246). On prostitution: "Three Centuries of Russian Prostitution," *pravda.ru*, April 30, 2004, http://www.pravdareport.com/news/society/sex/30-04-2002/42121-0/.

The case of Avdotya Arshinina is discussed in detail by the lawyer Aleksandr Lyubavskiy in *Russkiye ugolovnïye protsessï*, vol. 2 (St. Petersburg: Obshchestvennaya Pol'za, 1867), 193–222. A feuilleton published in the newspaper *Moskovskiy gorodskoy listok* reimagined the events at the masquerade that preceded her molestation while also cruelly mocking the poor girl's low-class French. To get around the censors, Avdotya is renamed Anyuta in the feuilleton, which is in and of itself a nasty reference to morose folk songs about lost or ill-fated love, such as that sung by the peasant heroine Anyuta in the popular comic opera *The Miller Who Was Also a Magician, a Swindler, and a Matchmaker*: "Through my entire youth / After all, I've seen no joy." The feuilleton reads: "Masquerade at the theater. *Female Domino:* 'Lesse mua, musye' [Laisse moi, monsieur]. *Moustache:* 'No, no, beautiful mask, I won't leave you.' *F. D.*, running off, says to herself: 'He's drunk.' *Moustache*, catching her: 'I love you. We're leaving.' *F. D.* to *Moustache:* 'Lesse, lesse mua.' To a *distinguished gentleman:* 'Come to my aid, sir.' *Gentle-*

man: 'Anyuta, is that you?'" (*Moskovskiy gorodskoy listok*, January 9, 1847, 26). The case seems later to have inspired pulp fiction. The plot of "Red Mask" (Krasnaya maska), a Nat Pinkerton detective tale from 1909, approximates Arshinina's circumstances. See http://az.lib.ru/r/razwlechenieizdatelxstwo /text_132_krasnaya_maska.shtml.

The official reports about the destruction by fire of the Bolshoi Petrovsky Theater are in RGIA f. 497, op. 2, d. 14484.

1   Quoted in Wiley, *A Century of Russian Ballet*, 83–84.

2   Meaning rubles pegged to the value of silver.

3   "In one spectacular trick, attributed to the dancer Amalia Brugnoli, dancers blithely hiked themselves onto the tips of their toes and perched there for all to see: toe dancing"; Jennifer Homans, *Apollo's Angels: A History of Ballet* (New York: Random House, 2010), 138.

4   RGALI f. 2579, op. 1, yed. khr. 1567, l. 165. Vasiliy Fyodorov gathered some eight hundred black-and-white photographs of Bolshoi performances and personnel. The two albums are in such brittle condition that even the employees of RGALI are cautioned against cracking them open. The collection has been microfilmed and partially published (V. V. Fyodorov, *Repertuar Bol'shogo Teatra SSSR, 1776–1955*, 2 vols. [New York: Norman Ross, 2001]), but nothing substitutes for a perusal of the original. The first album includes a painting of the Petrovsky Theater, torchlights denying the pitch-black of central Moscow in 1780, carriages snaking into view from the bottom of the frame. There are also designs for the ballets staged in Moscow by Marius Petipa, who gifted the French ballet tradition to Russia during his decades as second and first *maître de ballet* of the St. Petersburg Imperial Theaters.

5   Nataliya Chernova, "V moskovskom balete shchepkinskoy porï," *Sovetskiy balet* 4 (1989): 35.

6   S. T. Aksakov, *Sobraniye sochineniy*, 4 vols. (Moscow: Gosudarstvennoye izdatel'stvo khudozhestvennoy literaturï, 1955–56), 3: 538; also quoted in V. M. Krasovskaya, *Russkiy baletnïy teatr ot vozniknoveniya do seredinï XIX veka* (St. Petersburg: Lan', 2008), 346. The title of the ballet was *The Young Milkmaid, or Nisetta and Luke* (Molodaya molochnitsa, ili Nisetta i Luka). It was first performed in St. Petersburg in 1817.

7   RGALI f. 659, op. 4, yed. khr. 1298, l. 64.

8   Petrov, *Russkaya baletnaya kritika kontsa XVIII—pervoy polovinï XIX veka*, 152.

9   Ibid.

10   RGALI f. 659, op. 4, yed. khr. 1298, l. 64.

11 Ibid., l. 5; also quoted in Krasovskaya, *Russkiy baletnïy teatr ot vozniknoveniya do seredinï XIX veka*, 347.

12 RGALI f. 659, op. 4, yed. khr. 1298, l. 44; Muzey Bakhrushina f. 486, no. 124520/13.

13 Wiley, *A Century of Russian Ballet*, 154–55.

14 Adapted from the 1833 Taglioni vehicle *La Révolte au sérail*.

15 Marius Petipa, *Russian Ballet Master: The Memoirs of Marius Petipa*, ed. Lillian Moore; trans. Helen Whittaker (London: Chameleon Press, 1958), 46–47.

16 Mukhin, "kniga o balete," l. 178 (quoting *Moskovkiye vedomosti*).

17 Chernova, "V moskovskom balete shchepkinskoy porï," 36.

18 Information and quotations from the article, in this and the following paragraphs, from the copy held in RGALI f. 191, op.1, yed. khr. 2005.

19 Petrov, *Russkaya baletnaya kritika kontsa XVIII—pervoy polovinï XIX veka*, 164.

20 Ann Hutchinson Guest and Knud Arne Jurgensen, *Robert le diable: The Ballet of the Nuns* (Amsterdam: Gordon and Breach, 1997), 6.

21 Petrov, *Russkaya baletnaya kritika kontsa XVIII—pervoy polovinï XIX veka*, 157 (Vissarion Belinsky in *Moskovskiy nablyudatel'*).

22 "Baletmeyster Gerino," *Moskovskiye vedomosti* no. 99, v subbotu, dekabrya 10 dnya, 1838 [Saturday, December 10, 1838], 796.

23 RGIA f. 497, op. 1, d. 6378, l. 21 (letter of October 9, 1838, from Mikhaíl Zagoskin to Gedeonov).

24 Petrov, *Russkaya baletnaya kritika kontsa XVIII—pervoy polovinï XIX veka*, 157–59 (*Moskovskiy nablyudatel'* and *Severnaya pchela*.)

25 RGIA f. 497, op. 2, d. 9262, ll. 10ob.–11. Alexandra Sankovskaya's complaint against Guerinot is dated December 3, 1842, and included in l. 4 of this file. The matter was settled by December 29.

26 Letter of December 19, 1843, in "Perepiska A. N. Verstovskago s A. M. Gedenovim," *Yezhegodnik imperatorskikh teatrov* 2 (1913): 48; also quoted in Krasovskaya, *Russkiy baletnïy teatr ot vozniknoveniya do seredinï XIX veka*, 359.

27 RGIA f. 678, op. 1, d. 1017, l. 13.

28 RGIA f. 497, op. 1, d. 10618, l. 10 (verso). This and the following quotations from a twenty-six-page file titled "O proisshestvii pri Moskovskikh Teatrakh 29 ch. oktyabrya 1845" (Regarding the occurrence in the Moscow Theaters on October 29, 1845).

29 Ibid., l. 11.

30 Ibid., l. 11 (verso).

31 Ibid., l. 14 (verso).

32 Ibid.

33 Ibid., l. 16 (verso).

34 RGIA f. 497, op. 1, d. 10628, l. 64 (undated).

35 Quoted in Krasovskaya, *Russkiy baletnïy teatr ot vozniknoveniya do seredinï XIX veka*, 326.

36 Letter of December 19, 1843, in "Perepiska A. N. Verstovskago s A. M. Gedenovïm," *Yezhegodnik imperatorskikh teatrov* 2 (1913): 47–48.

37 Alexander V. Tselebrovski, "The History of the Russian Vaudeville from 1800–1850" (PhD diss., Louisiana State University, 2003), 260.

38 Information and quotations in this and the previous paragraph from M. I. Pïlyayev, *Zamechatel'nïye chudaki i originalï* (St. Petersburg: Izdaniye A. S. Suvorina, 1898), 313–15; the tale is also told by Mukhin, "kniga o balete," l. 154 ob., and Petipa, *Russian Ballet Master*, 27–30.

39 Petipa, *Russian Ballet Master*, 28.

40 The sentiment, dated September 22, 1898, of the poet, translator, and actor Dmitri Lensky; Muzey Bakhrushina f. 143, no. 148024. Lensky altered the text, changing the last word, "sins" (grekhi), into "fleas" (blokhi), turning it into a joke of sorts about Sankovskaya's flea-like jumping abilities. He might also be aligning "sylphide" with "syphilis."

41 RGIA f. 497, op. 1, d. 11475, l. 4.

42 RGIA f. 1297, op. 27, d. 750, l. 7.

43 Ibid., l. 13.

44 Ibid., l. 8.

45 Ibid., l. 14.

46 Ibid., l. 16.

47 RGIA f. 497, op. 1, d. 11475, l. 92.

48 RGIA f. 1297, op. 27, d. 750, l. 55.

49 Chernova, "V moskovskom balete shchepkinskoy porï," 33.

50 This and the following quotations from Muzey Bakhrushina f. 156, no. 73844, ll.1–2; the letter, which does not bear a date, is also quoted in Chernova, "V moskovskom balete shchepkinskoy porï," 35–36.

51 This and the following quotations from "Destruction of the Imperial Theatre, Moscow, by Fire."

4: IMPERIALISM

Following Verstovsky's retirement, the directorship of the Moscow Imperial Theaters changed frequently, passing from one often inadequate or indifferent nobleman to another: Leonid Lvov (L'vov) lasted from 1862 to 1864 in the post; Vasiliy Nekhlyudov from 1864 to 1866; Nikolay Pelt (Pel't) from 1866 to 1872; Pavel Kavelin from 1872 to 1876; Laventiy Auber (Ober) from 1876 to 1881; Vladimir Begichev from October of 1881 to May of 1882; and, for just two months after that, Yevgeniy De Salias-Turnemir. The situation stabilized under Pavel Pchelnikov, who served from 1882 to 1898. For two years, 1886–88, Pchelnikov reported in Moscow to the censorship-board chairman Apollon Maykov, who, like the repertoire inspector Ostrovsky, sought to remove the lesser-skilled ballet master Bogdanov from the Bolshoi. Pchelnikov, however, defended Bogdanov, which allowed him to hang on to his job until 1889. The tsar, Alexander III, was in on the intrigue, to Bogdanov's disadvantage.

Vladimir Telyakovsky took over the directorship of the Moscow Imperial Theaters from 1898 to 1901. Like his predecessors in the post, he served at the pleasure of the powerful intendants of the Imperial Theaters in St. Petersburg: High Chamberlain Andrey Saburov, who served from 1858 to 1862; Count Alexander Borkh (von der Borch, 1862–67); Stepan Gedeonov (the son of Alexander Gedeonov and the former director of the Hermitage Museum, 1867–75); Baron Karl Kister (former account manager for the minister of the court, 1875–81); the Francophile diplomat but Russophile theatrical reformer Ivan Vsevolozhsky (1881–99); and Prince Sergey Volkonsky (Wolkonsky, 1899–1901).

Alberto Cavos's life and times are recounted by his grandson Aleksandr Benue (Alexandre Benois) in *Moi vospominaniya v pyati knigakh* (Moscow: Nauka, 1980), 36–40. The smoking ban is described in RGIA f. 497, op. 2, d. 15906. The gas war involving Makar Shishko is described in RGIA f. 497, op. 2, d. 19317, which contains the Moscow Imperial Theaters incident reports for the year 1863; the arson and sugar bribe cases are in f. 497, op. 2, d. 25074, ll. 239, 414. The contracts for the French mechanic (Vaudoré) are detailed in f. 497, op. 2, d. 19321; those for Mikhaíl Arnold in d. 19322. RGIA f. 497, op. 2, d. 25120, describes the prohibition of excessive encores (more than three); and d. 25489 gives a sample list of the kinds of expenses deducted from benefit receipts. On Mademoiselle Rachel and the jennet: f. 497, op. 2, d. 14472.

On the coronations of the nineteenth-century tsars, I relied on the impeccable scholarship of Richard S. Wortman, *From Alexander II to the Abdication of Nicholas II*, vol. 2 of *Scenarios of Power: Myth and Ceremony in Russian Monarchy* (Princeton: Princeton University Press, 1995–2000), 19–57, 212–70, and 340–64. I also consulted the chronicle of imperial Russia in Stephen Kotkin, *Stalin*, 3 vols. (New York: Penguin Press, 2014–), 1: 56–60 (Tsar Alexander II's reforms), 61–62 (*okhranka*), and 66–67 (Crimean and Russo-Ottoman Wars).

My thanks to Sergey Konayev for his invaluable help with *Swan Lake* and its contexts, and for providing me with an advance copy of his edition of the original violin rehearsal score: P. I. Chaykovskiy, *Lebedinoye ozero. Balet v 4-x deystviyakh. Postanovka v Moskovskom Bol'shom teatre 1875–1883. Skripichnïy repetitor i drugiye dokumentï*, ed. and comp. Sergey Konayev and Boris Mukosey (St. Petersburg: Kompozitor, 2015). Thanks as well to Roland John Wiley for information related to *Don Quixote*; email communication, November 10–20, 2014. I drew in this chapter from his *Tchaikovsky's Ballets:* Swan Lake, Sleeping Beauty, Nutcracker (Oxford and New York: Clarendon Press, 1985), 25–62, 92–102, and 242–74; *The Life and Ballets of Lev Ivanov: Choreographer of* The Nutcracker *and* Swan Lake (Oxford and New York: Clarendon Press, 1997), 170–83; and *Tchaikovsky* (Oxford and New York: Oxford University Press, 2009), 100–102, 134–37, 369–71, and 413–17. I also benefited from Elizaveta Surits, "'Lebedinoye ozero' 1877 goda," http://www.ballet .classical.ru/surits.html; and Selma Jeanne Cohen, "The Problems of *Swan Lake*," in *Next Week, Swan Lake: Reflections on Dance and Dances* (Hanover, NH: University Press of New England, 1982), 1–18.

On Cesare Pugni, I referred to Ivor Guest, "Cesare Pugni: A Plea for Justice," *Dance Research* 1, no. 1 (Spring 1983): 30–28; on Ludwig Minkus, Robert Ignatius Letellier, *The Ballets of Ludwig Minkus* (Newcastle: Cambridge Scholars Publishing, 2008), 5–59. Alexander Gorsky's service record is preserved in RGALI f. 659, op. 3, yed. khr. 932. I also consulted E. Surits and E. Belova, eds., *Baletmeyster A. A. Gorskiy: Materialï, vospominaniya, stat'i* (St. Petersburg: Dmitriy Bulanin, 2000). RGIA f. 497, op. 8, d. 55, chronicles the 1901–05 shipments of the *Don Quixote* props from St. Petersburg to Moscow for Gorsky's innovative production. On the Kingdom of the Shades: Lynn Garafola, "Russian Ballet in the Age of Petipa," in *The Cambridge Companion to Ballet*, ed. Marion Kant (Cambridge: Cambridge University Press, 2007), 156.

The symbolism of Carl Fabergé Easter and spring eggs is discussed by Wortman, *From Alexander II to the Abdication of Nicholas II*, 278–81; see also "Imperial Eggs," Fabergé, http://www.faberge.com/news/49-imperialeggs. aspx. Fifty such eggs were produced from 1885 to 1916, though not all of them survive. On Rasputin, I relied on Joseph T. Fuhrmann, *Rasputin: The Untold Story* (Hoboken: John Wiley & Sons, 2013), 97–101 (boating accident), 103–04 (hemophilia and Rasputin's attempts to treat it through hypnosis), 192 (cartoon of Rasputin with the tsarina), and 223–24 (Rasputin's death).

1   RGIA f. 497, op. 2, d. 14480, ll. 2 ob.–3.
2   Ibid., l. 3 ob.
3   RGIA f. 497, op. 2, d. 14548, l. 8.
4   Ibid., l. 140 ob.

5   "Fact Sheet: La Vivandière," Language of Dance Centre, 2010, http://www.lodc.org/uploads/pdfs/LaVivandiere.pdf.

6   Tat'yana Belova, *Bol'shoy teatr Rossii: Istoricheskaya stsena* (Moscow: Novosti, 2011), 87.

7   Ibid., 12.

8   Wortman, *From Alexander II to the Abdication of Nicholas II*, 44.

9   [William Howard Russell], "Russia," *The Times,* Saturday, September 20, 1856, 7. The lovely flaxen-haired princess was not a princess at all, but Countess Anna Daschkoff. Her daughter Catherine recalled her being "one of the loveliest women at the Russian Court, and at the coronation of Emperor Alexander II was considered the most beautiful among all those who attended it. . . . She was radiantly beautiful, and, like all those whom the gods love, she was carried off young, dying in the full splendor of her youth and of her happiness, five days after my birth" (Princess Catherine Radziwill, *My Recollections* [London: Isbister & Company, 1904], 18 and 42). De Morny is the French statesman Charles Auguste Louis Joseph Demorny (1811–65).

10   Richard Wortman, "The Coronation of Alexander III," in *Tchaikovsky and His World,* ed. Leslie Kearney (Princeton: Princeton University Press, 1998), 278.

11   Wortman, *From Alexander II to the Abdication of Nicholas II*, 237.

12   Ye. O. Vazem, *Zapiski balerinï sanktpeterburgskogo Bol'shogo teatra, 1867–1884*, ed. N. A. Shuvalov (Leningrad: Iskusstvo, 1937), 181. Reference is to the coloratura soprano Zoya Kochetova, who sang the part of Antonida in the opera.

13   Ibid., 179; additional information in this paragraph from Wortman, "The Coronation of Alexander III," 289–90.

14   Unsigned, "Po povodu baleta A. N. Bogdanova," *Teatral'nïy mirok,* February 9, 1885, 2.

15   [F. B. Gridnin], "Khronika," *Teatr i zhizn',* January 21, 1885, 2.

16   [F. B. Gridnin], "Novïy balet. 'Prelesti gashisha ili ostrov roz' A. N. Bogdanova," *Teatr i zhizn',* January 22, 1885, 1–2.

17   RGIA f. 652, op. 1, d. 287, l. 1. The letter, dated May 11, 1885, is addressed to Ivan Vsevolozhsky.

18   V. A. Telyakovsky, Nina Dimitrievitch, and Clement Crisp, "Memoirs," *Dance Research* 8, no. 1 (Spring 1990): 39.

19   One of the directors of the Moscow Imperial Theaters, Evgeniy De Salias-Turnemir, balked at implementing reforms and resigned in 1882 after just two months on the job. His appeal for retirement is cast, in keeping with the nostalgic nature of Tsar Alexander III's reign, in

archaic eighteenth-century language. RGIA f. 497, op. 2, d. 24885, ll. 13 and 16.

20 RGIA f. 497, op. 2, d. 25072, l. 29.

21 RGIA f. 497, op. 18, d. 16, l. 3.

22 RGIA f. 468, op. 13, d. 675, l. 5 ob.

23 RGIA f. 497, op. 2, d. 25090, ll. 38–39. The investigation of the theft was extremely thorough (Vashkevich's mother, a railroad switch operator, was interrogated, along with a woman in St. Petersburg with whom he corresponded), but he kept his job.

24 RGALI f. 659, op. 1, yed. khr. 209, l. 1.

25 A. P. Chekhov, *Polnoye sobraniye sochineniy i pisem*, ed. S. D. Balukhatïy and V. P. Potemkin, 20 vols. (Moscow: Ogiz, 1944–51), 2: 370.

26 Telyakovsky, "Memoirs," 40. Alastair Macaulay observes that the ballet *Nathalie, ou la laitière Suisse*, which starred Marie Taglioni in the 1832 version choreographed by her father, remained in repertory in Russia, perhaps in part because audiences knew of the ballerina-milkmaid connection. Email communication, July 22, 2015.

27 Chekhov, *Polnoye sobraniye sochineniy i pisem*, 2: 370.

28 Wiley, *Tchaikovsky's Ballets*, 97. Wiley reports that additional "improvements" included "the introduction of special drama and singing classes; the publication of *The Yearbook of the Imperial Theaters* [Yezhegodnik imperatorskikh teatrov]; the founding of central libraries of music, theater, and production materials; the building of warehouses and other storage facilities; and the establishment of a photography studio within the imperial theaters."

29 Telyakovsky, "Memoirs," 40.

30 RGIA f. 652, op. 1, d. 523, l. 11.

31 RGIA f. 497, op. 2, d. 25297, l. 38; 1883 telegram from Pchelnikov to Vsevolozhsky, in which Pchelnikov requests permission to use the spare rubles in the budget to retain several of the employees that he had earlier sacked, to keep them housed and fed.

32 RGIA f. 497, op. 2, d. 25110, l. 2 (March 15, 1883) and ll. 5 ob.-6 (April 12, 1883). The quotations come from Vsevolozhsky to the minister of the court, Count Illarion Vorontsov-Dashkov (1837–1916), an intimate of Tsar Alexander III. According to the minister's head note on the April 12 letter, Vsevolozhsky's argument for the survival of the Bolshoi Ballet was "granted by His Majesty" on April 20.

33 RGIA f. 497, op. 2, d. 25074, l. 350 ob. The disparities between the earnings of the Bolshoi Opera and the Ballet are illustrated on ll. 315 ob.-316 of this file. In October of 1881, the seventeen Russian (as

opposed to French or Italian) opera performances brought in 25,056 rubles and 85 kopecks, and the nine ballet performances 6,160 rubles and 30 kopecks. In October of 1882, the twelve Russian opera performances earned 21,772 rubles and 20 kopecks, and the thirteen ballet performances 7,093 rubles and 70 kopecks. The disparities increased in November of the two years.

34 RGIA f. 497, op. 2, d. 25110, l. 3.

35 Yu. A. Bakhrushin, *Istoriya russkogo baleta* (Moscow: Sovetskaya Rossiya, 1965), 166.

36 RGIA f. 497, op. 2, d. 25110, l. 42 (October 10, 1883; Vsevolozhsky to the minister of the court).

37 Marius Petipa, *Russian Ballet Master: The Memoirs of Marius Petipa*, ed. Lillian Moore; trans. Helen Whittaker (London: Chameleon Press, 1958), 20.

38 Ibid., 50.

39 Ivor Guest, *The Ballet of the Second Empire* (London: Pitman, 1974), 170–71; my thanks to Alastair Macaulay for this reference, and for information in this paragraph and the next. Email communication, July 22, 2015.

40 August Bournonville, *My Theatre Life*, trans. Patricia N. McAndrew (Middletown, CT: Wesleyan University Press, 1979), 582.

41 Petipa, *Russian Ballet Master*, 50.

42 Elizabeth Souritz, "Moscow vs Petersburg: The Ballet Master Alexis Bogdanov and Others," http://harriman.columbia.edu/files/harriman/International%20Symposium%20of%20Russian%20Ballet%20%20Paper%20Souritz.pdf.

43 Wiley, *Tchaikovsky's Ballets*, 27.

44 The music for the Paul Taglioni version, called *Der Seeräuber*, came from the quill of the Bohemian Wenzel Gährich, who wrote at least nine other ballet scores, including one on the popular subject of Don Quixote and a Christmastime ballet for children, along with two operas and two vaudevilles. See Carl Friedrich Heinrich Wilhelm Philipp Justus, Freiherr von Lebedur, *Tonkünstler-Lexicon Berlin's von den ältesten Zeiten bis auf die Gegenwart* (Berlin: L. Rauh, 1861), 178–79; my thanks to Bruce Brown for this reference. The music for the Mazilier version is by Adolph Adam, composer of *Giselle*; and that for the Perrot and Petipa versions is credited to Cesare Pugni, although he evidently felt free to paraphrase Adam. Music by Léo Delibes became part of the Adam-Pugni–based performing edition.

45 RGIA f. 497, op. 2, d. 16897, l. 48 (letter of November 27, 1858).

Owing to the lack of precedent, ticket scalping was not illegal at the time. Of the rush for seats for *Le corsaire*, Verstovsky scorns the "hundreds of people desiring to cram themselves through the same hole," adding that, "in any public place, jostling, and dirt, and complaints are unavoidable."

46   This and the previous quotations from RGIA f. 497, op. 2, d. 17600, ll. 99–100.

47   Henry Schlesinger, *The Battery: How Portable Power Sparked a Technological Revolution* (New York: HarperCollins, 2000), 132 and 170–71.

48   RGIA f. 497, op. 9, d. 1585, ll. 19–24 (information and quotations).

49   RGIA f. 482, op. 3, d. 3, l. 202.

50   Ibid., l. 137 ob.

51   RGIA f 497, op. 1, d. 71 ("Vospominaniya E. P. Kavelinoy o teatral'noy zhizni Moskvï 1870 gg."), ll. 1–14 (information and quotations in this paragraph and the following).

52   Rodney Stenning Edgecombe, "Cesare Pugni, Marius Petipa and 19th-Century Ballet Music," *The Musical Times* 147, no. 1895 (Summer 2006): 48

53   He died on January 14, 1870.

54   Edgecombe, "Cesare Pugni, Marius Petipa and 19th-Century Ballet Music," 40.

55   RGIA f. 659, op. 4, d. 1128, 1. 44 (memorandum from the Imperial Court to the Directorate of the Imperial Moscow Theaters, November 10, 1869).

56   RGALI f. 659, op. 4, yed. khr. 3639, l. 7.

57   Arthur Saint-Léon, *Letters from a Ballet Master: The Correspondence of Arthur Saint-Léon*, ed. Ivor Guest (London: Dance Books, 1981), 113 and 120; see also Letellier, *The Ballets of Ludwig Minkus*, 22–23.

58   Roberto González Echevarría, *Cervantes' Don Quixote: A Casebook* (Oxford and New York: Oxford University Press, 2005), 67.

59   Neteatral, "Teatral'naya khronika," *Vseobshchaya gazeta*, December 16, 1869; quoted in V. Krasovskaya, *Russkiy baletnïy teatr vtoroy polovini XIX veka* (Leningrad and Moscow: Iskusstvo, 1963), 250.

60   RGIA f 497, op. 1, d. 71, l. 9.

61   [Unsigned], *Russkiye vedomosti*, January 25, 1870, 3 ("Moskovskiye vedomosti"). The criticism "boiled" in Gerber's heart. He felt underappreciated in Moscow, both by the press and by the bureaucrats running the Bolshoi, and on December 1, 1873, sent an impassioned letter of complaint to Gedeonov in St. Petersburg. His grievances included being passed over for awards, fines, and rudeness from the Italian musicians

with whom he had to work—all despite improving the quality of the orchestra and putting the score library in order. "I do all that I can, Your Excellency, and if I had the happiness of serving under your personal direction, then I am sure that Your Excellency would award me the Stanislavsky Ribbon. But from these gentlemen, who understand and accomplish nothing, there is no hope even of a kind word, never mind awards" (RGIA f. 497, op. 2, d. 23344, l. 56 ob.).

62 RGIA f. 497, op. 2, d. 22660, l. 1.

63 Krasovskaya, *Russkiy baletnïy teatr vtoroy polovinï XIX veka*, 255.

64 RGIA f. 497, op. 2, d. 24261, l. 7.

65 "I sought in vain to discover plot, dramatic interest, logical consistency, or anything which might remotely resemble sanity. And even if I were fortunate enough to come upon a trace of it in Petipa's *Don Quixote*, the impression was immediately effaced by an unending and monotonous host of feats of bravura, all of which were rewarded with salvos of applause and curtain calls" (Bournonville, *My Theatre Life*, 581).

66 RGIA f. 497, op. 2, d. 22646, l. 2.

67 RGIA f. 497, op. 2, d. 22036, ll. 1–19 (information and quotations in this and the preceding paragraphs). A report was also filed in 1869 about sparks flying from the smokestack leading from the steam room to the back of the theater. The pressure had been increased to fill the water tower needed for the bathing scene in the ballet *Le roi Candaule* and the fountain in *The Little Humpbacked Horse*. Firemen were summoned to the theater to "put out the smokestack," but it continued smoldering.

68 Bournonville, *My Theatre Life*, 585; he reports seeing one act each from *Cinderella*, *Le diable à quatre*, and *The Little Humpbacked Horse*.

69 I refer to the biographies of David Brown and Anthony Holden, and to recent Russian-language commentaries. See, for broader context, Simon Morrison, "Waist-Deep: In the Mire of Russian and Western Debates About Tchaikovsky," *The Times Literary Supplement*, May 1, 2015, 14–15.

70 *Swan Lake*, Tchaikovsky Research, http://wiki.tchaikovsky-research. net/wiki/Swan_Lake; letter of September 10, 1875.

71 P. I. Chaykovskiy, *Dnevniki 1873–1891* (St. Petersburg: EGO; Severnïy olen', 1993), 198; http://wiki.tchaikovsky-research.net/wiki/Letter_681 (December 7, 1877, to Sergey Taneyev). The *"moment of absolute happiness"* came during a concert performance of *Swan Lake* in Prague on February 9, 1888.

72 Alexander Poznansky, *Tchaikovsky: The Quest for the Inner Man* (New York: Schirmer, 1999), 175; see also Wiley, *Tchaikovsky's Ballets*, 40–41.

73 Skromnïy nablyudatel', "Nablyudeniya i zametki," *Russkiye vedomosti*,

February 26, 1877, 2; see also Krasovskaya, *Russkiy baletnïy teatr vtoroy polovinï XIX veka*, 199.

74   Krasovskaya, *Russkiy baletnïy teatr vtoroy polovinï XIX veka*, 199; see also Wiley, *Tchaikovsky's Ballets*, 55.

75   The initial hope was that Tchaikovsky would compose the music, and he even signed a contract with the Moscow Imperial Theaters to do so. But the deadline expired without a single sketch being produced. Partly to make amends, Tchaikovsky accepted the commission for *Swan Lake*.

76   RGALI f. 659, op. 3, yed. khr. 3065, l. 37; also Surits, "'Lebedinoye ozero' 1877 goda."

77   RGALI f. 659, op. 3, yed. khr. 3065, l. 35; also Surits, "'Lebedinoye ozero' 1877 goda."

78   N. D. Kashkin, *Vospominaniya o P. I. Chaykovskom* (Moscow: Muzgiz, 1954), 117. The composer received 400 rubles up front for the music, and then, upon submitting the first three acts to the Bolshoi on April 12, 1876, he requested the remaining 400 rubles due. The payment was "disbursed from the receipts for the first four performances of the ballet *Swan Lake* (accordingly, 100 rubles each evening)" (RGALI f. 659, op. 3, yed. khr. 3065, l. 36).

79   Chaykovskiy, *Lebedinoye ozero. Balet v 4-x deystviyakh. Postanovka v Moskovskom Bol'shom teatre 1875–1883*, 9.

80   Arlene Croce, "'Swan Lake' and Its Alternatives," in *Going to the Dance* (New York: Alfred A. Knopf, 1982), 184.

81   Chaykovskiy, *Lebedinoye ozero. Balet v 4-x deystviyakh. Postanovka v Moskovskom Bol'shom teatre 1875–1883*, 32.

82   Kashkin, *Vospominaniya o P. I. Chaykovskom*, 119.

83   Chaykovskiy, *Lebedinoye ozero. Balet v 4-x deystviyakh. Postanovka v Moskovskom Bol'shom teatre 1875–1883*, 87, 91.

84   Alastair Macaulay, "'Swan Lake' Discoveries Allow for a Deeper Dive into its History," *New York Times*, October 13, 2015.

85   Chaykovskiy, *Lebedinoye ozero. Balet v 4-x deystviyakh. Postanovka v Moskovskom Bol'shom teatre 1875–1883*, 210.

86   Nothing is known of his relationship with Hansen.

87   N. Panovskiy, "Bol'shoy teatr," *Moskovskiye vedomosti*, September 19, 1863, 3; see also Wiley, *Tchaikovsky's Ballets*, 46. The critique of Karpakova is perhaps too strong. August Bournonville saw both her and Sobeshchanskaya perform a benefit in Moscow in 1874, and praised the "matchless staying power and unmistakable skill of [the] two ballerinas with the curious names" in his memoirs (*My Theatre Life*, 584).

88   Mukhin, "kniga o balete," l. 255.

89 Ibid.

90 K. F. Val'ts, *65 let v teatre* (Leningrad: Academia, 1928), 73–75 (information and quotations in this paragraph and the following); see also Wiley, *Tchaikovsky's Ballets*, 47.

91 U rampï, "Pochemu balet padayet? II.," *Russkiy listok*, November 22, 1900, 3.

92 Ibid.

93 The standard formula was for the performer to receive one-half or one-quarter of the Bolshoi Theater box-office receipts, once the bookkeeper had deducted expenses specific to the benefit and issued the performer a claim check for presentation to the cashier. Alternative arrangements, including advance payments, required approval from the minister of the court. Karpakova's *Swan Lake* benefit earning is listed in RGALI f. 659, op. 4, yed. khr. 3508, l. 36.

94 Later this dance was inserted into *The Little Humpbacked Horse*.

95 P. I. Chaykovskiy, *Perepiska s N. F. von-Mekk*, ed. V. A. Zhdanov and N. T. Zhegin, 3 vols. (Moscow and Leningrad: Academia, 1934–36), 2: 298 (letter of January 14–15, 1880, from Nadezhda von Mekk to Tchaikovsky).

96 N. K[ashkin]., "Muzïkal'naya khronika," *Russkiye vedomosti*, March 3, 1877, 1.

97 Quotations in this paragraph and the next from Zub', "Bol'shoy teatr. Benefis g-zhi Karpakoy 1-oy—'Lebedinoye ozero,' balet Reyzingera, muzïka Chaykovskogo," *Sovremennïye izvestiya*, February 26, 1877, 1.

98 The liberalization began in 1858.

99 Val'ts, *65 let v teatre*, 108. In the draft of the Soviet-era memoirs from which these lines come, Valts adds that "none of this is in the current [circa 1926] production; everything is simplified" (Muzey Bakhrushina f. 43, op. 3, no. 3, l. 10 ob.). Since imperial-era ballet could not be seen as superior to Soviet-era ballet in any respect, Valts's complaint was excluded from the published text.

100 N. K[ashki]n, "Muzïkal'naya khronika," *Russkiye vedomosti*, February 25, 1877, 1; see also Wiley, *Tchaikovsky's Ballets*, 57.

101 And, Alastair Macaulay notes, simultaneously became part of productions in Russia, England, and the United States. Email communication, August 7, 2015.

102 Chaykovskiy, *Lebedinoye ozero. Balet v 4-x deystviyakh. Postanovka v Moskovskom Bol'shom teatre 1875–1883*, 28–29. Rothbart wore a more flamboyant and expensive costume in 1877: "Waist-length jerkin of colored satin on buckram base, trimmed in black velvet, lace and soutache

of foil and bullion fringe - 1 pc.; matching slacks - 1 pc. (31 rub[les]. 50 kop[ecks].). Sash with pockets trimmed in black velvet and satin, and a gilded buckle - 1 pc. (3 rub. 60 kop.) The outfit with webbing: hip-length jerkin of colored velvet on base of white paduasoy and colored silk, trimmed in beaded webbing, soutache, foil silk webbing, white ribbons of gros-de-Naples silk on thread with rings and hooks - 1 pc., matching overcoat - 1 pc. (145 rub. 79 kop.). Sash with a pocket trimmed in colored velvet, with tassels and a gilded buckle - 1 pc. (4 rub. 96 kop.)." Ibid., 27.

103 Titled *Watanabe*, it was to tell the tale of an ancient samurai clan known for fighting demons, dragons, and man-eating hags. The project had captured Tchaikovsky's fancy, and so, after cautioning Valts that the scenario was better suited to a spectacular *ballet-féerie* than an opera-ballet, he pledged to take it on. "I look at *Watanabe* as a great subject for a ballet and I'm prepared to write the best music I possibly can for this well-chosen, well-planned scenario," he told Valts. The composer had estimated completing it in time for the 1893–94 Bolshoi season. Muzey Bakhrushina f. 43, op. 3, no. 14.

104 Alexander Poznansky, *Tchaikovsky's Last Days: A Documentary Study* (Oxford and New York: Oxford University Press, 1996), 71.

105 Frank Clemow, *The Cholera Epidemic of 1892 in the Russian Empire* (London and New York: Longmans, Green, and Co., 1893), 55, https://archive.org/details/39002086311652.med.yale.edu.

106 Marius Petipa, *The Diaries of Marius Petipa*, ed. and trans. Lynn Garafola (Pennington, NJ: The Society of Dance History Scholars, 1992), 14.

107 Muzey Bakhrushina f. 205, no. 230, l. 2 ob.

108 RGIA f. 497, op. 18, d. 495, l. 2. An eyewitness fills in the details: "The Mariyinsky Theater came up with an interesting activity for the bird. She appears on the stage, sitting on a rock or flying, just when Rothbart wants to be invisible or to see what the swan maidens do in his absence. The owl, flying excitedly from place to place, reacts as though greatly impressed by the amorous dialogue and meeting between Odette and the prince" (G. A. Rimskiy-Korsakov, "Iz rukopisey o russkom balete kontsa XIX-nachala XX v.," in *Mnemozina: Dokumentï i faktï iz istorii otechest-vennogo teatra XX veka*, ed. V. V. Ivanov [Moscow: Indrik, 2014], 21).

109 Muzey Bakhrushina f. 205, no. 230, l. 2 ob.

110 Akim Volynsky, *Ballet's Magic Kingdom: Selected Writings on Dance in Russia, 1911–1925*, trans. and ed. Stanley J. Rabinowitz (New Haven and London: Yale University Press, 2008), 118. From a recollection passed to the critic by Ekaterina Geltser.

111 Ibid., 17 (from a 1911 appreciation).

112 Ibid., 19.

113 H.S.H. The Princess Romanovsky-Krassinsky, *Dancing in Petersburg: The Memoirs of Kschessinska*, trans. Arnold Haskell (New York: Doubleday, 1961), 74.

114 RGIA f. 652, op. 1, d. 404, l. 4; f. 497, op. 5, d. 1708, l. 51.

115 Wortman, *From Alexander II to the Abdication of Nicholas II*, 321.

116 Romanovsky-Krassinsky, *Dancing in Petersburg*, 77.

117 RGIA f. 497, op. 5, d. 1708, l. 108.

118 The target of the chicken attack was Olga Preobrazhenskaya (Preobrajenska, 1871–1962). See Coryne Hall, *Imperial Dancer: Mathilde Kschessinska and the Romanovs* (Phoenix Mill, Thrupp, Stroud: Sutton, 2005), 109.

119 Romanovsky-Krassinsky, *Dancing in Petersburg*, 58–59.

120 Wortman, *From Alexander II to the Abdication of Nicholas II*, 357.

121 Romanovsky-Krassinsky, *Dancing in Petersburg*, 59.

122 Wortman, *From Alexander II to the Abdication of Nicholas II*, 350.

123 *Memories of Alexei Volkov*, trans. E. Semonov Payot (1928); trans. Robert Moshein (2004), "Chapter Four: The Coronation of the Tsar," http://www.alexanderpalace.org/volkov/4.html.

124 Information and quotations in this paragraph from RGIA f. 652, op. 1, d. 523 (Pchelnikov's letters and telegrams to Ivan Vsevolozhsky, 1884–91).

125 "I hope to be better on Wednesday," his April 1, 1883, request concludes. RGIA f. 497, op. 2, d. 25346, l. 5.

126 RGIA f. 497, op. 2, d. 25074, l. 371.

127 Krasovskaya, *Russkiy baletnïy teatr vtoroy polovinï XIX veka*, 506.

128 Hence the fussiness of his petition for repairs to a fire-singed overcoat; RGIA f. 468, op. 13, d. 680, ll. 1–3 (1890).

129 Telyakovsky, "Memoirs," 41.

130 Tim Scholl, "The Ballet's Carmen," in *Don Quixote* [Royal Opera House program booklet] (London: ROH, 2013), 17.

131 Ibid.

132 G. Khummayeva, "'Peterburgskaya gazeta' protiv 'Don Kikhota' Aleksandra Gorskogo," *Vestnik Gosudarstvennogo khoroegraficheskogo uchilishcha Belorussii* 1, no. 2 (1994): 73–87 (information and quotations).

133 A. G., "Obrashcheniye k baletnoy truppe," August 1, 1902, in *Baletmeyster A. A. Gorskiy: Materialï, vospominaniya, stat'i*, 90.

134 Tat'yana Saburova, "Fotoetyudï Aleksandra Gorskogo," in *Moskovskiy Imperatorskiy Bol'shoy teatr v fotografiyakh. 1860–1917 gg.*, ed. L. G. Kharina (Moscow: Kuchkovo Pole, 2013), 282.

5: AFTER THE BOLSHEVIKS

On the murder of the last tsar and his family, I relied chiefly on Robert K. Massie, *The Romanovs: The Final Chapter* (New York: Random House, 1996), 3–11; and *Nicholas and Alexandra* (New York: Random House, 2012), 533–62. I also consulted Stephen Kotkin, *Stalin*, 3 vols. (New York: Penguin Press, 2014–), 1: 280–81, and derived my description of the revolution and civil war from pages 86–421 of his magisterial publication. For Gorsky in 1917–18 I used E. Surits, "A. A. Gorskiy i moskovskiy balet," in E. Surits and E. Belova, eds., *Baletmeyster A. A. Gorskiy: Materiali, vospominaniya, stat'i* (St. Petersburg: Dmitriy Bulanin, 2000), 49–55. Biographical information on Elena Malinovskaya is taken from the preface to her RGALI fond (1933); details about the price of the shoes used by the dancers of the Bolshoi Ballet in 1917–19 are in RGALI f. 648, op. 3, yed. khr. 31. I am most grateful to the Moscow dance critic Tatyana Kuznetsova for detailing by email (on January 3–4, 2015) the career and fate of her grandfather, Vladimir Kuznetsov. As the relative of a victim of the Stalinist repressions, Kuznetsova received access to his Cheka dossier. Kuznetsova relates that his "archive" consists of a last letter from Tomsk, a few photographs, and bureaucratese.

Most of the documents on the period immediately after the revolution are in the RGALI Bolshoi Theater fond, but I also made use of copies of protocols preserved in the library-archive of the Theater Union (Soyuz teatral'nïkh deyateley/STD) in Moscow. Biographical information on Geltser comes from Aleksandr Kolesnikov, "Yekaterina Gel'tser," in *Russkiye bogini*, ed. T. Derevyanko (Moscow: Act-Press, 2011), 118–33. I also drew from V. V. Makarov's unpublished 1945–46 monograph on the ballerina, including interview transcripts, a 1909 contract, and other materials: Muzey Bakhrushina f. 152, no. 205. F. 257, nos. 1–2, contain Geltser's undated letters to Sobeshchanskaya about learning the "Russian" dance. For her record of service from 1909 through 1917, I consulted RGALI f. 659, op. 3, yed. khr. 802. Details on Geltser and Mannerheim come from http://photo-element.ru/story/nappelbaum/nappelbaum.html (on the photograph taken of the ballerina in 1924); Jonathan Clements, *Mannerheim: President, Soldier, Spy* (London: Haus Publishing, 2010), 42 and 298 n. 13 (discounting the rumors that she had a son with Mannerheim).

I benefited throughout this chapter from Elizabeth Souritz, *Soviet Choreographers in the 1920s*, trans. Lynn Visson with Sally Banes (Durham and London: Duke University Press, 1990), esp. 142–53, 162–65, and 231–54. For political context on *The Red Poppy* I drew from Kotkin, *Stalin*, 1: 625–33, and especially from Edward Tyerman, "*The Red Poppy* and 1927: Translating Contemporary China into Soviet Ballet" (paper presented at the Columbia University symposium "Russian Movement Culture of the 1920s and 1930s," on February 13, 2015). Tyerman notes the relationship between *The Red Poppy* and the contemporaneous Meyerhold Theater production of Sergey Tretyakov's *Roar, China!*, a play that told of an English gunboat on the Yangtze River that threatens the destruction of a village as revenge for the drowning of an American hide-trader. The villagers are forced to sacrifice two of their own, by coin toss, to the English.

The rivalry between the designers Kurilko and Fyodorovsky is touched on in S. Chekhov, "Vblizi Mikhaíla Chekhova," in *Voprosï teatra: Sbornik statey i publikatsiy*, ed. K. L. Rudnitskiy (Moscow: VNII Iskusstvoznaniya, Soyuz Teatr. Deyat. RSFSR, 1990), 136.

1   "No newspaper, no program, no performance"; Marius Petipa, *The Diaries of Marius Petipa*, ed. and trans. Lynn Garafola (Pennington, NJ: The Society of Dance History Scholars, 1992), 64 (January 12/25, 1905).

2   R. H. Bruce Lockhart, *Memoirs of a British Agent* (London: Pan, 2002), 258–59.

3   Richard Pipes, *The Russian Revolution* (New York: Vintage Books, 1990), 781. Stephen Kotkin clarifies "that there is no solid, direct evidence of Lenin's involvement in the murder, or of his reaction to it." Email communication, November 29, 2015.

4   S. Rakhmaninov, *Literaturnoye naslediye*, ed. Z. A. Apetyan, vol. 1, *Vospominaniya. Stat'i. Pis'ma* (Moscow: Sovetskiy kompozitor, 1978), 57–61.

5   According to the intendant of the Imperial Theaters at the time, Vladimir Telyakovsky; see Sergei Bertensson and Jay Leyda, *Sergei Rachmaninoff: A Lifetime in Music* (Bloomington: Indiana University Press, 2001), 115.

6   Walter Duranty, "Russian Revolution 'Interrupted' Ballet," *New York Times*, March 22, 1923.

7   V. I. Lenin, "Declaration of Rights of the Working and Exploited People," Marxists.org, http://www.marxists.org/archive/lenin/works/1918/jan/03.htm.

8   Sally A. Boniece, "The Spiridonova Case, 1906: Terror, Myth, and Martyrdom," in *Just Assassins: The Culture of Terrorism in Russia*, ed. Anthony Anemone (Evanston: Northwestern University Press, 2010), 137.

9   Lockhart, *Memoirs of a British Agent*, 300.

10 RGALI f. 1933, op. 2, yed. khr. 12 (Ye. K. Malinovskaya, "Bol'shoy teatr po imeyushchimsya material. Vospominaniya"), l. 2.

11 This was Gorsky's 1903 version of the ballet, which derives from the

1885 Petipa-Ivanov version. The title is also translated as *The girl who needed watching.*

12 Surits, "A. A. Gorskiy i moskovskiy balet," 49.

13 "Otkrïtiye Gosudarstvennïkh teatrov," *Iskrï,* March 26, 1917, 96.

14 Alexandre Gretchaninoff, *My Life* (New York: Coleman-Ross, 1952), 118.

15 Surits, "A. A. Gorskiy i moskovskiy balet," 51.

16 Souritz, *Soviet Choreographers in the 1920s,* 89.

17 RGALI f. 659, op. 3, yed. khr. 932, l. 127.

18 Arkhiv Bol'shogo teatra/STD; "'Tayna ministerskoy lozhi' (iz gaz. 'Vremya' ot 10/V-1917 g.)."

19 RGALI f. 1933, op. 2, yed. khr. 12, l. 5.

20 RGALI f. 1933, op. 2, yed. khr. 58, l. 10.

21 Ibid., l. 3.

22 RGALI f. 1933, op. 2, yed. khr. 13, l. 2.

23 Ibid., l. 3.

24 Sergey Prokofiev, *Diaries 1915–1923: Behind the Mask,* trans. Anthony Phillips (London: Faber and Faber, 2008), 279; entry of April 7, 1918.

25 Rimskiy-Korsakov, "Iz rukopisey o russkom balete kontsa XIX-nachala XX v.," 76–77.

26 Roland John Wiley tangentially reports the absence of "standard bureaucratese"—permissions for Petipa's travel, for example—from the records on Petipa stored in St. Petersburg. Email communication, November 10, 2014. The papers that survived the ransacking of the apartment ended up in the theater collection established by the industrialist Alexei Bakhrushin.

27 L. Sabaneyev, "Bït' li Bol'shomu teatru?," *Ekran* 7 (November 15–17, 1921): 3. The author comes to the conclusion that the theater had outlasted its purpose even before the revolution.

28 P. N. Lepeshinskiy, *Na povorote* (Moscow: Gospolitizdat, 1955), 111–12.

29 Ibid. Although allowed to continue operating during the crisis, the Bolshoi could not count on the government to provide fuel to heat the theater and so was encouraged, by the theater division of the People's Commissariat for Enlightenment, to purchase firewood on the black market (RGALI f. 649, op. 2, yed. khr. 177, l. 14).

30 RGALI f. 1933, op. 2, yed. khr. 12, l. 6.

31 Asaf Messerer, *Tanets. Misl'. Vremya* (Moscow: Iskusstvo, 1990), 70.

32 RGALI f. 764, op. 1, yed. khr. 192.

33 Email communication with Tatyana Kuznetsova, Vladimir Kuznetsov's granddaughter, January 3, 2015.

34 RGALI f. 1933, op. 2, yed. khr. 13, l. 18.

35 *Protokol obshchego sobraniya artistov baletnoy truppï Gosudarstvennogo Bol'shogo teatra*, December 17, 1919, l. 1. Personal archive of Tatyana Kuznetsova.

36 Arkhiv Bol'shogo teatra/STD; letter of April 10, 1923 from Lunacharsky to the "M. G. O." (Moskovskaya gorodskaya organizatsiya).

37 Personal archive of Tatyana Kuznetsova.

38 Personal archive of Tatyana Kuznetsova.

39 Kevin Murphy, *Revolution and Counterrevolution: Class Struggle in a Moscow Metal Factory* (New York and Oxford: Berghahn Books, 2005), 71; additional information in this paragraph from 68–73.

40 RGALI f. 1933, op. 2, yed. khr. 13, l. 20.

41 RGALI f. 648, op. 2, yed. khr. 54, l. 81.

42 Bella Cohen, "The Women of Red Russia," *New York Times*, November 25, 1923.

43 RGALI f. 648, op. 2, yed. khr. 128, l. 19.

44 E. A. Churakova, "Fyodor Fyodorovskiy i epokha eksperimentov: 1918–1932," in *Fyodor Fyodorovskiy: Legenda Bol'shogo teatra*, ed. E. A. Churakova (Moscow: SkanRus, 2014), 83.

45 RGALI f. 658, op. 2, yed. khr. 351, l. 18; minutes of the Bolshoi workers' assembly, June 21, 1924.

46 *Vlast' i khudozhestvennaya intelligentsiya: Dokumentï TsK RKP(b) – VKP(b), VChK – OGPU – NKVD o kul'turnoy politike. 1917–1953 gg.*, ed. Andrey Artizov and Oleg Naumov (Moscow: Demokratiya, 2002), 31–34; and *Muzïka vmesto sumbura: Kompozitorï i muzïkantï v strane sovetov 1917–1991. Dokumentï*, ed. Leonid Maksimenkov (Moscow: Demokratiya, 2013), 40–45.

47 RGALI f. 648, op. 2, yed. khr. 185, l. 2.

48 RGALI f. 648, op. 2, yed. khr. 187, l. 106; minutes of the March 10, 1924, meeting of the council of artists.

49 Ibid., ll. 45, 48; May 24 and May 26, 1923.

50 RGALI f. 1933, op. 2, yed. khr. 13, l. 15.

51 The location of this affiliate changed, but it settled in the building of an abolished private opera enterprise. Malinovskaya had lobbied for it to be housed in a historic church on the river (RGALI f. 648, op. 2, yed. khr. 734, l. 21; December 8, 1934).

52 Arkhiv Bol'shogo teatra/STD; undated.

53 RGALI f. 648, op. 2, yed. khr. 187, l. 77.

54 Arkhiv Bol'shogo teatra/STD; RGALI f. 648, op. 2, yed. khr. 339, l. 1. Bryusov's draft resolution for the Central Control Commission is dated January 9, 1924.

55 RGALI f. 648, op. 2, yed. khr. 315, l. 19.

56 RGALI f. 648, op. 2, yed. khr. 315, l. 36.

57 Malinovskaya's two tenures as director of the theater effectively framed the existence of Glaviskusstvo, a political watchdog administration formed under the People's Commissariat for Enlightenment. It oversaw the Bolshoi in the late 1920s, during the worst of the ideological attacks mounted against the theater by the Communist Union of Youth and other proletarian organizations. See Sheila Fitzpatrick, "The Emergence of Glaviskusstvo: Class War on the Cultural Front, Moscow, 1928–29," *Soviet Studies* 23, no. 2 (October 1971): 236–53.

58 RGALI f. 648, op. 2, yed. khr. 124, l. 22; minutes of the December 22, 1923, meeting of Glavrepertkom.

59 RGALI f. 648, op. 2, yed. khr. 187, l. 34; Souritz, *Soviet Choreographers in the 1920s,* 83.

60 RGALI f. 648, op. 2, yed. khr. 695, ll. 1–2. Reed, an American journalist famous for his account of the Bolshevik coup, *Ten Days That Shook the World*, was buried a hero in the Kremlin Wall Necropolis in 1920. The libretto for the proposed opera about his socialist radicalism, adapted from a play by Igor Terentyev, sought to depart from old-fashioned opera conventions, but it was derided by the artistic and political council as a "kaleidoscope, the likes of which we haven't seen before." Terentyev was sent back to the drawing board, told that he needed "to show Reed's death at that moment when Russia had regained her strength, and to depict his burial on Red Square."

61 Cohen, "The Women of Red Russia."

62 This quotation, and information in the following paragraph, from Ivor Guest, *Ballet Under Napoleon* (London: Dance Books, 2002), 481; and from Alastair Macaulay, email communication, July 22, 2015.

63 Unsigned, "Quiet Tea Shop League Formed in Moscow to Get Peaceful Places to Talk of at Night," *New York Times,* January 15, 1928.

64 RGALI f. 2729, op. 2, yed. khr. 3, l. 1; letter of October 5, 1896.

65 Ibid., ll. 4, 6; 1897.

66 "Iz stenogrammï besedï E. Gel'tser s baletnoy molodezh'yu 16 iyunya 1937 g.," in *Baletmeyster A. A. Gorskiy: Materialï, vospominaniya, stat'i,* 124.

67 Yekaterina Geltser, "The Way of a Ballerina"; New York Public Library (NYPL) clipping file.

68 Elizabeth Souritz, "Isadora Duncan and Prewar Russian Dancemakers," in *The Ballets Russes and Its World,* ed. Lynn Garafola and Nancy Van Norman Baer (New Haven and London: Yale University Press, 1999), 108.

69 Irina Sirotkina, *Svobodnoye dvizheniye i plasticheskiy tanets v Rossii* (Moscow: Novoye literaturnoye obozreniye, 2012), 79 (quoting a 1924 article in the theater journal *Novaya rampa*). Additional information on the Duncan school in Moscow in this paragraph from 60–62.

70 RGALI f. 1933, op. 2, yed. khr. 111, l. 1. The quoted words come from an April 7, 1931, report on Isadora Duncan's art and its possible "Marxist" adaptation by the Bolshoi Ballet, with reference to the findings of the Duncan Commission of the Russian Theatrical Society.

71 Unsigned, "Pavlowa's Successor in Russian Ballet," *Musical America*, January 13, 1912; NYPL clipping file.

72 Sergey Konayev has reconstructed the 1913 film with the correct music. The version trafficked on YouTube is incorrect; the Schubert piano music it features is completely misaligned with the steps. See Sergey Konayev, "Muzïkal'nïy moment. Atributsiya, ozvuchaniye i pereosmïsleniye tantsev iz dorevolyutsionnïkh nemïkh lent," in *XVII Kinofestival' Belïye Stolbï-2013. Katalog*, ed. Tamara Sergeyeva (Moscow: Gosfil'mofund Rossii, 2013), 18–19.

73 Herbert Corey, "Lithe Grace of Pavlowa Is Missing in Mordkin's New Partner," *Cincinnati Times*, December 23, 1911; NYPL clipping file.

74 Vlas Mikhaílovich Doroshevich, "Pis'ma," in *Teatral'naya kritika Vlasa Doroshevicha*, ed. S. V. Bukchin (Minsk: Kharvest, 2004), http://az.lib.ru/d/doroshewich_w_m/text_1220.shtml. Reference is made to the delicate marble sculptures of female nudes produced by Antonio Canova (1757–1822).

75 Kolesnikov, "Yekaterina Gel'tser," 128.

76 Ibid., 129.

77 Akim Volynsky, *Ballet's Magic Kingdom: Selected Writings on Dance in Russia, 1911–1925*, trans. and ed. Stanley J. Rabinowitz (New Haven and London: Yale University Press, 2008), 86.

78 RGALI f. 648, op. 2, yed. khr. 321, l. 1.

79 "Novaya faza bor'bï v Kitaye," *Pravda*, January 9, 1926, 1; "Obïsk na sovetskom parakhode v Londone," *Pravda*, January 9, 1926, 1.

80 Sergey Prokofiev, *Diaries 1924–1933: Prodigal Son*, trans. Anthony Phillips (London: Faber and Faber, 2012), 427; entry of January 23, 1923.

81 RGALI f. 2085, op. 1, yed. khr. 68, l. 31.

82 Muzey Bakhrushina f. 467, no. 62, l. 4. The recollection is dated June 6, 1952; it appeared in print as M. I. Kurilko, "Rozhdeniye baleta," in *Reyngol'd Moritsevich Glier: Stat'i, Vospominaniya, Materialï*, ed. V. M. Bogdanov-Berezovskiy, 2 vols. (Moscow and Leningrad: Muzïka, 1965–67), 1: 105–09.

83   Muzey Bakhrushina f. 467, no. 45, l. 1 (June 1, 1952, recollection).

84   RGALI f. 2085, op. 1, yed. khr. 55, l. 7.

85   *Politbyuro TsK RKP(b) – VKP(b) i Komintern: 1919–1943 gg. Dokumentï*, ed. G. M. Adibekov (Moscow: ROSSPEN, 2004), 357 n. 1.

86   Tyerman, "*The Red Poppy* and 1927."

87   Muzey Bakhrushina f. 467, no. 676, l. 1.

88   Muzey Bakhrushina f. 467, no. 677, l. 6.

89   Messerer, *Tanets. Mïsl'. Vremya*, 122.

90   Muzey Bakhrushina f. 467, no. 677, l. 9.

91   Vik., "Krasnïy mak," *Pravda*, June 21, 1927. The music is discussed, negatively, by Yevg. Braudo, "Muzïka v 'Krasnom make,'" *Pravda*, June 21, 1927.

92   Quoted in Tyerman, "*The Red Poppy* and 1927."

93   Sadko [Vladimir Blyum], "*The Red Poppy* at the Bolshoi" ['Krasnïy mak' v Bol'shom teatre], in Marina Frolova-Walker and Jonathan Walker, *Music and Soviet Power 1917–1932* (Woodbridge, Suffolk, UK: Boydell, 2012), 195.

94   It was so popular, in fact, that it reached the "captive audiences" of the Gulag: *The Red Poppy* was performed by imprisoned dancers in at least one of the subarctic mining basin labor camps established by Stalin in the 1930s. The camps had cultural clubs, and some of the talent, artists who had been imprisoned for treasonous activities, escaped dangerous work in dangerous conditions by performing. Jake Robertson reproduces a photograph of a presentation of *The Red Poppy* in the late 1940s or early 1950s in Vorkuta ("Captive Audiences: The Untold Stories of Professional Theater in the Gulag Camps of the Komi Republic" [senior thesis, Princeton University, 2015], 186).

95   "Zapis' besedï i. o. zaveduyushchego Otdelom Vostochnïkh narodnïkh respublik VOKS tov. Erofeyeva s kitayskim poetom Emi Syao ot 6 marta 1951 goda," http://www.rusarchives.ru/evants/exhibitions/prc60-f/89.shtml. Quoted in part in Tyerman, "*The Red Poppy* and 1927."

96   RGALI f. 648, op. 2, yed. khr. 681, ll. 18–19. The ballet was called *The Soccer Player* (Futbolist) and was performed in Kharkov, Ukraine, before being presented, on March 30, 1930, at the Bolshoi. The scenario emerged from a 1929 competition for a ballet on a sports theme.

97   Muzey Bakhrushina f. 691, op. 1, no. 14; May 29, 1928, letter from Fyodorovsky to Lunacharsky.

98   RGALI f. 2622, op. 1, yed. khr. 98, l. 8 ob.

99   Unsigned, "Two Dancers Leap to Death on Moscow Stage as Solution of Both Loving Scenery Painter," *New York Times*, April 29, 1928; and

"Two Men Arrested in Moscow Suicides," *New York Times*, April 30, 1928. The event received viral coverage in the *Atlanta Journal Constitution*, *Los Angeles Times*, and *New York Herald Tribune*.

100 Ibid.

101 Geltser, "The Way of a Ballerina."

102 Kolesnikov, "Yekaterina Gel'tser," 132.

103 Ibid., 133.

104 RGALI f. 2729, op. 2, yed. khr. 3, l. 23.

105 Ibid., l. 37.

6: CENSORSHIP

On *Le pas d'acier*: Lesley-Anne Sayers and Simon Morrison, "Prokofiev's *Le Pas d'Acier* (1925): How the Steel was Tempered," in *Soviet Music and Society under Lenin and Stalin: The Baton and Sickle*, ed. Neil Edmunds (New York: Routledge, 2004), 81–104. On Viktor Smirnov, I consulted S. Konayev, "Po pvozvishchu Uzh. O sud'be librettista," in *Bolt* [Bolshoi Theater program booklet] (Moscow: GABT, 2005), 38–41. I also borrowed, on Shostakovich's second ballet, from Simon Morrison, "Shostakovich as Industrial Saboteur: Observations on *The Bolt*," in *Shostakovich and His World*, ed. Laurel Fay (Princeton: Princeton University Press, 2004), 117–61. For the peasant-worker assessment of *The Bright Stream* I am indebted to Ye. S. Vlasova, *1948 god v sovetskoy muzïke* (Moscow: Klassika—XXI, 2010), 155–64. The relevant material on the contract that brought *The Lady Macbeth of the Mtsensk District* to the United States is in the Gosudarstvennïy arkhiv Rossiyskoy Federatsii (GARF), f. 5283, op. 3, d. 694. The proof of David Zaslavsky's authorship of the one-two-punch *Pravda* denunciation of Shostakovich is furnished in a booklet by Yevgeniy Yefimov, which draws on Zaslavsky's papers. See *Sumbur vokrug 'sumbura' i odnogo 'malen'kogo zhurnalista'* (Moscow: Flinta, 2006). *Conditionally Killed* is the usual translation of the title of the Shostakovich revue *Uslovno ubitïy*, but a better rendering might be "dead for now," or "murdered for the time being."

Detailed information on Prokofiev's three Soviet ballets is given in Simon Morrison, *The People's Artist: Prokofiev's Soviet Years* (New York: Oxford University Press, 2009), 31–39 and 106–10 (*Romeo and Juliet*); 258–65 (*Cinderella*); 348–56 and 368–69 (*The Tale of the Stone Flower*). On Grigorovich, the Komsomol, and *The Stone Flower*, I relied on Christina Ezrahi, *Swans of the Kremlin: Ballet and Power in Soviet Russia* (Pittsburgh: University of Pittsburgh Press, 2012), 118–28. On Khachaturian's three ballets, I referred to Harlow Robinson, "The Caucasian Connection: National Identity in the Ballets of Aram Khachaturian," in *Identities, Nations and Politics after Com-*

munism, ed. Roger E. Kanet (New York: Routledge, 2008), 23–32. On *Happiness*, I also consulted Aram Khachaturyan, "[O baletakh]," in Khachaturyan, *Stat'i i vospominaniya*, ed. I. E. Popov (Moscow: Sovetskiy kompozitor, 1980), 131; Khachaturyan, *Noto-bibliograficheskiy spravochnik*, ed. L. M. Person (Moscow: Sovetskiy kompozitor, 1979), 15–16; and www.khachaturian .am/rus/works/ballets_1.htm. On Mikoyan, Stalin, and the thermal waters of the Crimean spas: Stephen Kotkin, *Stalin*, 3 vols. (New York: Penguin Press, 2014–) 1: 465–66; on the purges more broadly, I benefited from Robert Conquest, *The Great Terror: A Reassessment* (New York: Oxford University Press, 2008), including 246–47 (on Mikoyan), 306–07 (on Meyerhold and Raykh), and 431–35 (on Yezhov's downfall). The arrest and death of Marina Semyonova's diplomat husband is noted in her obituary in *The Guardian*, June 15, 2010, http://www.theguardian.com/stage/2010/jun/15/marina -semyonova-obituary. The 1948 scandal in the Union of Soviet Composers is assessed in numerous places, including, incisively, Leonid Maximenkov, "Shostakovich and Stalin: Letters to a 'Friend,'" in *Shostakovich and His World*, ed. Laurel E. Fay (Princeton: Princeton University Press, 2004), 43–58.

On the imperial print censor (Glavnoye Upravleniye po delam pechati) and Bogdanov's 1885 ballet *Svetlana, the Slavic Princess*, the source is RGIA f. 497, op. 6, d. 3679, l. 59.

1   "Stalin Angry," https://www.youtube.com/watch?v=1YsL4HXZN9E, accessed January 20, 2016.
2   RGIA f. 497, op. 18, d. 12, l. 1.
3   RGALI f. 648, op. 2, yed. khr. 653, l. 8.
4   Sergey Prokofiev, *Diaries 1924–1933: Prodigal Son*, trans. Anthony Phillips (London: Faber and Faber, 2012), 880–81; entry of November 14, 1929.
5   D. Gachev, "O 'Stal'nom skoke' i direktorskom naskoke," in Marina Frolova-Walker and Jonathan Walker, *Music and Soviet Power 1917–1932* (Woodbridge, Suffolk, UK: Boydell, 2012), 242.
6   RGALI f. 648, op. 2, yed. khr. 702, l. 21.
7   Richard Taruskin, *Defining Russia Musically* (Princeton: Princeton University Press, 1997), 94.
8   Olga Digonskaya, "Interrupted Masterpiece: Shostakovich's Opera *Orango*. History and Context," in *Shostakovich Studies* 2, ed. Pauline Fairclough (Cambridge: Cambridge University Press, 2010), 31. The librettist Alexei Tolstoy and Alexander Starchakov were the principal authors of *Orango*, Digonskaya explains, and it was their second-guessing, as opposed to Shostakovich's, that led to its cancellation. They missed the

June 1 deadline for the submission of the completed libretto to the Bolshoi. Digonskaya speculates that Shostakovich had disappointed Tolstoy and Starchakov by rejecting a blander operatic project called *A Partisan's Son. Orango* was the last-minute substitute. See ibid., 7–33.

9   Olga Digonskaya, "D. D. Shostakovich's Unfinished Opera *Orango*," in Dmitri Shostakovich, *Orango. Unfinished Satirical Opera. Piano Score* (Moscow: DSCH, 2010), 49.

10 From his farewell speech at the Bolshoi Theater, May 12, 1930, http://lunacharsky.newgod.su/lib/v-mire-muzyki/-novye-puti-opery-i-baleta.

11 Vlasova, *1948 god v sovetskoy muzïke*, 345.

12 According to Reuters, the items supposedly stolen included "an umbrella, two pairs of gloves, a pair of cufflinks and a roll of tape." The Bolshoi dismissed the matter as a "provocation." See "Soviet Ballerina Scoffs at Accusation of Theft," *New York Times*, June 30, 1958.

13 *Vlast' i khudozhestvennaya intelligentsiya: Dokumentï TsK RKP(b) – VKP(b), VChK – OGPU – NKVD o kul'turnoy politike. 1917–1953 gg.*, ed. Andrey Artizov and Oleg Naumov (Moscow: Demokratiya, 2002), 374–76.

14 Ezrahi, *Swans of the Kremlin*, 265.

15 Ravich., "Bol'shoi teatr na perelome ('Futbolist' na stsene mosk. Bol'shogo teatra)," *Rabochiy i teatr*, April 21, 1930, 12–13.

16 Asaf Messerer, *Tanets. Mïsl'. Vremya* (Moscow: Iskusstvo, 1990), 124.

17 RGALI f. 648, op. 2, yed. khr. 740, l. 15.

18 Janice Ross, "Leonid Yakobson's Muscular Choreography and *The Golden Age*" (paper presented at the Columbia University symposium "Russian Movement Culture of the 1920s and 1930s," on February 13, 2015).

19 Janice Ross, *Like a Bomb Going Off: Leonid Yakobson and Ballet as Resistance in Soviet Russia* (New Haven and London: Yale University Press, 2015), 113–14.

20 Manashir Yakubov, "Dmitri Shostakovich's Ballet *The Golden Age:* The Story of its Creation," in *Dmitri Shostakovich: New Collected Works, Vol. 60B*, ed. Manashir Yakubov (Moscow: DSCH, 2011), 358; additional details from 355–39. The original scenario, by Alexander Ivanovsky, is included in *Dmitri Shostakovich: New Collected Works, Vol. 60A*, ed. Manashir Yakubov (Moscow: DSCH, 2011), 8–10.

21 Letter of February 1930 from Shostakovich to Sollertinsky, in Elizabeth Wilson, *Shostakovich: A Life Remembered* (Princeton: Princeton University Press, 2006), 103.

22 Fedor Lopukhov, *Writings on Ballet and Music*, ed. and introd. Stephanie Jordan; trans. Dorinda Offord (Madison: University of Wisconsin Press, 2002), 11; on the *Dance Symphony*, see 69–96.

23 I. I. Sollertinskiy, "Kakoy zhe balet nam v sushchnosti nuzhen?," *Zhizn' iskusstva*, October 6, 1929, 5.

24 *Rabochiy i teatr*, quoted in Wilson, *Shostakovich: A Life Remembered*, 104.

25 D. D. Shostakovich, *Pis'ma I. I. Sollertinskomu*, ed. D. I. Sollertinskiy, L. V. Mikheyeva, G. V. Kopïtova, and O. L. Lansker (St. Petersburg: Kompozitor, 2006), 178; letter of November 17, 1935.

26 Ezrahi, *Swans of the Kremlin*, 59.

27 Vlasova, *1948 god v sovetskoy muzïke*, 160.

28 *Dmitri Shostakovich: New Collected Works, Vol. 64A*, ed. Manashir Yakubov (Moscow: DSCH, 2006), 8–9.

29 RGALI f. 648, op. 5, yed. khr. 5, ll. 1–8, esp. 1–2. See Ezrahi, *Swans of the Kremlin*, 59, for other quotations from this document.

30 Shostakovich, *Pis'ma I. I. Sollertinskomu*, 176; letter of October 30–31, 1935.

31 Maya Plisetskaya, *I, Maya Plisetskaya*, trans. Antonina W. Bouis (New Haven and London: Yale University Press, 2001), 11.

32 A. Zrlikh, "'Svetlïy ruchey' v Bol'shom teatre," *Pravda*, December 2, 1935, 6. On the Leningrad run, see Georgiy Polyanovskiy, "Novïy balet Shostakovicha," *Pravda*, June 6, 1935, 4.

33 Nicolai Leskov, "The Lady Macbeth of Mtsensk," *Hudson Review*, http://hudsonreview.com/2013/02/the-lady-macbeth-of-mtsensk/#. VQMyU0LWSIw.

34 This point from an essay by Richard Taruskin on the moral "lessons" of *Lady Macbeth* and the scandal it precipitated. The fame of the opera in the West, he argues, stems in part from the fact of its censorship, which has granted it the benefit of the moral doubt. "So ineluctably has the opera come to symbolize pertinacious resistance to inhumanity, that it is virtually impossible now to see it as an embodiment of that very inhumanity." But it should nonetheless be experienced "with hearts on guard." Taruskin, *Defining Russia Musically*, 509–10.

35 Nelli Kravets, *Ryadom s velikimi: Atovm'yan i yego vremya* (Moscow: GITIS, 2012), 222–23; biographical details on Atovmyan from 298–301.

36 *Muzïka vmesto sumbura: Kompozitorï i muzïkantï v strane sovetov 1917–1991. Dokumentï*, ed. Leonid Maksimenkov (Moscow: Demokratiya, 2013), 135–36.

37 See Platon Mikhaílovich Kerzhentsev, *Zhizn' Lenina. 1870–1924* (Moscow: Partizdat, 1936).

38 Quotations in this paragraph from [David Zaslavskiy], "Sumbur vmesto muzïki. Ob opera 'Ledi Makbet Mtsenskogo Uyezda,'" *Pravda*, January 28, 1936, 3.

39 [David Zaslavskiy], "Baletnaya fal'sh,'" *Pravda*, February 6, 1936, 3.

40 Leonid Maksimenkov, *Sumbur vmesto muzïki. Stalinskaya kul'turnaya revolyutsiya 1936–1938* (Moscow: Yuridicheskaya Kniga, 1997), 112.

41 Shostakovich, *Pis'ma I. I. Sollertinskomu*, 188.

42 Sulamif' Messerer, *Sulamif'. Fragmentï vospominaniy* (Moscow: Olimpiya, 2005), 103.

43 *Muzïka vmesto sumbura. Kompozitorï i muzïkantï v strane sovetov 1917–1991. Dokumentï*, 138.

44 Ibid., 139.

45 Ibid.

46 Prokofiev, *Diaries 1924–1933*, 411; entry of January 18, 1927.

47 Morrison, *The People's Artist*, 35.

48 RGALI f. 1929, op. 4, yed. khr. 302, l. 124; letter of November 30 and December 1, 1935.

49 Prokofiev, *Diaries 1924–1933*, 1027; entry of June 1–6, 1933. Besides Marina Semyonova, Prokofiev refers to the dancer Vakhtang Chabukiani, with whom he would work on his ballet *Cinderella*.

50 Morrison, *The People's Artist*, 37. The words are Radlov's, as reused by Prokofiev in a 1941 squib about the ballet for the journal *Sovetskaya muzïka*.

51 Ibid.

52 Rossiyskiy gosudarstvennïy arkhiv sotsial'no-politicheskoy istorii (RGASPI), f. 82, op. 2, d. 951, l. 1.

53 RGASPI f. 178, op. 5, d. 5, 8769; document provided by Leonid Maximenkov.

54 *Bol'shaya tsenzura: Pisateli i zhurnalistï v Strane Sovetov. 1917–1956*, ed. A. N. Yakovlev; comp. L. V. Maksimenkov (Moscow: Demokratiya, 2005), 463.

55 Ibid.

56 The URL *was* http://memoryfull.ru/purge/repressions.html.

57 On her survival of the Soviet penal camps, see Simon Morrison, *The Love and Wars of Lina Prokofiev* (London: Vintage, 2014), 257–79.

58 Morrison, *The People's Artist*, 49.

59 Translation by Vera Tancibudek from the December 30, 1938, program.

60 Morrison, *The People's Artist*, 108–9.

61 Ibid., 159.

62 Jennifer Homans, *Apollo's Angels: A History of Ballet* (New York: Random House, 2010), 352–53.

63 RGASPI f. 17, op. 125, d. 499, ll. 43–46.

64 Rossiyskiy gosudarstvennïy arkhiv noveyshey istorii (RGANI), f. 5, op. 36, d. 42, l. 61.

65   Agrippina Vaganova, *Basic Principles of Classical Ballet: Russian Ballet Technique*, trans. Anatole Chujoy (New York: Dover, 1969), 55; my thanks to Colby Hyland for this reference. Alastair Macaulay adds that the pedagogical method developed by Enrico Cecchetti (1850–1928), who danced and taught for Petipa in St. Petersburg and Diaghilev in Paris, likewise emphasizes *épaulement* and coordination, and that Vaganova borrowed from him. Email communication, December 1, 2015.

66   The opinion of Mikhaíl Khrapchenko, Kerzhentsev's successor as Chairman of the Committee on Arts Affairs; *Muzïka vmesto sumbura: Kompozitorï i muzïkantï v strane sovetov 1917–1991*, 193.

67   Valerie Hemingway, *Running with the Bulls: My Years with the Hemingways* (New York: Random House, 2007), 114.

68   David Satter, *It Was a Long Time Ago, and It Never Happened Anyway: Russia and the Communist Past* (New Haven and London: Yale University Press, 2011), 153.

69   Marina Frolova-Walker, *Russian Music and Nationalism: From Glinka to Stalin* (New Haven and London: Yale University Press, 2007), 378 n. 54.

70   TASS, "Priyom v Kremle uchastnikov dekadï Armyanskogo iskusstva," *Pravda*, November 5, 1939, 1.

71   G. Khubov, "'Schast'ye.' Balet A. Khachaturyana," *Pravda*, October 25, 1939, 6. A photograph of act 1 appears at the top of the page. See, for the composer's cautious thoughts on his achievement, Aram Khachaturyan, "Balet 'Schast'ye,'" *Izvestiya*, October 20, 1939, 3.

72   Information and quotations in this and the preceding paragraphs from RGALI f. 652, op. 6, yed. khr. 214. The file contains a collection of short articles on the ballet along with the scenario, assembled for publication by "Iskusstvo" through the Committee on Arts Affairs.

73   Quoted in Robinson, "The Caucasian Connection: National Identity in the Ballets of Aram Khachaturian," 28.

74   Constantine Pleshakov, *Stalin's Folly: The Tragic First Ten Days of WWII on the Eastern Front* (New York: Houghton Mifflin, 2005), 101.

75   L. D. Rïbakova, *Voyna i muzïka: Bol'shoy teatr v godï voynï* (Vladimir: Foliant, 2005), 163.

76   Quotations and information in this paragraph from Lepeshinskaya's 2004 interview for the newspaper *Izvestiya*, http://izvestia.ru /news/288937.

77   Rïbakova, *Voyna i muzïka*, 35.

78   Email communication, May 2, 2015.

79   "Balerina. K 70-letiyu so dnya rozhdeniya O. Lepeshinskoy," *Moskovskaya pravda*, September 28, 1986; Muzey Bakhrushina f. 749, op. 55, l.

5. Lepeshinskaya told the tale of her broken leg to interviewers over and over again; the medical records in her Bakhrushin Museum archive, and the letters from her fans wishing her a quick convalescence, all confirm her heroic service to the Bolshoi.

80   "Take Me on a Trip a Long, Long Time Ago," *Indypendent History* (blog), http://indypendenthistory.tumblr.com/post/53237349769/ballet -class-in-russia-during-world-war-ii.

81   Rïbakova, *Voyna i muzïka,* 103–04. The telephone exchange is with Natalya Sergeyevna Sadkovskaya.

82   Ibid., 91.

83   Ibid., 92; additional information in this paragraph from 93.

84   RGALI f. 656, op. 5, yed. khr. 9740. The last comment is a quotation from a 1928 poem by the futurist poet Vladimir Mayakovsky, "Sekret molodosti" (The secret of youth), which has harsh things to say about idlers. The ballet's scenario, by Isaak Glikman to a score by Stefaniya Zaranek (1904–62), was vetted, and rejected, on April 15, 1949. The composer's previous ballets and operetta projects had better results.

85   Such was the description of Razin in the preface to the scenario of the "ballet about the Volga" that was written by Nikolay Volkov for the composer Boris Asafyev and submitted for assessment by Glavrepertkom on March 2, 1939. RGALI f. 656, op. 5, yed. khr. 9687, l. 6.

86   Ezrahi, *Swans of the Kremlin,* 48.

87   "Obrucheniye v monastïre," *Vechernyaya Moskva,* January 17, 1941; in *Prokof'yev o Prokof'yeve: Stat'i, interv'yu,* ed. V. P. Varunts (Moscow: Sovetskiy kompozitor, 1991), 189.

88   RGALI f. 656, op. 5, yed. khr. 9685, l. 17.

89   Ibid., l. 2.

90   N. Volkov, "Skazka dlya baleta," *Za sovetskoye iskusstvo,* April 12, 1946, 4.

91   N. D. Volkov, *Teatral'nïye vechera* (Moscow: Iskusstvo, 1966), 397.

92   RGALI f. 656, op. 5, yed. khr. 9685, l. 10.

93   Volkov, *Teatral'nïye vechera,* 398.

94   RGALI f. 962, op. 3, yed. khr. 139, l. 3.

95   Ibid., ll. 15–16.

96   R. Zakharov, "Vdokhnovennïy trud," *Sovetskoye iskusstvo,* June 13, 1947, 3.

97   RGALI f. 2329, op. 3, yed. khr. 1928, l. 81.

98   Nicholas Thompson, "My Friend, Stalin's Daughter," *The New Yorker,* March 31, 2014, http://www.newyorker.com/magazine/2014/03/31/my -friend-stalins-daughter.

99   RGALI f. 3045, op. 1, yed. khr. 171, ll. 8–10; and f. 3045, op. 1, yed. khr. 170, l. 12.

100 T. Khrennikov, "Obrazï ural'skikh skazov v balete," *Pravda*, June 2, 1954, 6. The author, a party-minded composer often hostile to Prokofiev, knew little about dance, but that did not matter.

101 Harrison E. Salisbury, "Prokofieff Work Divides Moscow," *New York Times*, March 17, 1954.

102 In his memoirs, he claims that his "prickliness" had damaged his relationship with the minister of culture, Nikolay Mikhaílov, but also that he had been made into a "scapegoat." His return to the theater followed the appointment of Ekaterina Furtseva as minister, though she too would have him deposed. See M. I. Chulaki, *Ya bïl direktorom Bol'shogo teatra* (Moscow: Muzïka, 1994), 74–82 (on the "time out"), 82–83 (on his reappointment), and 126–32 (on his second dismissal).

103 Ibid., 116, and, for broader context, 91–92. See also Tat'yana Kuznetsova, *Khroniki Bol'shogo baleta* (Moscow: RIPOL klassik, 2011), 12.

104 *Muzïka vmesto sumbura. Kompozitorï i muzïkantï v strane sovetov 1917–1991. Dokumentï*, 553.

105 Danielle Fosler-Lussier, *Music Divided: Bartók's Legacy in Cold War Culture* (Berkeley and Los Angeles: University of California Press, 2007), 21.

106 *Muzïka vmesto sumbura. Kompozitorï i muzïkantï v strane sovetov 1917–1991. Dokumentï*, 552.

107 Osgood Caruthers, "Russians Cheer Bolshoi Ballet That Breaks Classical Pattern," *New York Times*, March 8, 1959.

108 *Muzïka vmesto sumbura. Kompozitorï i muzïkantï v strane sovetov 1917–1991. Dokumentï*, 513–16, esp. 514; RGANI f. 5, op. 36, d. 99, ll. 33–38.

109 Interview, February 15, 2015, Beijing, China. My thanks to Nicholas Frisch and Suhua Xiao for arranging and conducting this interview on my behalf.

7: I, MAYA PLISETSKAYA

From 1951 to 1955, the general director of the Bolshoi Theater was the choral conductor and composer Alexander Anisimov (1905–76); followed in 1955–59 by the composer Mikhaíl Chulaki (1908–89), and then, for two years each, Georgiy Orvid (1904–80), a trumpeter in the Bolshoi Theater orchestra in his youth, and Vasiliy Pakhomov (1909–89). After his "time out," Chulaki returned to the position from December 1963 to September 1970. He was replaced in 1970–72 by the opera conductor and pianist Yuriy Muromtsev (1908–75); then for 1973–75 by the composer and Communist Party official Kirill Molchanov; in 1976–79 by the actor and Communist Party official Georgiy Ivanov (1919–94); and for 1979–88 by Stanislav Lushin (b. 1938). Vladimir Kokonin (1938–2005), a longtime Ministry of Culture bureaucrat, led the theater in 1988–95, seeing it through the end of the Soviet Union and the resignation of Yuriy Grigorovich. He was replaced as general director by the dancer and choreographer Vladimir Vasiliev (b. 1940), who served from 1995 to 2000. Kokonin stayed on with the theater in the newly created position of executive director. That position was dissolved following the establishment of a Bolshoi Theater Board of Trustees in 2001. The overcommitted, internationally recognized conductor Gennadiy Rozhdestvensky (b. 1931) briefly replaced Vasiliev as general director in 2000, before Anatoliy Iksanov (b. 1952) took over. Iksanov had previously administered the Malïy Theater in Moscow and the Tovstonogov Bolshoi Drama Theater in St. Petersburg. He oversaw the major rebuilding and restoration of the theater in 2006–11, but the turmoil in the ballet cost him his post in 2013. He was replaced that year by Vladimir Urin (b. 1947), who came to the Bolshoi from the Stanislavsky Theater.

Following the departure of Grigorovich, the ballet was directed by Vasiliev, first in 1995–97 in an alliance with Vyacheslav Gordeyev, and then in 1997–2000 in an alliance with Alexei Fadeyechev and Nina Ananiashvili. Boris Akimov took over for 2001–03, followed by Alexei Ratmansky until 2008. Yuriy Burlaki ceded the position after just a year to Sergey Filin.

I relied in this chapter on notes taken during my May 5, 2015, afternoon with Grigorovich at his dacha in southeastern Moscow. Thanks to Ruslan Pronin and Suhua Xiao for arranging this visit; to Sergey Konayev, who provided access at the Bolshoi to the conductors' scores of *Legend of Love* and *Spartacus*; and to Matthew Honegger, whose research supplied some of the details on *Spartacus* and *The Golden Age*. On the Bolshoi Ballet's tour to London in 1956 and on Grigorovich, I consulted Christina Ezrahi, *Swans of the Kremlin: Ballet and Power in Soviet Russia* (Pittsburgh: University of Pittsburgh Press, 2012), 137–68 and 201–31. On *The Seagull*, I consulted S. Davlekamova, "Ozhidaniye," *Teatr*, no. 4 (1981): 21–30. On the failed coup of August 1991, I drew from Victor Sebestyen, "The K.G.B.'s Bathhouse Plot," *New York Times*, August 20, 2011. The information on Anatoliy Kuznetsov and *Swan Lake* come from his daughter Tatyana Kuznetsova, in conversation in Moscow on May 2, 2015. I am also grateful to her for her insights about Grigorovich's career. Details on Expo 67 come from http://www.collections canada.gc.ca/expo/053302_e.html.

1   Maya Plisetskaya, *I, Maya Plisetskaya*, trans. Antonina W. Bouis (New Haven and London: Yale University Press, 2001), 6.

2   RGALI f. 3266, op. 3, yed. khr. 6, l. 2.

3   Plisetskaya, *I, Maya Plisetskaya*, 6.

4   Ibid., 26.

5   Ibid., 27.

6   V. Gayevskiy, *Divertisment* (Moscow: Iskusstvo, 1981), 238.

7   *Maya: Portrait of Maya Plisetskaya,* directed by Dominique Delouche (1999; Pleasantville, NY: Video Artists International, 2009), DVD.

8   "If it's swans you want, go to the zoo"; Arlene Croce, "Ballets Without Choreography," 1967, in *Afterimages* (New York: Alfred A. Knopf, 1978), 328. Alastair Macaulay, who brought this source to my attention, is slightly more generous, calling "Plisetskaya's version of *The Dying Swan* a marvelous feat of poetic athleticism but not seriously moving"; email communication, September 24, 2015.

9   George Feifer, *Our Motherland, and Other Adventures in Russian Reportage* (New York: Viking, 1974), 66.

10   Ibid., 52.

11   Gordeyev was a principal dancer in the 1970s and 1980s. His wife, also a Bolshoi star, divorced him in 1989, "citing Soviet laws saying a spouse cannot be 'made to live with a homosexual'": Alec Kinnear, "Gordeyev: A Tough but Talented Taskmaster," *The Moscow Times*, May 30, 1995, http://www.themoscowtimes.com/news/article/tmt/338847.html.

12   Feifer, *Our Motherland*, 52–53.

13   Mayya Plisetskaya, *Trinadtsat' let spustya: Serditïye zametki v trinadtsati glavakh* (Moscow: ACT, 2008), 142–43.

14   Plisetskaya, *I, Maya Plisetskaya*, 35; additional information from 34.

15   Sulamif' Messerer, *Sulamif'. Fragmentï vospominaniy* (Moscow: Olimpiya, 2005), 114.

16   Plisetskaya, *I, Maya Plisetskaya*, 37.

17   Ya. Chernov, "Debyut molodoy balerinï," *Komsomol'skaya pravda*, April 6, 1944; STD.

18   RGANI f. 5, op. 17, d. 494, l. 55.

19   Plisetskaya, *I, Maya Plisetskaya*, 133. Formed in 1954, the KGB (Komitet gosudarstvennoy bezopasnosti/Committee for State Security), consolidated the secret police and intelligence-gathering operations of the NKVD and MGB (Ministerstvo gosudarstvennoy bezopasnosti/Ministry for State Security).

20   RGANI f. 5, op. 17, d. 494, l. 62.

21   The plot comes from Lope de Vega's play *Fuente Ovejuna* (1619).

22   John Martin, "Moscow's Ballet Attended by Tito," *New York Times*, June 5, 1956.

23   See, for example, V. Zlatogorova, O. Lepeshinskaya, and N. Shpiller, "V intimnoy blizosti so Stalinïm ne sostoyali" [We were not intimate with

Stalin], *Argumentï i faktï*, no. 43 (October 26, 1994), http://www.aif.ru/archive/1643162.

24 RGANI f. 5, op. 36, d. 24, l. 133.

25 Ezrahi, *Swans of the Kremlin*, 143; RGALI f. 2329, op. 8, yed. khr. 234, l. 30.

26 RGANI f. 5, op. 36, d. 24, l. 125.

27 RGALI f. 2329, op. 8, yed. khr. 234, l. 57.

28 According to Alastair Macaulay, who attended the 1986 press conference in London, where Ulanova tenderly recalled the experiences of 1956. Email communication, June 9, 2015.

29 RGALI f. 2329, op. 8, yed. khr. 234, l. 57.

30 Margot Fonteyn, *Autobiography* (New York: Alfred A. Knopf, 1976), 157. Fonteyn's worshipful biographer asserts that the "restrained English ballerina" fell for "the wild Russian soul." Through her contact with Ulanova, Fonteyn "broaden[ed] and loosen[ed] her neat contained style" (Meredith Daneman, *Margot Fonteyn* [London: Viking, 2004], 332).

31 A. V. Coton, "Contemporary Arts," *The Spectator*, October 12, 1956.

32 Margaret Willis, "Britain Welcomes the Bolshoi Ballet While US Waits its Turn," *Christian Science Monitor*, October 21, 1986.

33 RGANI f. 3, op. 35, d. 40, l. 126; May 22, 1958.

34 Ibid., l. 125; May 12, 1958.

35 Ibid., ll. 123–24; March 7, 1959.

36 Ibid., l. 128.

37 RGANI f. 5, op. 36, d. 99, l. 40; March 18, 1959, report from Polikarpov to the Central Committee. Lepeshinskaya commented as follows about Plisetskaya's memoir and its criticism of her dancing and closeness to Stalin: "I like that book! It was written with absolute sincerity. Sometimes it's a little harsh, but you know . . . you can understand where Maya's coming from! She had such a difficult childhood! How else could she relate to a ballerina whose husband was in the KGB?" She noted that she had called Plisetskaya in Munich to congratulate her on the publication of her memoir, praising her as "a ballerina of fantastic talent." "I didn't change," Lepeshinskaya concluded of their relationship, "but she did." Mariya Vardenga, "Lichnost'. Ol'ga Lepeshinskaya. Memuarï na puantakh," *Argumentï i faktï*, no. 43 (October 23, 1996): 8.

38 Stav Ziv, "The Legacy of Maya Plisetskaya, Cold War–Era Bolshoi Ballerina," *Newsweek*, May 4, 2015, http://www.newsweek.com/saying-farewell-swan-328275.

39 RGANI f. 5, op. 36, d. 99, l. 109; June 9, 1959.

40 On the NYCB trip to Moscow, Leningrad, Kiev, Tbilisi, and Baku, see Clare Croft, "Ballet Nations: The New York City Ballet's 1962 US State Department-Sponsored Tour of the Soviet Union, *Theatre Journal* 61, no. 3 (October 2009): 421–42.

41 RGANI f. 5, op. 36, d. 143, l. 140; August 29, 1962, Polikarpov to the Central Committee.

42 Ibid., ll. 68–69; June 6, 1962, Semichastnïy to the Central Committee.

43 Ibid., ll. 69–70.

44 Ibid., l. 139; August 23, 1962, deputy minister of culture A. Kuznetsov to the Central Committee.

45 Mayya Plisetskaya, "Iskusstvo shagayet v kosmos," *Molodyozh' Gruzii*, March 23, 1965; STD.

46 Mayya Plisetskaya, "Russkaya terpsikhora pokorila Ameriku," *Izvestiya*, December 30, 1962; STD.

47 Laird Borrelli Persson, "Haute Cuisine: Ballerina Maya Plisetskaya's Recipes from the Pages of *Vogue*," *Vogue*, November 6, 2014, http://www.vogue.com/3705317/haute-cuisine-maya-plisetskaya-recipes-vogue/.

48 Feifer, *Our Motherland*, 77.

49 Plisetskaya, *I, Maya Plisetskaya*, 245–46.

50 Muzey Bakhrushina f. 737, no. 7, l. 2; December, 1965.

51 Interview, May 5, 2015, Moscow, Russia.

52 Muzey Bakhrushina f. 737, no. 7, l. 3.

53 B. L'vov-Anokhin, "'Legenda o lyubvi' v Bol'shom teatre," *Teatr*, no. 9 (1965): 42.

54 Arlene Croce, "The Bolshoi Bows In," 1987, in *Writing in the Dark, Dancing in* The New Yorker (New York: Farrar, Straus and Giroux, 2000), 589, 592.

55 Tat'yana Kuznetsova, *Khroniki Bol'shogo baleta* (Moscow: RIPOL klassik, 2011), 155.

56 Interview, May 5, 2015, Moscow, Russia.

57 Grigorovich missed the deadline, but not egregiously; his *Spartacus* was premiered on April 9, 1968.

58 Quoted in Svetlana Borisovna Potemkina, "Osobennosti stsenarnoy dramaturgii baleta 1930–60 gg.: na materiale istorii sozdaniya baleta 'Spartak'" (PhD diss., Gosudarstvennïy institut iskusstvoznaniya [Moscow], 2013), 22; additional information in this and the next paragraph from ibid., 20–46, 59–64.

59 Quoted in ibid., 35.

60 Ibid., 63.

61 Muzey Bakhrushina f. 468, no. 1065, l. 1; translation from www .marxists.org/archive/lenin/works/1919/jul/11.htm.

62 Muzey Bakhrushina f. 468, no. 1065, l. 5.

63 Muzey Bakhrushina f. 548, no. 462, l. 2; Moiseyev's "rezhissyorskiy stsenariy" (directorial scenario) for the ballet. Additional information in the paragraph from ll. 4, 6, and 8.

64 Janice Ross, *Like a Bomb Going Off: Leonid Yakobson and Ballet as Resistance in Soviet Russia* (New Haven and London: Yale University Press, 2015), 275–76.

65 Interview, May 5, 2015, Moscow, Russia.

66 Ross, *Like a Bomb Going Off,* 250.

67 Ibid., 256.

68 Ibid., 269.

69 Christina Ezrahi (*Swans of the Kremlin,* 206) reports that Yakobson's 1956 *Spartacus* "was revived by the Kirov in 1976, 1985, and 2010. According to performance statistics up to 1987, it had received 197 performances. Apparently the ballet was a success at the box office."

70 Muzey Bakhrushina f. 548, no. 182, l. 3ob. The letter is dated January 4, 1957, eight days after the Leningrad premiere of *Spartacus.*

71 Ibid., l. 5.

72 Ibid., l. 8ob.

73 Muzey Bakhrushina f. 548, no. 268, l. 1ob.; letter to Yakobson from S. A. Reynberg, January 13, 1957.

74 Muzey Bakhrushina f. 548, no. 1, l. 8. The partial manuscript from which this quote is taken, "Moya rabota nad baletami 'Zhurale' i 'Spartak'" (My work on the ballets "Shurale" and "Spartacus"), became part of Yakobson's memoir and treatise *Pis'ma Noverru* (Letters to Noverre), which made it into print posthumously, in 2001.

75 Quoted in Potemkina, "Osobennosti stsenarnoy dramaturgii baleta 1930–60 gg.: na materiale istorii sozdaniya baleta 'Spartak,'" 83; additional information in this paragraph from 68 (Asafyev likening Khachaturian to Rubens), 71–87.

76 Joan Acocella, "Man of the People," *The New Yorker,* July 28, 2014, http://www.newyorker.com/magazine/2014/07/28/man-people.

77 Ezrahi, *Swans of the Kremlin,* 205. In Moscow in 1961, the two of them glared at each other across the table during a meeting of the artistic council of the Bolshoi Theater. Yakobson grumbled about Khachaturian refusing to meet with him; Khachaturian saw no point in doing so, since he had been betrayed. "[Yakobson] bought six piano scores and made one piano score out of them—so you can imagine what became

of the music!" Khachaturian alluded to the argument in Leningrad—"I stormed at him; he stormed back"—and a last-ditch effort at peace. "We came to an agreement, everything was confirmed, and then a slew of additional changes!" "Stenogramma obsuzhdeniya baleta 'Spartak,'" l. 10; March 16, 1961/Bolshoi Theater Museum.

78 Ezrahi, *Swans of the Kremlin*, 210.

79 Allen Hughes, "Ballet: Bolshoi Stages U.S. Premiere of 'Spartacus,'" *New York Times*, September 13, 1962.

80 Allen Hughes, "'Spartacus': Can It Be Understood Though Disliked?" *New York Times*, September 23, 1962.

81 Walter Terry, "The Bolshoi: 'Spartacus,'" *New York Herald Tribune*, September 13, 1962.

82 Walter Terry, "DeMille Out De-Milled," *New York Herald Tribune*, September 16, 1962. The Universal pictures blockbuster *Spartacus* (1960) was directed by Stanley Kubrick, not DeMille, though it was first shown in New York at the DeMille Theater.

83 W[alter]. T[erry]., "For the Bolshoi, Second 'Spartacus,' Warmer Crowd," *New York Herald Tribune*, September 14, 1962.

84 Terry, "The Bolshoi: 'Spartacus,'" *New York Herald Tribune*, September 13, 1962.

85 "Bolshoi, in Shift, Cancels 3 'Spartacus' Showings," *New York Times*, September 18, 1962.

86 "'Spartacus' Taken Out of Ballet Repertoire," *Los Angeles Times*, September 24, 1962.

87 Plisetskaya, *I, Maya Plisetskaya*, 233.

88 Ross, *Like a Bomb Going Off*, 257–58.

89 "Stenogramma zasedaniya khuozhestvennogo soveta. Soobshcheniye Yu. N. Grigorovicha o postanovke baleta 'Spartak,'" l. 5; June 27, 1967/ Bolshoi Theater Museum. Also quoted in Potemkina, "Osobennosti stsenarnoy dramaturgii baleta 1930–60 gg.: na materiale istorii sozdaniya baleta 'Spartak,'" 138.

90 "Stenogramma obsuzhdeniya baleta 'Spartak,'" l. 12.

91 Ibid., l. 20.

92 Interview, May 5, 2015, Moscow, Russia.

93 Ibid.

94 Gayevskiy, *Divertisment*, 219.

95 Plisetskaya, *I, Maya Plisetskaya*, 103.

96 Marina Harss, "Bolshoi Ballet—Spartacus—New York," *DanceTabs*, July 28, 2014, http://dancetabs.com/2014/07/bolshoi-ballet-spartacus -new-york/.

97   Gayevskiy, *Divertisment*, 212.

98   Joan Acocella, "After the Fall," *The New Yorker*, August 22, 2008, http://www.newyorker.com/magazine/2005/08/22/after-the-fall.

99   RGALI f. 648, op. 12, yed. khr. 45, l. 8 (invitations to the Cuban dance festivals)

100 RGALI f. 648, op. 12, yed. khr. 45, l. 4 (extension of Alonso's visa from forty days to four months).

101 RGALI f. 648, op. 12, yed. khr. 166, l. 4 (Plisetskaya's program booklet article), RGALI f. 648, op. 12, yed. khr. 45, l. 40 (Alonso's financial details).

102 Feifer, *Our Motherland*, 53.

103 Ibid., 63.

104 Plisetskaya, *I, Maya Plisetskaya*, 278.

105 M. I. Chulaki, *Ya bïl direktorom Bol'shogo teatra* (Moscow: Muzïka, 1994), 125–26.

106 Feifer, *Our Motherland*, 63.

107 Clive Barnes, "Maya Plisetskaya Leads Bolshoi Stars," *New York Times*, September 18, 1974.

108 Gayevskiy, *Divertisment*, 217.

109 Ibid., 216.

110 RGALI f. 648, op. 12, yed. khr. 289, ll. 2–3.

111 Ibid., l. 5. She expanded her criticisms in print: Ye. Lutskaya, "V protivorechii s partituroy," *Teatral'naya zhizn'*, no. 15 (August 1970): 15. Her thoughts would, in due course, be echoed by British and American critics, who deplored Grigorovich's decision to deracinate the national dances. Alastair Macaulay notes that he seems not to have had the courage to pursue the same policy in his 1984 staging of *Raymonda*, which has an "Oriental" as a villain. Email communication, September 24, 2015.

112 RGALI f. 648, op. 12, yed. khr. 289, ll. 7–8. Another learned critic, Nataliya Roslavleva, twisted herself in knots trying to praise the ballet. Grigorovich relied on "Tchaikovsky's manuscript" for guidance, yet he staged the ballet in an "entirely new way," yet he also "tastefully respected tradition and Ivanov's choreographic signature" ("Vernoye i spornoye. Novaya postanovka 'Lebedinogo ozera' v Bol'shom teatr SSSR," *Muzïkal'naya zhizn'*, no. 12 [June 1970]: 9).

113 According to the recollection of Elizabeth Souritz, who attended the general rehearsal. Email communication, May 2, 2015.

114 Interview, May 5, 2015, Moscow, Russia.

115 RGALI f. 648, op. 12, yed. khr. 289, l. 3.

116 *Spartacus* came up repeatedly in the discussions of *Swan Lake*. "Len-

ingrad," Lopukhov declared, "has surrendered its position to Moscow; they can't dance *Spartacus* there; the soloists are no better than the corps de ballet" (ibid., l. 8).

117 Bernard Gwertzman, "Controversial New 'Swan Lake' Given by Bolshoi Ballet in Soviet," *New York Times*, December 26, 1969.

118 Ibid.

119 Plisetskaya, *I, Maya Plisetskaya*, 360.

120 Ibid., 361.

121 "Stenogramma zasedaniya khuozhestvennogo soveta. Soobshcheniye Yu. N. Grigorovicha o postanovke baleta 'Spartak,'" l. 5.

122 RGALI f. 648, op. 12, yed. khr. 214, l. 4.

123 M. Kapustin, "Uznayem li mï Annu? Novïy balet R. Shchedrina," *Pravda*, April 5, 1968, 6; Chulaki, *Ya bïl direktorom Bol'shogo teatra*, 122–23.

124 Viktorina Kriger, "Iskusstvo molodosti," *Pravda*, June 6, 1972, 3; Hedrick Smith, "Bolshoi Ballet Scored in Pravda," *New York Times*, June 8, 1972.

125 Muzey Bakhrushina f. 737, no. 1613, l. 2; October 22, 1974.

126 Mayya Plisetskaya, "Baletu podvlastno vsyo," in *Rodion Shchedrin. Materialï k tvorcheskoy biografii: Sbornik retsenziy, issledovaniy i materialov*, ed. E. S. Vlasova (Moscow: Mosk. Gos. konservatoriya im. P. I. Chaykovskogo, 2007), 43.

127 Natalya Kasatkin and Vladimir Vasilyov choreographed it for Plisetskaya and her onstage partner, Fadeyechev, in 1967.

128 Information and quotations in the previous paragraphs from *Muzïka vmesto sumbura: Kompozitorï i muzïkantï v strane sovetov 1917–1991. Dokumentï*, ed. Leonid Maksimenkov (Moscow: Demokratiya, 2013), 635–37. The letter is signed "the artists of the ballet."

129 Laurence Senelick, "'A Woman's Kingdom': Minister of Culture Furtseva and Censorship in the Post-Stalinist Russian Theatre," *New Theatre Quarterly* 26, no. 1 (February 2010): 19.

130 Ibid., 18.

131 Galina Vishnevskaya, *Galina: A Russian Story*, trans. Guy Daniels (San Diego: Harcourt Brace Jovanovich, 1984), 303.

132 Senelick, "'A Woman's Kingdom,'" 16.

133 A. I. Adzhubey, *Furtseva: Yekaterina Tret'ya* (Moscow: Algoritm, 2012).

134 Senelick, "'A Woman's Kingdom,'" 23. Additional information in this paragraph from Adzhubey, *Furtseva: Yekaterina Tret'ya*, 198–201.

135 The joke is told by Bill McGuire, *Tales of an American Culture Vulture* (Lincoln, NE: iUniverse, 2003), 26.

136 Plisetskaya, *I, Maya Plisetskaya*, 362.

137 Ibid.

138 Ibid.

139 Interview, May 5, 2015, Moscow, Russia.

140 Ibid.

141 Ibid.

142 Ibid.

143 *Apparat TsK KPSS i kul'tura 1973–1978. Dokumentï*, ed. N. G. Tomilina, T. Yu. Konova, Yu. N. Murav'yev, M. Yu. Prozumenshchikov, and S. D. Tavanets, 2 vols. (Moscow: ROSSPEN, 2011): 2: 131.

144 Plisetskaya, *I, Maya Plisetskaya*, 291.

145 *Maya: Portrait of Maya Plisetskaya.*

146 Arlene Croce, "Folies Béjart," 1971, in *Afterimages*, 381.

147 Plisetskaya, *I, Maya Plisetskaya*, 287.

148 Ibid., 340.

149 Muzey Bakhrushina f. 737, no. 1297, 1. 2; in reference to a January 24, 1977, performance of *Ivan the Terrible* in Leningrad. According to the complaint, sent to Ulanova from an offended viewer, Soviet ballet had lost its restraint, as evidenced by the love scene between Ivan and Anastasia, which made viewers uncomfortable. Ivan's suffering after Anastasia's death, on the other hand, showed Grigorovich at his best.

150 Yuri Grigorovich and Sania Davlekamova, *The Authorized Bolshoi Ballet Book of The Golden Age* (Neptune City, NJ: T.F.H. Publishers, 1989); and Sergey Sapozhnikov, "Snova zvuchit muzïka Shostakovicha," *Sovetskiy balet*, no. 1 (January–February 1983): 5–7.

151 Martin Bernheimer, "Shostakovich Ballet: Bolshoi Opens with 'The Golden Age,'" *Los Angeles Times*, August 13, 1987.

152 Alexei Yurchak, *Everything Was Forever, Until It Was No More: The Last Soviet Generation* (Princeton: Princeton University Press, 2005).

153 RGALI f. 648, op. 19, yed. khr. 171, 1. 37. The Bolshoi Theater collected and archived its correspondence with viewers; this file includes letters about *Lady with the Lapdog* as well as Grigorovich's ballets. The author of the complaint against Plisetskaya boasts his longtime membership in the Communist Party.

154 Alastair Macaulay, "Grand Concerns," *The New Yorker*, April 11, 1988, 108.

155 Ibid. Arlene Croce describes the difference between meaningful and meaningless dancing in this sense in "Ballets Without Choreography," 319–31.

156 The expression comes from Stravinsky. See Igor Stravinsky and Robert Craft, *Memories and Commentaries* (London: Faber and Faber, 2002), 72.

157 Feifer, *Our Motherland*, 71.

158 Anna Kisselgoff, "Review/Dance; 'Seagull' and Finale End U.S.–Soviet Festival," *New York Times*, April 4, 1988.

159 On Plisetskaya as the world's prima ballerina, see Anna Kisselgoff, "Success Is What Sustains Her," *New York Times*, March 22, 1977.

160 V. Kukharskiy, "Vechno molodoy," *Pravda*, May 26, 1976, 3. The page, dedicated in full to the Bolshoi Theater, includes a tribute by Tikhon Khrennikov, "Zdes' tsarit muzïka" (Here music reigns). The tsars did not preside over the theater during the imperial period, composers did, and after the revolution, the Bolshoi found its proper role as "a true center for the building of multinational socialist musical culture." Yu. Kartashov, a lathe operator at the Kommunar plant, provides the worker-peasant perspective on the jubilee in an article called "Sodruzhestvo" (Concord).

161 S. Davlekamova, "Segodnya nado rabotat'!," *Sovetskaya kul'tura*, May 21, 1987; STD.

162 Judith Mackrell, "Your Biggest Bolshoi Ballet Moments—Open Thread," *The Guardian*, July 29, 2013, http://www.theguardian.com/stage/2013/jul/29/bolshoi-ballet-moments.

163 Anna Kisselgoff, "For the Bolshoi Ballet Director, Politics Looms as Large as Art," *New York Times*, July 11, 1990. Grigorovich hinted that his time was almost up at the Bolshoi, telling Kisselgoff that he was "trying to get an operetta theater for so-called experimental work," while also running "a choreographic workshop in an institute called the Dance Academy." These comments were parroted in the Soviet press; Grigorovich disavowed them. See Yu. Grigorovich, "Pis'mo v rekatskiyu. Dom-to obshchiy!," *Izvestiya*, October 20, 1990; STD.

164 Geyorgiy Melikyants, "Razval Bol'shogo teatra—prestupleniye pered russkoy kul'turoy," *Izvestiya*, March 14, 1995, 23.

165 Tat'yana Kuznetsova, "Ochen' nepriyatnïy tsar,'" *Kommersant*, October 11, 2012, 5.

166 Kuznetsova, *Khroniki Bol'shogo baleta*, 9–44 ("Epokha Yuriya Grigorovicha 1964–1995").

EPILOGUE

1 Yuliya Bedyorova, "Zerkalo parada," *Moskovskiye novosti*, October 31, 2011, http://www.mn.ru/culture/20111031/306530925.html. This paragraph and the following on the restoration of the Bolshoi Theater are adapted from Simon Morrison, "The Bolshoi's Latest Act," *NYRblog*,

November 12, 2011, http://www.nybooks.com/blogs/nyrblog/2011/nov/12/the-bolshois-latest-act/.

2 Alastair Macaulay, "A Transformed Theater in a Transformed Land," *New York Times*, April 7, 2014.

3 Anna Gordeyeva, "'Gospod' Bog sam znayet, shto delat' s Bol'shim teatrom': Interv'yu vedushchey balerinï Bol'shogo teatra Svetlanï Zakharovoy," *gazeta.ru*, August 1, 2014, http://www.gazeta.ru/culture/2014/08/01/a 6154185.shtml.

4 Arlene Croce, "Hard Work," 1975, in *Afterimages* (New York: Alfred A. Knopf, 1978), 141.

5 Joan Acocella, "Dance with Me," *The New Yorker*, June 27, 2011, http://www.newyorker.com/magazine/2011/06/27/dance-with-me.

6 Jennifer Homans, *Apollo's Angels: A History of Ballet* (New York: Random House, 2010), 547–49.

7 Wendy Lesser, "Ratmansky and Shostakovich," *The Threepenny Review*, no. 119 (Fall 2009), http://www.threepennyreview.com/samples/lesser_f09.html.

8 Valerie Lawson, "The Bolshoi Looks on the Bright Side of Life," *dance lines.com.au*, June 10, 2013, http://dancelines.com.au/bolshoi-bright-side-life/.

9 Sarah Crompton, "Flames of Paris, Bolshoi Ballet, Review," *The Telegraph*, August 16, 2013.

10 Putin declared 2016 "Prokofiev year," which freed up funds to mark the composer's 125th birthday: http://ria.ru/culture/20151209/1339037709.html.

INDEX

Note: Page numbers after 428 refer to notes.